CORPORATE
INTEGRITY
&
ACCOUNTABILITY

CORPORATE INTEGRITY & ACCOUNTABILITY

EDITOR

GEORGE G. BRENKERT
GEORGETOWN UNIVERSITY

SAGE Publications
Thousand Oaks ▪ London ▪ New Delhi

For information:

Sage Publications, Inc.
2455 Teller Road
Thousand Oaks, California 91320
E-mail: order@sagepub.com

Sage Publications Ltd.
1 Oliver's Yard
55 City Road
London EC1Y 1SP
United Kingdom

Sage Publications India Pvt. Ltd.
B-42 Panchsheel Enclave
Post Box 4109
New Delhi 110 017 India

Printed in the United States of America

Library of Congress Cataloging-in-Publication Data

Corporate integrity and accountability / George G. Brenkert [editor].
    p. cm.
Includes bibliographical references and index.
  ISBN 0-7619-2954-1 (cloth) — ISBN 0-7619-2955-X (pbk.)
1. Social responsibility of business. 2. Corporations—Moral and ethical aspects.
3. Corporations—Corrupt practices. 4. Business ethics. I. Brenkert, George G.
HD60.C638 2004
658.4′08—dc22   2004003256

This book is printed on acid-free paper.

04   05   06   07   10 9 8 7 6 5 4 3 2 1

Acquisitions Editor:	Al Bruckner
Editorial Assistant:	MaryAnn Vail
Production Editor:	Diane S. Foster
Copy Editor:	Publishing Servies
Typesetter:	C&M Digitals (P) Ltd.
Proofreader:	Libby Larson
Indexer:	Molly Hall
Cover Designer:	Janet Foulger

CONTENTS

ACKNOWLEDGMENTS

The essays presented in this book arose out of a twofold intention. First, the analysis of corporate integrity and accountability has acquired significant urgency and importance due to recent business scandals in the United States and other parts of the world, as well as the effects of globalization over the past several decades. The chapters in this book seek to contribute to the examination of these complex problems. Second, inasmuch as these issues have an international dimension, the reflections of individuals drawn from both sides of the Atlantic may contribute more meaningfully to this discussion than would those drawn from just one society. The authors of the chapters in this book reflect this intention as well. In addition, though they come primarily from universities, one-third of the papers are from those in business or nongovernmental organizations. In short, the chapters in this book were intended to advance the global discussion of corporate integrity and accountability and to do so through the trans-Atlantic perspectives of its authors.

All the chapters in this book were originally presented at the Trans-Atlantic Business Ethics Conference at Georgetown University in the fall of 2002. This was the second such conference, the first one having been held in the fall of 2000 in Budapest, Hungary, at the Budapest University of Economic Sciences. In developing the Georgetown conference, I had the important advice of Professor Laszlo Zsolnai, from the Budapest University of Economic Sciences, who was, unfortunately, unable to attend.

We were very pleased to have the financial support of both Levi Strauss & Co. and ING Group (the Netherlands). Without their financial support this conference would not have been possible. The Georgetown Business Ethics Institute as well as the McDonough School of Business (Georgetown University) also provided financial support. For the support and participation of all these individuals and organizations, I am very grateful.

—*George G. Brenkert*

1

THE NEED FOR
CORPORATE INTEGRITY

GEORGE G. BRENKERT

The nature of business and its place in society has been a topic of considerable importance for centuries. Economic, political, social, and ethical issues are all intertwined in this discussion. However, the last several decades have led to a situation of considerable irony, in which noteworthy achievements of business have been confronted with its great failures, and in which increasing discussion of corporate responsibility has been faced with the massive irresponsibility of some businesses. This book is about this complex, ironical, and important situation. It is also about the responses that some individuals and organizations have been urging as well as putting into place to address this situation. There is a great deal to be done. But movement in the right direction is important and needs to be supported.

In the last 20 or 30 years, business has grown considerably in extent and power. Globalization has been a part of endless discussions. Companies such as Wal-Mart have grown to be huge, dominating, worldwide organizations.

Based on corporate sales and country GDPs, it has been claimed that (in 2000) 51 of the world's 100 largest economic entities were corporations, not countries (Anderson & Cavanagh, 2000). Further, "the Top 200 corporations' combined sales are bigger than the combined economies of all countries minus the biggest 10" (Ibid.). The reach of Western capitalist organizations has penetrated China, India, and even Vietnam in ways unimaginable 30 or 40 years ago. The victory of capitalism and the demise of communism have been trumpeted throughout much of the world. As a result, at the end of the twentieth century, the "end of history" was announced, a "new economy" identified, and globalization (of capitalist business) said to be the order of the day. During this time, many business leaders stood out as models to be emulated. They were the new celebrities. Jack Welch, head of General Electric, was often referred to as one of the most admired CEOs in the United States. And leading businesses were honored. Enron was known for its social responsibility efforts, for having an admirable code of ethics, and for actions taken to protect the environment. Arthur Andersen was widely known for having sponsored ethics workshops for accountants in the early '90s. It was in the spirit of these times that, in 1997, Michael Novak wrote, "Like a proud frigate, the American business corporation is sailing confidently into the twenty-first century" (Novak, 1997, p. 1).

It has subsequently become clear to all that other things that were also occurring resulted in massive business failures. Major multinational corporations have been engaged in instances of self-destruction that have dramatically reduced the economic futures of their employees, suppliers, investors, and the communities in which they did business. Enron has become a shibboleth for a self-destructive, irresponsible company. WorldCom, Arthur Andersen, ImClone, Global Crossing, and Tyco are a few names among the many businesses that have failed, been driven into bankruptcy, or suffered huge losses. Towards the end of 2003, almost every day American banking, investment, and mutual funds companies were being charged with ethical and criminal misdoings. However, this exercise in self- and other-destructiveness has not been limited to the United States. In Europe, corporations such as Barings, Vivendi, Credit Lyonnais, and EM.TV & Merchandising AG, among others, have also suffered significant scandals. Likewise, Asian firms have not been immune to financial shenanigans and government inquiries. Even the president of South Korea has been tainted by scandals involving business corporations.

And while these scandals were going on, a good number of top American executives sought salaries and compensation packages of such extravagance that some have had to renounce, after their exposure, the product of their greed. Even the chairman of the New York Stock Exchange, Richard Grasso, lost his job, not because of anything illegal he did, but because of the view of many that his compensation package was unjustifiably large.

Finally, there have been significant protests around the world against globalization. Books have been written challenging "the False Dawn" of globalization (Gray, 1998). College students have led sit-ins at their campuses in protest of sweatshop conditions in the developing world. Ordinary people and workers have taken part in demonstrations in many places around the world against the effects of globalization on them. Disparities in incomes and wealth between developing and developed nations have grown, as well as similar disparities within developed nations. And though HIV/AIDS has not been attributed to major corporations, many businesses (and especially the pharmaceutical companies) have been seen as less attentive to this pandemic than is warranted.

A third development has taken place at the same time as these two contrasting trends: the significant increase in discussion, by academics, business people, members of nongovernmental organizations (NGOs) and international governmental organizations (IGOs), and even national governments, of the importance and value of corporate (social) responsibility. A confusing variety of terms has been used by those engaged in this discussion. Among the most frequently used terms are *business ethics*, *corporate citizenship*, *corporate sustainability*, *triple bottom line*, *stakeholder dialogue*, *corporate social responsibility*, and *corporate stewardship*. Though conflicting meanings may be attributed to these terms, and different issues thereby identified, there is also a great deal of overlap. At a minimum, all these discussions seek to answer the basic question of the nature and role of business in society.

Businesses have been urged to play an active and positive role in the communities in which they operate—for example, by protecting the environment, supporting local organizations, paying their fair share of the taxes, keeping prices in check, hiring the hardcore unemployed. In addition, they have been exhorted to provide their employees with safe working conditions, to produce safe products, and to market their goods in a responsible manner. All these activities have fallen under calls for corporate responsibility. Codes of ethics have been developed by business organizations, NGOs, and even the United Nations. The

European Union commissioned White and Green Papers on Corporate Social Responsibility. It is quite clear from a broad range of surveys regarding responsible investment, the treatment of customers, and the working conditions of employees that society increasingly looks at business through moral filters.

In short, we have a situation in which business has been phenomenally successful and in which there has been an extraordinary growth of discussion regarding business's responsibilities to its stakeholders, and yet, at the same time, considerable problems have arisen due to the irresponsibility of some businesses and the negative effects of business on society. The natural response is to ask what accounts for these contradictory results. What has gone wrong? Are there different things we should be doing?

Some have said that business ought not become engaged in social responsibility efforts but should instead focus on maximizing profits. If society is concerned about the environment, social problems, or the impact of business on society, then governments should pass the appropriate laws and regulations for business to follow, or private individuals should undertake philanthropic activities to correct these situations. Neither of these is the role of business. Hence, if problems remain, then private individuals, philanthropic organizations, and/or governments need to step up their efforts.

Though this view is widely held, even today, primarily in the United States (and Great Britain, perhaps) increasingly, it is a minority perspective. At the very least, the great explosion of talk by business itself about business's responsibilities to its stakeholders makes that response to our situation seem less plausible. Further, the reason that businesses have failed and their top executives accused of greed beyond measure has had nothing to do with their activities in the realm of social responsibility (at least as it relates to social problems). On the contrary, many of their failures have occurred in the heart of their accounting, investing, and business practices. It is not because they have undertaken socially responsible efforts that they have failed overall. They

have failed because they have mishandled their core business activities.

Others have contended, in light of the above contrasting trends, that corporate responsibility actions by businesses are undertaken only because of public relations concerns, or only because they are also profitable for companies. In such cases, these skeptics argue, businesses are not really engaged in operating in a socially responsible manner as much as they are acting to enhance corporate profitability simply by another route. Thus, corporate responsibility is simply a cloak worn when convenient by businesses that have little concern for the interests of others.

There are really two aspects to this objection. On the one hand, the point being made here is that since responsible behavior is treated by businesses as something external to how they define themselves, what they do by way of corporate responsibility activities is really little more than an "add on." It will disappear in bad times, and even in good times it will be viewed, even from within a business, with suspicion and mistrust. The other side of this objection is that responsibility measures have not been integrated into the core activities and the strategic designs of companies.

In short, the concern that lies behind both aspects of this objection is related to calls for businesses to "walk the talk," to operate in a manner that integrates into their very core activities the ways in which they (and others) have spoken about the responsibilities of business. If companies like those noted above can collapse and take with them the wealth of their stockholders, employees, suppliers, and communities, even though they spoke openly about the importance of corporate social responsibility, we need to take another, more fundamental look at the ways they are run and their relations to the communities in which they operate. We need to look more closely at the kinds of reasons they failed and what we can do to prevent future failures. We must seek to ensure that they act in ways that reflect what they (and others) have come to talk about.

In short, we need to consider to what extent and in what ways activities that fall under corporate social responsibility (or simply corporate responsibility) are integrated into corporations. This is but another way of saying that we need to examine the integrity of these organizations and not simply some of the activities and programs in which they engage that they may be treating as peripheral to who and what they are.

CORPORATE INTEGRITY

As might be expected, questions of integrity arise due to the gap that has been painfully exposed between the claimed actions of some corporations and what they have really done. The demand that corporations, organizations in general, and people in particular act as they say they will act is essential to the demand for integrity.

However, this way of putting things makes two important assumptions about corporate integrity. First, it assumes that corporations can have integrity. Second, it assumes that a corporation that does exactly what it says is one that exhibits integrity. The first assumption has been disputed, while the second assumption is, arguably, false.

Some argue that only individuals can have integrity. Corporations are legal fictions, they say, and legal fictions cannot have integrity. This is to take an overly restrictive view of corporations and integrity. Corporations are organizations of humans. They have purposes and missions that are not simply those of their members. They may go about pursuing those purposes and missions in more or less efficient and ethical manners. They may have dysfunctional cultures or flourishing cultures that support their employees. An organization that goes about what it is supposed to be doing in an efficient manner, whose culture is not dysfunctional, and that practices what it preaches would certainly seem to be an organization that exhibits at least some form of integrity. In such a case, integrity refers to the wholeness, consistency, or coherency of the organization in question. Given that corporations are run by human agents through structures and

rules that can be changed in light of ends or objectives that have been chosen, it seems plausible to attribute integrity in some moral form, though under the appropriate circumstances, to corporations as well.

However, it is just these circumstances that are crucial. It is possible that an organization did exactly what it said it would do, did it in some efficient manner and in accord with an end it adopted, and yet its actions could still be those of a very pernicious, insensitive organization. Perhaps it did business with tyrants, engaged in corrupt practices, and had little concern for the environment or its employees. It might be doing exactly what it says it will do. And though there would be no gap between the two, nevertheless that company would not be what is plausibly recognizable as a responsible corporation or one of integrity. That such a business could exist in some ongoing fashion may be less plausible today, given the amount of exposure to which business is subject. But in the past, we should remember, it was possible for a business openly to say that it does not hire blacks, or even more recently that it does not hire homosexuals.

These examples tell us that integrity involves more than simply doing what one says; what one says and does must also pass through some moral filter. As such, integrity is closely bound up with business ethics and forms of social responsibility. But this needs to be elaborated upon more fully.

A central feature of personal or corporate integrity is that it is different from simply following the law. The legal, or compliance, view of the responsibilities of business and those within business was given a considerable boost as a result of the previous corporate scandals of the '60s and '70s in the U.S. defense industry. In 1986, a Defense Industry Initiative (DII) was created in the United States as a mechanism whereby those defense industries that subscribed to it would create within their organizations various structures to encourage compliance with the law. This effort on behalf of corporations in the United States was expanded with the formulation of the U.S. Executive Sentencing Guidelines

(1991). These guidelines laid down the kinds of penalties corporations and their executives would be subject to if they violated the law. Written into this act was the allowance that if a corporation had an ethics program in place and had made a good faith effort to head off criminal acts by its employees, its fines and penalties could be dramatically reduced (cf. Paine, 1994).

As a result, in the '90s there was a great proliferation of corporate ethics offices. In 1991, the Ethics Officers Association was formed to provide support and networking opportunities for the ethics officers of those corporations that had instituted this position. Though there is considerable talk of ethics (and even some of integrity) in these contexts, the efforts of many of those in business and of corporations themselves were mainly to comply with these guidelines.

Though this legalistic approach to corporate (social) responsibility was felt by others to be important, it was also believed to be inadequate. It is crucial that businesses "walk the legal talk" and obey the law, but (as has often been pointed out) the law is itself incomplete in some areas, ill defined in other areas, and poorly enforced in yet other areas. Businesses can obey the letter of the law, but not the spirit of the law. Further, the distinction between law and morality is a widely recognized one. If business was focusing on the law, it wasn't fully focusing on business ethics or social responsibility. More was required.

The result was a call for something beyond mere compliance, something that would involve business ethics or social responsibility and would, at the same time, encourage corporations to do what many of them were claiming to do. One of the important ways in which this was addressed was by speaking of the importance of integrity within business as something in addition to simple compliance with the law. As a result, corporate integrity and integrity programs began to develop.

Though this places integrity in a particular context—that is, in contrast to compliance programs and the law—it does not tell us a great deal about what constitutes corporate integrity. In fact, there are at least three ways in which corporate integrity has been talked about.

Some link integrity with some specific value or principle. The ING Group, as well as Levi Strauss and Chiquita Brands International, are a few of many businesses that speak of integrity as one of their basic principles. However, others identify corporate integrity with a general way of acting morally. For example, De George has identified integrity with acting morally (De George, 1993). Corporate integrity then becomes virtually synonymous with corporate morality. To give an account of one is to give an account of the other. And yet others view integrity as an exemplary form of behavior; perhaps this is because so few of us do actually follow through and "walk the talk" or act consistently with our moral values. In this third view, those who act with integrity are people or organizations that are willing to defend difficult positions. As such, integrity involves the stuff of moral courage and even heroism.

This last way of viewing integrity is not as applicable in the current context as the others, since we want to know not simply what the very best, most exemplary business organizations would do, but what all business organizations ought to do. Further, we are interested not simply in how they ought to behave (however consistently that might be) in just one part of their activities but rather overall. Hence, it is the second sense of integrity that is most relevant when talking about corporate integrity, at least in the present context.

Needless to say, this last form of integrity has been the subject of a wide variety of approaches and different interpretations. Some focus on questions, quite generally, of corporate responsibilities to various stakeholders. What responsibilities does business have to each group of stakeholders and how should those be weighed in the balance? Others examine this question more specifically by asking how corporations should act in foreign lands where the same values do not seem to exist. How should executives be compensated? How might corporate codes of conduct be improved to address current ethical challenges that business faces? What forms of corporate governance, auditing requirements, and socially responsible investing should be associated with corporate integrity? These are among the questions that the chapters in this book discuss. What we find, in part, is that we need to know not only what corporate integrity is and how to foster it but also how to recognize when corporations have (or lack) integrity.

ACCOUNTABILITY

Most of what is discussed under business ethics or social responsibility is viewed as voluntarily undertaken by business. This is to say that these activities are not required or obligatory, but permissible—something a business may (or may not) do. The European Union White and Green Papers on corporate social responsibility were quite emphatic on this point. Of course, if business ethics or corporate integrity presupposes a defining difference between law and morality, then one would hardly expect otherwise. However, this distinction is also too simple in a number of ways.

To begin with, just because something is legally voluntary does not mean that it is morally voluntary. A business might be morally obligated to do something, such as not to fire an employee just before retirement so as to save on retirement costs due to that employee, even though it is legally permissible. It might also be morally obligated not to give its CEO a huge compensation package, even though to do so might also be legal. These actions are not morally permissible (or voluntary), even though they might be legally so—i.e., there might be no laws against either of these acts.

Second, normal moral behavior requires a certain set of conditions that help foster and promote it. These conditions do not define which act is morally right or wrong, but they are conditions that individuals typically require in order to respond as normal moral agents. These conditions may include the fact that one's peers (or superiors) are acquainted with one's actions, that they can bring some pressures of praise and blame to bear upon one, that one is susceptible to such pressures and not wholly indifferent or insulated against them, etc. These are

circumstances of accountability whereby one's responsibility for one's actions becomes known to other relevant individuals or groups and is either approved or disapproved.

Third, the very process of engaging in the reasoning whereby an individual, or a business, undertakes responsible (or ethical) actions requires discussion with others. The idea that a person arrives at his or her moral judgments solely through some inner monologue is an image many people harbor, but it belies how we really must arrive at moral conclusions and decisions. Our moral reasoning processes require other individuals and social institutions. We must consider how others will be affected by our actions and how they will see our actions. This generally involves some sort of dialogue with them. Further, morally to adopt a certain course of action is to be prepared to defend it to others and to give reasons—in short, to give an account of what one intends (or intended) to do. It is that account to which one appeals, after one's actions, to help explicate and defend what one has done. Similarly, corporate integrity is bound up with reasoning processes that involve other stakeholders as well as accounts that describe and justify what was done. In short, integrity at both individual and corporate levels is bound up with various accountability measures. How this gets worked out with corporations—through reporting mechanisms and auditing practices of certain sorts; measures to address information asymmetries, conflicts of interest, and codes of ethics; and forms of engagement with other institutions that seek to promote ethical and responsible behavior in business—is a major feature of current discussions in this area, as well as an important part of this book.

Finally, though people tend to conflate responsibility and accountability, they are different concepts. To say that a person is morally responsible for something means (roughly) that that person is morally obligated to do (or not to do) something. Of course, a person may also be causally responsible for something, which means that the person brought about (or had a significant hand in bringing about) something. But this is different from moral responsibility. For a person to be morally responsible for something is to say that there is something they are morally required to do and that, though they could have done something else, if they fail to do what is required (absent excusing conditions), they may be blamed and/or punished for having failed. In this sense, a father is responsible for the well-being of his children, and a woman may be responsible for fulfilling the duties of her job. In general, our responsibilities are to certain individuals or organizations, which may even have rights against us to act in particular ways. It is not always the case, however, that we are accountable to them. I may be responsible for my children, but I am accountable to my wife, the state, my church, etc., when it comes to my success or failure to fulfill these responsibilities. Similarly, corporations are accountable to their stockholders, as well as other stakeholders, for their performance in a wide variety of areas. And, here as well, a business may be responsible for its employees but accountable to the stockholders as well as other stakeholders (which may include those employees). Likewise, a company may be responsible for its treatment of the environment but not accountable to the environment (whatever that would mean). Instead, it is accountable to the community in which it operates, guardians of the environment, or the state.

Accountability refers, then, to a response (or account) one is required to give, the evaluation of the contents of that response, and the praise or punishment that may derive from the manner and the extent to which one's account is satisfactory. As such, accountability is bound up with the success or failure of a person or organization to fulfill their responsibilities. It is part of how we know and judge their success or failure. To say "we are going to hold you accountable" is to say that, at the end of the day, your fulfillment (or nonfulfillment) of your responsibilities will be monitored and evaluated. If you have been successful, you will be commended, or perhaps even rewarded, whereas if you have failed to do what you should have done, you will be punished in some manner. It is, in an interesting way, to say that we are going to take your responsibilities seriously. We are going to hold you to them.

It is worth noting that there is something of an asymmetry here in that we normally believe that people and organizations should fulfill their responsibilities and do not, as such, deserve commendation for that, though they do deserve condemnation and even punishment if they fail. However, in circumstances where significant numbers of people or organizations are not doing what is generally expected of them, praise and commendation may be appropriate as well. In some instances, however, people fulfill their responsibilities to an extent above and beyond the call of duty—this is the exemplary form of integrity—and then we believe that praise and commendation are especially in order. Mother Teresa did what was above and beyond the normal responsibilities individuals have. Hence, she was highly regarded and commended.

Accordingly, accountability involves at least the following four aspects: (a) some standard(s) according to which a person or organization is supposed to act; (b) a response from that person or organization given to some other person(s) or organization(s) regarding the fulfillment (or nonfulfillment) of those standards; (c) a determination regarding the manner and extent to which those standards were (or were not) fulfilled; and (d) some kind of evaluative response from another person or organization that commends or condemns that behavior. The standards in (a) can be explicit and legal, or they may be explicit or implicit and moral. In the explicit and legal case, we have what might be called compliance accountability.

The accountability that occurs with ordinary human agents relies on other people (and organizations) seeking explanations and justifications from them for why they have (or have not) followed various common moral standards. It also depends on other people's preparedness to praise or blame them as a result of their actions. This requires a community of moral agents. To modify a well-known phrase, it takes a community to foster moral behavior.

The difficulties and shortcomings within the business community in these regards have been increasingly evident. The heads of many businesses have not, in general, been willing to speak out about the ethical failures of other businesses, not to mention their own. They have not been prepared to blame, condemn, or chastise them for anything short of the most egregious behaviors. Stockholders have criticized management, but usually this has been for financial, rather than moral, shortcomings. We have also seen that boards of directors, e.g., in the case of Enron, have been reluctant to question top management. Other boards of directors have not, apparently, really known what was going on. In some cases they have even suspended parts of their own organization's code of ethics so that questionable activities might take place.

Accordingly, the situation we face does not obviously require new moral principles as much as their serious application. New laws and regulations may be required. For example, in the United States the Sarbanes-Oxley Act of 2002 attacked problems of corporate accounting behavior in a wide variety of ways. Among its many provisions are the following: Audit committees are required to have individuals with financial expertise who are knowledgeable of the organization's activities; "members of this committee must be independent directors without any compensation for service on the committee" (Lakey, 2003, p. 1); external auditors are barred from providing most other business services to the organization; individual auditors are to be rotated every five years; CEOs and CFOs are required to certify that financial reports are accurate and compliant; and, finally, policies must be developed and followed to protect whistleblowers. The destruction or alteration of relevant documents is a crime (cf. Lakey, 2003). However, these and other such laws and regulations will not, in the end, be a complete solution since people are always able to get around laws and regulations. Hence, there is also a need for monitors and outside examiners who will determine whether companies really do what they say they are doing and what they are required by law and morality to do. As the Clean Clothes Campaign has noted, there is "ample evidence of the failure of companies to actually implement the promises

made in their codes (in most cases workers are not even informed of the rights articulated in the codes . . .)" (Codes, 2004, p. 3).

Some companies have made efforts to address this issue. In Great Britain, Allied Domecq PLC has decided to set up an independent review board to assess company advertising, as part of its focus on corporate social responsibility. Chiquita Brands International has developed a long-term relationship with the Rainforest Alliance, which is a leading international conservation organization. In this partnership, "Chiquita has achieved [in 2000] Rainforest Alliance certification on 100 percent of its Latin American farms, covering more than 60,000 acres" (Corporate Conscience Award, 2003, p. 2). Chiquita is also working "to achieve compliance and third-party certification to SAI's (Social Accountability International's) Social Accountability 8000 international workplace standard in all of its owned banana divisions" (Conscience, 2003, p. 2). And Transparency International has developed what it calls "National Integrity Systems" that are designed to confront corruption, which might be said to be one form of lack of integrity. Partnerships of various kinds between businesses and NGOs seem to be part of an emerging trend that seeks to foster corporate integrity. For business, these partnerships may help resolve the issue of which standards to adhere to (which is central to the problem of integrity). And to the extent that these groups also engage in activities that seek to monitor the activities of businesses, they may, in part, also be addressing the accountability problem.

These are a few examples of legal and nonlegal, coercive, and cooperative measures that might be brought to bear as part of new forms of accountability required of business in the twenty-first century. It is worth noting, though it is not discussed in this book, that the issue of accountability has arisen not only for profit-seeking corporate organizations but also for nonprofit and nongovernmental organizations (not to mention governments). There is much that needs to be done in these other organizations as well.

ADDRESSING ISSUES OF
ACCOUNTABILITY AND INTEGRITY:
TRANSATLANTIC BUSINESS ETHICS

In light of the importance of accountability and integrity issues, not only in the United States but also in Europe (and other parts of the world), a transatlantic business ethics conference of leading thinkers and practitioners in business ethics was held at Georgetown University in the fall of 2002 on the topic of "Corporate Integrity and Accountability." The chapters in this book are the result of that conference and discuss many of the topics mentioned above. They represent the thinking of some of the very best business ethicists in both North America and Europe.

The papers have been grouped into four main areas. Since there are introductions to each of these sections, their contents will not be summarized here. What is worth noting briefly in this initial introduction are the different approaches to the twin main themes of corporate integrity and accountability that are evident between the U.S. and European approaches. These differences can easily be overstated since each side of the Atlantic has influenced the other side, and since there are important variations within each area. Still, they are noteworthy.

Regarding their similarities, the authors represented below tend to see similar problems, recognize the limits of compliance, accept different multiple approaches, and even share similar views on basic concepts such as integrity. Further, on both sides of the Atlantic, business ethics and corporate social responsibility, as fields of academic study, have undergone significant development in recent years. On both sides of the Atlantic, problems such as the following are recognized to be major issues that corporate integrity faces: conflicts of interest, information asymmetry, corruption, CEO compensation, etc. Likewise, authors on both sides of the Atlantic have defended, for example, greater transparency, auditor independence, and more modest executive compensation.

Differences between the two sides of the Atlantic include the following: terminological

preferences; the sources on which they base their views on business ethics; the styles of argumentation they employ; their estimations of the place of laws and rules in corporate responsibility; their views concerning the universality of moral principles; and their positions on the relations between business, government, and society and the extent to which government should be involved in corporate social responsibility (CSR).

A PricewaterhouseCoopers (PwC) survey (June 2003) indicates that there may be other differences as well. That survey indicated that "environmental impacts will continue to receive more attention by companies based in Europe, while for their U.S. counterparts, there will be a spotlight on governance; employee issues and benefits; and business ethics" (European, 2003, p. 2). A different PwC survey (February 2002) noted that North American CEOs "prioritize supporting community projects over workplace safety in their definition of CSR, while Central/ South American and European CEOs prioritize workplace safety highest" (Baue, 2002, p. 2). How significant (and real) these differences are may be a matter of considerable debate, but they tend to fall within the much broader agreement on issues noted above.

CONCLUSION

In the coming years, we may anticipate that questions of corporate integrity with regard to governance, reporting, and the integration of ethics and social responsibility measures into corporations will continue to grow in importance. It might be said that in addition to the triple bottom line of "people, profits and planet" that Elkington proposed as the focus of corporate activity (cf. Elkington, 1998), we require a quadruple bottom line of people, profits, planet, and procedures—procedures or processes that would integrate the first three into corporations so that they are organizations of integrity.

It should also be clear that though CSR and business ethics are treated as voluntary add-on considerations by many businesses, it is just this approach that leads to the self-destructive (and other-destructive) activities of businesses. CSR and ethics must be integrated into the daily and strategic activities of businesses. Businesses must be bound by reporting and accountability mechanisms if they are to develop the integrity that is both necessary and desirable for ethical business in a good society. An obvious extension of such views on integrity and accountability would be to nonprofit organizations and to government itself.

Finally, this book does not offer a single didactic thread running throughout all chapters. Instead, the chapters that constitute this book raise various issues and take different stances on a number of the broad topics that fall under the umbrella heading of corporate integrity and accountability. The fact is that there are different problems and different viewpoints on these twin topics, and though there are some common moral principles and values at work here, even these are plural in nature. It would be a grave mistake, however, to conclude, from these differences, that some courses of action are not better than others or that corporate integrity and accountability are not topics of great importance.

REFERENCES

Anderson, S., & Cavanagh, J. (2000). *Field guide to the global economy.* New Press.

Baue, W. (2002, February 1). *CEOs worldwide prioritize corporate social responsibility.* Retrieved December 2003 from SRI World Group Inc. at http://www.socialfunds.com/news/article.cgi/article769.html

Codes, monitoring, and verification. Why the CCC is involved. (2004). Retrieved February 2004 from http://www.cleanclothes.org/codes.htm

Corporate Conscience Award presented to Chiquita by Social Accountability International. (2003, October 8). Press release from Chiquita Brands International, Inc. Retrieved December 2003 from SRI World Group Inc. at http://www.socialfunds.com/news/release_print.cgi?sfArticleId=2185

De George, R. (1993). *Competing with integrity.* New York: Oxford University Press.

Elkington, J. (1998). *Cannibals with forks: The triple bottom line of 21st century business.* Stoney Creek, CT: New Society Publishers.

European and U.S. multinationals place different emphases on corporate sustainability. (2003, June). Retrieved December 2003 from Pricewater houseCoopers at http://www.pwcglobal.com/ext web/ncpressrelease.nsf/DocID/4330ED430 DF383AA85256D3B00529D16

Gray, J. (1998). *False dawn.* New York: New Press.

Lakey, B. M. (2003). Sarbanes-Oxley: When accountability comes knocking. *BoardSource 2003–10.* Retrieved October 14, 2003, from the Ethics Resource Center Web site at http://www.ethics.org/resources/article_detail.cfm?ID=833

Novak, M. (1997). *On corporate governance.* Washington, DC: The AEI Press.

Paine, L. S. (1994). Managing for organizational integrity. *Harvard Business Review, 2* (March–April), 106–117.

PART I

CORPORATE INTEGRITY CHALLENGED

The turn of the millennium brought a large number of business scandals that caused a great deal of economic, social, and personal distress. As a result, they have led people to rethink how businesses should operate and be monitored. However, they have also led many to reconsider how business ethics should approach business and people in business. Perhaps these scandals revealed weaknesses not only in business but also in business ethics and corporate social responsibility movements. The first several chapters speak to this issue of the relation of business ethics and business. In brief, they consider what business ethicists should be focusing on (Berenbeim), about what and to whom they should be speaking (Collins), what the nature of a better way of thinking about business might be (Wempe & Donaldson), and how integrity should be viewed in various dynamic social contexts such as business (van Luijk). These chapters open the door to the challenges that corporate integrity has posed for those thinking about business in a time of scandal. They should be read less with an eye searching for final answers regarding what to do than with one looking for important questions and issues to be considered.

Ronald Berenbeim contends that the recent business scandals have made much clearer what business ethics must focus on these days. If businesses such as Enron can engage in laudable sustainability programs regarding the environment, be a generous contributor to good causes, and still engage in the illegal and unethical activities it did, then the focus of business ethics must shift to the processes by which businesses govern themselves. Two of the crucial questions that emerge in this shift of attention are conflicts of interest and moral hazard (in Part II, questions of conflicts of interest will arise again as being of vital importance). However, the way to address these issues is not through legalistic compliance programs. Instead, broader, ethically infused programs are required that, among other things, permit individuals to raise ethical questions and that inform them about the proper understandings of the ethical issues they face. Top management must support these systems. Business ethics can then provide individuals and organizations with "systems and . . . methods for determining rules of conduct in making decisions where neither law nor the market offers clear guidance."

David Collins attacks the issue of fostering corporate ethics and integrity from a different, more traditional direction. He argues that an important part of the problem is that the reluctance of many in the business community to embrace corporate social responsibility (CSR) has not been adequately addressed. To develop his argument he briefly reflects back on the well-known case of Johnson & Johnson's handling of the Tylenol crisis it faced in the early '80s. This is a good example, he argues, of the importance of CSR and how it can be good for business and its reputation. Whether the ethical issues that business faces are ones of right and wrong, or of right and right, business frequently balks at CSR due to one (or more) of the six reasons that people such as Milton Friedman (and more recently David Henderson) have identified. Collins briefly summarizes these well-known reasons and urges that those who address issues of business ethics and CSR take them seriously since they are rooted in a set of four values that Collins identifies and claims are central to a liberal-democratic market society. More particularly, he challenges business ethicists to forge a more coordinated approach to the topics of business ethics and CSR. In addition, CEOs, boards of directors, and large shareholders must speak out more openly and forcefully on their behalf, something that has infrequently occurred even during the recent business scandals. In any case, the discussion of ethical issues that business faces must be done in terms that businesspeople are able to understand, and in ways that might move them to make important changes. In this way, Collins adds a further business and social dimension to the issues that were initially raised in Berenbeim's chapter.

Johan Wempe and Thomas Donaldson urge that our concern for the ethical challenges that business faces should focus not simply on the large ones (such as Enron), but also on much less famous and smaller ones (such as obesity in children). In addition, these challenges are misunderstood, they argue, if they are viewed as simply brought about by the greed of, and the breaking of rules by, the leaders of business. Instead, they contend, the situation is much more complex. Many of those who attribute ethical deficiencies to business these days are involved in a form of simplistic thinking, which leads them (and us) further astray in the rush to embrace additional rules and more sanctions.

They illustrate these views by discussing the possible link between childhood obesity and the placement of soft drinks in schools, the increased noise and air pollution that would be caused by an additional runway at Schiphol Airport outside Amsterdam (the Netherlands), and the manipulation of profits by high-paid executives at WorldCom and other businesses. They argue that current discussions of these kinds of issues are beset by a form of bipolar or monistic interpretation, an effort to place blame on someone, and the attempt to strengthen the rules surrounding such cases and to ensure greater compliance. Much of this last feature of these discussions is based on a view of the market that not only eradicates the notion of socially responsible business practices but also inadequately represents the imperfect markets in which corporations operate.

To remedy this situation, they argue, we must turn towards a more pluralistic view both of these situations and of the moral tools required to analyze them. For this, the notions of integrity and of social contracts may serve us well. The latter concept, in the form of Integrative Social Contracts Theory (a theory they briefly explain), maintains that companies have multiple responsibilities beyond their stockholders. In short, they defend a view of value pluralism not only within, but also between, the communities in which companies do business. Of course, such value pluralism will result in real dilemmas, which cannot simply be dismissed or easily skirted. This is one of the results of recognizing the complexity of the ethical challenges business faces. They place people's integrity in jeopardy, since they prevent them from the following threefold integrity project: the aligning of their values, norms, and ideals; the striving for coherence between words and deeds; and the making of a contribution to the greater whole. This integrity project they refer to as "working on wholeness."

To achieve integrity in the face of the real dilemmas they have described, Wempe and Donaldson present four possible strategies that stem from their views on value pluralism. Of these four strategies, they argue, only one will provide a real solution that is consistent with integrity, namely, the one that while recognizing "the worth of different conflicting values" seeks "to maximize the opportunities that exist for creating social added value."

The three preceding chapters offer three different suggestions on how we might better attempt to understand and correct the ethical failures that businesses have experienced in the past several years.

Henk van Luijk takes a rather different approach to arrive at a position not too distant from that of Wempe and Donaldson. He does this by taking us on an extended examination of the idea of integrity, in personal and social contexts, as well as in private, public, and corporate domains. This discussion enriches our understanding of integrity, both in corporate and noncorporate contexts.

After noting the use of *integrity* to refer to the wholeness of physical things as well as the unity of people in psychological contexts, van Luijk distinguishes between personal integrity (which involves sticking to your own personal standards), and social integrity (which involves sticking to socially given standards). Clearly there is a tension between these two forms of integrity. In this chapter, van Luijk focuses on social integrity, which is linked to his view of morality as a social phenomenon.

The realm of social integrity is a complex realm that includes both private and public domains. In both domains, the rights and interests that, in their respective domains, deserve respect define integrity. For example, in the private domain, integrity involves three different ethics: a transactional one (including principles of equality, reciprocity, and honesty); a recognitional ethics that addresses cases involving divergent claims and conflicting interests (principles of justice and beneficence are central here); and a participatory ethics whose basic principles are alertness (a moral sensibility for what can be and deserves to be better), decency, and emancipation (towards full citizenship).

In the noncommercial public domain, supra-individual interests are looked after by representative agencies, institutions, and functionaries that represent the democratically defined common good and public interests. Safeguards are needed in this realm, given the asymmetrical relation of power to be found here. This basic safeguard is the public democratic system itself. Accordingly, the two public domain characteristics are those of power and representation. The latter brings principles of dignity, trustworthiness, lack of greed, and openness. The former introduces principles of respect, care, and preparedness to serve actively. With these principles, social integrity and morality in the public domain can be articulated. Together they give rise to a type of ethics called representative ethics.

In the corporate domain, social integrity has been mistakenly equated with market morality. Since corporations move in both the private and public domains, they cannot simply be regulated by the principles of either the private or the public domains. Instead, they are subject to only those principles related to public power, first and foremost of which is the principle of openness to democratic control. The stress on transparency grows out of this basic public principle related to the corporate domain of social integrity.

This blurring of boundaries between private and public suggests that an institutional approach could add to a domain approach. Each of the above three institutions has its own managing task, objective, and one or two basic moral principles. Here we see that many new interrelations between basic institutions are developing—for example, public agents acting as market participants, while civil society representatives dominate the political debate. With this comes the rising prominence of respect and shared responsibility among these participants.

In this newly developing context, institutional integrity is not about power, money, or knowledge, but about where, in a current situation, through a joint effort, a normative balance can be established to foster well-being, justice, and democracy. Also important is the attempt to give them content in specific situations. This requires a joint effort. Integrity above all is an agreement.

In summary, these authors depict the situation business ethics faces (both as a topic and as a way of doing business) in the post-Enron era. It must look to corporate governance, address businesspeople with arguments that relate to ones that move them, and stop looking at these issues in bipolar ways by recognizing the complexity and pluralism that is part of them. This will give rise to problems and conflicts for which we need appropriate strategies. One of these might include the complex understanding of integrity, as a social phenomenon, with its category-spanning nature in the case of corporate integrity.

The chapters in Part I pose the problem of how to understand and to approach the problem of corporate integrity. While these chapters provide only the broadest answers to the problems they pose, the chapters in the parts thereafter address these problems more specifically.

2

WITTGENSTEIN'S BEDROCK

What Business Ethicists Do

RONALD E. BERENBEIM

"If I have exhausted the justification, I have reached bedrock and my spade is turned. Then I am inclined to say 'This is simply what I do.'" So wrote Wittgenstein about his work as a philosopher (as cited in Edmonds & Eidinow, 2001, p. 87).

Enron and the stream of cases that have followed in its wake have certain common elements that confront business ethicists with Wittgenstein's bedrock. Our spade is turned. What we do is much clearer than it was a year ago.

If companies and their leaders were not accountable for making ethical choices, there would be no such thing as business ethics. Because they are, there is. The business ethicist's essential project is to provide companies with systems and to supply business professionals with methods for determining rules of conduct in making decisions where neither law nor the market offers clear guidance. When this process of ordered choice works, the company develops principles that will govern similar future situations.

Business ethics, then, is not about good behavior per se. It is about using rigorous processes and methods for making behavioral choices. For this reason, other concerns such as sustainable development and citizenship—worthy objectives in their own way—have little meaning in the absence of organizational commitment to ethical decision making.

Enron, to cite the leading example, publicized its sensitivity to sustainable development issues. The company impressed socially responsible investors with its investment in alternatives to fossil fuels. Its wind energy investment was believed to be a forward-looking effort in this regard. Enron was also lionized as a model corporate citizen. The company's substantial beneficence to Texas institutions such as the

M.D. Anderson Cancer Center and the University of Texas Law School offers eloquent testimony to Enron's public spiritedness.

In the field of Corporate Governance (another one of business ethics' many tributaries), the company had a widely admired board consisting of non–business members whose broad experience and expansive vision afforded the public assurance that its interests would always be part of Enron's deliberations. In a stirring address to a 1999 Houston Conference on Corporate Governance, Enron's CEO Ken Lay said that "the responsibility of our board—a responsibility which I expect them to fulfill—is to ensure legal and ethical conduct by the company and everyone in the company" (Lay, 1999, p. 26). Of course, two Enron directors were the president and dean, respectively, of the aforementioned Anderson Cancer Center and the University of Texas Law School. Evidently, Ken Lay's awareness of one of business ethics' most rudimentary concepts— conflict of interest—was seriously defective. The same could be said for the directors who accepted contributions to their institutions.

Allowing for purposes of discussion that Lay's ignorance of the potential conflicts of interest of nonprofit sector directors is not unique, a chairman with his public relations instincts should have been alert to ways in which appearances can compromise board effectiveness. Indeed, Enron's generosity (if that is what it was) compromised the ability of certain independent directors to fulfill what Lay believed to be their primary role—"ensur[ing] legal and ethical conduct by the company and everyone in the company."

Avoidance of conflict of interest—the requirement that the company's directors and officers refrain from opportunities that potentially undermine a commitment of undivided loyalty to the company—is not something that you learn in church or on your parents' knees. While easily stated, individual situations may give rise to complex and perhaps even counterintuitive applications. Did the Enron directors whose nonprofit organizations were beneficiaries of Enron philanthropy have an unacceptable conflict of interest, or was it one that could be cured by full disclosure? Did the appearance of conflict render their decisions fatally defective? These are difficult questions for which we cannot be certain that good people or even highly moral individuals well versed in the law can find the right answers.

The same could be said for moral hazard—an individual's perception that either the cost or the benefit of the activity differs from the true social cost or benefit. (For a more complete discussion of moral hazard, see Pindyck & Rubinfeld, 1997.) For example, boards and CEOs failed to recognize the potential for moral hazard in options compensation. They did not see that options formulas gave senior executives an incentive to manage earnings at the ultimate social cost of market confidence. In some cases, this situation may have been further compounded by the acquiescence of directors who may have had real or potential conflicts of interest to these incentive plans. And the accounting, law, banking, and brokerage firms whose role it is to insist that their clients avoid moral hazard situations failed to do so. The result was conflict-ridden boards that readily acceded to managed earnings.

The failure of these institutions to play their proper role as guardians of the public interest explains much of the damage that Enron, WorldCom, and other companies were able to inflict. Indeed, commenting on what went wrong in the '90s, George Soros said that "we can identify two specific elements: a decline in professional standards and a dramatic rise in conflict of interest." In Soros's view, lawyers, accountants, auditors, security analysts, and bankers allowed the priority of client retention to trump the long-standing values of independence and adherence for those engaged in their calling to an independent code of professional conduct. The social principles of which these "values" are an expression are, as Soros puts it, the "anchor" of financial markets (Soros, 2002).

The pitfalls of conflict of interest and moral hazard are but two problem areas that underscore the need for companies to have an ongoing process for developing and refining their business conduct standards. Such systems are essential in global markets that depend significantly on a company's capacity for self-regulation. No laws can successfully deter wrongful conduct without an effective compliance response from business institutions. And compliance efforts that do not insist on an extra measure of prudence in company affairs beyond mere legal compliance are unlikely to be successful.

Since there ought to be widespread agreement on these points, one would think that business ethics would now be accorded new respect as an essential element in business education and practice. Of course, this is not so. Enron and related cases have been used to argue that you can't teach business ethics. In all honesty, I must admit in this regard that Jeffrey Skilling would be a severe challenge to whatever pedagogical skills I may have. Recently, business ethics has been derided as little more than a hugely profitable public relations gambit to assure an anxious public and those few board members who care that all is well (cf. Marino, 2002).

In brief, the argument is that you can't teach people to be ethical—only parents and religious institutions can do that. Indeed, you cannot even cultivate a capability to be morally articulate. If anything, more effort needs to go into the teaching of "business law"—which is a real thing.

These attacks ignore the need to remedy deficiencies in subjects such as the understanding of conflict of interest and moral hazard. They also overlook the important contribution that business ethics has made through the development of the compliance system to the improvement of business practice. U.S. compliance systems began as part of the Defense Industry Initiative. Following the adoption of the U.S. Organizational Sentencing Guidelines, firms outside the defense industry instituted them as well.

As U.S. companies became increasingly active in global markets, they found that the compliance model was useful in helping to achieve common standards of business conduct in global operations. With the approval of the OECD Anti-Bribery Convention by 35 countries in 1997, the compliance model attracted interest from non-U.S. companies. Compliance systems are simple in structure, and regardless of the company or the culture in which they are used, they rely on four key elements: (a) top management commitment; (b) code of conduct; (c) implementation through discussion and training; and (d) communication systems for reporting and documenting questionable practices.

As a word—and even more as a mentality—the term *compliance* is out of favor. For many, it implies the imposition of an excessively rule-based informer-and-enforcement culture, but good compliance systems have none of these features.

What distinguishes a good compliance program from a bad one is simply this: A company with a good system affords an opportunity for people to talk with some level of comfort and literacy about ethics. The managers do it by articulating the values to which the company is committed. The code is the product of an ongoing dialogue between the company and its employees, and it is periodically revised to incorporate the changing concerns of managers and workers. Discussion and training sessions enable the organization to be aware of issues when and where its people confront them and to formulate rules and methods for dealing with these problems. And far from being "snitch-lines," whistle-blowing channels are used by employees to seek advice in difficult situations and for the organization to get early warnings about potentially dangerous situations.

Successful compliance systems can be found in all cultures. Indeed, a good compliance program is the best possible tool for securing adherence to core business principles in diverse cultures. In my work on the World Bank project on East Asian company anticorruption programs, I have seen many companies in that region adopt compliance systems. Effective programs operating in East Asia, whether North American, European, or Asian, use similar approaches—especially in discussions of situations that the company has actually confronted—to formulate the best possible response to problems.

But the most important thing to be said about compliance programs is that they work for the limited purpose for which they are intended. No "rogue employee" in a large company with an effective compliance system has destroyed that company or even caused it serious harm. The one recent example of an employee who bankrupted a company was Nicholas Leeson of Barings. A few years ago I saw a television interview with Leeson. In so many words and with a tone of regret, he said that he could not believe that his activities had gone unnoticed. If Barings had adopted a compliance program, perhaps the bank would still be in business and Leeson might have been spared an extended stay in a Singapore jail.

There is little evidence that Enron, to cite just one example, had a compliance system worthy of the name. Although, as stated earlier, compliance systems can only prevent or limit the damage that a rogue employee can inflict on the company or stakeholders, I don't know of a company with a highly regarded compliance system that is in trouble.

To date, there are no compliance programs that exercise truly effective oversight of senior executive and director conduct, but we have the next best thing. Directors and CEOs that are truly committed to their companies' compliance systems are a fairly safe bet to stay out of jail.

At the heart of this director–CEO support is an understanding that ethics and compliance systems constitute a company's acknowledgment that regulation and enforcement are not just the job of legislators, prosecutors, and judges. It is the company's duty as well. Recognition of that fact is the single most important act of corporate citizenship. Without such an understanding, a company would not have a governance system worthy of the name, and it would lack the necessary capability for identifying those market failure situations where the exercise of moral restraint is essential for sustainable companies.

Finally, it is worth noting that all the companies that have failed so catastrophically had the best legal advice. I am not here to deride the importance of law, but it has its limitations. People go to lawyers to find out what the rules are and whether the act that they are contemplating runs afoul of the rules. These are the individuals who think that our courses afford them instruction on how far they can go before they can get into trouble. They aren't interested in the underlying principles to which the law gives imperfect expression. The people who are now on their way to jail do not find themselves in this situation because of poor legal advice. Their problem is a lack of moral curiosity for which a better understanding of ethics is the only cure.

This brief survey suggests that ethical business decisions are much more likely in companies where managers and workers are able to discuss with ease and fluency the ethical choices that they confront. The absence of such opportunities in some companies resulted in their catastrophic failure and a crisis of confidence in business institutions. The business ethicist's project is to help organizations build the institutional mechanisms and to provide employees with the analytic methods for this ongoing dialogue. We owe considerable gratitude to the cavalcade of scoundrels who have helped us, in Wittgenstein's phrase, to reach the point where the "spade is turned" and we are now inclined to say "this is simply what I do."

REFERENCES

Edmonds, D., & Eidinow, J. (2001). *Wittgenstein's poker*. London: Faber & Faber Ltd.

Lay, K. (1999). What should a CEO expect from a board? In D. Koehn (Ed.), *Corporate governance: Ethics across the board* (p. 26). Houston, TX: University of St. Thomas.

Marino, G. (2002, July 30). The latest industry to flounder: Ethics Inc. *The Wall Street Journal*, p. A14.

Pindyck, R. S., & Rubinfeld, D. L. (1997). Moral hazard. In *Microeconomics*. Upper Saddle River, NJ: Prentice Hall.

Soros, G. (2002, September 2). Busted. *The New Republic*, 18–21.

3

TYLENOL REVISITED: FRIEDMAN AND THE CURRENT CSR DEBATE

DAVID COLLINS

I n late September 1982, seven people died in the western suburbs of Chicago as a result of taking Extra Strength Tylenol capsules laced with cyanide. Strange as it may seem, this was the beginning of what has come to be regarded as an outstanding example of Corporate Social Responsibility, or CSR. I was a member of the executive team charged with responding to this terrible tragedy and I want to make its story the starting point for this chapter.

At the time this tragedy occurred, the analgesic Tylenol was the country's leading nonprescription pain reliever and Johnson & Johnson's (J&J) largest selling product. It was also one of the most profitable of the thousands of products made by this global health care company.

We received word of the poisonings midday on a Thursday in late September 1982. By Saturday, we had determined that the poison had been inserted after the product reached the store shelves, not in our plants. Nevertheless, the following Tuesday, concerned that the capsules would be used by copycats as weapons to harm others, J&J withdrew all consumer capsules from the market worldwide. In total, over 30 million bottles were returned and destroyed. The out-of-pocket cost was in excess of $140 million.

Seven weeks later, J&J reintroduced Tylenol capsules with a triple safety seal package. This launch met with outstanding success and support from the public. Six months later Tylenol had regained most of its leading market share. The company and its chairman, Jim Burke, were widely applauded for acting responsibly. And the Tylenol example is still frequently cited today with approval.

As this example demonstrates, socially responsible action can often be good for the business and is often good for the reputation of the company and its senior executives. Even in the current climate with its focus on scandalous corporate behavior, this holds true. Recently, *BusinessWeek* ("The Good CEO," 2002) carried a cover story spotlighting the good CEOs from six public companies. As these stories showed, there is often, though not always, tangible business and personal benefits from CSR. So why isn't a commitment to social responsibility universally embraced by the business community? I suggest there are a number of valid reasons for this that need to be understood and addressed. Identifying these gaps in the approach to promoting CSR will in turn suggest an agenda for future consideration and action.

First, a disclaimer: I approach this as a businessman, not an academic. I do this because efforts to affect the behavior of business folks must reflect, be tailored to, and be in the language of the real day-to-day life of the businessperson. Expressing the rationale for CSR in the language of the academy is not well designed to gain the attention of business people. Rather, one must stand in the shoes of the senior corporate executive and understand what they see when faced with the challenge of CSR.

Let me be clear on what I'm talking about. It's not about the Enron, WorldCom, or Tyco kinds of decisions. CSR, in my mind, is not about choosing right versus wrong. It's about choosing right versus right! Sometimes this means choosing between what's legally permissible and what's morally acceptable. At other times, it means making a choice between two arguably moral courses of action. For example, look at the Tylenol episode. If J&J had decided *not* to withdraw the product, but to take smaller remedial measures, this would not have been wrong. Going further, it would have been an acceptable course of action, one subsquently taken by a number of companies in similar situations.

But what CSR is always about, in my view, is choosing between two competing social and personal values. It is always a values-based decision and reflects the values priority of the executives and their organization. And because this is the case, the choice of a course of action can be the source of endless and frustrating debate between the business and interested outsiders. I experienced this at J&J when dealing with the single-minded advocates for withdrawal from South

Africa during the apartheid era, critical of our decision to remain in that country.

Further, once embarked on the search for an appropriate socially responsible course, the business will frequently find itself in a "damned if you do, damned if you don't" situation. This seems to be the dilemma facing GE today in its Hudson River clean-up case.

Is it any wonder then that business would seek shelter in Milton Friedman's position that the social responsibility of business is to make a profit—period! And leave all those social good works to other players in society (Friedman, 1970).

In fact, the Friedman position has more attraction than simply serving as a shield for the hassled businessperson. While he is, in my experience, the most well known exponent of the "profit only" point of view, he is not alone. Just last year, Mr. David Henderson, former chief economist at the Organization for Economic Cooperation and Development, published a long pamphlet entitled "Misguided Virtue" strongly advocating similar views. And one of the gaps in the drive to promote CSR is, in my view, the failure to engage and deal seriously with the arguments that Friedman advances, in the language and the arenas that business folks use and frequent. And they should be engaged because they are good arguments, ones that can be persuasive to senior executives in large publicly held companies. Let me illustrate.

Friedman raises six objections. The first is based on the agency theory of corporate governance. Corporate managers, according to this theory, are agents of the shareholders and consequently are obliged by contract to pursue the shareholders' interests—which is to make a profit. Any diversion of funds or effort to other socially worthy causes is a violation of that fiduciary agency duty.

The second argument is the "taxation without representation" one. According to this idea, if an executive can divert resources to causes other than making a profit, this effectively deprives shareholders, customers, and employees of a share in those diverted resources—shareholders of increased dividends, customers of price reductions, and employees of wage gains. Friedman characterizes this as taxation and points out that none of these constituents have any "say" in these decisions.

The third argument is the "skills" argument. Taking a page from the book of Adam Smith, in his *Wealth of Nations* (1776/1985) treatise, Friedman questions the skill of business executives to make these decisions. Since they are not economic issues (an arena where the executive is presumably an expert) but rather social issues (where he/she has no particular expertise), it is impossible to have any confidence that an appropriate decision will be made.

He adds to this a fourth point—trust. Why should we allow these essentially social decisions to be made by someone who is not accountable to society by some established social or political mechanism? The force of this argument can be appreciated if you visualize how you would feel if the business in which you invested or for which you worked spent part of its charitable funds supporting the Ku Klux Klan.

Friedman's fifth argument is that any business engaging significantly in these activities risks loss of shareholders, customers, and employees, each of whom might elect to place their economic fortunes in more trustworthy hands. While examples of this are rare, there are some. The Control Data Corporation of Minneapolis is often cited as an example. This case of waste of corporate assets in pursuit of worthy societal goals is concisely covered in the June 27, 1989, issue of *Financial World* in the article "The Do-Gooder."

Friedman's last argument is based on "forced conformity." He posits that a market economy is based on voluntary unanimity. In his words, "in an ideal free market resting on private property, no individual can coerce any other. All cooperation is voluntary and all parties to such cooperation benefit or they need not participate." But the idea of a corporation acting in a socially responsible way is built on the political principle of conformity. Since the only decision is that of the executive, the other players—shareholders, customers, and employees—are forced to agree, that is, to conform. This extension of an essential political principle into the economic arena threatens, in

Friedman's view, the foundations of the free market and indeed of the free society itself. Friedman thus calls it "a fundamentally subversive doctrine."

Whatever one thinks of the individual arguments Milton Friedman puts forward, it seems to me that as a whole they must be taken seriously. Here is a list of the values he is speaking up for:

1. sanctity of contract;

2. preservation of the institution and free use of private property;

3. the democratic political process and its proper place in society;

4. the clear allocation of responsibility and accountability between the public and the private sectors of society.

The interesting thing to me is that almost all of Friedman's arguments—the arguments, remember, of a renowned economist—are political in nature.

There is another forceful argument—one rooted both in economics and in the sound ordering of society—that needs to be advanced and understood. It could be called the "eye on the ball" argument. The economist Herb Stein and the theologian Michael Novak address this point. Stein points out that efficiency in maximizing the nation's product is the goal that business is best qualified to achieve. Novak phrases it as creating new wealth and asks who will meet this challenge if business does not because its "eyes"—its talents and resources—are devoted elsewhere.

These, I suggest, are substantial arguments and ones the CSR movement needs to engage and address in terms and in ways that reach the busy decision makers in the business community.

But the drive for CSR must go further. It is not enough to answer the arguments against CSR. It must also advance the arguments in favor of such behavior. Why should corporate managements risk going beyond the bottom line to direct their talents and resources to meet these legitimate public expectations? Some have suggested religious faith as a motive; others say it's good for business, or it's a requirement of good citizenship, or it's necessary if we are to preserve the freedoms we have enjoyed in our market economy. These are all good reasons, but they need to be developed and presented in a business-friendly language. At Johnson & Johnson, this was done in 1946 by then-CEO General Robert Wood Johnson when he published his famous Credo and its justification in a short book entitled *Or Forfeit Freedom*. In doing this, the general established a tradition of speaking out for CSR, which has been followed to this day by his successors.

One of the problems in advancing the cause of CSR as I have advocated is the lack of a coordinated approach to the subject. While there are thousands and thousands of initiatives in this area—at universities, think tanks, NGOs of all stripes, and business-based organizations of all sizes—many of these efforts are conducted without regard to, or even knowledge of, the others. Where then is the businessperson to turn to? Which of the many available voices should they listen to? And importantly, where will they find effective "cover" when their choice attracts the often-inevitable criticism from dissidents? Why can't there be a consortium of major proponents of CSR to do things such as conduct research, maintain a library, evaluate and critique proposals, and coordinate or at least collect information on the multiple activities underway?

The Business Roundtable took a small step in this direction several years ago by sponsoring an in-depth survey and study of CSR practices among its members. Unfortunately that report seems to have been shelved after its initial publication. This suggests another gap in the efforts to promote CSR—the reluctance of CEOs and boards to speak out publicly in defense of it. Indeed, in the *BusinessWeek* article on "The Good CEO," it was noted that one prominent executive refused to be interviewed because "talking to the media" did not in his judgment advance the interests of his company. This is not an unusual reaction. This is unfortunate, I believe, because if CEOs will not speak out on these issues, if the only voices heard are those outside the business, it's going to be hard to

persuade businesspeople, particularly the newer entrants to the workplace, that CSR is a legitimate goal and that they have permission to use a values-based approach to their decisions.

And while the challenge of getting CEOs to speak up is large, the challenge of getting large shareholders—mutual funds, pension plans, insurance companies, etc.—to accept a suitable measure of responsibility for the social responsiveness of their corporate holdings is even greater. It always puzzled me as a business executive why, in most debates about the social responsibility of corporate business, the enormous influence and sometimes-active role of these large shareholders was not on the table. In my view, again standing in the shoes of the businessperson, it should be. And along with this, we should consider the responsibilities that NGOs, religious groups, and other corporate activists bear for the consequences of the positions that they advance for corporate action. Just as it is appropriate to ask the business sector to go beyond self-interest in promoting a good society, so too is it fair to ask these other influential players to transcend their special interests in this worthy pursuit.

Finally, I present two more "gaps" or areas for exploration and illumination. The first is the difficulty in reconciling the permissions and demands of different countries and cultures. Is "when in Rome" an appropriate standard, or is "cultural imperialism" more appropriate? Or is there something in between? And how can we reconcile the domestic repercussions of the one and the competitive implications of the other? And a further aspect of this is whether the need for and appropriateness of CSR activities varies by country or culture. Is there less of a need in countries where the government plays a greater role in the society than in the United States? Is the relative freedom of the local market economy related to the social responsiveness of its business sector? For the operating executive in today's global economy, these can be the substance of day-to-day operational decisions.

The second gap is the question of the difference between public and private companies when it comes to CSR responsibilities and responses. Even Friedman notes that there is or may be a big difference between the two in the appropriateness of CSR activities. Is there a difference, and if so, what and why? I sense that understanding the answers to these questions can help in illuminating the challenges and opportunities for promoting CSR activities of our large, publicly held corporations.

I want to close by emphasizing how practical and important the need is for business to be socially responsible. We in business have numerous and vocal critics who are ready to challenge business and our free-market economy. In many cases they have the ear of the media and of ambitious politicians who are all too willing to upset the balance between government regulation and the freedom of markets that characterizes our unique American form of market economy. This balance is essentially founded on trust. This is why business cannot be singularly focused on maximizing profits to the exclusion of its other social responsibilities and why filling the "gaps" I have mentioned merits the attention and efforts of all of us.

REFERENCES

The do-gooder. (1989, June 27). *Financial World.*

Friedman, M. (1970, September 13). The social responsibility of business is to increase its profits. *New York Times Magazine.*

The good CEO. (2002, September 23). *BusinessWeek.*

Smith, A. (1776/1985). *The wealth of nations.* New York: Random House.

4

THE PRACTICALITY OF PLURALISM

*Redrawing the Simple Picture of Bipolarism
and Compliance in Business Ethics*

JOHAN WEMPE

THOMAS DONALDSON

Corporate "Watergates" such as Enron, Global Crossing, Tyco, and WorldCom have shaken the foundations of trade and industry. Even today in the fall of 2003, financial markets continue to reel from the impact of the trust-collapse that such Enron-like scandals created. But smaller ethical challenges, too, litter the pages of business media throughout the world, and they also take a toll on confidence in business. For example, in California a debate recently raged about the alleged role of the soft drink industry in the problem of childhood obesity. Kids like sugar, but too much of it makes for patterns of serious disease in later life. In turn, critics argue that the soft drink industry has shamelessly neglected kids' health. In Europe, Amsterdam's Schiphol Airport has been targeted by people living in the neighborhood and by

nongovernmental organizations (NGOs). The growth of the airport stimulates the economy but at the same time causes air and noise pollution for people living in the vicinity.

The blame for such seeming insensitivity, whether in the giant Enron-like scandals or the smaller criticisms of business practice, is directed invariably at a handful of leaders at the tops of the organizations: at the Lays (Enron), the Skillings (Enron), the Ebbers (WorldCom), and the Duncans (Arthur Andersen). It is directed at the big fish: the CEOs, CFOs, and partners of accounting or banking firms who, presumably driven by greed, doctor books, invent evasive schemes, and then cash in big. And what was the nature of the bad actions of these "greed-heads"? We are told they broke the rules; their greed trumped their sense of law abidance. What is the solution for a world in which greedy people break the rules? We need more rules, more clearly stated, and more punishment for these big fish rule breakers. In a word, we are told that we need tougher "compliance" for high-level corporate executives.

In this chapter we agree that greed and rule-breaking are bad. But the simple picture of evil people who need to be warned louder and hit harder in order to make them comply with laws and rules is little more than a comfortable mirage. Many clues immediately raise doubts about the veracity of the picture. For example, in at least a few notable instances, it is not clear that executives who destroyed their companies actually *did* break formal rules. What is more important is that hundreds or thousands of people—and not only the big fish at the top—were usually involved in facilitating these sorts of disasters. Not all of them will fit comfortably in the "greedy" category. A more complex picture is needed.

We maintain in these pages that standard discussions of moral problems in organizations have a common flaw, namely, a form of simplistic thinking. This simplistic thinking spawns a second flaw, namely, the rush to embrace compliance and legal systems as robust solutions. From the standpoint of such a compliance approach, the prescribed medicine for ethical disease seems always to be more rules, more controls, and more sanctions.

We will argue, in turn, that it is essential to think more complexly about ethical problems in organizations. We advance pluralism in contrast to monolithic or bipolar interpretations. To this purpose, we draw upon the concept of integrity as elaborated by Kaptein and Wempe (2002) in their recent book *The Balanced Company: A Theory of Corporate Integrity*, as well as the social contracts approach taken by Donaldson and Dunfee (1999) in the book *Ties That Bind*. Our argument suggests, in particular, that a proper notion of *integrity* entails a pluralistic value theory. This pluralistic value theory can help situate problems in a more detailed context, and the social contracts approach promises practical solutions. Finally, we show how pluralism can be put in the service of the creative solution of business ethics dilemmas.

We examine first three typical examples of ethical debates in which companies played pivotal roles. We intentionally use a cross section of examples to show how the issues extend beyond mere incidents and how the embedded analytical problem is a structural one.

THREE TYPICAL CASES

Overweight Adolescents

In the United States, politicians, including President Bush, are focusing attention on healthy living and eating habits. Many Americans are overweight and do not get enough exercise, and the problem even extends to children. Being overweight is one of the most important causes of death in the United States. A link can be made between obesity and a hurried lifestyle, quickly eating a fast-food breakfast while going to work or school. Even with changes in family structure, as children do not always eat at home or end up eating what is in the refrigerator when they feel like it. This seems to be a problem that is prevalent mainly in the United States. However, other societies are quick to follow the example of the "American Way of Life." In California, this topic has recently been made the subject of political discussion. How children are brought up is becoming the focus of increasing attention. The soft drink industry in particular is taking the rap for this. A connection is being made between the sponsoring of schools and the availability of a certain brand of soft drink. Children, not yet able to view the situation critically, are imperceptibly enticed. Once they are accustomed to a certain brand, they are not likely to switch to another product. There is also the subconscious image that soft drinks are healthy. The school's reputation also helps to promote the soft drink brand. If consumed in normal quantities, soft drinks do not cause health problems. However, this is a product that can easily be consumed in large quantities. If a child consumes soft drinks all day and does not get sufficient exercise, this considerably increases the chance of the child becoming overweight. The senior management of the companies in question are faced with a difficult choice. The intention of corporate citizenship is to actually help schools and community centers. And in reality, these schools and community centers are dependent to a certain extent on resources provided by these companies. Of course, the marketing activities are aimed at increasing turnover. The large soft drink companies separate their marketing activities from their corporate citizenship programs. And, with regard to the marketing, consumers are free to purchase any product they choose. In addition, parents have a responsibility to their children. After all, this is a product that is harmless when consumed in normal quantities. Should the corporate citizenship programs be stopped, and should the companies' marketing policies be changed?

Noise and Air Pollution
Caused by Amsterdam Airport

In the Netherlands, as in many other countries, the air and noise pollution caused by the national airport, Amsterdam Airport Schiphol, is the regular subject of heated discussions. In time, Schiphol Airport will be privatized. However, at present, it is run as a company with different government bodies owning the shares. When Schiphol was established, the location chosen was a thinly populated area a stone's throw away from Amsterdam. The presence of the airport had a positive effect on the economy in the area surrounding Schiphol. Schiphol now offers work to more than 100,000 people. However, the indirect effects are much more extensive. The small villages around the airport have grown into towns. Amsterdam, originally geared towards the seaport, turned to embrace the air. Many large companies opened offices on the Schiphol side of Amsterdam. Schiphol is embroiled in fierce competition with the airports of London, Frankfurt, Paris, and Rome. The expectation is that only a few European airports will be able to continue to fill a "mainport" function. A mainport is where large transatlantic flights originate. Passengers and cargo are flown from smaller airports to a mainport. The loss of the mainport function would have huge economic consequences for the region. A solution in the form of a fifth runway was chosen to better spread out the noise pollution. However, the use of a new runway has meant that other people have had to deal with noise and air pollution. To limit the damage for those living around the airport, Schiphol has begun a sizable sound insulation project. All homes affected by the noise pollution from the new runway will be insulated with Schiphol footing the bill. The plans for expansion met with considerable criticism from NGOs and those living in the surrounding area. The NGOs are of the opinion that Schiphol's growth in this densely populated area must not continue. Those living in the surrounding area feel they are being robbed of their peace and quiet.

Schiphol's management is faced with a difficult choice. They have to deal with the expectations of the NGOs and those living in the surrounding area. The air traffic is a serious nuisance. At the same time, the general public wants to fly to faraway destinations for their holidays. In addition, business people want to fly comfortably. The loss of the mainport function would not mean that there would be fewer flights. Schiphol's competitors would be all too happy to snap up the airport's customers. Tremendous economic interests are at stake. Schiphol has made considerable business activity possible, and many employees are dependent on the airport for their income.

Manipulation of Profits at WorldCom

Many angles of the profit manipulation at the telecom company WorldCom have been discussed in the media. Some facts and observations are presented briefly below.

WorldCom was one of the most successful telecom companies in the second half of the '90s. The senior management of the company firmly believed in the demand for network capacity. The Internet revolution would lead to a huge increase in the traffic on the telecom networks. WorldCom therefore made large investments in the network. The telecom company built its own fiberglass cable connections between large European cities. Countless companies were acquired, including the much larger U.S. telecom company MCI. The banks and shareholders did not see any problem with the company's enormous investments and acquisitions. In mid-2002, WorldCom's debts amounted to some $30 billion. In 1999, the company had a market value of more than $100 billion. Banks were very willing to grant loans for the investments, and shareholders lined up for share issues to finance the acquisitions. After the stock market crash, in which the telecom companies in particular took a beating, investors and banks became more critical. Was the cash flow sufficient to carry the sky-high interest charges? If WorldCom got to the point where it could no longer comply with the loan conditions, the company's creditors could pull the plug on the company. For customers, this would be a good reason no longer to do business with WorldCom. Banks will not be likely to grant new credits, and investors will avoid the company's shares. Under all this pressure, the senior management of WorldCom collapsed. The company had booked maintenance costs amounting to $3.8 billion as investments, which created a profit of $1.3 billion. But, in fact, the company was incurring a significant loss.

The accounting scandal at WorldCom was not a one-off incident. Similar accounts of misappropriation of funds have taken place at other telecom companies. For example, Global Crossing and Qwest allegedly purchased totally unnecessary network capacity from each other, in order to keep the turnover artificially high and to present a distorted view of the company's results to investors. Similar problems also emerged outside the telecom sector. In particular, the Enron scandal has received considerable attention. The energy company transferred assets to special companies not included in the books, while the company remained responsible for the risks. After the scandal emerged, Enron also took the accounting firm Arthur Andersen down with it when it fell. The auditor must have known about the misappropriation of funds in the books but

approved them anyway. Legal action followed the discovery that one of the accountants had destroyed evidence, which led to the demise of the entire multinational.

The consequences for the companies involved were tremendous. Thousands of employees lost their jobs. The shareholders watched the value of their shares plummet. The banks were forced to accept significant losses. However, the effects of these scandals extended even further. They have had enormous consequences for the U.S. economy and, indirectly, for the world economy. Confidence in the U.S. business community fell. Investors got rid of their American shares en masse. As a result, the United States' sizable trade deficit is no longer compensated by an influx of foreign currency. Consequently, the value of the dollar compared to the euro and the yen dropped, which meant that the import prices for the United States increased and imports from abroad fell. In view of the vast social impact, it is understandable that the bookkeeping scandals have received significant attention in the media and politics.

In the discussions arising from these scandals, a link has been made to the excessive incomes of senior managers. Because their bonuses depend on the company's stock market results, figures are manipulated or just plainly misstated. An accusatory finger is also being pointed at the accounting firms. Their independence is up for discussion. They knew, or should have known, about the misappropriation of funds. Politicians and the media are falling over one another to demand more and more effective rules, stricter controls, and harder sanctions.

THE FAULT LINE OF ETHICAL INTERPRETATION

Albert Einstein is reputed to have once said, "Things should be made as simple as possible . . . but no simpler." These three cases may be used to show how a recurring failure of ethical interpretation is a form of oversimplification. In each of the aforementioned cases, the popular explanations avoid a pluralistic interpretation in favor of either a monolithic or bipolar one. This happens not only in the interpretation of the empirical facts and causes but also of the value assessments. Unfortunately, monolithic or bipolar interpretation inevitably leads to a myopic view of remedies centered on the power of compliance systems. The result is a three-step syndrome consisting first of bipolarism; second, assignment of blame; and finally, the recommendation for more compliance.

Pluralistic Versus Bipolar or Monistic Interpretations

In each of the aforementioned cases, a complex interrelationship exists among empirical factors. For example, in the Schiphol case, factors include public health, traffic density around Schiphol airport, and confidence in commercial companies. Yet the tendency in the discussions about such cases is to highlight only one or two of their factors and also to classify the factors involved as straightforward causal forces, i.e., simple causes in simple, cause-effect relationships. By reducing the problem to simple empirical factors, a bipolar value trade-off can then be emphasized, usually between a human interest on the one hand and profit on the other. So, for example, the pursuit of profits by the soft drink industry is said to be in conflict with the health of young people. Likewise, the economic significance of Schiphol is said to be in conflict with a healthy environment for people living in the surrounding area. The greed of senior managers at Enron or WorldCom is said to be in conflict with the truthful reporting of financial data. It is surprising how many well-received analyses of business ethics problems implicitly assume such a bipolar trade-off of values. In a high percentage of these bipolar values conflicts, a social value is contrasted to that of commercial advantage, and the resulting bipolar conflict is used to explain why the actors in the cases find themselves under pressure to compromise ethics. The assumption is that a choice for commercial interests equals a choice against the fundamental social value at issue.

Blame

The discussion of values surrounding such cases is most often directed at determining the locus of blame. Blame thus becomes the monistic issue of ethical analysis. We seek to identify a person or persons (or, in a few instances, a whole company) who can count as guilty. And once we have found this locus of guilt, everyone can relax. At last, we know whom to blame. By keeping things simple in this manner, we make our problem manageable. The problem can be solved by simply removing the bad persons and starting afresh or, if we anticipate future bad acts, by imposing sanctions and punishments that will deter the "bad" people who might consider engaging in them. Once the blaming, punishing, and establishing rules and sanctions are finished, we can return to business as usual.

By focusing on blame and isolating a finite set of bad actors, it is possible to ignore the contributions made wittingly or unwittingly by the "blameless," i.e., the people who are not bad. A bipolar distinction between the blameless and the blamable inevitably neglects even the casual role sometimes played by the presumably innocent. In the disasters at Enron, WorldCom, Adelphi, Global Crossing, Tyco, etc., almost all attention has been focused on the greedy individuals at the top, on the Lays, the Skillings, and the Ebbers. But this neglects the fact that hundreds if not thousands of other—sometimes very ordinary—people were necessary to make what happened happen. It seems odd to imagine that they were all "evil" people. All three cases previously described deal with a social problem where we hesitate to blame ordinary people, and for good reason: Blaming the innocent is self-contradictory. Again, in the example concerning the nuisance caused by the airport, it is primarily the ordinary members of the general public who want to go on holiday by plane to faraway destinations. Finally, consider WorldCom. At the end of the '90s, the stock market grew into a type of pyramid scheme in which everyone wanted to profit from the Internet boom. Companies had to show profit figures of more than 10 percent, and preferably even better profit forecasts. By means of acquisitions and major investments (such as the UMTS investments of telecom companies), the companies conjured up visions of future profits for their shareholders. Companies that did not participate in the pyramid scheme were punished by the stock market. Ordinary investors, who certainly did not participate directly in the financial shenanigans that eventually brought disaster, were nonetheless all too happy to talk at parties about their successes on the stock markets when the prices were going through the roof. The level of their scrutiny was low, and less scrutiny served investors' self-interest. Expectations for numbers were continually bumped up. A CEO had to show at least 15 percent. Not all such investors were "evil."

THE FAILURE OF THE COMPLIANCE/MARKET MODEL

An interesting consequence ensues. A monolithic emphasis on blame inevitably leads to policy prescriptions for better compliance. This happens because when causes for bad events are parsed neatly between the "blamable" and the "blameless," or between the "innocent" and the "evil," the obvious challenge becomes how to handle the blamable/evil ones. It seems obvious that someone who has already committed evil must be punished or removed, while the evil person who has not yet committed evil, but who might do so, must be deterred. People who act only in their own interest and are not guided by ethical motives will not act simply because it is the "right thing to do." They must be deterred by punishment. Hence we find refuge in designing systems that appeal to the rational calculation of harm and benefit.

The compliance view of companies is in fact directly based on (misguided) market thinking as developed in the Western world in recent centuries. Companies imagine wrongly that self-interested businesspeople can be made to comply using a combination of market forces and legal and corporate compliance systems that appeal entirely to their rational calculation of harm and benefit. This market/compliance model eradicates the notion of socially responsible business practice. Businesspeople are driven by market forces. Their actions are bounded by law and enforced by sanctions. The market/compliance model often appeals for justification to the writings of Adam Smith.[1] It is true that Adam Smith had little confidence in the good intentions of the business community (Smith, 1976) and had greater faith in the self-interest of businesspeople. He speaks of an "invisible hand" that will lead to the general interest being served optimally (Smith, 1976).[2] Now if this were all there was to Adam Smith's message, it would seem to follow that self-interest in business is all we need. Market forces appeal to the self-interested businessperson, and when they are ineffective we need only add in systems of rules and punishments (legal sanctions or corporate compliance systems). The compliance approach appears to fit in seamlessly with this conception. Competition serves to maximize prosperity. Laws, external and internal control systems, and sanctions prevent the "free rider" behavior of companies themselves and their management. Thus, optimal prosperity is achieved.

Modern market economic theory teaches that market forces guarantee that companies that deliver their products and services in the most efficient way will ultimately survive. In order to base the search for solutions to the major social issues on a market model, consumers and shareholders must take account of their companies' purchase and investment decisions. In this context, companies are seen as the amoral instruments of the final consumers, who will see to it that the companies behave responsibly or else they will not buy from those companies. The question remains, however, whether consumers' knowledge and insight can be trusted when it comes to the complex interrelationships that populate modern business. For example, is it realistic to expect that individual consumers and shareholders take account of social interests when making decisions about purchases or investments? In fact, the role of the consumer and the (individual) investor is systematically ignored in the cases concerning the negative effects of frequent soft drink consumption, the environmental damage resulting from the frequent use of air travel for holiday and business purposes, and pressure on companies to achieve high profits. Of course, neither consumers nor investors knowingly intend to contribute to the creation of these kinds of societal problems. Their actions may, moreover, have unintended side effects. Still, confidence in market forces fails particularly in situations where unintended side effects of choices occur. This happens in situations such as the following, where it is difficult to rely on market forces:

- The socially undesirable effect becomes visible when it is the result of the actions of numerous parties and involves numerous causal relationships or interactions.
- Individual advantages result in collective disadvantages (the tragedy of the commons).
- Short-term advantages result in long-term disadvantages.
- Local advantages must be weighed against disadvantages elsewhere.
- Personal or group advantages result in disadvantages for others.

As we saw earlier, the often unconsciously employed monolithic logic of blame drives us to the remedy of market/compliance systems, even though, as we now see, these are inadequate. We are driven thus to a regimen of publicizing rules as well as the punishments or rewards that are the consequence of disobeying or obeying rules. And in those cases where blame is assigned beyond a group of individual bad actors, it is directed at compliance systems, whether legal or corporate. Failures of legal and corporate control systems thus become the second-order locus of blame.

Years ago, Lynn Sharp Paine correctly distinguished between adopting an "integrity" strategy and a "compliance" strategy (Paine, 1994). A compliance strategy assumes a negative image of people and organizations. People have the tendency to pursue their own self-interest, even when this is at the cost of others.

The three "typical" case analyses described at the beginning make this point. In each the behavior of companies is directly understood on the market/compliance model as stemming from the profit motive, the greed of senior management, and management's unwillingness to follow the law. The community involvement programs of the soft drink industry are, in fact, refined marketing techniques. The health of young people is made secondary to the profit pursuits of the company. Companies are in fact a danger to society, because they are driven by profit even when this is at the cost of the general interests of society. The ultimate explanation for the behavior of companies is the greed of senior management. This conduct can be controlled by rules, supervision of compliance, and sanctions. Companies look for the limits to what is legal and will even exceed these boundaries if they are not held in check by laws and an adequate control system.

The special errors of oversimplification identified above can be corrected, but in order to do so we must change our analytic stance. By adjusting the lens through which we see the function of corporations in society, we can see the common errors made in responding to corporate ethics problems. Moreover, we can begin to develop a more effective strategy for solving them. To a large extent, assigning blame is a distraction from the fundamental question of what companies should be doing.

SOCIAL CONTRACT THEORY

Social contract analysis using Integrative Social Contracts Theory (ISCT) shows that companies have economic responsibilities extending beyond making money for their investors. They also possess duties as economic citizens of a free market, duties that if shunned by economic participants will eventually destroy the fruits of the "invisible hand." In particular, companies have economic obligations because they are participants in market systems that demand at least a minimal amount of cooperation to ensure overall efficiency and the working of the invisible hand. In ISCT, *hypernorms* are defined as norms so fundamental that they play a second-order role in evaluation; in particular, they are used to judge and evaluate first-order or ordinary norms. The *economic hypernorm*, discussed in *Ties That Bind* (Donaldson & Dunfee, 1999), requires companies to have certain duties, the sharing of which preserves the economic efficiency of shared institutions, such as markets and regulation. These hypernorms imply, for example, the following duties:

- Engaging in fair competition and avoiding monopolies
- Respect for intellectual property
- Avoiding nepotism and "crony capitalism"
- Not abusing government relationships
- Providing nondeceptive information to the market (including transparency of relevant information)
- Avoiding bribery
- Respecting environmental integrity
- Honoring contracts, promises, and other commitments[3]

Social contracts analysis reveals that companies must go beyond even this purely "economic" collection of duties. If companies did nothing more than obey the law, pursue profits, and adhere to the preceding obligations, they would never be able to speak to or contribute to the solution of a host of social problems. Companies have a duty to contribute to the interests of specific constituencies or stakeholders other than investors, such as employees or persons who live near the corporation.[4] What is more, companies play a role in creating and alleviating social problems. The cases at the beginning of this chapter—unhealthy eating habits, excessive mobility, and the volatility of the stock market—are examples of this. Corporations are also directly involved in other major social issues such as global climate change, combating poverty, fighting corruption, dealing with AIDS in Africa, and maintaining biodiversity on the planet. They are frequently called to account for these issues, and some companies acknowledge their responsibility—which

is not unlimited—in these areas. Corporations understand that something more than money is at stake, and so do the members of society. Their mutual responsibilities are a reflection of the implicit "social contracts" that pervade the economic arena. Mere confidence in market forces and external compliance systems, a confidence that relies finally only on the pains and pleasures of the pursuit of self-interest (both individual and corporate), falls far short of providing solutions for major social issues.

To a certain extent, in *Ties That Bind*, Donaldson and Dunfee assume a negative view of the "moral free space," that is, the room for a community to define its own norms. The diversity of values between communities is something that cannot be avoided, and this is acceptable when these freedoms are limited by hypernorms. We would like to go a step further here. We assert that a plurality of values is a positive thing. Value polytheism establishes a condition for achieving social added value. The hypernorms that we hold dear, such as the sanctity of life and of human rights, work to create the very conditions that make integrity and social added value possible.

DILEMMAS

In the three cases presented at the beginning, we witnessed a syndrome of misleading simplicity, one in which problems are always described as a bipolar conflict between a single social or moral value (public health, a healthy living environment, transparent business practices, the distribution of wealth, maintaining biodiversity, sustainable use of energy resources, etc.) on the one hand, and commercial interests on the other. The social value is put under pressure because the economic interests exert too much pressure on those involved. In reality, however, it involves a conflict between numerous values. In the soft drink case, it concerns consumers' freedom of choice, the interests of the schools, the economic interests of the soft drink industry (employment, interests of suppliers, shareholders, governments), and care for the public health, in particular that of young people. In the case of Schiphol airport, it involves consumer freedom (people want to decide themselves whether and, if so, how they wish to travel), the importance of the airport for the economy, and the importance of a healthy environment for those living in the vicinity. In the accounting affairs, it concerns the freedom of senior executives to negotiate their own employment terms and conditions, the proper functioning of the global economy, independence of boards, and the confidence that accounting standards and auditing rules guarantee reliable presentation of reality in the business reporting. It is not about a single value that comes under pressure but, in fact, numerous values that are all legitimate. The economic interests should not be seen as an obstacle to achieving the social value. There is a social value underneath the commercial interests: Prosperity and the proper functioning of the economy are social values. Just like all the other social values, these also compete with the other conflicting values for precedence.

It is important to realize that these are real dilemmas. Dilemmas, in our view, are not simply difficult issues. A dilemma concerns situations where we are morally obliged to act and to refrain from acting at the same time. It may be that we are required to act to achieve a certain end but that other counter-effects render the action unacceptable. It is sometimes possible to resolve a dilemma by prioritizing the relevant duties involved insofar as some are prima facie stronger than others (see Ross, 1930), but often it is impossible. Practical hurdles can make it impossible to prioritize. Perhaps there is an order of priority and good reasons to make trade-offs, but we lack sufficient knowledge, insight, information, and the analytical skills to successfully make such trade-offs (see McConnel, 1987). In that instance, we could try to resolve these dilemmas with still further research to fill the gaps in our knowledge and insight. This impossibility to come to a rational decision can also be due to the incomparability of the values, norms, and ideals that are at stake.

There is much discussion about the question of whether dilemmas truly exist. Are we faced

with conflicting moral obligations that cannot be realized simultaneously and where the realization of the one offers no excuse for neglecting the other, or is it a case of difficult issues that we simply have to think through better in order to judge which deserves priority?

One argument against the existence of true dilemmas is that such situations would amount to a logical inconsistency. On the one hand, obligations have to be honored. On the other hand, "ought implies can." We are not bound by impossibilities (see McConnel, 1987). Another argument that is often advanced against the existence of true dilemmas concerns the unacceptable consequences of accepting their existence. To do so would undermine all ethics. According to the critics, we should hold on to the ideal of coherence, as without it ethical reflection is meaningless or even impossible. On the one hand, we argue that different norms and values apply that cannot be reduced to one measure. On the other hand, ethical reflection requires that decisions be made rationally. If the choice for a given criterion is ultimately arbitrary, both the meaning and possibility of ethics are undermined. From a theoretical perspective, it is difficult to understand dilemmas. In everyday practice, however, a pressing need for understanding dilemmas is felt. As McConnel observes, "Common sense and ordinary moral discourse are on the side of the friends of dilemmas" (McConnel, 1996, p. 37).

STRATEGIES FOR "RESOLVING" DILEMMAS

The question is whether it is possible to resolve these kinds of dilemmas by formulating one fundamental criterion against which all values and norms can be weighed. If this is not possible, it seems that we will have to accept that norms and values are ultimately relative or subjective in nature. Dilemmas put people's integrity (and as we will see shortly, also that of organizations) in question. People who are confronted with dilemmas oscillate between conflicting demands. The notion of integrity offers a way out of this choice. Integrity means "working on wholeness" in three respects: first, by aligning values, norms, and ideals; second, by striving for coherence between words and deeds; and finally, by making a contribution to the greater whole. We define integrity in this respect in process terms. This is inherent to the character of dilemmas. "Wholeness" is a situation that can never be realized for mortals on all fronts in a sustainable manner. What does integrity mean in concrete terms? Do the dilemmas that arise between values, norms, and principles get solved of their own accord as long as we are dealing with persons or organizations of integrity? Because integrity means "working on wholeness," there can never be a solution in terms of a tangible result.

Several strategies can be followed for "resolving" a "real" dilemma:

Strategy A: A possibility is to do nothing. None of the conflicting values are realized.

Strategy B: A simple choice can be made for one of the two values.

Strategy C: Sometimes a compromise can be sought where both values are partially realized. It implies falling short with respect to both values at the same time.

Strategy D: A new value, norm, or interest can be developed that transcends the original conflicting values, norms, and interests.

Figure 4.1 depicts the possible strategies for solving dilemmas.

An important reason for the acuteness of moral dilemmas can be found in the supposition that honoring one of the conflicting values means rejecting the other value. However, we believe that

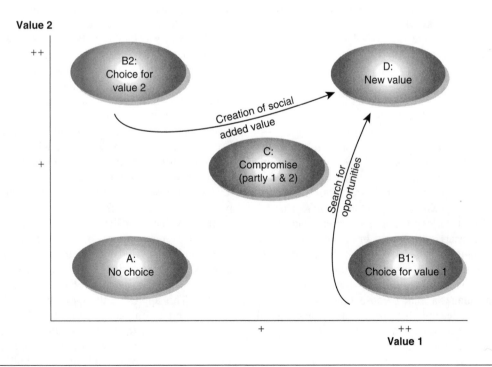

Figure 4.1   Strategies for the solution of dilemmas
SOURCE: Adapted from Kaptein & Wempe, 2002

in the face of dilemmas, value pluralism can provide a basisfor working on "wholeness" in the three senses discussed. Value pluralism recognizes the validity of a plurality of values, norms, and ideals. This is not to suggest that all values, norms, and ideals are equally good or that mistaken responses to moral issues are no longer possible. Value pluralism should be distinguished from moral relativism and moral subjectivism. At the same time, the choice that must be made among constant values, norms, and interests is not an arbitrary one. Value pluralism holds that people find valuable a diverse range of irreducible values, norms, and ideals that regularly clash. This is, in short, what lies at the basis of moral dilemmas. That a choice has to be made—for example, due to a scarcity of resources (time, money)—does not imply that the obligation that is not fulfilled or the value that is not honored is no longer valid. Choosing one value does not necessarily imply a rejection of the other conflicting value. Value pluralism holds that norms (of both the utilitarian and deontological kind) and ideals ultimately rest on values. A characteristic of values is that they are not mutually exclusive.

VALUE PLURALISM AND VALUE CREATION

Value pluralism holds that norms (of both the utilitarian and deontological kind) and ideals ultimately rest on values.[5] This is the value pluralism found in the "moral free space" of Integrative Social Contracts Theory (Donaldson & Dunfee, 1999). Charles Hampden-Turner and Fons Trompenaars, both experts in the field of strategic intercultural management, have conducted extensive research on managing intercultural differences. In their view, values exist by virtue of differences. Something is a value because it possesses a distinguishing feature that we see as a fundamental interest. Clashes can arise between the things we value. This can readily be seen in products.

Consider the differences incorporated into an automobile. We wish it to be *high-performing* yet *safe,* to *economize on fuel* yet *accelerate*

sharply, to be *sporty* yet *reliable,* to give *freedom* to the driver yet *reassert control* in emergencies, to be *compact* yet *roomy* inside, to *absorb* the impact of a collision so that occupants *escape* that impact. We want it to be *low-cost* yet *distinctive.* Clearly this list of values is full of contrasts. A car that performs more sluggishly is safer; acceleration uses up fuel; a compact car, all things being equal, is less roomy; and so on. These values are in tension with each other. The conventional wisdom is that we must choose between these values, so that a Volvo, for example, is safe and reliable but not high-performing and sporty. But if we look deeper, we see that despite some trade-offs, automobiles are considerably safer *and* better performing, more fuel-saving *and* more responsive to the throttle than they were just a few years ago. The industry consistently improves *both* values-in-tension (Hampden-Turner & Trompenaars, 2000, p. 8).

According to Hampden-Turner and Trompenaars, the clash between values is the source of value creation. Conflicts between values should thus be seen as a challenge. This applies not only to products but also to processes aimed at producing these products. "Value conflicts and clashes emerge within research, development, manufacturing, marketing, distribution, and after sales service departments, and many conflicts erupt *between* them" (Hampden-Turner & Trompenaars, 2000, p. 9). In launching a new pharmaceutical product on the market, the approach of a marketer is different from that of a medical researcher. Every professional has her own values and, with it, her own professional culture. Value conflicts can arise not only between national cultures but also between corporate cultures. At the same time, the various professionals must work together; they create space for one another or they impede one another. This applies in the same way to departments within a company and to national cultures. In most instances, it is possible to search for new perspectives in which the conflicting values can be considered together and new values, norms, and interests become visible. For the process aimed at uniting clashing values,

Hampden-Turner and Trompenaars use the term *reconciliation*, which entails creatively bridging these conflicting values to as great an extent as possible. The development of new insights can be specified with the term *flow*.

Hampden-Turner and Trompenaars' description of conflicting cultural values also applies to conflicting moral values. Conflicts between particular rights and the common good, for example, can often be "resolved" in practice. The solution has to be sought in reconciling clashing demands and the development of new values, norms, and interests. In doing so, it is important not to treat each situation as an isolated case. The reconciliation of clashing demands can consist in frankly admitting to the impossibility of meeting all demands, expressing regret, showing compassion for the victim, striving for minimum damage, and seeking a way to compensate damages. It can also involve seeking creative compromises. On top of this, it can lead to new insights. The dynamics of values thus becomes visible. This approach often means making oneself vulnerable, being willing to learn from mistakes, and being open to better ideas.

INTEGRITY AND THE MAXIMIZATION OF OPPORTUNITIES

Dealing with moral dilemmas places demands on behavior but in particular on the disposition of the person or organization involved. This person or organization is to stand up and make known the values he believes in. The person or organization of integrity does not hide behind others and makes sure forces beyond him do not control him. Over and above this, he or the organization has the disposition to search for concordance in the different demands and an open attitude towards developing new values. A person or organization of integrity strives towards understanding and realizing the respective conflicting values, norms, and ideals as an interconnected whole.

Against the background of the alternative responses to dilemmas, we can now describe the choice a person or organization of integrity would make.

For a person or organization of integrity, strategy A is never acceptable. The person or organization in question actually leaves the choice to others and, in doing so, actually relinquishes his autonomy. He becomes a plaything of the forces around him or the organization and lets it happen.

Strategy B is unappealing to a person or organization of integrity. It implies that only one value is realized and the other is negated, which raises doubts about how strongly one feels about the value that is not realized. A choice for B requires a clear explanation for the absolute importance of the one value or interest over and above the value that is ignored.

The compromise strategy C is similarly unattractive for a person or organization of integrity if it simply appeases others superficially. In seeking an optimal solution (strategy D), it must be clear that the person or organization in question is confronted with a tragic dilemma that forces him to choose but that he is trying to fulfill all moral obligations to the best of his abilities. Only if these requirements are met is it clear that he takes both values to heart. The search for the correct balance is expressed in the willingness to enter into dialogue and to subject choices to discussion. Often strategy D leads to a new perspective and the development of a new value.

Integrity concerns a disposition that is aimed at holding on to values, norms, and ideals. The search for an appropriate course of action involves a willingness to analyze and discuss one's choices and to seek richer solutions. *Richness* refers to finding solutions that do justice to the different values at stake. By combining where possible the positive dimensions of the one-sided (strategy B) alternatives, we gain sight of an optimal solution (strategy D). Integrity is visible in the dispositions, conduct, and ambitions that are aimed at continuous improvement and in striving for an optimal (or more optimal) solution. Integrity implies holding on to values, norms, and ideals; openness to other values, norms, and ideals in words and deeds; and striving for improvement. Integrity is therefore expressly nonrelativist. The notion of *improvement* is an explicitly normative concept. Integrity leaves room for other norms and values.

BACK TO THE CASES

Let us return to the three cases and comparable major social issues for which companies are held co-responsible. Market thinking and the compliance approach make these major social issues seem as if they can be reduced to simple causal associations for which individual companies can be called to account—at least when consumers and shareholders find it worthwhile. By taking on their social responsibilities, these companies can distinguish themselves on the market. Where that is not possible, the government can correct companies by means of legislation and an efficient system of controls and sanctions. The market/compliance approach is amoral. People are driven by market forces and laws and are not expected to take responsibility for societal problems. The compliance character of this view even leads to anxiousness, risk avoidance, and inaction. It is better to do nothing than to take the risk of acting against the law (strategy A). However, the major social issues we are discussing are extremely complex. Numerous values apply and are operative in these issues. Moreover, these issues rise far above the responsibilities that companies have. They can be resolved only when commerce, social groups, and governments join their efforts. People need to have an open attitude towards these major social issues and a willingness to accept responsibility for these issues. The integrity approach presents a vision that makes it possible to recognize the worth of the different conflicting values and thus maximize the opportunities that exist for creating social added value.

The integrity approach requires a particular attitude from all parties involved. It is about finding similarities and searching for opportunities to support each other in contributing to the solutions of the major social issues. This is diametrically opposed to a view steeped only in the simple logic of markets and compliance.

NOTES

1. Smith, himself a moral philosopher, would probably reject much that is proclaimed in his name today.

2. Adam Smith was much more sophisticated than the thumbnail sketch of his view (above) indicates. As Patricia Werhane has shown, Smith believed that neither markets nor laws could satisfy the full extent of a businessperson's responsibilities (cf. Werhane, 1991).

3. Donaldson, Thomas. (2002, July 10). Congressional testimony for the hearing "Penalties for White Collar Crime: Are We Really Getting Tough on Crime?" of the Senate Judiciary Committee Subcommittee on Crime and Drugs, Room SD-226.

4. This point is made increasingly not only by business ethicists but also by traditional financial theorists (cf. Jensen, 2002).

5. Values describe what drives people and organizations, what we together find important. Norms describe what we expect from one another, what we consider normal. Norms therefore have a more restrictive character than values.

REFERENCES

Donaldson, T. (2002, July 10). Congressional testimony for the hearing *Penalties for white collar crime: Are we really getting tough on crime?* of the Senate Judiciary Committee Subcommittee on Crime and Drugs, Room SD-226.

Donaldson, T., & Dunfee, T. (1999). *Ties that bind: A social contracts approach to business ethics.* Cambridge, MA: Harvard Business School Press.

Hampden-Turner, C., & Trompenaars, F. (2000). *Building cross-cultural competence: How to create wealth from conflicting values.* New York: John Wiley.

Jensen, M. C. (2002). Value maximization, stakeholder theory, and the corporate objective function. *Business Ethics Quarterly, 12*(2), 235–256.

Kaptein, M., & Wempe, J. F. (2002). *The balanced company: A theory of corporate integrity.* New York: Oxford University Press.

McConnel, T. C. (1987). Moral dilemmas and consistency in ethics. In C. W. Gowans (Ed.), *Moral dilemmas.* New York: Oxford University Press.

McConnel, T. C. (1996). Moral residue and dilemmas. In H. E. Mason (Ed.), *Moral dilemmas and moral theory.* New York: Oxford University Press.

Paine, L. S. (1994). Managing for organizational integrity. *Harvard Business Review, 72*, 107–117.

Ross, W. D. (1930). *The right and the good.* London: Oxford University Press.

Smith, A. (1976). *The Glasgow edition of the works and correspondence of Adam Smith.* New York: Oxford University Press.

Werhane, P. (1991). *Adam Smith and his legacy for modern capitalism.* New York: Oxford University Press.

5

INTEGRITY IN THE PRIVATE, THE PUBLIC, AND THE CORPORATE DOMAIN

HENK VAN LUIJK

Integrity is a keyword in present-day ethical discourse. It is a rich concept that contains various related meanings. It is also a complex concept, because its current meanings do not always fit together smoothly. With regard to the reception of the term, integrity is used, as a key moral notion, in some domains more easily than in others. In the private domain, integrity has been used as a hallmark of moral excellence. So too in the public domain, where public functionaries, given their specific role and discretionary power, are expected to act with integrity. This is less so, however, in the corporate world. There, at least in some western European regions and languages, the preferred concept to express normative expectations, is "corporate social responsibility." This can be seen simply as a semantic preference without serious implications. It can also be the case, however, that integrity contains various implications that deserve to be

applied to the corporate as well as to the private and the public domain. This is the basic thesis of my contribution. To articulate it more distinctly, I first pose some introductory questions.

Is integrity a moral obligation? Can governmental agencies impose moral excellence on their functionaries? Can an institution of public administration oblige its employees to more than administrative duties? Or is the duty to act with integrity itself a moral duty, independent of who is imposing it? And if integrity is an inherently moral notion, what does it add to the basic moral rule(s) that "evil should be avoided and good be done," *malum est vitandum et bonum faciendum,* as was said in Scholastic philosophy, or *neminem nocere,* "Do not hurt anybody," as Roman law formulated its ground rule? Is integrity more than what contemporary ethics has in mind when it states that being moral means taking into account the rights and interests of all relevant individuals? Is somebody who lives up to this principle acting with integrity, or is more required to deserve that qualification? And if so, does it count only in the public domain, or in other domains as well?

These are too many questions to tackle all at one time. Some ordering is needed. I try to achieve this by, first, mapping some varieties of integrity. I then list basic features of morality and integrity in the private, the corporate, and the public domain. Finally, I point to recent shifts in these domains and their mutual relations and to possible repercussions on our ideas about integrity.

Varieties of Integrity— Personal and Social

Originally, integrity was not an exclusively moral notion. Its first meaning was physical: wholeness, intactness, or not being violated. It can be said of the body, left untouched in a fistfight; of the virginity of the bride; of a territory, not invaded by the enemy; and even of the early dawn, *integro die,* the early moments of the day not yet worn out. Beyond this meaning, the term represented a psychological state of inner equilibrium and consistency between words and deeds (Taylor, 1985; McFall, 1987; Benjamin, 1990; Carter, 1996; Dobel, 1999). Only gradually did moral overtones emerge. Integrity now stands for complying in an exemplary way with specific moral standards. But much remains to be explained.

The physical meaning of the term should not detain us for long. It refers to regions that hardly require moral discussion, for what is intended here is, first and foremost, a material wholeness that deserves to be held intact, to be protected and defended. Infringements occur, but they are unsuited, and that is about all that should be said, with the possible exception of the medical domain, where opinions about the integrity of the body can very well cause moral discussions.

More complicated is the psychological meaning, for here several qualifications intermingle. Reasonably constant is the meaning that says for

integrity to be at stake, two conditions should be fulfilled. In the words of Patrick Dobel, "First, it demands consistency between inner beliefs and public actions. . . . Second, integrity presupposes that people have the reflective capacity to make a commitment. . . . Third, integrity assumes a oneness or unity in the moral life of individuals" (Dobel, 1999, pp. 3–4). To a large extent, these are formal conditions. They come down to "Say what you intend to do, and do what you say."

But more seems implied here. The inner unity that is referred to as spiritual or mental integrity requires physical as well as character-linked capacities. In the very beginning of his book *Public Integrity,* Dobel provides a list of requirements: "physical buttresses such as levels of energy, strength, health, and endurance, and aspects of character and temperament such as optimism, courage, caution, empathy, imagination, conscientiousness, and self-discipline" (Dobel, 1999, p. 4). Regarding this list he adds that integrity, next to consistency between words and deeds and the reflective capacity to commit oneself, supposes also a unity in the *moral* life of individuals. People create consistency and coherence in their personal existence by attuning their divergent roles with the central values they adhere to and with the bonds and duties they have accepted. In doing so, they show not only mental but also *moral* integrity.

From here onward, however, I concentrate on the moral meaning of integrity.

An articulation of the notion of moral integrity can be achieved by a closer look at the often-used distinction between personal and social integrity. The terms are applied with different nuances, but, in general, *personal integrity* refers to "sticking to your personal standards" whereas *social integrity* stands for "observing socially given standards." McFall adds, "If we grant that there are cases where the claims of personal and social morality conflict, and where the conflict may be justifiably resolved either way, without loss of integrity, then we do not claim (1) that every person should, under the same circumstances, do the same thing, nor (2) that there is a moral duty to be impartial" (McFall, 1987, pp. 19–20). She adds that one's personal standards do not have to be shared by everyone and stresses that personal integrity is not necessarily impartial. With my personal standards as a guide, I may privilege certain individuals or groups and not others, as long as I do not violate anybody's fundamental rights. I give special attention only to categories and causes that, according to my personal convictions, deserve this attention. With regard to social integrity, however, standards are at stake that we expect everybody to observe. Here impartiality is a basic requirement.

Something peculiar occurs in the commonly accepted distinction between personal and social integrity. The distinction presents itself as a clear symmetrical dichotomy. In the personal form, integrity presents itself as commitment to self-imposed and self-accepted standards and obligations concerning issues outside the normal region of social requirements and legitimate expectations. Personal integrity is located in a morally free space, not riddled with binding social expectations, except the minimum standards of decency that apply to each individual within a given community. In this free space, a person can build a strong moral personality, authenticity, and identity by freely assuming standards and commitments for no other reason than that in doing so he or she becomes the moral person he or she wants to be. Personal integrity deserves moral respect in that it shows the ultimate dimensions of common morality. It has the merits of exemplarity.

In its social form, integrity presents itself as the consistent, impartial and selfless fulfillment of legitimate social expectations. People showing integrity in this sense deserve appreciation, for they contribute in a substantial way to the maintenance of the moral order and the social system.

What is peculiar is that this seemingly clear and symmetrical distinction between personal and social integrity introduces, at one and the same time, a tension in our thinking, for the two varieties often are seen as standing in an asymmetrical relation to each other. Implicitly, but nonetheless unmistakably, personal integrity is given moral priority, as being encompassing and ultimately decisive. Should this qualification be correct, this would have serious consequences for our ideas about moral integrity. A ranking order would emerge, consisting of first-class and second-class, or at least higher and lower class, integrity. But is this qualification correct? Only partially.

Moral integrity is linked to committing oneself to, and accepting responsibility for, standards, norms, and values, be they self-chosen or socially given. To accept responsibility means to accept standards as binding. By an act of appropriation—the term stems from Paul Ricoeur—you seal the standards with your personal hallmark and make them an intrinsic part of your moral identity. This act of appropriation applies to all consciously accepted standards, whatever their origin, be they self-chosen, socially imposed, or legitimately expected. But through the process of appropriation, nothing is yet decided regarding moral priority. The only thing that can be said is that the mature moral actor will accept *all* his or her standards as morally binding.

At the background of this discussion looms the image of the Kantian moral actor as his own moral master and lawgiver. The image is persistent. Schneewind even states that the whole history of modern moral philosophy can be described as "the invention of autonomy," as he puts it in the very title of his book (Schneewind, 1998). But gradually we have come to recognize that the image is essentially one-sided. Sure, the mature moral actor is master of his own moral identity but not the master of all his moral standards. We should understand *personal* integrity to be the moral identity that somebody chooses for him- or herself in the morally free space that, as a social concession, is left within the texture of social exchanges. *Social* integrity stands for the responsibility that someone accepts vis-à-vis socially given standards. But we should not attach different moral weights to the two elements of the dichotomy. In both varieties, personal appropriation is a sign of moral maturity. Moral priority would prevail only when self-chosen standards deserve greater moral weight than socially given standards—or vice versa, of course. And that has, as yet, not been proven.

Neglect of this distinction can be seen in Patrick Dobel's study *Public Integrity* (1999). His subject is the morality and integrity of public functionaries. Be they elected, appointed, or career executives, the basic moral structure of the function is always the same. Public functionaries are required to meet, in their behavior and decisions, the obligations of the function, that is, the standards that come with the functional responsibilities. At the same time, Dobel states, every decision a functionary takes implies a complex interaction of *three* mutually supporting domains of judgment: obligations of office, personal commitment and capacity, and political prudence. All public functions have to seek a balance between institutional, personal, and prudential dimensions. But the key lies, Dobel contends, in the hand of personal integrity as a normative ideal that people always should strive towards. Whatever the obligations of a role or function are, at the end of the day it is the individual that commits him- or herself to them. They remain *mentally signed obligations,* in last resort dependent on somebody's personal integrity.

In this way, self-chosen moral identity and the personal appropriation of moral standards can be conflated. This can lead to a myopia that ultimately only sees the moral actor as master of his own standards, with socially given moral standards as second-rate. Where this occurs, there is a need to rehabilitate social integrity. In the moral free space, there is every possibility to develop one's own moral identity. A person working on it can be deeply respected. But in social exchanges, integrity is not primarily a matter of personal moral excellence but of an accepted responsibility.

So there seems to be no reason to give moral priority to personal integrity above social integrity, as both require similar acts of proper appropriation. But because personal integrity belongs to the socially conceded free space of moral authenticity, there *is* reason to consider social integrity, not as the morally more important but certainly as the more encompassing and pervading subject. This is due to the fact that standards that people are expected to adhere to,

and responsibilities that they are required to assume, are more demanding and intriguing than standards they freely impose upon themselves. So from here onward my attention will mainly be directed to forms of social integrity.

This focus of attention is linked to a conception of morality as basically a social phenomenon, as one of the most important instruments we have at our disposal—next to law, politics, religion, education, and the market—to keep social relations in balance. Other conceptions are possible—for instance, morality seen as an instrument to bring to perfection one's personal identity, with social repercussions coming to the fore only as a consequence of personal virtuousness. Here I choose a social and functional approach to morality, in the conviction that social and societal equilibrium is too important a task to make it dependent on virtuousness alone.

This brings us to an interesting conclusion with regard to one of the questions I raised at the beginning, namely, the question of whether integrity adds something to morality. The answer is yes on the level of personal integrity but not on the level of social integrity. Personal integrity is located in the region "beyond the call of duty." It exceeds what somebody can reasonably be required to perform. In the ethical jargon, it belongs to the realm of the *supererogatory.* This, by implication, also answers another preceding question. Nobody, not even public authorities, can impose on others personal integrity as a duty. Social integrity, on the contrary, is another term for the adequate fulfillment of mutually recognized obligations. In the sphere of personal morality, integrity does add something, but in the social sphere of the private as well as the public domain, integrity coincides with morality as such.

THE AUTHORITY OF SOCIAL STANDARDS

When it comes to social moral identity, standards are largely externally defined and authoritatively imposed as binding expectations. Social integrity is not a self-designed duty with progressive perfection as perspective, but the consciously accepted responsibility to seek a balance in social expectations. A socially integrated person, acting with integrity, is aware of the expectations he is allowed to cherish regarding his own life and of the social expectations he is expected to fulfill. He or she is prepared to contribute to an effective equilibrium of expectations that is marked not by a moral maximum but by a social optimum.

Then the questions arise: Who or what supports those expectations? And what is the moral authority of the bearers? These are questions about the *sources of moral authority.*

Over time, these questions have received shifting answers. Just as Western moral philosophy can be described as "the invention of autonomy," so, at least in the Western world, the evolution of sources of moral authority can be characterized as "the democratization of morality." There has always been a need for moral regulation, but for generations the regulative authority has been attributed to localized entities of varying composition: the monarch, the church, the government, the family, tradition, the autonomous moral actor, or public debate. The conceptual roots of the locus of authority are successively found in divine sovereignty, the order of creation, the hierarchical universe, natural law, reason, social contract, or power-free discussion. This is not to say that the various instances have succeeded each other smoothly. The current pattern of moral authority is a varying mixture of old and new, heteronomous and autonomous, and individual and communitarian elements. We can leave the reconstruction of individual historical configurations and their successions to the sociology of morality. Nevertheless, we may speak of an ongoing process of the *democratization of morals,* because, in the course of time, the accent has more and more been put, at least within the Western moral tradition, on an equal moral voice for everyone and on the right of individual consent. This is an important observation. A more and more democratic moral authority implies that social integrity supposes not only a mature appropriation of socially offered standards, but also a contribution to the factual filling in and interpretation of these standards from the side of the several parties expected to comply with them.

Bearers of moral authority show a multitude of forms, as institutions, organizations, and exemplary figures. They do not speak with one tongue. Their reach varies, and so does the weight of their claim or their binding force. Their authority can remain restricted to a professional group, a functional unity, or a specific organization. In those cases, we face social expectations in the form of a professional ethics, business ethics, or public ethics. In other cases the reach is sensibly wider. Social expectations then regard everybody's environmental behavior, or the respect for human rights that is required from every person in all circumstances. Social integrity bears the characteristics of the domain in which it is in force.

The Private, the Public and the Corporate Domain

It is up to the sociology of social stratification to map the different domains that define the social playing field. For us, a basic classification will do. The basic distinction between the private and the public domain will suffice for our primary purpose.

Not that this distinction is without problems. I point to two of them. First, it is important to notice that the distinction between the private and the public does not coincide with the aforementioned distinction between the personal and the social domain. "Private" and "public" are both subcategories of "social." The social domain contains private as well as public relations. Think of the private relations between teacher and pupil, producer and consumer, and doctor and patient on the one hand, and the relation between government and parliament, or public administration and citizen, on the other. Next, we should recognize that the term *the public domain* can be used in a physical as well as a metaphorical sense. In a physical sense, one speaks of "the city as public domain" (Hajer, 1989). What is at stake there is city planning, infrastructure, and spatial provisions that have to be organized in such a way that all parts of the population are enabled and encouraged to make use of them. But when we talk here about ethics and integrity in the public domain, we do not talk about decency in the city park or safety in the mall, even if the availability of public provisions may play a role at a given moment.

How, then, can we characterize, for our purpose, integrity in the private and in the public domain? Integrity in both cases represents a form of social integrity that, as I stated earlier, can be described as the consciously accepted responsibility for a well-balanced attitude and practice vis-à-vis legitimate social expectations regarding rights and interests of all concerned parties. Rights and interests are included in the description, because that is what (social) morality is about: respect for everybody's rights and interests and for the providing of a well-balanced ranking of them. Integrity in the private and in the public domain is defined by the rights and interests that, in their respective domains, legitimately deserve respect, and subsequently by the moral principles that give substance to this respect. I leave out, for the moment, the corporate domain but will return to it in due course.

Which moral expectations are at stake in the basic domains we here consider? The question raises issues of method as well as of content.

INTEGRITY IN THE PRIVATE DOMAIN

The private domain covers the extended and densely populated region where particular entities enter into relations and transactions with others, each with its own rights and interests. These entities may either be individuals or groups, organizations, or institutions. Their rights and interests are not only legitimate, until the contrary is duly proved, but also particular in the sense of standing on their own as nonderived and self-distinctive. In this private domain, particular entities regulate their mutual relations on the basis of legitimate particular rights and interests. This does not imply that no external intervention in these relations can be made (for example, by the government) on behalf of the common good. But this is an *intervention,* hopefully justifiable, in a domain that wants to be seen as based upon self-regulation. In a liberal democracy, the autonomy of the private domain is primary. Needless to say, *private* does not here coincide with "belonging to the sphere of one's privacy." The private domain is a social arrangement.

To find out what social integrity and morality mean in a given domain of action, one can use a method that is similar to the one commonly in use when organizations, of various kinds, attempt to define their basic values. Take the example of a private organization—say, a professional association—that wants to develop an ethical code. In order to arrive at a well-balanced document, the organization has to determine what it considers to be its set of basic values. It must identify "the organization's essential and enduring tenets—a small set of general guiding principles; not to be confused with specific cultural or operating practices; not to be compromised for financial gain or short-term expediency," as Collins and Porras describe them (1996, p. 73). Experience teaches that defining basic values and the leading moral principles that are implied in them forms the most demanding but also the most exciting part of a code design. In these three or four concepts, the organization expresses its basic moral identity, the ultimate touchstone of all corporate decisions, and the moral qualities to which the organization is prepared to be held accountable in all its performances. How is such a set of basic values arrived at?

Several questions of a descriptive as well as a normative nature have to be asked. Who are we? What is the business we are in? Which are our core objectives? What are our primary relationships, who are our competitors, and which regulatory agencies are intervening in the course of our activities? These are mainly descriptive issues. Questions of a normative nature include the following: Who are our stakeholders? Given the business we are in, what, from a moral point of view, do we ourselves want to be as an association? What are our basic moral tenets and beacons? What are the principles we need to adhere to if we want our behavior to be recognized as fair, honest, and orderly and if we want, for our part, to contribute to a well-balanced moral optimum?

A careful self-definition, together with a proper analysis of the social texture and a solid moral alertness, will normally suffice for a particular organization or association to arrive at a specific set of basic values. Things become more complicated when basic values are at stake for a whole domain of action, say, the private domain, for here the level of generality is higher and the specificity of a single entity, corporation, or association is lacking. Methodologically, a hold can be found in the types of relationships that prevail in the field, the rights and interests that are generally recognized as legitimate, and the pattern of actions that people can undertake towards each other.

Elsewhere I have tried to sketch the morality of the private domain in some detail, using a typology of varieties of ethics and of concomitant moral principles (van Luijk, 1993, 1994, 2000, pp. 38–42, 84–96). Here I restrict myself to the main lines.

In the vast domain in which particular entities meet each other, action patterns of single players are, with regard to their intentional structure, self-directed, other-directed, or other-including. The first two varieties do not require much moral comment. A self-directed action is one that intends the author of the action and the recipient of the effects of that action to coincide (e.g., in the development of a career path, or an investment made at the stock exchange). From a moral point of view, such actions are morally acceptable as long as nobody else is hurt in his or her rights or legitimate interests. With regard to other-directed, altruistic actions, with which the actor intends results that exclusively benefit someone other than him- or herself, such a behavior can be praised as highly laudable, but it cannot be required morally, for heroism is not a moral duty. In both action patterns, self-directed and other-directed, relationships between players, if any, are plain and straightforward.

It is in the realm of other-including actions that relationships between players and realization of interests become more complex.

The weakest form of inclusion of the other occurs where actors, each with their own interests, happen to be present and active *simultaneously on the same playing field.* The basic moral requirement here is *equality,* meaning that every actor should permit every other to be active as well, admitting her the same amount of freedom and action space as he claims for himself, without having to feel obliged, however, to foster the interests of the other as a distinct objective, independent of the pursuing of his own interests.

More often other-including actions are of a certain *cooperative* or *interdependent* nature. In all these cases we need the cooperation of one or several other players in order to reach our goal. Every time we make a deal, work out a balance of interests, or enter into a transaction with somebody, we are acting within the pattern of an other-including action in a strict but neutral, almost descriptive sense. It is a factual relation that is at stake, "nothing personal," as when I need a plumber to repair my dishwasher, or make use of the skills of a famous soloist to satisfy my musical needs and interests. Here two more moral requirements are at stake, next to the principle of equality: the principle of *reciprocity,* which says that everyone in the deal should contribute his fair share (hence, no free-riding or parasitism), and the principle of *honesty,* which says that our words and deeds should be trustworthy (therefore, no cheating or misleading information, no promise breaking, and no changing of the rules during the game). Together, the principles of equality, reciprocity, and honesty constitute what I call *transactional ethics.* They rule that part of the private domain where the pursuits of interests by relatively abstract equals can be combined to the advantage of all parties involved. They are "abstract equals" because the equality remains restricted to the fact that all players or actors are equal to each other as being "pursuers of interests."

Other patterns of actions, relationships, and interests can be noted within the private domain.

One appears in the case of *conflicting* interests. Actors here present themselves as pursuers of interests that cannot be combined to the advantage of all, not even through negotiating a compromise. Interests in this part of the private domain are difficult to reconcile. The relation between the actors is *asymmetrical,* in the following sense. One actor presents herself as bearer of a strong claim, if not an explicit moral right, and so acts as *claimant,* while the other finds himself under the obligation to recognize the claim and so acts as *duty-bound vis-à-vis the claimant.* One cannot save a natural park and use it for the construction of a new city district at one and the same time; neither can economic development be promoted on an equal footing with the healthy growth, both physical and social, of children when economic development requires the use of child labor. Once the moral weights of the various rights and interests have been determined in accordance with standards generated by proper moral instances, the duty-bound actor finds himself under the moral obligation to recognize the strongest claims as such and to act accordingly. The part of the private domain that is characterized by divergent claims and conflicting interests is ruled by what I indicate as *recognitional ethics,* where people find themselves under the often severe moral requirement to give precedence to rights or interests of others, even if they strongly conflict with their own interests. Recognitional ethics is the ethics of human rights and of acknowledged basic needs.

The basic moral principles that play a leading role in recognitional ethics are the principles of *justice* and *beneficence.* Regarding the principle of justice, various interpretations have been developed. They are partly complementary, but also partly mutually exclusive. Accordingly, when applying the principle, one will have to be clear about its range and meaning in the given circumstances. But all interpretations share the intention to build a dam against an easy trade-off of fundamental rights and basic needs against allegedly far-reaching utility functions. In this sense, the basis of justice is found in respect for the dignity of living beings. The principle of

beneficence too has been interpreted in more or less extensive forms (Frankena, 1973, p. 47). I think that it makes sense to have the principle say six things: avoid doing harm, repair or compensate the harm you did, prevent harm being done by others, avoid bringing about conditions that generate harm, repair or compensate harm done by others, and do good wherever and whenever you can. There is clearly a progression of increasingly demanding requirements implied in this formulation of the principle. But it is too easy to contend that only the first two or three rules can be constructed as moral obligations, the other ones belonging to the realm of the supererogatory, of behavior "beyond the call of duty." All six sub-principles deserve to be taken as possible moral guidelines, applicable according to the circumstances.

There is, finally, one more realm noticeable within the private domain in which a specific type of ethics, or social integrity, can be detected, linked this time to the acceptance of *shared interests.* This type of ethics does not regulate relations between single participants in the social fabric among each other primarily, but rather relations between each of them (individually or collectively) and the common interest and public welfare. Public welfare is seen here as a collective good with which comes a collective obligation in more than one sense. It is a duty for each citizen and for all citizens collectively to take part, in one way or another, in the development and maintenance of the public welfare. It is also a shared responsibility of citizens and public administration together. The type of ethics in force here can be referred to as *participatory* ethics. Its leading moral principles are *alertness,* that is, a moral sensibility for what can be and deserves to be done better; *decency,* for this society does not leave the unfortunate ones in a backward position; and *emancipation,* towards full citizenship for all notably. Participatory ethics is the ethics of individual and collective citizenship. It sees public possibilities as a shared duty of cooperativeness.

Acting with integrity in the private domain requires adherence to the principles of a transactional, recognitional, and participatory ethics and the willingness to be assessed according to these principles. What integrity means in specific circumstances and in the occurrence of a single moral dilemma has to be elaborated on the spot. But with the taxonomy sketched here it might be possible to get a reasonably articulated hold on the varieties of actions and principles involved in social integrity in the private domain. Can something of the kind be developed for the public domain as well?

INTEGRITY IN THE PUBLIC DOMAIN

It can be done, and it has been done repeatedly (Applbaum, 1980; Dobel, 1999; Hampshire, 1999). Jane Jacobs does it extensively and thoroughly in her book *Systems of Survival: A Dialogue on the Moral Foundations of Commerce and Politics* (1992). She describes what she calls "two moral syndromes," the commercial syndrome and the guardian syndrome, roughly coinciding with the market and the government, or trade and administration. For both syndromes she develops some 15 moral and prudential imperatives, some of them of a rather unexpected character. For example, with regard to the guardian syndrome, one finds not only "shun trading, be obedient and disciplined, respect hierarchy, be loyal, treasure honor," but also "make rich use of leisure, take vengeance, deceive for the sake of the task, be fatalistic," not imperatives to follow unreflectively. I point to them just to show that generating imperatives as touchstones for integrity in the public domain has been attempted earlier by carefully analyzing the cluster of action patterns and relations that characterize acts and decisions of the public administration and of administrative functionaries such as politicians, public administrators, and officers.

More usual is an approach via the principles of correct administration, such as legality, legal security, and equality before the law, or via basic values of political morality, such as justice, liberty, equality, utility, legitimacy, and democracy

(Applbaum, 1999, p. 68). However, the former largely remain enclosed within the confines of administrative law, whereas the latter mainly indicate a general direction. Without further analysis of their roots, both remain too unspecific to serve as guidelines. Therefore I attempt, on the basis of general characteristics of the public domain and the interests at stake there, to find a moral hold enabling us to fill in the concept of social integrity in this specific field.

We came to see the private domain as the terrain on which particular individuals, groups, organizations, and institutions take care of the organization of particular rights and interests, with the help of commercial, social, legal, and moral ordering instruments. In a similar way, the public domain is the terrain on which, in a noncommercial way, supra-individual interests are looked after by representative agencies, institutions, and functionaries that represent the duly defined common good and public interests, while bound by person neutrality and role relativity (Applbaum, 1999). *Person neutrality* and *role relativity* imply that the duties of the representative agencies and the actors acting within them are not linked, one-to-one, to the person who is in charge of the common good or the public interests, but to his or her role. Following Brian Barry (1970), I use *public interests* as an administrator's concept par excellence for when an institution or political action is to be defended; *common good* is used in the context of an appeal to individual people to do something that is not primarily in their net interests or is possibly even contrary to them. "A system of rewards to encourage work or of punishment to discourage law-breaking might well be supported by saying that it was 'in the public interests' but hardly that it was 'for the common good'" (Barry, 1970, p. 203). Supra-individual interests present themselves in two ways: first, as the interest involved for "everybody" in certain collective goods, such as security and care being provided within a given society, and second, as a right or interest of a particular individual, not as an isolated entity but as citizen among citizens. In this sense, citizenship is a supra-individual quality, rooted in individuals, and civil rights are a collective good. In the public domain, priority is given to civil rights and supra-individual interests. Agencies within the public domain do not protect private interests primarily but foster general welfare and the common good.

In the public domain, under the notions of public interests and the common good, public functionaries and administrators, politicians, agencies, and institutions meet each other and meet citizens and groups representing private interests in many forms and on different levels, from interstate and suprastate relationships to the service-seeking citizens at the counter of the city welfare service. However, when it comes to articulating social integrity in the public domain, it seems that two factors are pivotal in all relationships, namely representation and power. They give rise to some distinct moral principles and a specific type of ethics.

Those active in the public domain find their legitimacy in that they represent the protection and promotion of the public interest and the common good, issues too important and too encompassing to leave them to private initiatives and individual responsibilities. Public activities always are, or always should be, marked by the common good and general welfare. That is what society has appointed its functionaries for, and why it has established public institutions. That is why it has permitted some specific powers, such as the monopoly of violence and a series of lawgiving and discretionary powers, to be concentrated in the hands of a restricted number of institutions and functionaries. That is also what gives public functionaries and institutions a characteristic dignity. A relation with a public functionary, administrator, or institution is a relation with an official or agency representing the common good, and never with just another person. That is what person neutrality and role relativity are about, the safeguarding of the representative quality of the office, not to be overgrown by personal preferences or judgments. This does not mean that a public functionary ceases to exist as a person. It means, as Dobel (1999) has rightly noted, that every act of a public functionary

requires a complex interaction of *three* elements: obligations of office, personal commitment, and political prudence. A single person (taken as such) is insufficiently qualified to bear responsibility for a public decision.

With representative authority comes power, and with power comes asymmetry. Exclusive possession of power makes non-possessors dependent, and dependence can evolve into inferiority. Therefore safeguards are needed. The fundamental safeguard in the public domain is the democratic system itself. By attributing legitimacy to its functionaries and by duly controlling them, it forms a counterbalance against public power running wild and degenerating into abuses. But equally important are moral safeguards, principles that help protect the rights and interests of those subjected to public powers and keep intact the dignity of those in power.

Several principles can be identified as linked to the two characteristics of the public domain, representation and power.

With representation comes dignity, in the sense of one of Jane Jacobs' moral imperatives for the guardian syndrome quoted above "treasure honor," but also trustworthiness as avoidance of arbitrariness, and lack of greed, for no functionary is supposed to work primarily for his or her own profit. Openness—in the double sense of being accessible to those dependent on public services and open to democratic control and democratically uttered wishes and demands—is similarly required. With power comes respect for those dependent on you, care to apply power equally, and preparedness to serve actively, not waiting for desires and needs to be expressed by others, but taking an active responsibility for the fostering of the common good by showing initiative in defining and realizing it.

With the help of the principles of dignity, trustworthiness, lack of greed, openness, respect, care, and preparedness to serve, social integrity and morality in the public domain can be articulated. Single functionaries and administrators can and should value their own behavior according to these principles. At the same time, the principles serve as a yardstick to measure, on the basis of democratic procedures, not only single public functionaries but also agencies and institutions. Together the principles give rise to a specific type of ethics that I refer to as *representative ethics*.

Earlier I characterized social integrity and morality in the *private* domain with the help of *three* types of ethics. Given the all-pervading structure of representation and power in the public domain, it seems that here *one* type of ethics is sufficient. It makes sense, however, to point to a special link between *participative* ethics in the private domain on the one hand and the *representative* ethics of the public domain on the other. In representative ethics, *rights* of citizens prevail; in participative ethics, *civil duties* with regard to the accomplishment of the common good are at stake. The two are closely connected, but not in the sense of reciprocity, as is the case in transactional ethics. Rights of citizens do not depend on the degree to which they contribute to the common good, for duties in participative ethics are real but unenforceable, and rights are due to citizens because they are citizens, not because they are exemplary citizens (van Luijk, 1994). Nevertheless, participative and representative ethics, taken together, form a solid basis for public/private partnerships on behalf of the common good.

Under the heading "ethics in public administration," other questions are commonly raised that, up to now, in this sketch of representative ethics, have been left unanswered. Is it permitted to governmental officials to do things that are plainly forbidden in the private domain, such as lying in public or misleading the press on behalf of the public interest (Applbaum, 1999; Winston, 1994)? Or is a public functionary morally allowed to do things that are not permitted by the rules of her office? In the first case, let it suffice here to say (in line with the elaborated principles of representative ethics) that there might be plausible utilitarian justifications for dirty hands, but only under the condition, expressed in the principle of openness, that the official proves able to withstand the criticisms of democratic control. Similarly with the second question, a public functionary may decide to deviate from the rules of her office, for reasons of personal convictions or on the basis of an idiosyncratic definition of the common good (e.g., when she grants a permit to an applicant, knowing that her superior, as standard practice, declines such a request, without even looking at the single case). Here also the ultimate criterion remains openness and democratic control, for the most serious infringement on social integrity in the public domain is concealment of actions. At the end of the day, once her action comes out in the open, she may rightly appeal to her personal integrity, but, according to the principles of social integrity, she will have to accept a legitimate reproach or even sanction, supposing, of course, that the control is truly democratic and the sanction not authoritatively imposed by a single superior.

Now that I have sketched the contours of social integrity in the private and in the public domains, the question that remains to be addressed is, what about integrity in the *corporate* domain?

INTEGRITY IN THE CORPORATE DOMAIN

Is there a reason to devote a specific section to integrity in the corporate domain? Is the corporate domain distinct from the private and the public domains to such an extent that it deserves a separate treatment? The answer has to be elliptical: no, the corporate domain is not located in an area totally outside the private and the public domain, but yes, it seems sufficiently specific to deserve explicit attention. Much depends here on the way we define the corporate domain and, more basically, on the theoretical framework we apply to determine the functions and objectives of corporations.

It seems fair to say that the *corporate domain* is formed by the relations that corporations establish with each other, and with other entities of various natures, in view of continuity and profit making, on the basis of a free market system.

Especially since Coase's seminal article "The Nature of the Firm" (1990), economic theory has pictured the firm as an umbrella over a network of contracts. Firms are seen as single production functions engaged in separate activities that are coordinated by market exchanges. Now there are costs involved in negotiating and concluding a separate contract for each exchange transaction. To lower these transaction costs, a *firm* is created as a coordination device for situations in which long-term contracts are both possible and desirable (Rowlinson, 1997, pp. 24–25). Gradually, by the economic theory of the firm, a mechanism of responsibility displacement was set in motion, in two steps: Responsibility was taken away from persons in the firm and confined to hierarchical authority (Jackall, 1988), and subsequently the firm was deprived of responsibility altogether by conceiving it as a legal fiction or artifact enabling an anonymous but overall effective striving for profit maximization. Individuals and functionaries within the firm act as representatives of an economic goal setting, not as private persons, let alone as autonomous and responsible persons. They are reduced to uniform and largely anonymous profit seekers and profit makers. Alan Wolfe puts it bluntly when he states, "A firm is a device through which human beings, who have moral obligations, come together for the purpose of ridding themselves of their capacity to exercise moral obligations" (Wolfe, 1993).

From various sides, attempts have been made to correct this one-sided picture by emphasizing the firm as a social institution, a distinct constellation of economic interests and social relations, backed up by the legal machinery. In the early decades of the twentieth century, Max Weber deserves to be mentioned in this respect (Weber, 1922/1978), as well as, later on, Peter Drucker, who in *Concept of the Corporation* (1972) has a long chapter entitled "The Corporation as a Social Institution" (pp. 130–208). Recent contributions come from disciplines such as economic sociology (Swedberg, 2003), institutional economics (Hodgson, 1988, chap. 9), and organizational theory (for an overview, see Scott, 1998). What they have in common is, negatively, the thesis that when it comes to analyzing social relations, especially with regard to firms, economists must be qualified as "sociological babes in the wood," as Mark Granovetter puts it (1985). Positively, they share the conviction that the firm should be seen as the institutionalization of economic interests embedded in social and structural relations, while at the same time stressing the importance of treating people in the organization as mature adults and granting them professional responsibility and personal prospects. People in organizations are seen as adult actors with a moral competence (Pearsons, 1995).

With regard to varieties of social integrity, the enlarged view of the firm has several consequences. Firms today are facing seemingly contradictory but equally legitimate demands:

> to get things done effectively, efficiently, and profitably;

> to incorporate features from their surroundings that will endow them with legitimacy;

> to comply with requirements that do not remain restricted to either the private or the public domain but that are located at the interface of the two.

For this reason, social integrity in the corporate domain exceeds what we have come to know as "market morality." Given the embeddedness of corporations as social institutions in surroundings that endow them with legitimacy, with regard to market morality, two assumptions play a role, more or less explicitly. The first consists of the restriction of market morality to what we have come to understand as transactional ethics and its accompanying principles of equality, reciprocity, and honesty. The second assumption consists of the idea that corporate activities take place exclusively within the private domain. Both assumptions are seriously truncated.

The assumption that corporations can restrict themselves to complying with the principles of a transactional ethics, which is only one of the three types of ethics that are valid in the private domain (leaving aside both recognitional and participatory ethics as moral guides in the corporate domain), is an unduly limited view of corporate integrity, as can be shown by pointing to the rise of stakeholder theory in business ethics. It becomes increasingly clear that the moral definition of the corporate domain is directly linked to the number and nature of stakeholders that corporations are expected and prepared to acknowledge. I propose to define *stakeholders* as "those individuals and groups who can legitimately expect that a corporation is prepared to include their rights and interests in its decision processes," rights and interests that are commonly summarized under the "Triple P" of People, Planet, and Profit (Elkington, 1999). This stakeholder perspective introduces the principles of a recognitional ethics, justice and beneficence, in the texture of corporate integrity. Corporations that prove hesitant or even unwilling to include a reference to human rights in their company code are insufficiently aware of the rights-recognizing implications of the stakeholder model. On the other hand, corporations that take seriously the rights and interests of their stakeholders may expect to be endowed with a public "license to operate."

Something similar is the case with regard to participatory ethics. Participatory ethics and its concomitant principles of alertness, decency, and emancipation, together cumulating in *cooperative* citizenship, are included in the texture of corporate integrity, as soon as it makes sense to talk about *corporate* citizenship. Corporations have the right to be recognized and protected by the law, and they are entitled to various kinds of public support that enable them to function properly, as there is a material infrastructure of communication, and protection by the law through a well-functioning legal system. In return for this "gift of society," corporations can reasonably be expected to contribute their fair share to the common good, not only by paying taxes, but also by accepting the principles of participatory ethics, moral alertness, decency, and promotion of emancipatory processes on both an individual and a global level.

Along these lines it can be shown that the principles contained in the *three* types of ethics

within the private domain all apply, in one way or another, to the corporate domain as well. But how about the second assumption, which states that corporate activities take place exclusively within the private domain?

BLURRING BOUNDARIES, SHIFTING RELATIONSHIPS

The fact that not only the principles of a market morality but also the principles that are implied in the two other types of social integrity in the private domain apply to corporations does in itself not change the nature of the corporation. It remains a distinct constellation of economic interests and social relations, backed up by legal machinery. It is the entity that comes to the fore in what I referred to earlier as "the enlarged view of the firm." The simultaneous applicability of three types of ethics in itself changes not the nature but the normative context of the firm. On top of that, however, there seems reason to state that, today, the very nature of entities operating on the market is changing as well.

This does not count for market entities only. The state or the government, as representative par excellence of the common good, is also undergoing substantial changes, to such an extent that we must speak of blurring boundaries between the market and the state, a dichotomy that often is equated, albeit incorrectly, with the distinction between the private and the public. What causes this blurring of boundaries and its concomitant shift in relationships?

An important factor is the emergence of what nowadays is called "civil society" (Cohen, 1982; Cohen & Arato, 1992; Dubbink, 2003; Fullinwider, 1999; Keane, 1998; Schnapper, 2000; van Gunsteren, 1998). Among the many possible definitions I quote here the one John Keane offers when he states, "Civil society . . . is an ideal-typical category (an *Idealtype* in the sense of Max Weber) that both describes and envisages a complex and dynamic ensemble of legally protected non-governmental institutions that tend to be non-violent, self-organizing, self-reflexive, and permanently in tension with each other and with the state institutions that 'frame,' constrict and enable their activities" (Keane, 1998, p. 6). Civil society, therefore, is a normative as well as a descriptive notion. To Keane's definition should be added that a "permanent tension" exists not only between the various institutions of civil society and state institutions but also, and even more so, between civil society and institutions of the market.

State, market, and civil society are often referred to as the three *basic institutions* of society. This can be a clarifying notion to help one get hold of the basic organizing factors in social life. Where necessary, I will use it in that sense. Sticking, however, to our previously chosen concept of "domains," it is important to note that "civil society" does not simply add a numerical third domain to the domains of the private and the public. As an in-between institution that partly bears traits of a semipublic representative of the common good and partly represents (legally protected) private rights and interests, it brings about new configurations of interrelationship that coexist with the existing more-traditional bonds and boundaries between market and state.

Equally important to note is that the three basic institutions present themselves as unequal in power, origin, and outlook. In many developed democracies, we witness a withdrawal of government, out of sheer necessity, back to its basics, the burden of taking responsibility for the bringing about of *every* common good simply surpassing its capacities. Civil society, for its part, emerges from a growing democratic maturation of well-informed citizens. The market, with its history of centuries, enters the scene today as technically innovative and socially conservative. It seems the least prone to actively participating in new configurations.

To articulate more clearly what is at stake, it seems defensible to characterize each of the basic institutions by its own managing task, its own objective, and one or two specific principles:

- The *market* is meant to manage *property* in view of *the safeguarding and growth of prosperity and well-being of its participants* under the guidance of the principles of *reciprocity* (including equality and honesty) and *efficiency.*
- The *civil society* is meant to manage *knowledge and expertise* in view of the fostering of *democratic citizenship* under the guidance of the principles of *transparency and emancipation.*
- The *state* or *government* is meant to manage *power* in view of *maintenance and growth of the common good* under the guidance of the principles of *fairness and commitment to all,* especially the unfortunate.

Now what are the moral implications of the institutional reshuffling that we are witnessing? Are new requirements emerging that add up to, if not partly replace, the principles we have already found? I restrict myself to some remarks regarding the corporate domain.

The situation corporations find themselves in, at the present moment, is marked by new partners, old habits, and radical demands. Newcomers, such as nongovernmental organizations and interest groups, "anti-globalists" and environmentalists among them, enter the field with specific information at their disposal and a firm commitment to their cause. Governmental agencies feel urged to concentrate on their basic task—the creation and application of effective legal arrangements—more than on the building and managing of state-directed welfare institutions. And the corporate world, bound by the innate social conservatism of the market and the traditional inward gaze of its institutions, stresses the indispensability of its economic efforts to general well-being, while recoiling from radical demands they are increasingly facing.

All parties mentioned have their proper place, role, and range of action. It is in the corporate domain, however, where changes seem most disturbing, for the new institutional configuration affects not only the context but also the nature of the corporation itself. Corporations, especially large corporations and their organizations, turn out to become monsters in the literal sense of the word *monstrum,* a being belonging to two different and seemingly irreconcilable spheres, such as a mermaid or a Minotaur (van Gunsteren, 1994). More and more corporations are pulled into the public domain, gradually acquiring a semipublic status. Without becoming a public agent they are explicitly seen as a partner in the fostering of the common good and are judged accordingly.

The institutional reshuffling brings with it a radical rearrangement of responsibilities and requirements, guided by principles that, to a large part, are complementary to the principles we already discovered. Given the blurring of institutional boundaries and the concomitant reconfiguration of the basic institutions, the principles that accompany this process will not exclusively be valid for just one institution but will count for other ones as well. Sometimes, however, a principle can be located more specifically.

Several principles must be presented as particularly suited to cover newly emerging relations and partnerships between the basic institutions of society and the various entities that constitute them, entities that, for lack of a better term, I shall refer to as *specific institutions*. I see five principles that deserve to be highlighted.

First, there is the principle of *self-respect* that applies to every single specific institution, be it a corporation, an NGO, a governmental agency, a hospital, a pension fund, a newspaper, or a university. Each one is required to show moral self-respect, for the increasing complexity of the social fabric demands a reinforcement of moral awareness of all parties involved. Self-respect is shown when a specific institution clearly states its basic values and objectives and declares itself prepared to be held accountable for its statements. To this end, the specific institution has to materialize its moral identity in devices such as a code, internal training programs, peer reviews, newly established partnerships, and the like. Self-respect evaporates if not rooted in self-imposed and publicly proffered obligations.

Next, there is the principle of *respect for other parties*. Especially now that relationships are shifting, respect for other parties cannot simply be stated but must constantly be maintained through an ongoing exchange of ideas and convictions with even distant parties, and even more so through the willingness to negotiate with others about everyone's interests and legitimate claims. When it comes to showing respect for other parties, negotiation is a more solid, and a more demanding, medium than dialogue.

Closely related to the principle of respect for other parties is the principle of *openness and transparency*. At stake here is the question of how accessible, and how controllable, a specific institution proves to be for participatory arrangements. The ongoing discussion about "corporate governance" mainly circles around issues such as correct, timely, and complete information and who has a say in major decision processes—in other words, around openness and transparency.

The fourth principle may sound more controversial. It is linked to what I pointed to as the innate social conservatism of the market and of market institutions such as corporations. I call it the principle of *legal firmness*. It should be understood against the background of the preference that market participants show for being autarkic, self-supporting, or at least self-regulative. What the principle of legal firmness stresses is that, at the end of the day, legal authorities have to guarantee the smooth and effective functioning of different social partners in view of the common good and, in case such a functioning is not, or not sufficiently, provided, to firmly impose adequate behavior by legal means. The principle of legal firmness is the positive flipside of a healthy distrust in every party's good intentions.

The fifth principle, finally, is probably the most encompassing and certainly the most demanding one. I call it the principle of *courageous modesty*. It implies the acknowledgment that, in the present state of affairs, no single specific institution is able to take care of its own interests, let alone to live up to the social expectations it is facing, without the support and cooperation of other specific institutions that belong either to the market, to the state, or to civil society. This is the modesty part of the principle, as well as the encompassing one. The courage part of the principle, and simultaneously the most demanding one, consists in the recognition that single insufficiency does not imply a discharge of responsibility. What De George (1990) calls "the principle of ethical displacement" comes into play here. By this he means that "what appears as a dilemma for an individual on a personal level may only find a solution, for example, on the corporate level, in the sense that personal dilemmas may require changes in corporate structure. Corporate dilemmas, in turn, may require changes in industry structures to guarantee fair conditions of competition. Industry dilemmas may require changes in national policies. And national business dilemmas, such as handling pollution, may require changes in structures on an international level" (Enderle, Almond, & Argandoña, 1990, pp. 27–28). In this way of presenting it, the principle of displacement still looks like a fairly rectilinear progression to a next higher level of solution, while remaining within the realm of business. I am afraid that this is a too simple presentation of what we are facing today. Solutions are no longer found by taking one step higher. They are often hidden in untrodden and highly complex areas where much is new and unproven, areas that present an intertwinement of institutional perspectives, with the contradictions and seemingly insurmountable obstacles that go with it. To take some steps in these areas requires courage, for the responsibility remains, but one certainly loses command. If there is a path nonetheless, it can be found only by following the footsteps of those who did not hesitate to take the lead.

Self-respect, respect for other parties, openness and transparency, legal firmness, and courageous modesty are the principles that come to the fore when we try to determine what social integrity in the corporate domain implies, once we come across the shifting relationships and the blurring of institutional boundaries that characterize the present-day state of corporate affairs. There is no guarantee that these are the only principles, or even the most central ones. One can try to elaborate specific principles of integrity by analyzing thoroughly domains for which they are supposed to be valid. A guarantee of their validity can come only from a common recognition. One thing that may have become clear by now is that integrity, ultimately, is based upon an agreement.

REFERENCES

Applbaum, A. I. (1999). *Ethics for adversaries: The morality of roles in public and professional life.* New Jersey: Princeton University Press.

Barry, B. (1970). *Political argument.* London: Routledge & Kegan Paul. (Original work published 1965)

Benjamin, M. (1990). *Splitting the difference: Integrity in ethics and politics.* St. Lawrence: University Press of Kansas.

Carter, S. L. (1996). *Integrity.* New York: Basic Books.

Coase, R. H. (1990). The nature of the firm. In R. H. Coase (Ed.), *The firm, the market and the law.* Chicago & London: The University of Chicago Press. (Original work published 1937)

Cohen, J. H. (1982). *Class and civil society: The limits of Marxian critical theory.* Amherst: The University of Massachusetts Press.

Cohen, J. H., & Arato, A. (1992). *Civil society and political theory.* Cambridge: MIT Press.

Collins, J. C., & Porras, J. I. (1996). *Built to last: Successful habits of visionary companies.* London: Century Ltd. (Original work published 1994)

De George, R. (1990). Using the techniques of ethical analysis in corporate practice. In G. Enderle, B. Almond, & A. Argandoña (Eds.), *People in corporations: Ethical responsibilities and corporate effectiveness. (Issues in business ethics: Vol. 1).* Dordrecht/Boston/London: Kluwer.

Dobel, J. P. (1999). *Public integrity.* Baltimore & London: The Johns Hopkins University Press.

Drucker, P. (1972). *Concept of the corporation.* New York: The John Day Company. (Original work published 1946)

Dubbink, W. (2003). *Assisting the invisible hand (Issues in business ethics: Vol. 18).* Dordrecht/Boston/London: Kluwer.

Elkington, J. (1999). *Cannibals with forks: The triple bottom line in 21st century business.* Oxford, UK: Capstone. (Original work published 1997)

Enderle, G., Almond, B., & Argandoña, A. (Eds.). (1990). *People in corporations: Ethical responsibilities* and corporate effectiveness (*Issues in business ethics: Vol. 1*). Dordrecht/ Boston/ London: Kluwer.

Frankena, W. K. (1973). *Ethics*. Englewood Cliffs, NJ: Prentice Hall. (Original work published 1963)

Fullinwider, R. K. (Ed.). (1999). *Civil society, democracy, and civic renewal*. Lanham, MD: Rowman & Littlefield

Granovetter, M. (1985). Economic action and social structure: The problem of embeddedness. *American Journal of Sociology, 91*: 481–510.

Hajer, M. A. (1989). *De stad als publiek domein* [The city as public domain]. Amsterdam: Wiardi Beckmanstichting.

Hampshire. S. (Ed.). (1980). *Public and private morality*. Cambridge, UK: Cambridge University Press. (Original work published 1978)

Hodgson, G. (1988). *Economics and institutions: A manifesto for a modern institutional economics*. Cambridge, UK: Polity.

Jackall, R. (1988). *Moral mazes: The world of corporate managers*. New York/Oxford, UK: Oxford University Press.

Jacobs, J. (1992). *Systems of survival: A dialogue on the moral foundations of commerce and politics*. New York: Random House.

Keane, J. 1998. Civil Society: Old Images, New Visions. California: Stanford University Press.

McFall, L. (1987). Integrity. *Ethics, 98*, 5–20.

Pearsons, G. (1995). *Integrity in organizations: An alternative business ethics*. London: McGraw-Hill Book Company Europe.

Rowlinson, M. (1997). *Organizations and institutions: Perspectives in economics and sociology*. Houndmills, Basingstoke, England: Macmillan Business.

Schnapper, D. (2000). *Qu'est-ce que la citoyenneté?* Paris: Gallimard.

Schneewind, J. B. (1998). *The invention of autonomy: A history of modern moral philosophy*. Cambridge, UK: Cambridge University Press.

Scott, R. (1998). *Organizations: Rational, national and open systems* (4th ed.). Englewood Cliffs, New Jersey: Prentice Hall.

Swedberg, R. (2003). *Principles of economic sociology*. Princeton, NJ & Oxford, UK: Princeton University Press.

Taylor, G. (1985). *Pride, shame, and guilt: Emotions of self-assessment*. Oxford, UK: Clarendon Press.

van Gunsteren, H. (1994). *Culturen van besturen* [Cultures of administration]. Amsterdam: Boom.

van Gunsteren, H. (1998). *A theory of citizenship: Organizing plurality in contemporary democracies*. Boulder, CO: Westview.

van Luijk, H. (1993). *Om redelijk gewin* [For reasonable profit]. Amsterdam: Boom.

van Luijk, H. (1994). Rights and interests in a participatory market society. *Business Ethics Quarterly, 4*(1), 79–96.

van Luijk, H. (2000). *Integer en verantwoord in beroep en bedrijf* [Acting with integrity and responsibility in professional and business life]. Amsterdam: Boom.

Weber, M. (1978). *Economy and society: An outline of interpretive sociology* (2 vols.). Berkeley: University of California Press. (Original work published 1922)

Winston, K. I. (1994). Necessity and choice in political ethics: Varieties of dirty hands. In D. E. Wueste (Ed.), *Professional ethics and social responsibility*. Lanham, MD: Rowman and Littlefield.

Wolfe, A. (1993). The modern corporation: Private agent or public actor? *Washington and Lee Law Review, 50*(4).

PART II

FINANCIAL REPORTING AND ACCOUNTABILITY

I f corporate integrity is the aim, we need to know what specific obstacles stand in the way, and how they should be analyzed and evaluated. Further, we must ask what can be done to resolve the problems and issues that have led to the recent scandals. What are businesses, large and small, doing along these lines? Answers to these questions are important for investors, business partners, and the general public. Discussion of these issues is the common theme of the chapters in Part II.

Norman Bowie argues that many of the current ethical problems business faces stem from "the existence of widespread conflicts of interest and the abuse of information asymmetry." The absence of such problems, Bowie contends, is essential to corporate integrity. And though only a few corporations have collapsed due directly to such ethical and legal troubles, he contends that they are bound up with other activities, such as the inflation and manipulation of earnings and the culture of greed, that are "endemic to the system." Accordingly, Bowie's chapter spotlights conflicts of interest and the abuse of information asymmetry. (For discussion of a problem related to that of human greed, the reader may refer to O'Higgins, Chapter 17, where excessive executive compensation is the focus of attention.)

Bowie presents several examples of both conflicts of interest and the abuse of information asymmetry and discusses why they are wrong and what can be done to resolve these problems. One primary solution involves disclosure, that is, transparency. However, this is not a sufficient answer, since it does not address issues of trust or the costs to stakeholders involved. Another response would be to make accountants government employees with civil service protection. But Bowie acknowledges that it is highly unlikely that this step will be taken. The requirements laid out in the Sarbanes-Oxley Act of 2002 offer another partial solution, namely, the rotation of auditors and the making of various conflicts of interest illegal. These reforms are then placed in an international context. Bowie contends that some form of external political regulation that is international in nature, but less adversarial and less rule-bound than in the United States, also needs to be adopted. Bowie notes that the abuse of excessive executive compensation escapes the preceding analysis. In response, he defends a position that relies on Rawls' views regarding the determination of justice, as well as Aristotle's views on character. In conclusion, Bowie reflects on the role of the business ethicist as being one who can help shape current debates over business ethics. Bowie maintains that this would consist of identifying relevant universal moral standards and serving as an ethical nonexpert in negotiating the implementation of those standards.

The independence of auditors from their audit clients, which is intended to ensure the reliability and credibility of the financial reporting process, is the focus of the chapter from **Thomas Dunfee, Alan S. Glazer, Henry R. Jaenicke, Susan McGrath,** and **Arthur Siegel.** Without the reliability and credibility of audits, corporate governance is weakened and trust in the financial reporting system undermined. The authors examine the kinds of relationships between auditors and their clients that may compromise the objective and impartial decision making of auditors. Two important dimensions of this independence are "independence of mind" and "independence in appearance." Accordingly, central to the analysis of auditor independence in this chapter is the notion of conflict of interest. Conflicts of interest may be of a number of different kinds (actual, latent, or potential). They may arise out of a multitude of situations. A wide variety of cognitive biases, about which people (and auditors as well) may be unaware, may contribute. It is possible to reduce or eliminate such conflicts of interest by revealing them, obtaining consent from affected parties, installing controls, or eliminating them. To address problems associated with auditor independence, they propose an Auditor Independence Conceptual Framework (AICF). Eschewing the more traditional rules-based approach taken by auditing in the United States, the authors adopt an approach that rests on general principles. This framework, in turn, rests upon a concept of "independence risk." Having detailed five typical types of threats to independence that are basic elements of AICF, they propose that those involved in auditing use this framework to assess the independence risk they face. Since this risk will have to be balanced against other costs and benefits, the authors indicate, not unlike part of Bowie's recommendation, that laws, regulations, public policy, and the judgment of audit committees themselves will have to be involved. The chapter concludes by showing how this framework might be used to resolve current auditor independence issues and to evaluate the pros and cons of these issues.

The chapters by Bowie and Dunfee et al. both focus on current issues regarding the integrity of auditors and financial reporting of corporations. In his chapter, **Georges Enderle** expands the area of reporting beyond the financial to include the social and environmental responsibilities of businesses. The recent problems of corporations such as Enron and WorldCom are not, he maintains, simply problems (at the micro level) of a few individuals but involve failures of the regulatory framework and macro-level issues. Indeed, these kinds of problems need to be addressed at the individual, organizational, and systematic levels. Hence, he discusses financial reporting but does it in the context of a "three-level conception" of business ethics. Trust can be developed only through an approach that involves truth or transparency with regard to the responsibilities of the providers, certifiers, and users of financial reports. The Global Reporting Initiative, and particularly its Sustainability Reporting Guidelines (2002), is presented as one widely recognized and commendable form that the reporting of financial, as well as social and environmental, dimensions of a company may take. Nevertheless, Enderle offers five critical comments regarding this approach to accounting. In light of his critical discussion of this broader view of reporting, he discusses what financial and sustainability reporting can learn from each other. Finally, drawing upon the preceding discussion, Enderle compares two different concepts of the company that may influence corporate reporting (the hierarchical and the balanced concept) and argues that we need to adopt the latter as the firm of the future. In doing this, he invokes Amartya Sen's concept of a "capability approach" and his "goal rights system" view to begin to fill out the details of a balance concept of the firm.

Josep Lozano takes a rather different approach to the issue of the accountability that each of the preceding authors in Part II discussed as a way to foster corporate integrity. He notes new developments in the direction that accountability has been taking, but argues that for these developments to work, the companies instituting them must carefully think through such issues as how they see their role in society and what values they support. In short, they must confront their identity, integrity, and fundamental purpose. This approach, he contends, is superior to focusing on corporate scandals and on ideas that we do not want to promote. Accordingly, by taking the topic of corporate success seriously, which includes that of corporate integrity, we can forge a path to understanding accountability.

Many businesses operate with a one-dimensional view of success, which focuses on economic and financial results. Lozano rejects this view. Those who focus so narrowly, to the exclusion of everything else, have a kind of "teleopathy" (a sickness of purpose). Instead, corporate success is a social construction of a company's own internal definition together with that of the society in which it operates. As such, there is a direct relation between success and accountability. Accountability is not simply another technique for providing information, or management of risks and reputations, but a learning process that defines the company. As Lozano says, "In a nutshell, accountability is not a question of metrics but of vision." Accordingly, accountability must be set within the broader framework of corporate social responsibility (CSR).

Unfortunately some business managers exhibit a form of CSR myopia. They adopt a narrow view of the firm. Against this, Lozano notes, there are tremendous pressures today in the direction of increased CSR. However, there are at least three different views of CSR with regard to the role of business and society. The third view of "business in society," the one Lozano adopts, is in line with triple bottom line thinking and embraces new spheres of responsibility and accountability. The development of this complex vision of business in society is one that will require the transformation of some individuals and companies towards greater social legitimacy.

In this view, an accountable company must also be one in which its members have a particular mindset that includes viewing people as active, responsible beings instead of passive objects, as being capable of forging relationships and taking on commitments, and as being able to work with values. With regard to organizations, Lozano contends, accountability involves clarifying ways and procedures to gather relevant information, as well as careful corporate reflection on its relations to stakeholders. For this, accountability needs to become not simply an instrument for management of interactions with stakeholders, but an opportunity for learning and innovation. Transparency will be an essential part of this process whereby businesses engage in ongoing dialogues with their stakeholders. The upshot should be aimed at fostering the accountability not only of businesses themselves but also of other institutions in society. And this development is intimately related to the broader question of the place of business in creating the good society. In seeking to answer this question, each business creates for itself and society a space of personal, professional, and corporate integrity.

In the final chapter of Part II, **Laura Spence** draws our attention to the importance of small firms with regard to issues of corporate integrity and accountability. In general, small firms are overlooked or assumed (mistakenly) to be similar to large firms. For these small firms, the role of owner-manager is the most important. There is not the separation of ownership and control as in large firms, and they are typically not focused on profit maximization.

In this context, the meaning of accountability is different, Spence maintains, than in large firms, though the meaning of integrity seems to remain the same. For example, at one level, accountability refers to reliable financial accounts on the financial status of the corporation (an economic account) reported to appropriate bodies. But at another, more basic, level it entails a relationship in which people are required to explain and take responsibility for their actions. It is this view of accountability that Spence finds most prevalent in small firms. This relationship, or socializing approach to accountability, acknowledges the interdependence of oneself and others. It also involves a moral perspective that is typical of the small firms she studied.

Spence found that issues of integrity arose primarily with regard to client/competitor relationships, whereas issues of accountability arose primarily with regard to employees. The upshot of her survey is that accountability differs between large and small firms. In large firms, accountability is a formal, individualizing process that involves competence in monitoring and auditing procedures. In small firms, accountability involves interdependence, reciprocal instrumental interests and claims, and a reciprocal sense of personal obligation and friendship.

As indicated previously, integrity concerns arise, in the small firm, primarily with regard to clients and customers. These firms are too small, Spence claims, to do anything but be honest and act with integrity. Drawing on Lynn Sharp Paine's views on corporate integrity, Spence maintains that a high degree of moral accountability is part of small firm integrity. Additionally, moral conscientiousness, in the form of independence and autonomy of action, is at stake here. These are important motivators for the small firm owner-manager. However, moral commitment and moral coherence (additional characteristics of corporate integrity, according to Paine) seem less relevant to small firms. Those pertain more readily to large firms. Spence notes that there is much more to be discussed, not only on the level of small firms but also with regard to the large firms that are more the focus of the other authors in this book.

In summary, the chapters in Part II give us five rather different perspectives on the nature of accountability and how it can, or should, be fostered in both small and large firms. They make clear the complexity involved. Accountability demands finely tuned corporate procedures not only on financial levels but also on social and environmental levels. It requires social laws and regulations on both a national and an international level, demands corporate visions of their identity and place in society, and also necessitates that we make adjustments for the size of the firm.

6

Why Conflicts of Interest and Abuse of Information Asymmetry Are Keys to Lack of Integrity and What Should Be Done About It

Norman E. Bowie

For many years we have lectured the world about the success of our capitalist/democratic system. More specifically, the United States has bragged about its transparency and honesty. And during the mid and late '90s, its rhetoric was backed with apparent financial success. In 2001, U.S. superiority was severely challenged. The United States inaugurated a president who did not win the popular vote and whose victory in the electoral college (an embarrassing relic) was itself contested and ultimately decided by the Supreme Court, whose members are not elected. That was followed by the horrifying terrorist attack that exposed our vulnerability to religious intolerance and hatred. At year's end, the collapse of Enron exposed widespread misconduct in corporate America with the complicity of the regulatory mechanisms. The Enron scandal was the prelude to a seemingly endless string of scandals that stretched throughout 2002 and well into 2003. It is not too farfetched to say that the stock market decline in the first six months of 2002 was almost entirely the result of investor distrust in the integrity of the financial reports of many of America's major corporations. The boom of the late '90s was a mirage, not the result of irrational exuberance as Alan Greenspan said, but rather a house built on lies and deception that could not stand once exposed to the light.

Of course, the exposure of our own system's inadequacies does not negate the criticism that was being made concerning the lack of transparency that existed in many markets around the world. Corruption is corruption is corruption. The fact that America is deeply involved in it does not make the corruption go away. We are all in the same mud together. Thus, when we consider issues of integrity and accountability, our task must be to analyze the problem and come up with solutions.

AN ANALYSIS OF CORPORATE INTEGRITY

In English, *integrity* is defined as (a) steadfast adherence to an ethical code, honesty; (b) the state of being unimpaired, soundness; (c) the quality or condition of being whole, undivided (*The American Heritage College Dictionary,* 1993). I frankly think that definition applies better to individual integrity than to corporate integrity. I propose that we come at the notion of corporate integrity from the other end—by examining what went wrong in American financial markets and then defining *integrity* as the opposite of what went wrong. I hope to demonstrate that many of our problems result from the existence of widespread conflicts of interest and the abuse of information asymmetry (a kind of violation of fairness). If this diagnosis is correct, then I argue that corporate integrity is a matter of avoiding conflicts of interest and of not abusing information asymmetry (of treating one's stakeholders fairly). I will then conclude with some comments on accountability, particularly on the issue of whether accountability can be achieved by self-regulation or whether it must be achieved by external political regulation. I argue that any external regulation ought to be international in character because regulation of that kind is more appropriate to a world where international business is so important. I also believe that U.S. participation in international agreements—rather than "going it alone" or trying to impose its standards on the world—would be a first step in showing that the United States is a cooperative player in the world order and not its dictator.

I turn to an examination of the problems that came to the surface with the collapse of Enron and continued with WorldCom, etc. Let us begin with Enron and its auditor Arthur Andersen (who ironically gave $5 million in the late '80s and early '90s to introduce ethics into America's business schools).

THESIS

My thesis is simply stated: The abuse of asymmetrical information and the existence of conflicts of interest have led to a decline in trust that threatens the very existence of capitalism.

THE CRISIS: REAL OR IMAGINARY—OR HOW MANY ROTTEN APPLES IN THE BARREL?

Some in the business community have argued that business is basically honest and that we have a few rotten apples. I reject that view. It is true that relatively few top executives have committed fraud, although some surely have. However, the inflation and manipulation of earnings is not limited to a few errant firms but is endemic to the system. So is a corporate culture characterized by personal greed and arrogance. We cannot change human greed. We can eliminate conflicts of interest. I will maintain that conflicts of interest and the abuse of asymmetrical information are the common threads behind many of the corporate scandals and that they have become a common practice in business. Moreover, the widespread existence of conflicts of interests and the abuse of information asymmetry has undermined trust in capitalism itself.

I include a few quotations to show that I am not alone. *BusinessWeek* had a special issue on the "Crisis in Accounting" in its January 28, 2002, issue (Nussbaum, 2002). The title of the lead article was "Can You Trust ANYBODY Anymore?" The first line in the article read, "The scope of the Enron debacle undermines the credibility of modern business culture." A month later they had an additional special issue, "The Betrayed Investor" (Vickers & McNamee, 2002). Here are some additional quotations:

> Ultimately, say analysts and commentators from a variety of disciplines, the public fascination with Enron expresses an anxiety over whether trust people place in their employers, political leaders, and even capitalism as it is currently practiced is misplaced. (Stevenson, 2002)
>
> Enron is a systematic failure implicating the range of institutions from accounting firms to boards of directors that are designed to justify broad public confidence in the functioning of what is supposed to be a mature capitalist system—confidence that is indispensable, given the rapidly broadening demographics of stock ownership. As an economic scandal—a scandal in the private sector—it may be the worst in American history. (Will, 2002, p. 64)

I also believe the market has spoken on this issue. In early December 2001, the stock markets had recovered most of the losses suffered after the September 11 terrorist attacks. Then they fell dramatically, and in early August of 2002,[1] they were at lows for the year and for the NASDAQ at lows not seen in over five years. Why? The economic news in the first quarter had been upbeat, interest rates were low, and inflation was and is virtually nonexistent. Yet stocks continued to fall. I submit that the only logical explanation for this during the December 2001 through August 2002 time period is failure of investor confidence resulting from the unending reports of inflated revenues, accounting irregularities, and revelations of conflict of interest where the interests of the ordinary investor were sacrificed. Is there any longer any doubt that the unethical and illegal treatment of stockholders hurts the bottom line?

ANALYSIS OF THE CRISIS

The first step in the argument is to show that most of the issues surrounding Enron, Arthur Andersen, and the subsequent disclosures of financial impropriety are nearly all cases of either the existence of conflicts of interest or the abuse of asymmetrical information. Before beginning, a clarification of terms is in order.

CONFLICTS OF INTEREST

Two definitions of a *conflict of interest* are prominent in the philosophical literature. Michael Davis has defined *conflict of interest* as follows: "A person has a conflict of interest if a) he is in a relationship of trust with another requiring him to exercise judgment in that other's service and b) he has an interest tending to interfere with the proper exercise of that judgment" (Davis, 1982, p. 21). Tom Beauchamp has proposed a similar definition: "A conflict of interest occurs whenever there exists a conflict between a person's private or institutional gain and that same person's official duties in a position of trust" (Beauchamp, 1992, p. 9).

One of the requirements of accounting codes of ethics and the recently passed Sarbanes-Oxley Act is that accountants be independent. That means that there should be no relationship between the accountant and the client that results in a conflict of interest. Unfortunately the accounting profession is enmeshed in an immediate conflict of interest. The client it audits pays the accounting firm. If you want to be asked back, you have an incentive to accept management's interpretation of anything in the gray area. (There is also a temptation to accept anything that violates Generally Accepted Accounting Principles (GAPP), but the disincentives of being caught are stronger here. However, the disincentives did not deter executives at WorldCom.)

Arthur Andersen violated auditor independence in far more egregious ways. Perhaps the most egregious conflict of interest was the fact that they helped structure the off-the-book partnerships they would later approve as auditors. It would be the financial shenanigans with these off-the-book partnerships that would ultimately bring down Enron. Andersen also was hired to do some of Enron's internal auditing—auditing that they would later review as the outside auditor. This is a clear conflict of interest and violates the ethical norms of the accounting profession.

Another conflict of interest involved revolving-door hiring practices. Andersen would hire Enron staff and Enron would hire Andersen staff. The conflict of interest involved with this revolving-door practice is well known in government, and rules have been put in place to prohibit government regulators from taking positions in the industries they regulate for a certain number of years. All these activities clearly meet both the definitions of *conflict of interest*. Nearly all the sins of Arthur Andersen can be described as sins resulting from acting on an actual conflict of interest and violating their professions' ethical code, which requires auditor independence.

Of course, conflicts of interest are not limited to Enron and Arthur Andersen. One of the most serious conflicts of interest that is nearly universal in the investment industry occurs when analysts who rate stocks are also involved in securing investment banking for the firm. The Merrill Lynch settlement with the State of New York after an investigation by New York Attorney General Eliot Spitzer provides an excellent example. Merrill Lynch analysts were shown to recommend a stock in order to secure investment business through the issuing of IPOs or to sustain the price of an IPO that Merrill Lynch had initiated. Specific charges of conflict of interest have been lodged against Merrill's star analyst Henry Blodget. He is accused of having "misled investors by fraudulently promoting the stocks of companies with which the firm had investment banking relationships" (Elstrom, 2002, p. 44). As an analyst, he had an obligation to provide objective investment advice, and that obligation morally should have trumped any obligation to increase the investment banking business at Merrill Lynch.

Another example is provided by the case of analyst Jack Grubman of Salomon Smith Barney. He maintained bullish "buy ratings" on WorldCom from early 1999 to mid 2001. The stock went from $80 to $13 in that time and WorldCom eventually went bankrupt as a result of accounting fraud. It wasn't that Grubman was stupid; he was a star. Rather, he acted upon a conflict of interest at the expense of the small investor and WorldCom employees. Grubman was an advisor to WorldCom's then-chairman Bernard Ebbers, and his ratings generated substantial profits for both Salomon and Grubman himself. Grubman unjustly put his own interests ahead of his obligations to provide objective advice to clients (Elstrom, 2002; Rosenbush, 2002).

Moreover, the problem is not simply limited to a few rogue traders. It is endemic in the industry. According to an analysis by First Call, of the analyst calls at the ten largest investment banks, there were 57 sell recommendations versus 7,033 buys. Seventy percent of all analyst calls are buys. And further research by Matthew Hayward has established that companies get higher ratings from the analysts they bank with than they do from analysts they do not bank with. It should be noted that Grubman had a buy on practically all the companies he covered. Eleven of sixteen analysts still had a buy or strong buy on Enron on November 8, 2001, even though Enron had taken a $1.2 billion reduction in shareholder equity and was under an SEC probe.

The moral wrong of the conflict of interest was exacerbated by the abuse of information asymmetry. At the center of the investigation were a series of damning E-mails including the following: "Nothing interesting about this company (GoTo.com) except banking fees," and "The whole idea that we are independent from banking is a big lie" (Vickers, 2002, p. 38). Many investors were unaware of the fact that the analysts' salaries were dependent on the amount of investment banking business they brought in. They also did not know, of course, that the analysts did not really believe these stocks should be a "buy." Private memos and E-mails now show that the analysts actually believed many of these stocks were really "dogs." Information asymmetry of that sort is also deceptive and perhaps fraudulent. Worse, these analysts knew these stocks were not a strong buy and privately disparaged them. This is a perfect segue to a more general discussion of the abuse of information asymmetry.

ABUSE OF ASYMMETRICAL INFORMATION

An abuse of asymmetrical information exists when one person has information that another person does not have and does not share that information with the other when the other person has a legal and/or moral right to the information. It should be pointed out that one of the assumptions of efficient markets is the existence of perfect information and the absence of information asymmetry. Insider trading is a paradigm case of the abuse of information asymmetry, and it is considered illegal and immoral on grounds of fairness. Persons with inside information know that the information will move a stock in a certain direction and trade on that information to make a profit that is not open to all. That is why there is so much interest in Martha Stewart's selling of ImClone. Another example of the abuse of insider information occurs when inside executives sell their shares in a firm while pretending to employees and the investing public that all is well. One of the most telling criticisms of a number of Enron officials and other executives at other financially stressed companies is that these officials sold their stock because they had inside information on the bad news before it was made public. Even if the legal requirements were met, that seems to be unfair (Berman, 2002).

Morally speaking, the worst cases of the abuse of asymmetrical information are fraud. The mammoth WorldCom scandal seems to be a clear-cut case of accounting fraud. Fraud occurs when a person deliberately lies or distorts the facts so that other people believe what is known not to be the case.

With Enron, the ethical violations were primarily abuse of information asymmetry violations. A *Wall Street Journal* article on December 5, 2001, begins with the headline "Behind Enron's Fall: A Culture of Operating Outside Public's View." Fraud involves lying and deception that are especially unethical instances of information asymmetry. Any Kantian understands why. Christine Korsgaard has put the point this way:

According to the Formula of Humanity, coercion and deception are the most fundamental forms of wrongdoing to others—the roots of all evil. Coercion and deception violate the conditions of possible assent, and all actions which depend for their nature and efficacy on their coercive or deceptive character are ones that others cannot assent to. . . . Physical coercion treats someone's person as a tool; lying treats someone's *reason* as a tool. That is why Kant finds it so horrifying; it is a direct violation of autonomy. (Korsgaard, 1996, pp. 140, 141)

Enron was guilty of this deception. They had a separate floor where they would create the appearance of doing energy trades whenever investors were in the building. But no such trades were taking place and the floor was not usually used for that purpose. Thus they deceived stockholders and investors. They also deceived their employees. They encouraged employees not to sell Enron stock, and for a brief time the employees were not permitted to sell stock in their retirement plans. In the meantime, some Enron executives who had inside information were selling their stock. A similar situation existed at Qwest. As Qwest ran into trouble and its stock began to decline, executives, including CEO Nacchio and founder Anschulz, sold their stock while employees were encouraged to hold on to their stock (Grover & Palmeri, 2002). Thus the rich saved their retirement income while lower-paid employees were left much worse off or even destitute. Some of my students argue that Enron employees should have been smarter and should never have invested so much of their retirement income in Enron stock. This argument strikes me as callous. These employees were strongly encouraged to place their retirement funds in Enron stock, and they trusted management to give them good advice. Is loyalty to one's company and trust in one's superiors vices that should be avoided, as some of my MBAs seem to argue?

Asymmetrical information that involves deception is clearly wrong, as is asymmetrical information that is unfair or creates an injustice. Recall our definition of *abuse of asymmetrical information*. It contained a legal criterion, but it also contained a moral criterion. We now operationalize that moral notion in terms of fairness. Robert Frank has demonstrated the importance of perceptions of fairness with respect to pricing (Frank, 1988). Firms that ignore these perceptions of fairness risk making strategic errors. Charges of unfairness and injustice are endemic in the current crisis. A few quotations should set the tone. Robert Barbera, chief economist of Hoenig and Company, commented that

> the moral outrage today focuses on risk. Basically investors and workers are incensed at being snookered into taking risks they didn't understand and wouldn't have willingly accepted. Enron lied to shareholders and workers about the risks they faced. Venture capitalists brought high-risk start-ups public without clearly informing investors of the dangers. And more broadly greedy executives and financiers have been shifting risk to other people without their informed consent, undermining their security. (Vickers & McNamee, 2002)

And Paul McCulley, chief economist at Pimco (an investment firm), stated, "It's a case where the rich guy took the upside and stuffed the poor guy with the downside" (Stevenson, 2002).

Occasionally a person has the courage to issue a sell on a stock or a sector, but the price can be the loss of his or her job. Mike Mayo was a star analyst for the firm of Credit Suisse First Boston. He had the courage to recommend in the spring of 1999 that clients sell bank stocks. He was right but was fired because Credit Suisse First Boston's bank customers were furious. The complete account of this sorry tale is described in the February 5, 2001, issue of *Fortune* in the article "The Price of Being Right" (Rynecki, 2001). The cost has been high. "Robert Barbera, chief economist at Hoenig & Co. figures most of the 26% operating earnings growth reported by the S&P 500 companies from 1997–2000 was the result of accounting shenanigans" (Vickers & McNamee, 2002).

As the number of companies that have engaged in these practices increases, perhaps it would be useful to summarize the tricks of the trade that are used to disadvantage those who are on the wrong side of this information asymmetry. These tactics enable companies to inflate earnings—tactics sometimes referred to as "buffing the company." Since the public has not been aware of these practices and since the existence of these practices violates the notion of a level playing field, they represent an abuse of information asymmetry. Many, many companies use a device called pro forma accounting to report on the financial health of the company. Pro forma earnings do not conform to GAAP, and there is no standardization across companies. Also, since management prepares the pro forma earnings reports, we shall just say that they tend to be overly optimistic. SEC Chief Accountant Lynn E. Turner calls pro forma earnings "EBS earnings—for everything but the bad stuff" (Henry, 2001).

There are many ways to make the earnings of the company sound better than they are. In the big bath, companies write off costs now in order to inflate revenue later. Cisco, Daimier Chrysler, and Kodak have played that game. Other companies have lent customers large amounts of money so that they can continue to buy their products. However, things are much worse if these customers go bankrupt and companies like Motorola, Lucent, and Nortel lose both customers and the value of the loans they made.

There is also the complicated issue of stock options. The liability of these options is kept off the books. However, following the simple laws of supply and demand, the more stock options that are out there, the greater potential for the dilution of the stock held by the general public. Sanford Bernstein has said that to prevent dilution "companies would have to spend a staggering $53 billion a year to buy back their own stocks. That figure is equivalent to an amazing 13% of operating earnings—51% for tech companies" (Fox, 2001).

In summary, I believe this array of examples confirms the view that the concepts of a conflict of interest and abuse of information asymmetry account for many of the reported scandals and scams.

WHAT SHOULD BE DONE?

There is a philosophical literature concerning conflicts of interest and how to resolve them. The first step in eliminating conflicts of interest is disclosure. If you admit a conflict of interest, then people are alerted and can decide for themselves whether to continue the relationship.[2] *BusinessWeek* of June 10, 2002, reported that in light of the revelations of conflict of interest in the investment business, many clients are shifting their accounts to firms that do little or no investment banking—to Edward Jones of St. Louis, for example. These clients no longer trusted their brokerage firms to put their interests first. On the other hand, in many real estate transactions, the same attorney represents the buyer and the seller. The transaction is routine and the expertise of the attorney may more than compensate for any concern about a conflict of interest. Here is another example. Richard L. Cook was appointed to a one-year term to Virginia's highest environmental post while retaining his position with the DuPont Corporation. It should also be noted that Virginia and DuPont had been in an adversarial relationship with respect to the environment not long before Cook was appointed. Why was he appointed? Because all parties agreed that he was the best person for the job and all parties trusted him to be impartial.

Suppose each investment firm was totally transparent concerning the various relationships their analysts have. Some investors might stay with the large firm because of the advantages that go with size or because they have a number of relationships with the large firm that they cannot get in a smaller one. These investors would believe either that the conflicts of interest are more apparent than real in their case or that the benefits of the relationship outweigh any costs of being taken advantage of in the conflict of interest situations. However, other investors will feel uncomfortable with the appearance of a conflict of interest and choose to go to a smaller firm where the conflicts do not exist. This is what seems to be happening after the fact.

But is pure disclosure sufficient for dealing with conflicts of interest? In many cases, I think

not for two reasons. First, in many cases for disclosure to work, there has to be a trusting relationship among all the parties. Often that trust is missing. Consider the former chairman of the SEC, Harvey Pitt, who has been accused of being in bed with the industry and of having his own inherent conflict of interest. As an attorney, he represented the major accounting firms including Arthur Andersen. He also has a political philosophy with respect to government regulation that many, including most Democrats, do not share. Pitt could never overcome the distrust because his actions seemed to exacerbate the appearance of a conflict of interest rather than diminish it. Due to the lack of trust, his position became untenable and he was forced to resign.

Second, full disclosure will not help in cases where there is a high risk that a potential conflict of interest will become actual at great cost to the party taken advantage of. Indeed, conflict of interest situations can be put on a continuum from high risk to low risk that the conflict will become actual. As Tom Beauchamp has pointed out, "some influences clearly distort judgment, others have some reasonable probability of doing so, and others have some distant probability of doing so" (Beauchamp, 1992, p. 10).

Let's apply this continuum to the practice of accounting. We need to start with the fact that our current practice involves an inherent conflict of interest. The Supreme Court has ruled that the client of the public accounting firm is the investing public. The job of the public accounting firm is to attest to the accuracy of the financials of publicly held firms. However, it is the publicly held firm that hires the accounting firm, pays them, and can fire them. Thus an accounting firm is tempted to accept management's interpretation of the financials so that they can retain the account. But of course their overriding obligation is to the investing public. Thus we have a conflict of interest.

Interestingly, the recent financial scandals have transformed what seemed to be a low risk of a potential conflict of interest becoming actual to a high risk in the minds of the public. To restore investor confidence, something must be done. One way to avoid a conflict of interest is to make accountants government employees with civil service protection and to pay for them through a tax on the corporations they audit. This suggestion is highly controversial, but the arguments against it rest mainly on a political philosophy that wants to limit government—both the regulation by government and the number of government employees. Since business would lose much of its de facto control over auditing, it has another reason to be opposed. And the accounting firms would be opposed because a significant reason for their existence would disappear. Public accountants would be the employees of the government rather than the employees of accounting firms. So despite its merits, this idea does not seem practical in the current political climate.

Another way to end the conflict is to rotate auditors every few years. It should be pointed out that the *Economist* recommended in its January 19, 2002, edition that there should be compulsory rotation of auditors. The Sarbanes-Oxley Act of 2002 did not go so far as to require that audit firms be rotated, but it did state that the lead partner or the audit partner responsible for reviewing the audit could not perform that function after performing that function for the previous five years. In addition, the act did mandate a study of the mandatory rotation of registered public accounting firms.

A clear-cut way for eliminating either the appearance of a conflict of interest or an actual conflict of interest is by prohibiting the conflict of interest. Normally this is done through legislation. The Sarbanes-Oxley Act of 2002 addressed and attempted to eliminate a number of conflicts of interest.

Title II Sections 201–209 of the law address the issue of audit independence. In an attempt to prevent public accounting firms from providing both audit and nonaudit services that result in a conflict of interest, accounting firms doing the audit are prevented from providing certain other services. Without those prohibitions, there is always the danger that the accounting firm will compromise the audit in order to obtain or retain the nonattestation business. Specifically prohibited by the act are (a) bookkeeping or other services related to the accounting records

or financial statements of the audit client; (b) financial information systems design and implementation; (c) appraisal or valuation services, fairness opinions, or contribution-in-kind reports; (d) actuarial services; (e) internal audit outsourcing services; (f) management functions or human resources; (g) broker or dealer, investment adviser, or investment banking services; (h) legal services and expert services unrelated to the audit (Sarbanes-Oxley Act of 2002).

Other provisions address conflict of interest abuses surrounding analysts who both provide analysis for the investing public and assist their firms with other financial activities such as bringing IPOs to market or providing investment banking services. That provision is designed to address the situation where analysts gave positive recommendations on company stocks so that their firms could gain investment banking business. Under this provision, investment firms are prohibited from retaliating against analysts who make negative calls on the investment firms' clients. Prepublication clearance is prohibited. Also, any conflicts of interest must be disclosed in any securities analysis. I note here that the disclosure of such conflicts of interest in the present climate of distrust will completely vitiate the analysis.

Important problems with the abuse of asymmetrical information are addressed as well. Title IV Sections 401–409 related to enhanced financial disclosures are attempts to reduce information asymmetry between management and the investing public. Executives are prohibited from selling company stock during certain periods called *blackout days* and all stock trades must be publicly reported within two days. Company officers and directors are prohibited from misleading, manipulating, or coercing any independent or certified accountant. The statute of limitations for fraud has been extended, and the penalties for fraud and other white-collar crimes have been increased. The CEO must attest to the accuracy of the financial statements. In general, the law aims to provide the investing public with more and better information and to increase the penalties on those who seek to mislead or interfere with providing more and better information as defined under the law.

There has been considerable discussion as to whether or not the law will be successful in dramatically reducing the abuses we have discussed. Much authority for implementation rests with the Securities and Exchange Commission and with the yet-to-be-established Public Company Oversight Board. Early reports on the actions of the Securities and Exchange Commission are good. For example, on January 15, 2003, the SEC promulgated regulations that deal to some extent with the use of pro forma earnings. However, rules and regulations are subject to the law of unintended consequences, and they provide challenges for lawyers to meet the letter of the law without meeting the spirit of the law.

Rather than focus on the oft-repeated charges against the efficacy of law and regulation as a solution to moral problems, I prefer to address an issue that is less discussed but nonetheless very significant. Our reaction to corporate scandals and accounting fraud has been primarily from the perspective of the United States. We have looked at the issue, taking as a starting point our traditions for dealing with such issues. However, we need to consider regulations in an international context. Given the multinational context of business, we need to work with other countries to establish international standards.

Although the United States has been the recent focus of attention, conflicts of interest and the abuse of information asymmetry are not unique to the United States. They are international issues. A story in the May 6, 2002, *BusinessWeek* is titled "The Corporate Cleanup Goes Global." And in 2003, Ahold in Europe was implicated in a major accounting scandal. The *BusinessWeek* story reports that changes are being demanded in such places as Germany, France, Italy, Scandinavia, Russia, South Korea, Hong Kong, and Japan (Rossant, 2002). A call to raise standards around the world has been issued by Jeffrey E. Garten, dean of the Yale School of Management. He also calls for the "creation of a global accounting framework" (Garten, 2002). He specifically recommends that the New York Stock Exchange and NASDAQ work with exchanges in London, Frankfurt, Hong Kong,

and Tokyo for common standards on corporate governance. More recently he has advocated that accounting needs to be modernized to deal with the new economy and that, in the process of modernization, "the best ideas from around the world must be combined into one high-grade set of international standards" (Garten, 2002).

Combining standards into one high-grade set of international standards means giving up the idea that American standards are best. Americans operate in an environment where government and business relations are adversarial. This adversarial relationship is intensified by the fact that our legal system itself is based on a very adversarial model. Cooperation between prosecution and defense and between government and business is suspect. I cannot imagine a cabinet-level position in corporate responsibility in the United States. Yet one already exists in the United Kingdom. Nongovernmental organizations (NGOs) work with business in Europe as society struggles to obtain sustainable business and to implement triple bottom line accounting that seeks to measure the environmental and social responsibility aspects as well as the financial aspects of firm behavior. Addressing corporate scandals and accounting fraud may need to take place in a less adversarial atmosphere if it is to be successful.

Americans are also very rule-oriented in their response to ethical malfeasance. We pass detailed laws and within the corporation make detailed rules, such as never take a supplier to lunch if the cost of the lunch exceeds $10 per person. I have been told that the GAAP rule for the accounting of derivatives runs on for 20 pages. That approach has not worked well here, and as the international community seeks to develop a set of *international* accounting rules, we can assume the rule-based approach will not work there. We would do well to consider the English model that focuses on the spirit of the law rather than the specific rules. Another way to make this point is to distinguish between principles and rules and to argue that we should be faithful to principles rather than blindly follow rules. It should be noted that in many of the exposés, the players insisted that they had followed the rules and thus done nothing illegal. Such a legalistic response totally misses the moral point.

AN EXCEPTION TO THE ANALYSIS

Although the concepts of conflict of interest and the abuse of asymmetrical information cover many of the cases of corporate abuse, one abuse lies outside these two categories. This abuse has to do with the excessive—some would say obscene—compensation that most executives receive. Some aspects of compensation abuse do fall under our categories. Insider trading that augments the value of one's stock is an abuse of asymmetrical information. Enlarging one's compensation through a conflict of interest as a number of so-called analysts did is also wrong. Failing to report the value of stock options can also be an abuse of asymmetrical information when the investing public is not able to determine the value of those options and thus the drag of those options on future profitability.

However, in this section we are focusing simply on the charge that corporate executives are paid too much—even if the executive earns that compensation without being in a conflict of interest and without abusing asymmetrical information. The issue of excessive executive compensation has a long history. All the major publications—*Fortune, BusinessWeek,* and the *Wall Street Journal*—have been tracking executive compensation for more than a decade. One of the baselines for tracking is the gap between the pay of the average factory worker and the average CEO. This gap has risen steadily and consistently for over a decade, peaking in 2000 at over 400 to 1, up from a ratio of 42 to 1 in 1980 (Borrus, 2003). Over the past two years, executive compensation has declined to the level of 1996 (Lavelle, 2003). As a result of this decline, the ratio of executive compensation to the compensation of the average worker declined to just more than 200 to 1. However, it should also be pointed out that the decline in compensation was due to the spectacular hits in pay and bonuses that some executives took. It should be noted that median pay for the 365 CEOs in the sample set increased by 5.9 percent (Lavelle, 2003). Similar results were found in the *Fortune* data set of 100 CEOs (Useem, 2003). This new data continues a long history. *Newsweek* (July 22, 2003) reports that executive pay is up 233 percent in a decade. Options equal 16 percent of outstanding shares in the top 200 corporations. And even as some executives faced pay decline, a new wrinkle arose. Some companies that were cutting their contributions to employee pensions were taking special care to protect the pensions of their top executives. In some situations, should the company go bankrupt, the employees would lose their pensions but the top executives would not (Schultz & Francis, 2003).

One of the items of most concern is that many companies that had been under indictment or challenge for accounting scandals or other misdeeds have been the most egregious with respect to excessive compensation. Tyco is the pacesetter here. Tyco produced three of the top six earners in the 2002 *Fortune* list. Dennis Kozlowski, now under indictment for tax evasion, was among the six. So was his indicted former CFO Mark Swartz, who made $136 million. Then, to complete the trio, the person hired to clean up the scandal, Ed Breen, was paid $62 million. By the way, the new CFO made $25 million, as did a Tyco division head. Asia Global Crossing forgave $10 million of a $15 million loan plus $2.75 million in severance pay to its CEO but stopped severance pay to laid-off workers. Charles Conway, CEO of Kmart, sought bankruptcy court approval for a $6.5 million bonus and to forgive a $5 million loan. Robert McGinn, fired one month before the start of an SEC investigation, got a settlement that included $3.5 million in cash, $7 million in restricted stock units, and an annual pension of $870,000 (Elstrom, 2002).

There is an understandable reluctance to deal with these issues through the law. Attempts to do so have failed. *Fortune* has put the point admirably:

> In 1989, Congress tries to cap golden parachutes by imposing an excise tax on payments 2.99 times base salary. Result: Companies make 2.99 the new minimum and cover any excise tax for execs.

In 1992, Congress tries to shame CEO's by requiring better disclosure of their pay. Result: CEO's see how much everyone else is making and then try to get more.

In 1993, Congress declares salaries over $1 million to be non tax-exempt. Result: Companies opt for huge stock option grants while upping most salaries to $1 million. (Useem, 2003, p. 59)

The ethical issue here is how much is enough? Some argue that markets set executive compensation and that there is not much that can or should be done about it. I believe that the claim that markets set compensation is mistaken as a matter of fact. Executive pay is not set by the market; it is set by boards of directors who look at industry averages and then put their CEO above average. Besides, many of the members of boards of directors are CEOs or retired CEOs. None will undervalue the contribution of the CEO to corporate success. And sitting CEO board members have no interest in punishing a CEO who may well sit on their boards. Anyone who thinks the market for executive compensation functions like a standard labor market is naïve.

Thus the "How much is enough?" question needs to be settled by normative arguments that use concepts like fairness and virtue. First, I am not aware of *any* ethical theory that would justify current executive compensation. Even libertarianism, the most likely theory, insists that compensation not be achieved by deception or fraud and that there should be a correlation between compensation and achievement. In many cases, one or both of these conditions do not hold. Utilitarianism will not work either, not with the law of diminishing marginal utility applied to compensation itself. (Some have tried to avoid this conclusion by arguing that rich people may have expensive tastes so the marginal value of an extra $100 is not worth less to them than to a poor person. That argument is so patently absurd it does not deserve an answer.)

Probably the best theory to evaluate executive compensation is some version of deontological theory, specifically some version of justice theory. There is a tendency to think that when a company does well it is the CEO that makes it happen. A bad CEO can weaken or destroy a corporation, but a successful corporation depends on the cooperative efforts of all those in the corporation. It is unfair that so much of the gain goes to the CEO. Yet the data clearly show that top executives have gained far more than the average worker. If all workers were to be put in the Rawlsian original position, where no one knew whether he or she would be the average worker or a CEO, I cannot imagine a CEO who took the veil of ignorance seriously approving of the current distribution of income between the top executives of the company and the average worker.

Also, there is an issue of character. Aristotle argued for the virtues of courage and temperance and against the vices of greed and avarice. CEOs and other corporate executives need to be less greedy. As *Fortune* put it, "Have they no shame?" (Useem, 2003). Greedy executives should be ostracized by their peers. Greedy CEOs need not be invited to the country club. The failures of character in so many CEOs have the danger of creating a class struggle—something the United States has avoided thus far. But some of us remember that during the '60s corporate executives were not masters of the universe. In fact, they were held in low esteem. The best students were not in the business colleges, but in the liberal arts, medicine, and engineering. Corporate executives should think about that and exercise the virtue of prudence as well.

FINAL THOUGHTS

There is not much a philosopher business ethicist can contribute to the specifics of what accounting standards the Public Company Accounting Oversight Board should adopt. Nor can he or she specify the rules of corporate governance. A few general comments from philosopher business ethicists might help shape the debate, however. First, although countries have different standards and to a certain extent these standards should be respected, there are some universals that should not be overlooked. What are some of these universals? Transparency is a necessary condition for financial success at the firm level. A company can despoil the environment or treat its employees badly and its stock price may not be hurt that badly. But if a company is found to mislead investors, the penalty of that unethical behavior goes right to the bottom line. Indeed, a number of companies that have deceived their shareholders are either bankrupt or close to bankruptcy. Another universal goes by different names, but the names all express the same idea. Accountants refer to independence. Auditors would speak of arm's-length transactions. Agency theorists would address the obligations to principals. And business ethicists would urge the avoidance of conflict of interest. There is some cultural variation in what these terms mean, but in every culture there is a distinction between a corrupt transaction that benefits oneself and one's cronies and an impartial business transaction.

There are also norms of fairness. Again, the details may vary from culture to culture, but all cultures have a distinction between what is fair and what is not fair. In a well-functioning capitalist economy, there are limits on the opportunism associated with information asymmetry. It should come as no surprise that so many of the corporate scandals involve either conflict of interest or abuse of information asymmetry. Capital markets everywhere depend on trust. To have the requisite trust, there must be transparency, independence, impartiality, and norms of fairness.

A second contribution from business ethicists is that there is no substitute for sitting down and actually negotiating the standards. It is one thing to assert the existence of universal norms. It is quite another for the representatives of countries involved to sit down and identify the same list of universals. And it is still another feat to then implement those universals in the context of international business practice.

Lastly, I would like to indicate how important it is that these negotiations include thoughtful ethical nonexperts in these matters. Political scientists have long noted the capture theory of regulation where the regulators are representatives of the industries that are regulated. To really protect the public and promote transparency, we need to make sure that the standards are not simply the standards of accountants and investment bankers. Maybe there is a role for business ethicists after all.

NOTES

1. After August 2002, it is hard to disaggregate the impact of the scandals from the impact of the international situation on stock prices.

2. In cases where the person who is disadvantaged cannot leave the relationship, full disclosure is of no help in resolving the moral dilemma. Also, it is acknowledged that in many cases full disclosure is not sufficient for eliminating the moral dilemma.

REFERENCES

American Heritage college dictionary. (1993). Boston: Houghton-Mifflin.

Beauchamp, T. L. (1992). Ethical issues in funding and monitoring university research. *Business and Professional Ethics Journal, 11*(1), 5–16.

Berman, D. (2002, August 12). Before telecom industry sank, insiders sold billions in stock. *The Wall Street Journal*, pp. A1, A7.

Borrus, A. (2003, February 24). A battle royal against regal paychecks. *BusinessWeek.*

Byrnes, N., & Henry, D. (2001, November 26). Confused about earnings? *BusinessWeek*, 76.

Davis, M. (1982). Conflict of interest. *Business & Professional Ethics Journal, 1*(Summer), 17–28.

Davis, M. (1991). University research and the wages of commerce. *Journal of College and University Law, 18*(1), 29–39.

Elstrom, P. (2002, May 13). Rainmaker in a firestorm. *BusinessWeek*, 44.

Executive pay. (2003, April 21). *BusinessWeek*, 86–90.

Fox, J. (2001, June 25). The amazing stock option sleight of hand. *Fortune*, 86–92.

Frank, F. (1988). *Passions within reason.* New York: W.W. Norton.

Garten, J. E. (2002, May 13). Corporate standards: Raise the bar around the world. *BusinessWeek*, 30.

Grover, R., & Palmeri, C. (2002, March 25). QWEST: The issues go beyond accounting. *BusinessWeek*, 68, 70.

Henry, D. (2001, May 14). The numbers game. *BusinessWeek*, 100–110.

Henry, D. (2002, July 15). An overdose of options. *BusinessWeek*, 112–114.

Korsgaard, C. (1996). *Creating the kingdom of ends*. New York: Cambridge University Press.

Lavelle, L. (2003, April 21). Executive pay. *BusinessWeek*, 86–90.

Liesman, S., & Weil, J. (2001, July 13). Disappearing act: Spate of write-offs calls into question lofty 1990's profits. *The Wall Street Journal*, pp. A1, A4.

Morgenson, G. (2001, December 23). Chills in the balance-sheet shadows. *The New York Times*, section 3, pp. 1, 12.

Nussbaum, B. (2002, January 28). Can you trust ANYBODY anymore? *BusinessWeek*, 30.

The real scandal. (2002, January 19). *The Economist*, 9.

Rosenbush, S. (2002, August 5). Inside the telecom game. *BusinessWeek*, 34–40.

Rossant, J. (2002, May 6). The corporate cleanup goes global. *BusinessWeek*, 80.

Rynecki, D. (2001, February). The price of being right. *Fortune*, 126–141.

Sarbanes-Oxley Act of 2002. (2002). Public Law No. 107–204, 116 Stat. 745.

Schultz , E. E., & Francis, T. (2003, April 24). Executives get pension security while plans for workers falter. *The Wall Street Journal*, pp. A1, A10.

Stevenson, R. W. (2002, February 17). Why a scandal became a spectacle. *The New York Times*, section 4, p. 1.

Useem, J. (2003, April 28). Have they no shame? *Fortune*, 57–64.

Vickers, M. (2002, April 22). Can this man make Wall Street behave? *BusinessWeek*, 38.

Vickers, M., & McNamee, M. (2002, February 25). The betrayed investor. *BusinessWeek*, 105–115.

Will, G. (2002, January 28). Events, dear boys, events. *Newsweek*, 64.

7

AN ETHICAL FRAMEWORK
FOR AUDITOR INDEPENDENCE

THOMAS W. DUNFEE

ALAN S. GLAZER

HENRY R. JAENICKE

SUSAN MCGRATH

ARTHUR SIEGEL

"There was a lack of auditor independence."—Juror David Schwab, explaining the vote to convict Arthur Andersen (Weil, Barrionuevo, & Bryan-Low, 2002).

The early twenty-first century financial crisis, driven in large part by lack of confidence in capital markets and concerns about massive hidden frauds, raised the issue of the credibility of the information contained in companies' financial statements. Many of the proposed solutions were designed to increase the objectivity and independence of those involved in the financial reporting process. For example, individuals within a company who are responsible for the preparation of the company's financial statements should be free from undue pressure from senior management. Research analysts should be independent of their firms' investment banking arms and should not be compensated for business brought into the firm. Independent members of a company's board of directors should play key roles and have exclusive authority over executive compensation and other critical governance areas.

In this chapter, we take a look at one important dimension of independence: the independence of auditors from their audit clients. Long a familiar principle, auditor independence has taken on renewed importance in light of the public controversies and negative publicity currently surrounding the accounting profession. The highly publicized criminal conviction of Arthur Andersen involved jurors speaking of Andersen's lack of independence from Enron, one of its largest audit clients. The U.S. Securities and Exchange Commission (SEC) has recently charged firms with and is investigating other instances of alleged independence violations. The number and magnitude of recent corporate financial reporting misstatements have caused the U.S. Congress and the public to question the independence of auditors. In the wake of these accounting failures, the Sarbanes-Oxley Act (Sarbanes-Oxley), adopted by the U.S. Congress in 2002, contains several provisions designed to strengthen the independence of auditors.

Auditor independence is critically important for the effective operation of financial markets. Auditor independence emphasizes objectivity and impartiality on the part of those conducting audits. Two dimensions of auditor independence are critical to making the concept operational. *Independence of mind* refers to the absence of the influence of biases or personal interests of an auditor that might result in a failure to make objective judgments. Although this attribute is critical, it is also hard for outsiders to assess accurately. For that reason, the second dimension, *independence in appearance*, is an important complement. Regardless of the auditor's state of mind, if a relationship with an audit client would cause a well-informed investor or creditor rationally to doubt the auditor's objectivity, there is a failure of independence in appearance.

Questions about auditor independence arise in many situations—for example, when an auditing firm generates a large percentage of its revenue from a single audit client or derives significant consulting fees from an audit client,

when an auditor's family member is in a sensitive senior position at an audit client, or when an auditing firm or an auditor has a direct financial interest in an audit client. Maintaining the independence of auditors is important because it helps ensure that audits improve the reliability of financial statements prepared by companies' managements and enhances the credibility of the financial reporting process. Those outcomes, in turn, promote investor confidence and optimal capital allocation.

Although an important area in accounting, there has not been a great deal written about auditor independence in the general business ethics literature. This is surprising because the issue is a classic application of conflict of interest analysis. In this chapter we (a) provide a brief overview of conflict of interest as an ethical concept and note its foundations in ethical theory and its consistency with the findings of cognitive psychology, (b) consider the role of auditor independence in the economy, (c) describe and discuss a proposed conceptual framework for auditor independence based on identification of threats and safeguards leading to an assessment of independence risk, and then (d) show how the framework can be used in resolving some of the major independence issues being debated today.

AUDITOR INDEPENDENCE AND CONFLICT OF INTEREST ANALYSIS

Positioning auditor independence in applied ethics is straightforward. Auditor independence invokes issues of conflict of interest. A conflict of interest arises when a person owes a duty to another, the proper performance of which is actually or potentially influenced by a personal interest or bias, or by an obligation to another party. Duties generally arise from contractual obligations, public sector requirements, employment and other relationships, and, very commonly, from professional roles. The general responsibilities of auditors to act objectively and to perform audits with competency and due care arise from their professional roles. Some of an auditor's specific obligations are imposed by law or contract; others stem from the actions of professional bodies and general social norms.

Conflicts of interest may be categorized on the basis of how likely they are to occur (Davis, 1982; Gaa, 1994). According to Gaa, an *actual conflict* is virtually certain to occur, a *latent conflict* involves a reasonable probability that the conflict will happen, and a *potential conflict* involves some chance that the conflict will be realized. For example, an auditor working for both a private client and a state tax authority on the same tax return is involved in an actual conflict of interest. A latent conflict arises where a member of an audit client's senior management is in the auditor's immediate family or is the auditor's close friend. A potential conflict arises when an auditing firm generates consulting fees from an audit client and could conceivably either be auditing records pertaining to the consulting assignment or be concerned about the loss of business that might occur if the auditing firm has to oppose management concerning a financial reporting issue.

Conflict of interest analysis is founded on the traditional ethical theories used in business ethics. Because the core of the conflict of interest concept is based on a breach of duty, it is a straightforward violation of deontological, or duty-based, theories. The source of the duty is generally clear, and the critical issue is whether that duty has been breached. Auditors' duties to maintain independence from their clients derive from SEC regulations, from the actions of professional associations and other oversight bodies, and from general professional norms.

Similarly, consequential and utilitarian theories are violated whenever auditors are so influenced by biases, self-interests, or mutually exclusive obligations that they fail to perform up to professional standards. Such audit failures can result in undetected financial statement misrepresentations and inefficient investor or creditor decisions and, when aggregated across multiple auditors, may damage the credibility of capital markets with a resultant misallocation of capital.

The ultimate result is that the goal of maximizing outcomes or utilities is not met.

Finally, contractarians also would condemn violations of auditor independence that result in a loss of auditor objectivity. Gaa (1994) noted that there appear to be extant social contracts (Dunfee, 1991) establishing general expectations for the performance and behaviors of auditors. Those expectations derive both from the profession itself and from society more generally. They set broad parameters based on the role of auditors in society, which is to perform audits of financial statements to help ensure that such statements are reliable and credible for the effective functioning of capital markets. The regulatory authority of the states and the SEC buttresses those expectations.

When potential and latent conflicts of interest exist, there are standard ways in which the anticipated conflict can be mitigated. One common method is full disclosure or transparency. A ready example is the requirement that research analysts disclose whether their firms have investment banking relationships with the firms whose stocks they tout. So long as there is full and accurate disclosure, the party whose interests might be compromised has the option to do business with another who is not similarly subject to an apparent conflict. An even stronger method for resolving an anticipated conflict is to obtain the express consent of the party at risk. Usually, the conflicted party fully discloses and then, before proceeding with the professional engagement, obtains formal approval from the party at risk. The most effective mitigation of an anticipated conflict occurs when the conflicted party eliminates the circumstances or relationships creating the conflict or completely severs the professional relationship. Another alternative is to install controls, such as peer reviews, to help ensure that the conflict of interest does not influence the services performed.

Results from research in cognitive psychology provide evidence of the difficulties auditors face in maintaining objectivity. In the last several decades, researchers have documented a wide variety of biases that distort human judgment.

They include overconfidence bias, confirmation bias, self-serving bias, optimism bias, recency and vividness bias, hindsight bias, and in-group bias.[1] The findings concerning a number of these biases are quite robust. In addition, the line of research has been extended in the accounting literature to studies of auditors, with results supporting the presence of some of these biases in auditors acting in various professional capacities.

Those results are significant in two ways. First, they show that the quality of auditors' judgments may be affected by commonly known cognitive biases. Second, and most important, auditors may be affected by those biases without realizing their influence. This means that auditors who think of themselves as objective professionals who would never allow their technical judgment to be affected by outside influences may, nonetheless, be subject to influences that they do not and cannot fully appreciate. For example, people generally are subject to an overconfidence bias, whereby they overestimate their knowledge and personal attributes. This has been established by studies asking people to estimate the percentage of correct answers they have given on an exam or their own percentile on positive attributes. For example, in a survey of 1 million high school students, 70 percent thought they were above average in leadership ability; only 2 percent thought they were below average (Prentice, 2000a, p. 1613, note 68).

Auditors have been found to have this overconfidence bias regarding task knowledge and skills. When asked to estimate their performance on questions from CPA exams and training manuals, practicing CPAs consistently overestimated their own performance (Kennedy & Peecher, 1997). Auditors also may be overconfident, and hence biased, when making judgments during an audit. For example, they may think that they do not need to call on their firms' technical consultants because they overestimate their own knowledge of accounting issues.

Practicing auditors also have been shown to be subject to a confirmation bias, which involves an individual preferentially seeking evidence to confirm a hypothesis (Bamber, Ramsey, & Tubbs, 1997; Heiman-Hoffman, Moser, & Joseph, 1995). For example, an auditor who tends to believe that a financial statement component is already accurate will be less likely to conclude that the component is misstated than an auditor who does not begin with that assumption. This bias has been found to affect the decisions of internal auditors reviewing control systems that they have previously helped to install (Plumlee, 1985). A confirmation bias may also apply when an auditing firm that has provided consulting work to an audit client subsequently reviews that work as part of its audit.

One of the most important biases in the context of auditor independence is the self-serving bias. This involves a tendency to interpret information in a manner consistent with one's economic or psychological self-interest. Ponemon (1995) found this bias applicable to accountants in a lab study of litigation support judgments. Other laboratory research found that CPAs tended to favor positions in takeover negotiations that their audit clients preferred (Haynes & Jenkins, 1998). Prentice (2000a, p. 1637) refers to the "substantial body of behavioral literature demonstrating the pervasive and corrosive impact of the self-serving bias upon auditors" and, after considering the arguments and findings to the contrary, ultimately concludes that "the greater weight of evidence clearly indicates that auditors act in a self-serving manner" (p. 1648). These findings, so consistent with our basic knowledge of human nature, have implications for what one may reasonably expect others to believe about auditors and therefore may predict likely concerns of investors and creditors about the credibility of financial reports.[2]

THE CRITICAL ROLE OF AUDITOR INDEPENDENCE IN THE ECONOMY

The Staff Report of the Independence Standards Board (ISB), *A Conceptual Framework for Auditor Independence* (Jaenicke, Glazer, Siegel, McGrath, Towers, & Dunfee, 2001), concluded that the goal of auditor independence is to enhance the reliability and credibility of the financial reporting process. Both qualities are critically important. The reliability of financial statements, in the sense of full consistency with accounting rules and standards, is necessary but not sufficient to support effective capital markets. Even though a company's financial statements may in fact provide full and fair disclosure of its financial position, results of operations, and cash flows, investors may not use them if they are not confident of their reliability. After all of the recent publicity questioning the independence of research analysts, corporate board members, and other financial professionals, it seems reasonable to assume that investors' confidence may indeed depend, at least in part, on their perception of the independence of auditors certifying a company's financial statements.

The independence of auditors also is an important component of effective corporate governance. The independence of board members is now widely seen as a critical governance element because board members who are independent are less likely to have conflicts of interest with senior management and, therefore, are a better line of defense against self-serving senior managers. Independent board members, especially those serving on audit committees, have direct interaction with the company's auditors and rely on them to help meet the board's oversight responsibilities. That reliance further highlights the need to ensure that auditors themselves are independent.

Auditor Independence Conceptual Framework

In this section we describe an Auditor Independence Conceptual Framework (AICF) derived from the Independence Standards Board's conceptual framework project.[3] There are many potential uses for such a framework. First and foremost, individual auditors and senior managements of auditing firms can use it to determine whether any of their client relationships pose problematic risks to independence.

Audit committees should find this framework particularly helpful as more responsibility is being placed on them as a result of the recent financial scandals. Professional societies and standard-setting bodies should find its guidance helpful for establishing new rules. A value not to be underestimated is the role such a conceptual foundation can play in educating the general investing public and other interested stakeholders concerning the importance, nature, and meaning of effective independence. A final aspect is its value in demonstrating connections to related professionals, such as those concerned generally with business ethics. The AICF is fully consistent with the ethical principles and lessons from cognitive psychology described previously.

Two major alternative approaches exist for developing a framework for auditor independence. One is to base a framework on specific rules, such as a requirement that auditors cannot audit clients in which an auditor holds an investment or in which an auditor's close relative is a key employee. The independence requirements of the SEC (2000) employ a rule-based approach. To the extent that an overall philosophy is associated with such a framework, it would have to be induced from the scope and nature of the specific rules.

The rules-based approach has the advantage of specificity. Nothing is left abstract or generalized; all elements are grounded in specific elements of the rules. Those who wish to use the framework can actively apply specific rules. That type of rule-based framework, of course, does have limitations. In particular, it can lead to an "if it is not prohibited it must be allowed" philosophy, a very dangerous situation because new situations cannot always be anticipated by the existing rules. Also, not every situation seemingly permitted by the rules will leave all auditors with the ability to be objective. For example, current SEC rules do not prohibit auditors from auditing companies in which an in-law is chief financial officer. Many auditors, however, would have trouble being objective in that situation.

The alternative approach is to first develop a conceptual framework based on general principles and a cogent philosophy, leaving until later the process of fleshing out how those principles and philosophy apply to specific situations. This approach provides flexibility, avoids having to try to anticipate a complete set of problems or speculate about special circumstances, and assists in ensuring that rules have a consistent and coherent underlying philosophy. Users of this type of framework—including standard-setters, auditing firms, audit committees, and regulators—would be able to adapt it more easily to new and unique circumstances. Many potential solutions to independence issues exist, and it is often very difficult to specify, in advance of a new set of circumstances, which is the best solution. Allowing discretion in deciding how to resolve independence issues to those charged with protecting auditor independence seems not only desirable, but also essential.

We now describe the basic elements of the AICF, which adopts the second approach. Its foundation rests on a concept called independence risk—the likelihood that a particular relationship with an audit client involves factors or influences capable of compromising an auditor's judgment to a degree such that necessary objectivity is lost. Because we also are concerned with independence in appearance, factors and influences that would cause the loss of an auditor's credibility also are included in independence risk. The overall approach is as follows. First, threats to auditor independence must be identified and assessed. Then, existing and potential safeguards must be identified and evaluated with consideration of costs and benefits. Finally, an assessment of the impact on independence risk is made. The principles of threats, safeguards, and risk ground the analysis.

A sensible, pragmatic approach to assessing independence risk must begin with an analysis of factors having the potential to compromise auditors' objective judgments. Only after specific factors, which the AICF calls threats to independence, are identified can regulators, auditors, professional bodies, audit committee members, and other independence decision makers consider the controls, called *safeguards* in the AICF, that mitigate those factors.

ANALYZING THREATS TO INDEPENDENCE

Many types of threats to independence are well recognized, and the AICF—like auditors' codes of ethics in Canada (Canadian Institute of Chartered Accountants, 2002) and also internationally (International Federation of Accountants, 2001)—discusses a nonexhaustive list of those threats. Following Gaa (1994), we believe that norms developed within the accounting profession over time under the umbrella of public policy and regulation help to establish the boundaries of problematic versus acceptable threats. For example, auditors' objectivity can be impaired simply because auditors are paid by their clients. Auditors may feel a pull to accede to the wishes of a client if they believe that disagreeing with the client would endanger the client relationship. Nevertheless, the long tradition of fee-for-service in the United States and in many other countries reflects the conclusion that the mere existence of a fee-for-service relationship does not result in *unacceptable* independence risk. Presumably the benefits of having a market in privately provided auditing services outweigh the costs associated with the increased independence risk.

In some cases, however, professional and auditing firm norms may not be sufficient to establish boundaries between acceptable and unacceptable independence risk. For example, one current issue concerns threats to independence that exist when fees from a single audit client are so large that an auditing firm, a segment of the firm, or individual auditors within the firm become financially dependent on that client. A conceptual framework like the AICF provides independence decision makers with a formal way of addressing this and other difficult issues.

The AICF describes five typical types of threats that should be considered in assessing independence risk. A major lesson from the cognitive psychology literature is that a *self-interest* threat is always a concern. Auditors may favor, perhaps without even realizing it, their own financial, emotional, or other personal interests in ways that cloud their professional judgment and impair their objectivity. This threat has been widely cited in debates about the amounts and types of consulting services provided by auditing firms to their audit clients. If, as was the case with Andersen's audits of Enron, an auditing firm receives significant fees from providing consulting advice to an audit client, individuals conducting the audit or others in the firm may consider the possibility of lost consulting income in deciding whether to challenge management over issues related to the audit. A self-interest threat also exists if the audit fees themselves are large, regardless of the size of the consulting fees derived from the client.

Another type of threat soundly grounded in the cognitive psychology literature is that of *self-review*. One well-known example of the difficulties people have when they review their own work is the case of authors proofreading their own writing. Editors catch obvious errors that authors, despite multiple readings of their own manuscripts, have failed to correct. This type of confirmation bias may arise in various auditing contexts when an auditing firm reviews its own work. To counter the possible effects of self-review threats, SEC rules prohibit individuals in auditing firms from maintaining the accounting records of audit clients because, when those individuals or others in the firm review those records as part of the client's audit, there would be a natural tendency to assume that the record keeping had been done correctly.

Problems created by a third type of threat, *advocacy*, also are well known in other fields. For example, under the view that one individual cannot adequately serve two masters, lawyers are prohibited from representing parties who are litigating with each other or whose interests are in conflict. This threat is evident in the studies by Haynes and Jenkins (1998) cited previously, which found that auditors' findings were biased toward positions in takeover negotiations favored by their clients. An auditing firm that sells an audit client's products or underwrites an audit client's securities faces an advocacy threat because the firm is representing and promoting the audit client in dealings with other parties. As a result, individuals in the firm may not make objective decisions in their capacity as the client's auditors.

A *familiarity* or *trust* threat exists when auditors are influenced by close relationships with individuals who are employed by or closely associated with their audit clients. For example, people in Enron's finance and accounting departments had previously worked at Andersen, and some Enron managers had close ties with Andersen personnel from their college days. Such relationships, and practices that encourage them (such as joint vacations or extensive entertaining), may result in auditing firm personnel identifying with an audit client to such an extent that they come to think of the client as "we" rather than as the subject of an objective review. This invokes the in-group favoritism hypothesis that, when making judgment calls, people tend to favor members of their own group without fully realizing what is occurring (Messick & Bazerman, 1996). The required practice of rotating lead partners off specific audit engagements after a specified period of time is an implicit recognition of the potential effects of the familiarity threat.[4]

A final example of a threat to independence is *intimidation*. Although usually not rising to the level of physical threats, intimidation from a client or someone in the auditing firm may take the form of a complaint to an auditor's superior or a request that an auditor be removed from the audit. That action, or the fear of that action, may affect the objectivity of the auditors involved. For example, Enron's management complained about one of Andersen's technical specialists who had objected to some of Enron's accounting methods. Andersen, apparently concerned about maintaining a good relationship with one of its largest audit clients, removed the specialist from the audit. Although we can only speculate about how that action was perceived by other Andersen auditors, intimidation threats can take many forms, including explicit or implicit threats of poor performance reviews, terminations, reductions in compensation, or transfers to undesirable locations or assignments.

These examples are not intended to illustrate all of the circumstances that could potentially affect auditors' judgments. Instead, they should help audit committees, auditing firms' senior management, professional bodies, and others concerned about auditor independence identify threats to independence. To act consistently with the philosophy underlying the AICF, independence decision makers must take an aggressive position in judging what audit client relationships might constitute a threat and the significance of those threats. In today's climate, it is no longer sufficient to assume that the "good and honest professionals" in auditing firms can overcome most threats to their objectivity. Restoring confidence to a skeptical investing public requires a much more proactive stance, one that assumes that even subtle or unconscious biases can threaten auditor independence and lead to a loss of both the auditing firm's and the audit client's credibility.

The AICF encourages independence decision makers to be as specific as possible in identifying threats arising from a particular relationship. For example, Sarbanes-Oxley requires audit committees to approve the extent and types of nonaudit work being done by the company's auditing firm. To be truly proactive in guarding against independent risk, audit committees also need to understand how the auditing firm's policies, procedures, and values ensure an appropriate emphasis on independence. Such an understanding comes from knowledge about factors such as how partners in the auditing firm are compensated, what controls exist in the firm when it provides nonaudit services to audit clients, how important the client's fees are to the engagement partner and the practice unit of the firm, and how much socializing goes on between auditing firm and company personnel.

An auditing firm's obligations to help identify threats arising from relationships with audit clients are discussed in ISB Standard No. 1, *Independence Discussions with Audit Committees* (1999). That rule requires auditing firms to report to clients' audit committees, in writing, "all relationships between the auditor and its related entities and the company and its related entities that in the auditor's professional judgment may reasonably be thought to bear on independence." We recommend that auditing firms act proactively and aggressively in a manner similar to that advocated for client audit committees. Probing discussions about auditor independence among members of board audit committees and auditing firms' senior managements greatly increase the likelihood that all significant potential threats will be identified.

Although the AICF requires an aggressive stance in reducing independence risk, it recognizes that costs and other factors also are relevant. Certainly, the likelihood that a specific relationship will in fact increase independence risk is an important consideration. Details are important. For example, an auditing firm that provides a valuation for the sale of an audit client's immaterial asset that will not be the subject of auditing procedures is unlikely to be influenced in any significant way by a self-interest threat, whereas it might be if the asset is material and likely to be subject to auditing procedures. Moreover, despite the threats that do exist, audit clients may realize efficiencies when they use their auditing firms for certain nonaudit services. Those services should be prohibited only if the increased independence risk is too great to be tolerated. That judgment might be made through regulation on a broad basis as a matter of public policy. It also could be made by an audit committee based on a particular set of facts and circumstances.

ANALYZING THE EFFECTIVENESS OF SAFEGUARDS

The next elements of the AICF are safeguards that, taken together, mitigate threats to independence. Safeguards include laws and regulations promulgated by regulators, standard setters, courts, and professional associations; policies and procedures adopted by auditing firms and audit clients; and training and education programs for auditors and client officials. Examples of the wide variety of safeguards currently in place in the United States include the following:

- A professional code of ethics for CPAs that stresses values such as independence, objectivity, integrity, and a commitment to the public interest
- Rules restricting or prohibiting certain activities and relationships promulgated by the professions, by the SEC, and in Sarbanes-Oxley
- Auditing firms' consultation requirements to ensure that auditing firms' technical specialists—those with a deep understanding of and expertise in the sometimes overwhelming body of accounting and auditing concepts and rules—are involved in particularly difficult issues
- Concurring review requirements to ensure that an additional audit partner is involved in and concurs with an engagement team's conclusions
- Audit partner rotation requirements to ensure that partners do not build an entire career around their relationships with one client
- SEC rules requiring publicly held companies to report certain circumstances surrounding and the reasons behind a change in auditors, thereby discouraging opinion shopping and intimidation of auditing firms
- Periodic internal and peer reviews of completed audits

Although it is beyond the scope of this chapter to identify and discuss all possible types of safeguards, we can describe a few common ones and show how they are employed in response to typical threats.

An effective ethics program developed by auditing firms or professional bodies, especially if reinforced by regular training and encouragement, can help minimize independence risk by helping individual auditors anticipate nonobvious sources of bias in their own personal situations. As noted in the previous section, many threats to independence are based on the possibility that an individual will be affected by a cognitive bias. To be effective against those types of threats, ethics programs should be targeted specifically at identifying biases at the individual rather than at the firm level. Although we believe that profession- and firm-based ethics programs hold great potential for dealing with individuals' cognitive biases, we agree with Prentice (2000a, pp. 1654–1655) that existing programs are insufficient to counteract the more powerful sources of bias. In order to be truly effective as safeguards, auditor independence ethics programs should focus on the subliminal aspects of bias and have the full support of auditing firms and leaders of the profession. Significant financial and creative resources need to be employed to develop effective ethics programs directed at sensitizing individual auditors at all levels.

Auditing firms have developed a wide variety of other policies and programs that serve as safeguards. The ethics literature, however, emphasizes that the culture of an organization has a large impact on the ethical behavior of the organization's managers (Vidaver-Cohen, 1993, 1998). The words and deeds of an auditing firm's management are critical to creating a firm culture in which ethical behavior is a top priority. Only through hands-on leadership that emphasizes appropriate values and ethical principles can a firm's senior management establish an appropriate "tone at the top" that supports independence.

Auditing firms also can get the message across that ethical behavior is important by acknowledging and rewarding, as a regular part of performance reviews, individuals who act in ways consistent with the firm's ethical principles. Individuals who violate those principles should be disciplined; if exceptions are made for "rainmakers," any positive messages are lost.

It is understandable that an auditing firm rewards people for bringing in new clients, selling additional services, and building client relationships. Nevertheless, these activities should not be the only—or even the most important—skills that the firm encourages its people to develop. If taken too far, firm personnel may focus on pleasing their clients rather than on maintaining their independence.

Safeguards implemented by clients' audit committees also help ensure auditor independence. For example, audit committees should review carefully the nature and likely impact on independence of all nonaudit services performed by the company's auditing firm. By themselves, however, client safeguards may not be sufficient to ensure auditor independence, especially if the client is very large or if the auditing firm or individual auditors are dependent on the client. Safeguards within auditing firms often are needed to supplement clients' safeguards. For example, in the case of a very large client, an auditing firm might include a special review by disinterested firm partners to ensure that the difficult decisions made by the partner and concurring reviewer assigned to the client represent the conclusions of the firm and its best technical specialists, not merely those of two individuals in the firm.

Other examples of client safeguards are clients' own ethics codes and programs. In some ways, these are mirror images of auditing firms' codes and programs. For example, a client's senior management and board can help ensure that the company's key financial personnel understand the company's commitment to full and fair financial reporting. McGrath, Siegel, Dunfee, Glazer, and Jaenicke (2001) proposed a series of questions that audit committees can ask auditing firms to assess how seriously a firm takes independence risk.

Other safeguards are imposed by regulators and standard setters—for example, requiring disclosures of potential conflicts. As noted previously, Independence Standards Board Standard No. 1 requires auditing firms to provide a written report to clients' audit committees identifying all circumstances that may reasonably be thought to bear on their independence.

Complete prohibition of certain practices or relationships is another type of potential safeguard. Seemingly clear-cut and decisive, prohibitions may be deceptively complex. For example, many people have called for a prohibition against auditing firms providing any consulting services to their audit clients. On first impression, this safeguard seems to remove a major potential threat to independence. The prohibition, however, is only operational with a reasonable and clear definition of

consulting. In fact, auditing firms have provided a wide variety of services for clients, such as tax planning and due diligence reviews for acquisitions. Despite the potential negative effects of a familiarity bias, an auditing firm may have unique expertise in performing those services because of the information and experience gained while conducting the client's audit. It may be less effective and more expensive, and represent only a minimal reduction in independence risk, for audit clients to obtain certain consulting services from other sources. In addition, an auditing firm may learn information from a consulting assignment that allows it to conduct more effective audits in the future. We believe that targeted, well-defined safeguards are likely to be more effective in lowering independence risk and achieving the worthy goals of auditor independence than sweeping, generalized prohibitions.

Another type of safeguard is the legal system in the United States, which provides strong incentives for auditing firms to reduce independence risk in order to reduce litigation costs. The possibility of litigation and the resulting loss of reputation are often held out as sources of assurance that auditors will be objective in performing their professional duties. Neither the threat of loss of reputation nor the threat of litigation, however, is a fine-grained enforcer. Andersen's reputation appears to have swung dramatically from good to bad in a relatively short time. Its problems also may have tarnished the reputations of other auditing firms, even though presumably they should have been distinguishable from Andersen based on their own experience and policies. Prentice (2000a, p. 1656) concludes that "(r)eputation is often not a sufficient motivation for auditors to preserve their own objectivity and independence." Nor have civil damages in the tens and hundreds of millions of dollars prevented audit failures.

ASSESSING INDEPENDENCE RISK

After identifying specific threats posed by a particular relationship and evaluating the effectiveness of existing safeguards, the AICF directs independence decision makers to assess independence risk. Although a precise measurement of independence risk is not feasible, the basic idea is to determine whether, for a specific relationship, there is a reasonable possibility that the auditor's objectivity and professional judgment—or the perception thereof—will be negatively affected in a significant way. In today's environment, it seems appropriate for independence decision makers to apply a high standard to guard against the likelihood that the reliability and credibility of the client's financial statements will be compromised.

If existing safeguards appear to be insufficient, the decision maker should investigate whether additional safeguards, perhaps specific to the particular relationship, could further mitigate the threats to independence. The approach suggested in the AICF can help with that assessment because, after the specific threats are properly understood, it becomes easier to develop targeted safeguards to mitigate them. For example, if a specific familiarity threat is identified, options include removing the affected auditor from the client's audit, having technical specialists in the auditing firm monitor the audit closely, disclosing the circumstances to the audit client, and obtaining the consent of independent members of the client's audit committee. Of course, if targeted safeguards are not effective in sufficiently mitigating the threats that have been identified, the auditing firm should not accept the company as an audit client or, if the company is already an audit client, the firm should resign from the engagement.

In choosing among available safeguards, independence decision makers should evaluate each in light of its cost versus its effectiveness in mitigating threats to independence. In considering what safeguards to mandate, government regulatory bodies and legislatures should consider the likely costs and benefits of the required interventions. Requiring costly safeguards is not in the best interests of investors if cheaper safeguards are sufficiently effective in mitigating threats to independence. On the other hand, the cost of a potential safeguard should not be used

as an excuse to tolerate an unacceptably high level of independence risk. The costs associated with the failures of Enron, WorldCom, and other large companies should make clear that the benefits from reducing the chances of massive audit failures can be enormous.

Consistent with the emphasis on the credibility of financial reports, independence decision makers need to consider the views and interests of investors, creditors, and other stakeholders in sound financial reporting. Groups such as the Association for Investment Management and Research (AIMR), pension fund managers, mutual fund managers, and others can offer valuable insights into how to identify threats and implement effective safeguards.

IMPLICATIONS FOR THE CURRENT ENVIRONMENT

The recent financial scandals have renewed the focus on corporate governance reforms, including management compensation and incentive systems, and on strengthening auditor independence. The New York Stock Exchange has adopted additional listing requirements, and the SEC has issued new rules requiring CEOs and CFOs of large, publicly traded companies to certify the accuracy of their companies' financial statements. In addition to extending that SEC requirement to all SEC registrants, the Sarbanes-Oxley Act seeks to improve the accuracy of corporate disclosures; imposes additional restrictions and requirements on companies, auditors, and research analysts; and strengthens oversight, enforcement, and sanctions applicable to those groups.

Several provisions of Sarbanes-Oxley attempt to help ensure that auditors are independent of their audit clients (U.S. Congress, 2002, Title II and Sec. 303). They include the following:

- The formation of the Public Company Accounting Oversight Board, which has been given authority to (a) establish new or adopt existing auditing, quality control, ethics, independence, and other standards for auditors and (b) inspect accounting firms and impose sanctions for rule violations

- Prohibitions on providing specific nonaudit services to audit clients, such as financial information systems design and implementation, and certain internal audit outsourcing
- A requirement that audit committees appoint the auditors, make clear that they report to the committee, and preapprove all services, including permitted nonaudit services
- Client rotation of audit and reviewing partners after five years
- Enhanced reporting by auditors to audit committees of information about clients' accounting policies
- Increased SEC funding
- Directives to the General Accounting Office (GAO) to study mandatory auditing firm rotation and the effects of the recent consolidation of auditing firms
- Making it unlawful for companies to fraudulently influence, coerce, manipulate, or mislead auditors for the purpose of rendering companies' financial statements misleading

One issue that is not addressed either by Sarbanes-Oxley or the SEC's current rules is the fundamental conflict of interest that exists when audit clients pay the auditor's fees. (Adding to this threat, historically, clients' CFOs or their designees—often people with direct and frequent contact with the auditors because of their financial statement responsibilities—negotiated audit fees and recommended their approval to the audit committee.) As described previously, that fundamental conflict of interest poses threats to independence, threats that have become more significant as the size of some annual audit fees has grown. For example, in 2001 Citigroup, General Electric, and Merrill Lynch each reported paying audit fees in excess of $20 million. Although those fees may not be material in a quantitative sense to any of the largest auditing firms, the loss of such a large client would still be a major event.

Unfortunately, Sarbanes-Oxley does not provide effective safeguards for the threats that arise in these circumstances. Current SEC rules raise

red flags only when total fees from a client exceed 15 percent of the auditing firm's total revenues. The use of this ceiling fails to address situations in which audit fees are under the 15 percent threshold for the auditing firm as a whole but are highly significant to a specific line of business within the firm, to a specific office, or to a specific partner or other key member of the audit team. For example, losing a large client can have significant consequences to a lead engagement partner or other senior professionals involved in the audit. Such potential consequences include lower income, fewer promotion opportunities, relocation to a different office, and loss of prestige, perhaps even professional embarrassment, within and outside the firm.

The AICF described in this chapter can assist in addressing this issue because it directs independence decision makers to assess the specific types of threats to auditor independence and their significance. Audits for which fees are significant to a firm, an office, or an individual pose an obvious self-interest threat to the auditors involved. In addition, a client who pays a fee that he or she knows is significant may use that knowledge as a weapon to intimidate the auditors. Those self-interest and intimidation threats reinforce cognitive biases, such as overconfidence, confirmation, and self-serving.

In the current environment, we believe that new safeguards are necessary in this, and in other, situations to ensure that auditors are independent and that investors, creditors, and other interested parties perceive them to be independent. Additional safeguards that should be considered include the following:

- Mandatory rotation of all key audit engagement personnel, not just the lead engagement partner
- Improving auditing firm compensation and promotion policies to ensure that technical expertise, integrity, and diligence in performing audits are rewarded more than fee production
- Actions strengthening auditing firms' cultures to help ensure that auditors know that their firms will stand behind them when audit clients are unhappy or use intimidation tactics—that is, their incomes will not be reduced, their promotions

will not be jeopardized, and a transfer will not be their reward for disagreeing with clients

- Policies to ensure that auditing firms refuse additional nonaudit work from an audit client if total fees from the client are already significant
- Joint audits—dividing up audits of the largest clients between two auditing firms
- Mandatory rotation of auditing firms

Each of these safeguards has costs and benefits that must be carefully weighed when analyzing its desirability. For example, while it is hard to argue against rewarding auditors for performing good audits rather than for being top salespeople, auditing firms must be sufficiently profitable to attract and retain bright people capable of understanding multinational businesses operating in a variety of fields and the accounting rules that apply to them.

The desirability of mandatory rotation of auditing firms has been debated from time-to-time, and Sarbanes-Oxley directs the General Accounting Office to evaluate this safeguard thoroughly. Some believe that mandatory rotation can mitigate familiarity, intimidation, and self-review threats that arise from long-standing relationships between auditors and their audit clients. Others, however, believe that the effects of those threats will still be felt, but in different ways. A nine-year rotation requirement has been the law for many years in Italy, and its unfortunate effects include the troubling aspects of heightened competition accompanied by the worst aspects of human nature. For example, major auditing firms in Italy are believed to have assigned partners and others to "romance" key officials and directors of companies that will be required to select new auditors in the next year or two. We can speculate about what those partners are promising potential new clients, but it is not likely that, in every case, it is the best and toughest audit. In addition, self-interest and self-review threats may be compounded with mandatory firm rotation because clients may try to ensure that the auditing firm agrees with its accounting policies prior to its appointment, resulting in a process sometimes called "opinion-shopping." Mandatory auditing firm rotation may not mitigate intimidation threats

from audit clients but may simply shift the timing of such threats from points during the audit to some time prior to the firm's appointment.

Requiring auditing firm rotation also may reduce the quality of audits. An auditing firm's knowledge of a client and its businesses, risks, people, internal controls, and accounting policies is much greater in second and subsequent audits than in the initial audit and, therefore, those subsequent audits may be better. An auditing firm cannot necessarily compensate for this learning curve by, for example, adding more professionals to its first audit of a client because it takes time and experience to gauge the quality of the interactions with client personnel. Although the specific personnel assigned to an audit client do change over time, and some knowledge may be lost, the continuity of experienced personnel and the information retained in firm files help ensure that much of an auditing firm's knowledge of its audit clients is preserved and passed on to newly assigned auditors. That cumulative knowledge is greater, and assumes greater importance, as clients become more complex and more geographically dispersed. Another factor that might lower audit quality under a mandatory rotation requirement is the possibility that an auditing firm about to rotate off an audit client might not spend enough money to obtain a complete understanding of the client's operations—for example, a new computer system—because the investment would soon be worthless.

Another possible safeguard, joint audits, could increase investor confidence in the financial reporting process and reduce self-interest and self-review threats. But they also could result in a Gresham's Law race to the bottom if auditing firms try to impress clients by demonstrating how "reasonable" they are compared with their co-auditor. Sharing audit responsibilities could lead to unproductive competitive behavior and finger-pointing that could reduce an audit's quality.

The desirability of these and other new safeguards will take time to evaluate. Our purpose in this chapter was not to advocate one solution over another but to illustrate the complexity of the issues and to show how a conceptual framework such as the AICF can provide a disciplined process for assessing and resolving them. Such a process should focus on matching the scope and effectiveness of restrictions and other required safeguards to the significance of the threats facing auditors and their audit clients, with adequate consideration of costs and benefits. A conceptual framework also reminds us to keep in mind the ultimate goal of auditor independence—to support investors' reliance on the financial reporting process and to facilitate the optimal allocation of capital—and to be mindful of the unintended consequences that could result from well-intentioned efforts to resolve independence issues.

NOTES

1. For summaries of some of this research, see Bazerman, Loewenstein, and Moore (2002) and Messick and Bazerman (1996). For a specific application to securities fraud litigation, see Prentice (2000b).

2. This is not to suggest that there are a large number of instances in which auditors' professional judgments are corrupted by a self-serving bias. We assume the contrary: Most auditors are able to guard against such tendencies, and their training and professionalism will result in their acting appropriately, particularly in carrying out the auditing function. Nonetheless, it is reasonable to anticipate that the influence of these factors will result in occasional failures of judgment and that professional standards, such as those supporting the concept of independence, are part of the portfolio of essential mitigating devices. We do not agree with Bazerman, Morgan, and Loewenstein (1997), who claim that auditors may find it psychologically impossible to achieve effective independence, because the authors do not recognize the significance of safeguards already in place or the possible salutary effects of additional ones. In addition, they propose no viable alternative to the current model.

3. Our interpretation and application of the ISB staff framework reflects the authors' opinions and should not be considered an official document of the ISB, its staff, or any other entity. The ISB framework is available from http://www.cpaindependence.org.

4. The threat is recognized explicitly, and controls mandated, in ISB Standard No. 3, *Employment with Audit Clients* (2000).

REFERENCES

Bamber, E. M., Ramsey , R. J., & Tubbs, R. M. (1997). An examination of the descriptive validity of the belief-adjustment model and alternative attitudes to evidence in auditing. *Accounting, Organizations and Society, 22*(3–4), 249–268.

Bazerman, M. H., Loewenstein, G., & Moore, D. A. (2002, November). Why good accountants do bad audits. *Harvard Business Review,* 96–102.

Bazerman, M. H., Morgan, K. P., & Loewenstein, G. F. (1997). The impossibility of auditor independence. *Sloan Management Review, 38*(4), 89–94.

Canadian Institute of Chartered Accountants (CICA). (2002). Public Interest and Integrity Committee. Exposure draft of Auditor Independence Standard. Toronto. CICA available from http://www.cica.ca

Davis, M. (1982). Conflict of interest. *Business & Professional Ethics Journal, 1*(4), 17–27.

Dunfee, Thomas W. (1991). Business ethics and extant social contracts. *Business Ethics Quarterly, 1*(1), 23–51.

Gaa, J. C. (1994). *The ethical foundations of public accounting* (Research Monograph No. 22). Vancouver: CGA-Canada Research Foundation.

Haynes, C. M., & Jenkins, G. J. (1998). The relationship between client advocacy and audit experience: An exploratory analysis. *Auditing: A Journal of Practice and Theory, 17*(2), 88–104.

Heiman-Hoffman, V. B., Moser, D., & Joseph, J. A. (1995). The impact of an auditor's initial hypothesis on subsequent performance in identifying actual errors. *Contemporary Accounting Research, 11*(2), 763–779.

Independence Standards Board (ISB). (1999). *Independence discussions with audit committees* (Standard No. 1). New York: Independence Standards Board.

International Federation of Accountants (IFAC). (2001). *Code of ethics for professional accountants.* London: IFAC. Available from http://www.ifac.org

Jaenicke, H. R., Glazer, A. S., Siegel, A., McGrath, S., Towers, R. T., & Dunfee, T. W. (2001). *A conceptual framework for auditor independence.* Staff report of the Independence Standards Board. New York: Independence Standards Board. Available from http://www.cpaindependence.org

Kennedy, J., & Peecher, M. E. (1997). Judging auditors' technical knowledge. *Journal of Accounting Research, 35*(2), 279–293.

McGrath, S., Siegel, A., Dunfee, T. W., Glazer, A. S., & Jaenicke, H. R. (2001). Assessing your audit firm's independence: Guidance for audit committee members. *Corporate Board Member.* Available from http://www.boardmember.com

Messick, D. M., & Bazerman, M. H. (1996). Ethical leadership and the psychology of decision making. *Sloan Management Review, 37*(2), 9–21.

Plumlee, R. D. (1985). The standard of objectivity for internal auditors: Memory and bias effects. *Journal of Accounting Research, 23*(2), 683–699.

Ponemon, L. A. (1995). The objectivity of accountants' litigation support judgments. *Accounting Review, 70*(3), 467–488.

Prentice, R. A. (2000a). The SEC and MDP: Implications of the self-serving bias for independent auditing. *Ohio State Law Journal, 61*(5), 1597–1670.

Prentice, R. A. (2000b). The case of the irrational auditor: A behavioral insight into securities fraud litigation. *Northwestern University Law Review, 95*(1), 133–219.

United States Congress. (2002). Sarbanes-Oxley Act of 2002 (Public Law No. 107–204, 116 Stat. 745). Washington, DC: U.S. Congress. Available from http://www.congress.gov

United States Securities and Exchange Commission (SEC). (2000). *Final release: Revision of the commission's auditor independence requirements* (Release Nos. 33–919; 34–43602; 35–27279; IC-24744; IA-1911; FR 56). Washington, DC: SEC. Available from http://www.sec.gov

Vidaver-Cohen, D. (1993). Creating and maintaining ethical work climates: Anomie in the workplace and implications for managing change. *Business Ethics Quarterly, 3*(4), 343–358.

Vidaver-Cohen, D. (1998). Moral climate in business firms: A conceptual framework for analysis and change. *Journal of Business Ethics, 17*(11), 1211–1226.

Weil, J., Barrionuevo, A., & Bryan-Low, C. (2002, June 17). Andersen win lifts U.S. Enron case. *Wall Street Journal,* p. A1.

8

THE ETHICS OF FINANCIAL REPORTING, THE GLOBAL REPORTING INITIATIVE, AND THE BALANCED CONCEPT OF THE FIRM

GEORGES ENDERLE

Reporting of corporate conduct is crucial for both the companies who send out the reports and the investors, consumers, business partners, competitors, and public agencies who receive and utilize these reports. In their reports companies represent themselves to the public, conveying, explicitly and implicitly, an image of their activities and philosophies, trying to enhance their reputation, and possibly rendering accountability for their deeds and objectives. On the other side, the receivers may check the quality of the reports, needing at least some truthful information for their own decision making and holding the companies accountable for their conduct.

While this describes the general purpose and focus of corporate reporting, many questions still need examination in light of globalization and recent corporate scandals. How accurate and comprehensive are financial reports? Do they reveal "the substance" of corporate performance rather than hiding it behind a plethora of formalities? How trustworthy and reliable should these reports be? Who is responsible for their veracity? Should companies report not only on financial and economic performances but also on social and environmental performances? In what respects are the latter different from the former, and thus in need of very special approaches and measurement techniques? What features do they have in common? Are there particular challenges for corporate reporting, given the fact of globalization? Are there legitimate differences in reporting among cultures and continents? What concepts of the company are involved in various types of reporting? To what extent do these concepts really matter for adequate reporting?

In the following, I attempt to discuss many of these questions.[1] The first part of this chapter addresses the ethics of financial reporting by focusing on the fundamental requirements of transparency and trust, and the responsibilities of the providers, certifiers, and users of financial reports. In the second part, after a brief presentation of the Sustainability Reporting Guidelines 2002, I offer several critical remarks and ask what financial reporting and sustainability reporting can learn from each other. In the third part, I attempt to link the issue of comprehensive corporate reporting to the understanding of the company. The common underlying theme throughout this chapter is the threefold corporate responsibility in the economic, social, and environmental respects and its implications for the concept and the reporting of the company.

THE ETHICS OF FINANCIAL REPORTING

Before the Enron and Andersen scandals, relatively little public attention was paid to the truthfulness of financial reporting. Of course, no one believed every company was beyond any suspicion of misrepresenting its activities. But, by and large, it was taken for granted that the reports certified by publicly recognized auditors sufficiently and accurately reflected companies' financial performances. Recently, however, this confidence has been greatly shaken. Serious doubts and even cynicism about current reporting practices have spread, particularly among investors (who nowadays make up approximately 50 percent of the U.S. population). The ethics of reporting has become a vital problem of the financial sector. This is the case not only in the USA where the "earthquake" of this crisis of confidence broke out, but also in Europe and indeed worldwide.

It would be naïve to assume that this problem could be fixed by tough punishment of CEOs and CFOs alone or by only sharpening the regulatory

framework and strengthening its enforcement. At stake is a much more complex problem that calls for a more comprehensive and sophisticated approach. Truthfulness of and trust in the financial reporting system depend on far more than the actions and decisions of individuals or sophisticated "mechanisms" for the whole system. As the Enron and Andersen events have shown (see Enderle, 2004b), far-reaching failures occurred at the individual (or micro) level of top managers, directors of corporate boards, management accountants, auditors, financial analysts, other employees, and members of supervisory boards and public agencies, including politicians. Yet, it would be shortsighted to blame only individuals. The crisis has also revealed serious insufficiencies at the systemic (or macro) level. The regulatory framework did not prevent but encouraged the establishment of several crucial conflicts of interest (particularly in the auditing and investment industry), the tempting call of which could be resisted only with extraordinary moral power. Many accounting and investment rules were vague, providing insufficient guidance in complex matters. In many instances the enforcement of the existing framework was half-hearted or even totally lacking. Moreover, to expect the financial reporting system to function well by relying solely on the individual "players" and the "rules of the game" would be a grave mistake. The Enron and Andersen cases clearly demonstrate the importance of organizations, with their objectives, structures, policies, and cultures (at the meso level), in influencing individuals and systems. Indeed, other companies in the energy, accounting, and banking industries and the professional associations of the certified public accountants and the investment managers and researchers have, in varying degrees, affected the quality of and confidence in the financial reporting systems.

Therefore, truthfulness of and trust in the financial reporting system cannot be a matter of either personal or institutional ethics alone. Rather, this complex problem challenges and requires both personal and institutional ethics, the latter including organizational as well as systemic ethics. In short, a three-level approach is needed that pays due attention to the indispensable roles and responsibilities of persons, organizations, and systems (see Enderle, 2003). Consequently, concepts of truthfulness and trust should take this complexity into account. If they are modeled exclusively on the basis of interpersonal relations (as is the case with a vast part of the literature on trust) or of anonymously functioning systems (see particularly sociological approaches), they will be inadequate to capture the core ethical issues of financial reporting.

Trust is generally a three-part relation: A trusts B to do X (see Hardin, 2002, 9 ff.). In the case of financial reporting, doing X concerns truthful reporting not only as a process but also and above all as the outcome of this process. The numbers are expected to be correct, accurate, comprehensive, objective, and understandable and to adequately reflect real processes and states of affairs of the reporting organization. A modern term for such truthfulness is *transparency*, meaning the reporting is "transparent" to the underlying financial "reality"; it does not hide substantial parts of this reality or deceive those who receive and need the reports.

Truthfulness and trust are issues that have shown up throughout the entire history of humankind and have been discussed in all ethical traditions (see Bok, 1999, 2001). It therefore comes as no surprise that they affect the modern financial sector too. Indeed, these core concepts appear to have moved to center stage of attention and importance due to the dynamics and complexity of financial markets, the wide and increasing range of financial instruments, and the dominating role of the financial sector on the whole economy and society at the national and international level. All these new developments offer a myriad of possibilities for false and deceptive financial reporting, which have not been matched with an increasing moral commitment to truthfulness and trust. This discrepancy between the seriousness of the problem and the need to deal with it might be a major reason why the ethics of finance has become an urgent task.

Given the scope of this chapter, only some essential features of the ethics of financial reporting can be presented. It includes five parts, which, for the sake of introduction, are treated separately but, in fact, are interrelated.

Structuring the Field

For the ethics of financial reporting, it is crucial to have a comprehensive and differentiated view of the field to which ethics should be applied. Financial reporting involves providers, certifiers, and users of financial statements and is the result of complex structures and procedures. It depends on the rules set up and enforced by the governmental and regulatory bodies (at the macro level), the proper application and interpretation of the rules by the providers', certifiers', and users' organizations (at the meso level), and the behavior of the individuals involved in reporting (at the micro level). The structuring of the field (as it relates to the United States) can be summarized in the following matrix (see Table 8.1).

Transparency and Trust

Trust in the financial reporting system is the fundamental requirement for the proper functioning of the system and can be considered a "public good," from which all participants in the system benefit, but which is being eroded by those who deceive. Trust is based on the truthfulness or "transparency" of financial reporting. This means that the numbers must be honest. They should reflect real processes and states of affairs of the company under consideration in an adequate manner, that is, according to appropriate rules of reporting. Moreover, they should be generated by trustworthy people who are competent and motivated by the knowledge that they are being trusted and by a moral commitment to honor this trust (see Hausman, 2002). In short, transparency and trust are the outcome of a combination of factors at the macro, meso, and micro level.

If financial reporting is inadequate and deceiving, trust will shrink or may even collapse. As a result, investment activities will drop and possibly come to a halt, with far-reaching consequences for

Table 8.1   Structuring the Field of Financial Reporting

	Providers	*Certifiers*	*Users*
Macro level	Governmental and regulatory bodies that set up and enforce the rules (Congress, SEC, FASB, Intern. Accounting Standard Board, boards of accounting)		
Meso level	Companies Firms issuing new securities Investment research divisions Professional associations of accountants and investment researchers	Auditing companies Public Company Accounting Oversight Board (since July 2002) Credit rating agencies Professional associations of accountants and auditors	Investor firms Creditor firms (banks, etc.) Government agencies (collecting taxes, etc.)
Micro level	Corporate management aided by management accountants Board of directors Chief financial officers Investment researchers	Internal auditors External auditors	Individual investors Individual bank employees Government officers Investment researchers

the economy and for individual businesses as well. It is noteworthy that the vital importance of transparency and trust can be argued for from both the perspective of consequences (that without transparency and trust, the system would break down) and the perspective of principles (that honesty should be lived up to for its own sake).

Responsibilities of the Providers

Financial reporting can be trustworthy only if its processes and outcomes are reasonably transparent. Therefore, the providers have a moral and legal responsibility to ensure transparency. First of all, the reporting rules must be conducive to fulfill this responsibility. For example, they have to prevent conflicts of interest that are built into or tolerated by the system, such as conflicts between auditing and numerous nonauditing functions and conflicts between investment research and investment banking. Moreover, they have to set clear standards for dealing with huge information asymmetries to which companies and individuals are exposed in the financial sector. (See Norman Bowie's chapter that deals with the problems of conflicts of interest and asymmetric information.) From the ethical

perspective, it is unfair and thus unacceptable solely to blame the players for wrongdoing when the rules of the game are deficient or misleading or even encourage unethical behavior. (As for the impact of law, regulations, and Supreme Court decisions on financial reporting, see Lerach, 2002.)

Second, the letter and the spirit of the rules can be followed only if the reporting organizations as such embrace this commitment. Corporate governance and culture have to be shaped in such a way that the "substance" of financial performance becomes transparent to the certifiers and users of financial reporting. In support of the companies, the professional associations of accountants and investment researchers play an indispensable role in enhancing the professional ethos by multiple provisions and activities such as ethical codes and ethics training.

Third, the moral responsibility of the individuals is equally crucial and cannot be replaced by mechanism, policies, and cultures. Instead, individuals must follow the letter and the spirit of the rules with competence and moral commitment. Here "moral commitment" is understood in a modest sense—that is, to live up to the ethical principle of honesty in providing adequate financial statements while being supported by the culture of the employer organization and the regulatory framework. This ethical requirement contrasts with the attitude of moral carelessness (i.e., that "anything goes") and also differs from the expectation of "heroic behavior." Under special circumstances, it might be praiseworthy to take a bold ethical stand against a prevailing misleading organizational culture or a deficient regulatory framework (for example, by blowing the whistle). But, in general, the ethical quality of organizations and systems should be such that heroic behavior of individuals is unnecessary.

Responsibilities of the Certifiers

The truthfulness of financial reporting in the complex financial sector should not rely on the providers alone, but must be certified by independent auditors as well. The strict separation of the providing function and the certifying function should be a hallmark of a modern society characterized by high degrees of division of labor and specialization. Here again, with regard to certification, the rules must be such that they lead to the stated purpose: to strengthen rather than impair the independence of the auditors. If there are conflicts of interest built into the system that seriously affect their independence, auditors and auditing firms experience too much pressure to give up their professional responsibility of impartiality. It comes as no surprise that under the present rules in the United States (in June 2002), the principle of independence has been violated in many instances.

Standing at the interface between the providers and users of financial reporting, the certifiers are accountable to the public and therefore can exert their task properly only if they are, and are perceived to be, independent. Conflicts of interest in fact and in appearance should be avoided. Having said this, many difficult ethical issues remain open, which cannot be addressed in this chapter (see chapter by Dunfee et al., "An Ethical Framework for Auditor Independence," in this volume). Suffice it to underscore that independence can be maintained only if it is an

essential feature of both the personal commitment of the auditors (at the micro level) and the policies and cultures of the auditing firms and the auditing profession as such (at the meso level).

Responsibilities of the Users

Financial reporting is also dependent on the users' expectations and behavior. If the users as organizations and individuals pay only lip service to the fundamental importance of transparency and tend to place the entire responsibility on the shoulders of the providers and certifiers, the financial reporting system cannot function properly with the necessary level of trust. Therefore, the users have to engage in contributing to the establishment and enforcement of fair and effective rules of financial reporting, which enhance the confidence in the system.

The users of financial reporting, be they organizations or individuals, may focus their attention particularly on three sensitive areas. First, they should distance themselves from the unquestioned belief in financial numbers that has spread in financial markets in recent times and instead seek out and scrutinize the underlying economic basis of those numbers. Second, they should not focus exclusively on short-term financial performance, but adopt a longer-term perspective as well. Third, they may nurture and express more realistic expectations regarding corporate performance and consequently discourage dishonest corporate communications and behavior.

THE GLOBAL REPORTING INITIATIVE (GRI) AND ITS SUSTAINABILITY REPORTING GUIDELINES

Short Introduction

While financial reporting is over 50 years old and currently exposed to increasing public attention and scrutiny, nonfinancial reporting of companies is relatively young. It has taken on a variety of forms in recent years and is far from providing a well-established and generally accepted framework. But, compared to the early '90s, considerable progress has been made, particularly with regard to the Global Reporting Initiative (GRI), which will be briefly discussed as an outstanding example of this broader development.

The GRI was launched in 1997 as a joint initiative of the U.S. nongovernmental organization Coalition for Environmentally Responsible Economies (CERES) and the United Nations Environment Program. Its goal was to enhance the quality, rigor, and utility of sustainability reporting. The initiative has enjoyed the active support and engagement of representatives from business, nonprofit advocacy groups, accounting bodies, investor organizations, trade unions, and many more. Together, these different constituencies have worked to build a consensus around a set of reporting guidelines with the aim of achieving worldwide acceptance (SRG, 2002, p. i).

The guidelines are for voluntary use by organizations for reporting on the economic, environmental, and social dimensions of their activities, products, and services. In its first phase, GRI has focused on corporations, with the expectation that governmental and nongovernmental organizations will follow in due course. According to GRI, a number of key trends has fueled GRI's swift progress: expanding globalization; the search for new forms of global governance; reform of corporate governance; global role of emerging economies; rising visibility of and expectations for organizations; measurement of progress toward sustainable development; governments' and financial markets' interest in sustainability reporting; and the emergence of next-generation accounting. Already over 2,000 companies worldwide are using the guidelines. This kind of reporting is seen as having numerous benefits as a proactive critical management tool; as a key ingredient for the engagement of internal and external stakeholders of the company; as a warning of trouble spots—and unanticipated opportunities—in supply chains; in communities, among regulators, etc.; and as a means to assess the societal and ecological contributions of the organization, to name a few. GRI recognizes that many challenges lie ahead and much work remains; however, it maintains that the confluence of need and opportunity will further advance the development of generally accepted sustainability principles (SRG, 2002, pp. 1–5).

Compared with the GRI document of June 2000, the Sustainability Reporting Guidelines of 2002 have been improved considerably. Among the substantive changes, two should be specifically mentioned in this context. The content and organization of the reporting principles have been developed into a comprehensive and consistent set of principles that provides a firm foundation and clear profile of sustainability reporting (see Figure 8.1). And the indicators regarding economic, environmental, and social performance, along with integrated indicators, have become more concise and more systematically organized, which substantially increases the grasp and utility of the reporting.

Critical Remarks

There is no doubt that the promotion of international harmonization in the reporting of relevant and credible corporate environmental, social, and economic performance information to enhance responsible decision making—as stated in the mission of GRI—is an urgent need and a crucial means to support global progress towards sustainable development. GRI and its Sustainability Reporting Guidelines, therefore, deserve close attention, critical examination, and constructive support by businesses, governments, NGOs, and academia.

GRI goes beyond traditional reporting approaches in at least three respects: It not only focuses on financial information but also includes economic,[2] social, and environmental information; it promotes a multi-stakeholder approach as opposed to the exclusive focus on shareholders; and it complements the common stakeholder approach by addressing the reporting content directly and specifying it systematically.

Despite the novelty and considerable progress advanced by GRI, there are several serious questions that need further scrutiny.

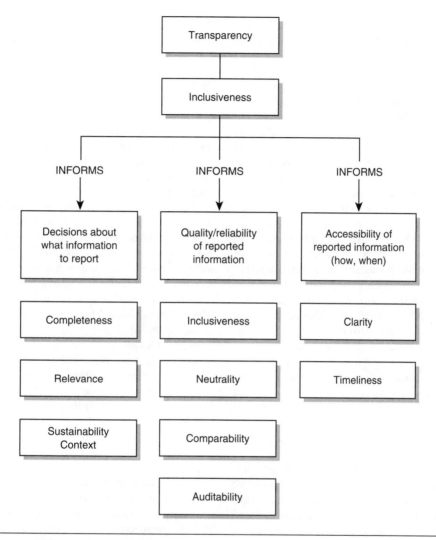

Figure 8.1 GRI Reporting Principles

First, the concept of *performance* seems to be understood mostly as "impact" rather than as "activity" of the organization (with the exception of some social indicators regarding policies, procedures, management systems, etc.). Thus economic performance is equated with the direct economic impact on customers, suppliers, etc., in terms of monetary flow. *Environmental performance* means the impact of the organization's activities on the environment—for instance, on energy and biodiversity. *Social performance* is defined as the impact on society—for instance, on indigenous rights and political contributions. However, by concentrating on the impact of the organization, one loses sight of its activities. While the impact of an organization concerns its effects (or consequences or outcome), which can lie in the economic, social, or another realm, the activities chiefly regard the processes (or the causes of the impact) which might be of primarily economic, social, or another nature. As the most striking example, profit generation, which was an aspect of economic performance in the draft of 2000, is conspicuously absent in the guidelines of 2002. Moreover, "net employment creation," "labor practices and decent work," and "strategy and management" are not considered activities but are seen only in terms of their social (not social *and* economic) impact.

Second, the *distinctions* among economic, environmental, and social performance (i.e., impact) are *sometimes blurred*, as the previous examples show. For instance, net employment creation has not only a social but also an economic impact. One can also question whether "competition and pricing" and "product responsibility" primarily concern social, rather than economic, performance. In addition, the same outcome can have simultaneously different impacts. For instance, "training and education" and "health and safety" may have not only social but also economic consequences (say, as investment in human resources). If these are valued only in social terms, their economic impact is ignored and consequently not accounted for (see Enderle & Tavis, 1998). With regard to social performance, GRI may consider two more aspects: (a) compliance with the tax law, which, perhaps, can be integrated in the category of economic performance, similar to the way compliance indicators are integrated in the environmental and social categories; and (b) respect for social customs and cultural heritage in different regions and countries, which is an increasingly important issue in the multicultural business environment.

Third, a further problem lies in the *widely heterogeneous informational basis of measurement*. Within each category there are several aspects with many indicators. Economic indicators are in a given currency; environmental indicators in tons, kilograms, volumes, joules, etc.; social indicators in numbers of employees, standard injuries, lost days, average hours of training per year, policies excluding child labor, etc. On what basis can the overall performance of a company be measured? It might be possible to compare the overall performance within the same company at two points in time, provided that the value changes of the indicators point in the same direction. But if the changes point in different directions (e.g., an increase in tons and a decrease in joules), the changes and the indicators (e.g., of use of materials and energy) have to be made comparable in order to aggregate the values. This is particularly difficult with regard to environmental and social indicators as well as the overall performance measurement.

Fourth, related to the informational question is the *evaluative* question. What normative standards should be used to determine the weights and scales of different indicators? GRI seems to offer a purely descriptive approach that only reports the organization's economic, environmental, and social performance. It is then up to the organization and the users of the report to evaluate the performance from the ethical perspective. Obviously, the selection of categories, aspects, and indicators already involves some moral judgment (since they are considered to be important for sustainable development). But, given this basis, no further ethical evaluation, for instance in terms of minimal ethical requirements, is proposed. Without doubt, this reservation of judgment has good reasons. It seems, however, questionable that such a value-free position can and should be maintained in the long run because the reporting unavoidably will be interpreted from an ethical perspective. If the ethical perspective of the organization sharply contrasts with the ethical perspective of, say, critical groups in society, the reporting might miss its objective and be counterproductive. As a possible solution to this problem, it might be worthwhile to consider Amartya Sen's capability perspective that is pluralistic in dealing with the aggregation over heterogeneous components and advocates "partial ordering" over the alternative states of affairs (Sen, 1999, chap. 3). What Sen has developed for the evaluation of institutions and public policies in the global context seems to be applicable to corporate reporting as well.

Fifth, as GRI is about the organization's economic, environmental, and social impact, one might clarify the meaning of *impact* in this context. The term does not mean the random outcome of uncontrollable processes. It rather designates the effects or consequences of corporate conduct, which affect not only the economic but also the environmental and social spheres and for which, supposedly, the company is to be held accountable. Beyond this, it remains open whether the consequences are the result of persistently pursued policies, intended or unintended side effects, or a mix of both. Moreover, it does not indicate how economic, environmental, and social performance might be interrelated, for instance, in a hierarchical manner in which environmental and social performance are taken as means to achieve the end of economic performance, or in a different manner. These are important questions about the conception of the company to be discussed in the final section.

A Brief Comparison Between Financial Reporting and Sustainability Reporting

As mentioned at the beginning of this chapter, reporting of corporate conduct is crucial for the companies that send out the reports and for those who receive and utilize them. This holds true for financial and sustainability reporting alike. However, they differ in many respects. Financial reporting has a long history while sustainability reporting has been developed in the last few years. The first kind concentrates exclusively on financial performance, is subject to a compulsory set of rules and regulations, and varies substantially from country to country. The second kind comprehends economic, environmental, and social performance, works on a voluntary basis without legal enforcement, and resolutely aims at international harmonization of standards.

Nevertheless, both kinds of reporting may learn from each other. They serve parallel and essential functions that enrich each other, and they may coordinate their processes, as GRI

encourages them to do. As early as 1993, Ciba Geigy began to publish separate reports (financial reviews, corporate environmental reports, reports on social responsibility, and summary reports). Ten years later, GRI listed several hundred companies, which, in varying degrees, use the sustainability reporting system (SRG, 2002). From the recent turmoil in financial reporting, sustainability reporting can draw several lessons. Reporting needs ethics and cannot properly function without a high level of trust based on truthfulness and transparency. It must be supported by appropriate rules, corporate governance and culture, and the moral commitment of the individuals involved in the reporting system. While GRI appears to be aware of the importance of credibility, this crucial issue probably needs even more emphasis because voluntary reporting (as with laws) is no guarantee for truthfulness. As financial reporting builds on three pillars (the providers, the certifiers, and the users of the reports, depending on their respective responsibilities), sustainability reporting with its identifiable contents should equally rely on such a system of checks and balances. Consequently, the provision of independent assurance (the equivalent of financial auditing) should be enhanced and the voices of the users (similar to the investor community) strengthened. (Numerous attempts to enhance the voices of consumers with social and environmental concerns have been made in recent years; see, for instance, CEP, 2000; Cortina, 2002.) As the history of financial reporting indicates, there is a long way to go to set up a necessary infrastructure that can make sustainability reporting really sustainable.

What can financial reporting learn from sustainability reporting? The broader perspective of GRI and its multi-stakeholder approach can raise the awareness of the risks and opportunities that are relevant to financial reporting as well. The eleven reporting principles of GRI (see Figure 8.1) may help to better define the task and profile of financial reporting. Over time, financial performance measurement increasingly can benefit from the measurement of economic, environmental, and social performance. And the resolutely global approach of GRI may bring financial reporting closer to common international standards and procedures in order to pursue the overarching goal of sustainable development.

TOWARDS A NEW CONCEPT OF THE COMPANY

The role of companies in the ethics of financial reporting and the Global Reporting Initiative leads one to examine the concept of the company that underlies and shapes corporate reporting.

With the broader focus on companies' economic, environmental, and social performance, it seems that a kind of "conceptual crossroads" has been reached where two distinct concepts of the company are posed: the strictly hierarchical concept and the balanced concept of the firm (Enderle, 2002; Enderle & Tavis, 1998).

The *strictly hierarchical concept* states that the company has one purpose, namely to maximize its economic objectives under the constraints of law and basic moral norms. Social and environmental activities and consequences are considered mere means to achieve economic goals. It goes without saying that this concept goes beyond the models of profit maximization and the maximization of shareholder value by providing corporate objectives with rich economic content: the creation of wealth and employment, the provision of marketable products and services to consumers at a reasonable price commensurate with quality, the making of profit, etc. Social and environmental performances have no value in themselves but are instrumentalized in view of the economic ends. In other words, they are pursued because and only because a "business case" can be made for them. This implies that they are used as long as they contribute to achieving the economic goals of the company, and they are dropped as soon as they fail to do so.

In contrast, the *balanced concept of the firm*[3] conceives of the company as a multipurpose organization including not only economic but also some social and environmental goals that are *interrelated in a circular way*. Being a multipurpose organization does not contradict the far-reaching disentanglement of social functions in modern society in which business, government, and the civil sector have large degrees of relative autonomy. Rather, it reflects the fact that business organizations are, willy-nilly, involved in other-than-economic spheres as well, in terms of both activities and consequences (or impact). In addition to economic responsibilities, these involvements also entail social and environmental responsibilities. According to the balanced concept of the firm, they should be clearly stated, along with economic responsibilities, not only as means but also as ends. In such a way, they provide long-term guidance and can motivate the company, its leaders and its employees, to proactive behavior. It should be noted that the recognition of those performances as ends does not exclude their use as means. (See Sen's discussion of human rights, which can and should be considered as ends and means as well; Sen, 1999, chaps. 2, 10).

The term *responsibility* points to the evaluative or normative-ethical question of corporate behavior. It is suggested to use De George's distinction of minimal ethical requirements, positive obligations beyond the minimum, and aspirations for ethical ideals (De George, 1993, chap. 10) and apply it to the economic, social, and environmental realms. For instance, a minimal ethical requirement in the economic realm would be to respect the life and rights of your competitors. A positive obligation beyond the minimum in the social realm would consist in helping the community in the company's neighborhood affected by a natural disaster. It is noteworthy that a company can be "ethical," or balance its economic, social, and environmental responsibilities in many different ways, provided that it respects the minimal ethical requirements in all three realms. It is confusing to talk about an "ethical" or "unethical" corporation without distinguishing these three levels of ethical demand.

In order to further specify corporate responsibilities, it is proposed that one apply Amartya

Sen's "capability approach" and his ethical framework of a "goal-rights-system" to the balanced concept of the firm (see Table 8.2; Sen, 1999). "Capabilities" or "real freedoms that people enjoy" would be the ethical standards, applicable primarily to the minimal requirements while having a guiding function for social obligations and ethical ideals. To illustrate, a minimal requirement in the social realm might involve the opportunity to receive basic education. This might require corporate policy to support local schools and to ban child labor, and the economic

facility of having access to finance may inspire a local group to establish a micro-credit bank (for further elaboration, see Enderle, 2004a).

A further question is how to balance economic, social, and environmental responsibilities in different business situations. The answer is twofold. Economic, social, and environmental performances of companies are closely interwoven and partially overlap. When they overlap, the same business strategy can achieve two (or more) kinds of outcome (or *impact* in GRI terms). "Hitting two birds with one stone" by fulfilling, say, economic

Table 8.2   Specifying Corporate Responsibilities in Terms of Capabilities of Individuals

Responsibilities of the Company	*Real Freedoms That People Enjoy (Amartya Sen)*
Economic responsibilities	*Basic capabilities* such as freedoms to satisfy hunger, to achieve sufficient nutrition, to obtain remedies for treatable illness; opportunities to be adequately clothed and sheltered, to enjoy clean water and sanitary facilities.
	Economic facilities: Opportunities to utilize economic resources for the purpose of consumption, production, or exchange; economic entitlements dependent on the resources owned or available for use as well as the conditions of exchange; distribution of entitlements; availability and access to finance.
Social responsibilities	*Political freedoms*, broadly conceived (including civil rights): Opportunity to determine who should govern and on what principles; freedom to scrutinize and criticize authorities; freedom of political expression and an uncensored press; freedom to choose between different political parties; freedom to enjoy local peace and order; etc.
	Social opportunities: Opportunities to receive basic education and health care in order to live a long and healthy life and to better participate in economic and political activities.
Environmental responsibilities	Environmental components involved in economic facilities, political freedoms, and social opportunities.
Regarding all relationships	*Transparency guarantees* deal with the need for openness that people can expect: the freedom to deal with one another under guarantees of disclosure and lucidity (as basic requirements for trust).
	Protective security is needed to provide a social safety net for preventing the affected population from being reduced to abject misery, or even starvation and death (unemployment benefits, statutory income supplements, famine relief, emergency public employment, etc.).

and environmental responsibilities, a company can achieve positive economic and environmental consequences at the same time without additional costs. This "win-win situation" occurs more often than one might believe, but it requires entrepreneurial imagination. Thus its opportunities should be taken to the fullest extent possible, which is probably the most important challenge of putting business ethics into practice.

More difficult to handle is the second situation in which different types of responsibility *diverge.* One faces a trade-off, for instance, between a considerable improvement of environmental performance and a substantive increase of costs. One has reached the "apex point," after which the increase in one kind of responsibility is only possible with the decrease in another kind of responsibility (i.e., a "win-lose situation"). Here two steps are recommendable. First, the apex point should be moved to the "right" as far as possible. This can be achieved by measures taken by companies (e.g., new technologies, training), industries (self-regulation), or governments (regulation). Second, when the apex point cannot be moved further, but the social or environmental need continues to exist, the costs for addressing this need should be clearly stated and fairly shared with other social actors.

To conclude, I have argued for the crucial importance of truthful and trustworthy corporate reporting, which is an essential interface between business and society. Recent corporate scandals have showed that the ethics of financial reporting should not be taken for granted. Rather, it needs keen attention on the side of the providers, certifiers, and users of reporting. Moreover, companies are more than financial entities, featuring broader economic, social, and environmental performances. But if these dimensions don't get measured, they don't get managed. Hence corporate reporting should be extended to sustainability reporting. This widened perspective calls for a conception of the firm which has a broader than financial purpose and balances its economic, social, and environmental responsibilities.

NOTES

1. Given the limited scope of this chapter, I refer the reader to several other writings in which I investigate these issues in more detail (Enderle, 2002, 2003, 2004a, 2004b; Enderle & Tavis, 1998).

2. The Sustainability Guidelines characterize the conceptual difference between the traditional financial performance and the economic performance as follows: "Broadly speaking, economic performance encompasses all aspects of the organisation's economic interactions, including the traditional measures used in financial accounting, as well as intangible assets that do not systematically appear in financial statements. However, economic indicators as articulated in the Guidelines have a scope and purpose that extends beyond that of traditional financial indicators" (SRG, 2002, p. 45).

3. The view of a "balanced concept of the firm" differs from the various stakeholder concepts of the firm, which are increasingly discussed in management theory and business ethics. While the former approach primarily focuses on the contents of ethically responsible corporate conduct, the latter concentrates on the groups of people ("stakeholders") who are affected by corporate conduct, to whom the firm is supposed to be responsible or accountable, and with whom the contents of responsibilities may be negotiated. Yet by listening to, and negotiating with, the stakeholders, the question about the specific contents of corporate responsibilities is not answered yet. In contrast, the balanced concept view emphasizes the question of what the company ought to do in economic, social, and environmental terms. By addressing directly these different responsibilities, the potential conflicts and overlaps in terms of contents can be better captured than with the stakeholder approach; if interpreted in an elitist fashion, however, it may fail to listen to the voices of the stakeholders. Therefore, it seems fair to say that both approaches are complementary, though not contradictory.

REFERENCES

Bok, S. (1999). *Lying: Moral choice in public and private life* (3rd ed.). New York: Vintage Books.

Bok, S. (2001). Deceit. In L. C. Becker & C. B. Becker (Eds.), *Encyclopedia of ethics* (2nd ed.) (pp. 378–381). New York: Routledge.

Bowie, N. E. (2002). *Why conflicts of interest and abuse of information asymmetry are keys to lack of integrity and what should be done about it.* Paper presented at the Transatlantic Business Ethics Conference on September 27–29, 2002, at Georgetown University, Washington, DC.

Cortina, A. (2002). *Por una ética del consumo. La ciudadanía del consumidor en un mundo global.* Madrid: Santillana/Taurus.

Council on Economic Priorities (CEP). (2000). *Shopping for a better world: The quick and easy guide to all your socially responsible shopping.* New York: CEP.

De George, R. T. (1993). *Competing with integrity in international business.* New York: Oxford University Press.

Dunfee, T. (2002). *An ethical framework for auditor independence.* Paper presented at the Transatlantic Business Ethics Conference on September 27–29, 2002 at Georgetown University, Washington, DC.

Enderle, G. (2002). Algunos vinculos entre la ética corporativa y los estudios de desarrollo. In B. Kliksberg (compilador), *Ética y desarrollo. La relación marginada* (pp. 345–372). Buenos Aires: El Ateneo. (Spanish translation of *Corporate ethics at the beginning of the 21st century.* Paper presented at the international meeting "Ethics and Development" on December 7–8, 2000, Inter-American Development Bank, Washington, DC.

Enderle, G. (2003). Business ethics. In N. Bunnin & E. P. Tsui-James (Eds.), *Blackwell companion to philosophy* (pp. 531–551). Oxford: Blackwell.

Enderle, G. (2004a). Global competition and corporate responsibilities of small and medium-sized enterprises. *Business Ethics—A European Review, 13,* 51–63.

Enderle, G. (2004b). Confidence in the financial reporting system: Easier to lose than to restore. In X. Lu & G. Enderle (Eds.), *Developing business ethics in China.* Notre Dame: University of Notre Dame Press. Forthcoming.

Enderle, G., & Tavis, L. A. (1998). A balanced concept of the firm and the measurement of its long-term planning and performance. *Journal of Business Ethics, 17,* 1121–1144.

Global Reporting Initiative (GRI). Retrieved February 2004 from http://www.globalreporting.org

Hardin, R. (2002). *Trust and trustworthiness.* New York: Russell Sage Foundation.

Hausman, D. M. (2002). Trustworthiness and self-interest. In T. Cosimano, R. Chami, & C. Fullenkamp (Eds.), Managing ethical risk: How investing in ethics adds value. *Journal of Banking and Finance, 26*(9), 1767–1783.

Lerach, W. S. (2002). Plundering America: How American investors got taken for trillions by corporate insiders. *Stanford Journal of Law, Business and Finance,* Autumn.

Sen, A. (1999). *Development as freedom.* New York: Knopf.

Sustainability Reporting Guidelines (SRG). (2002). Retrieved February 2004 from http://www.globalreporting.org

9

WHAT IS A SUCCESSFUL COMPANY?

A Path to Understanding Accountability

JOSEP M. LOZANO

We know what we are, but know not what we may be.

—*Hamlet,* act 4, scene 5

WHY DO WE NEED A BAROMETER?

In recent years, many companies have started to tie accountability into new auditing and reporting practices that promise commitment to transparency and relationships based on trust (SustainAbility, 2002). These new practices are all very well. But if they are to be workable, the companies instituting them must at the same time rethink their definitions of how they see themselves and their relationships with what we might call the "outside world." Because accountability is more than simply developing new instruments for appraisal or new forms of communication, we cannot even begin to discuss accountability if we are not prepared to question how we view the company as a social actor, what society can expect of it, and indeed what it is legitimate to ask for. In graphic terms, "a barometer is only valuable on the basis of a meteorological theory. There is no point in measuring barometric pressure, unless you have an accurate theory about the relationship between atmospheric pressure and the weather" (Mackenzie, 1998, p. 1398).

We must not forget, then, that the meaning of accountability is bound up with a particular view

AUTHOR'S NOTE: This paper forms part of one of the lines of research of ESADE's Institute for the Individual, Corporations and Society (IPES), which is sponsored by the Caixa Sabadell Foundation.

of the company rather than being intrinsic or standing alone. From where we stand, accountability must be understood within the context of the development of corporate social responsibility (CSR) or the Stakeholder Corporation (Wheeler & Sillanpää, 1997). Of course, we must reflect on the importance of developing new models, tools, and methodologies in accountability. But, because it is impossible to measure, evaluate, or give account of anything without values, we must avoid a narrowly technological or instrumental standpoint on methodology. Accountability, then, as an activity is neither neutral nor naïve. Everything a company says about itself reveals its basic values: its stance on its contribution to society, how it focuses relationships with its stakeholders, in short, its identity. "Who are *we*? Why are *we* here? What values do *we* support? What are *our* obligations as an organization? What is a good life for *us* [emphasis in original]? These are questions that deal not with superficial appearances, but with identity, integrity, accountability, and fundamental purpose" (Pruzan, 2001a, p. 55).

There is a growing trend these days to justify the need for new forms of accountability and for recovering trust and integrity by pointing the finger at corporate scandals. Although understandable, this is not necessarily wise, for two reasons: first, because taking scandals as a reference point focuses debate on what we want to prevent rather than what we want to construct; and second, because this focus ignores the existence of many companies whose corporate traditions already enshrine an acceptable and credible ethos on which the foundations of new forms of accountability could be laid.

As regards scandals, however, there is a third point to make, which may on the face of it appear paradoxical. In the not-too-distant past, many of these scandalous—and often now defunct—companies were being lauded by public opinion and business circles alike as prime examples of "successful" enterprises. What relationship, if any, was there between that vision of success and subsequent scandals?

Now any discourse about companies, or by companies, is bound to include a posture on success, what it means, as well as on what a "good" company is or should be. In this context, the interest of accountability lies not only in that it spells out what we should know about and what we should look for in a company, but also (if we take accountability seriously) in that it makes us rethink our vision of the company and its role in society. In other words, it forces us to question our definition of corporate success and logically also our definition of the accountability with which this is associated.

WHAT DOES SUCCESS MEAN?

Questioning the meaning of success is relevant in any consideration of accountability. A one-dimensional view of corporate success that includes only economic and financial results will evaluate company actions as if these happen in isolation from the social and environmental context, sometimes even narrowing down to just short-term financial results. I have already touched on the paradox of the scandals that could blight companies previously considered as "successful," where it seemed that success and scandal rested on the same practices. Gellerman was referring to a similar process when he raised the question of why "good" managers make bad ethical choices. He said,

> ambitious managers look for ways to attract favorable attention, something to distinguish them from other people. So they try to outperform their peers. Some may see that it is not difficult to look remarkably good in the short run by avoiding things that pay off only in the long run. [. . .] The sad truth is that many managers have been promoted on the basis of "great" results obtained in just those ways, leaving unfortunate successors to inherit the inevitable whirlwind. (Gellerman, 1986, p. 89)

Great results for whom? From what standpoint? With what criteria? Accountability cannot distance itself from these questions.

The ambivalence of the very idea of success is also highlighted by Goodpaster when he suggests that there is a malaise or disorder that may be a feature of the corporate world. It affects both people acting in corporate contexts and companies acting in social contexts. This malaise, *teleopathy* ("sickness of purpose"), can be defined as an uncritical obsession with results that blinds one to everything else.

> Teleopathy in its most abstract form is a suspension of "on-line" moral judgment as a practical force in the life of an individual or group. It substitutes for the call of conscience the call of decision criteria from other sources: winning the game, achieving the goal, following the rules laid down by some framework external to ethical reflection. These other sources generally have to do with self-interest, peer acceptance, group loyalty, and institutional objectives that themselves may have broad social justification (Goodpaster, 1991, p. 95).

There may therefore be various perceptions of professional and corporate success (some of which could be singularly unhealthy). This depends on the various sources used to build up each vision of success.

It behooves us then to recall that the meaning of corporate success is neither unequivocal nor one and indivisible, but rather a social construction (Berger & Luckmann, 1967). This construction depends both on a company's internal definition of success and on how success is recognized and legitimized by society. Accordingly, perverse and one-dimensional visions of professional or corporate success can help explain why certain irresponsible actions flow from corporate practices, and cannot be considered as lamentable and unnecessary exceptions to the rule according to which "good" managers and companies seek "good" results. In the final analysis, success is not in fact a question of results or data with intrinsic value but rather a cultural phenomenon affecting our attitudes and practices, pushing us in a given direction and lending purpose to our actions.

I believe that there is a direct relationship between our understandings of success and accountability. We demand accountability only for what we believe we can legitimately expect—and ask—of a company because a corporation's raison d'être determines the ends it seeks. There can be no accountability without reference to the corporate raison d'être. "Business and public leaders are realising that good answers to complex questions can be found by supplementing the narrow language of efficiency, control and profit with multidimensional and qualitative measures that explicitly recognise the values the organization shares with its stakeholders" (Pruzan, 1998, p. 1380).

I think that the fundamental issue for accountability today is the recognition that we are looking at complex organizations operating in complex societies. This is why we should question the reductionism of success seen in purely financial terms; "because the language of money reduces complexity it cannot express complexity" (Pruzan & Thyssen, 1990, p. 138). However, accountability is not limited to providing a more complex and comprehensive response to increased social demands and expectations of companies. Accountability is not simply another technique (however sophisticated) or tool for improving management of corporate risks and reputations. Accountability is an opportunity, the opportunity to configure a learning process (Lozano, 2000a) that reveals and reworks a company's vision of the future. As a process, it defines the kind of company one wants to build and the contribution one wants it to make; this is what emerges in the way the company renders account for its actions. In this respect, accountability involves much more than simply providing information; it involves building a corporate license to operate[1] through interaction with other social actors. Accountability cannot be reduced to the development of measurement techniques, tools, and processes (even though without these it could not exist). Accountability presupposes reflective action based on dialogue and inquiry. Why is this so? The answer is that accountability in a complex society is impossible without making explicit the corporate purpose and the kinds of relationships that the company wishes to build in its social context.

In a nutshell, accountability is not a question of metrics but of vision. This vision concerns how a company sees itself and its role in the world. On the basis of this vision, we can then establish what is meant by corporate success and in consequence what the company has to account for, and to which of its stakeholders this account should be given. This is what makes me believe that accountability is not merely a question of providing a flood of data.[2] What accountability is really about is the ability to provide meaningful data from credible sources (Lonergan, 1973). In this way, accountability contributes, among other things, to building corporate trust and commitment. This is why I believe we now need to clarify spheres of accountability, in much the same way as Walzer (1983) spoke of spheres of justice. We could see relationships with stakeholders as spheres of accountability. And accountability could be seen as a way of building relationships and dialogue with stakeholders (Lozano, 2000b). This link between company vision, relationship with stakeholders, and accountability is what makes us set accountability within the framework of CSR.

ACCOUNTABILITY WITHIN THE FRAMEWORK OF CSR: REFRAMING THE POSITION OF BUSINESS IN SOCIETY

Is there such a thing as CSR myopia? In the same way as Levitt (1960) spoke of "marketing myopia," perhaps we should now speak of CSR myopia. There are managers and companies who have such a narrow view of their businesses that they do not see how CSR can become an intrinsic component in corporate identity. Today, for example, we could not imagine a company without a marketing approach, because marketing is an essential aspect of management. But this has not always been the case. What Levitt pointed out was that, in his day, the adoption of a marketing approach signaled the gulf between forward-looking and myopic companies. There have been times in the history of management when a single question like this became crucial. In other words,

in making the decision whether to take it seriously or not, a company is anticipating something that will become generally accepted. That question today is whether CSR as an issue is vital to the future of every company. A few years hence, we may be saying that in our day, there were some myopic companies that did not realize how CSR had become a vital cog in company management.

Whether a company is myopic or forward-looking in relation to CSR is an issue linked to the increasing demands and pressures that are pushing companies in this direction, a seemingly constant feature of recent years.

- There is a demand for greater transparency, linked to increased surveillance by NGOs and the pressure exerted by social movements.
- There has also been an increase in institutional and political proposals (ranging from the Global Compact to the EU's Green Paper) to promote CSR, and a greater concern by some governments (with the risk of restricting the problem to a debate on the need for more regulation).
- The number of responsible consumers is also rising. Many shoppers take their personal and civic values with them when they enter the supermarket, considering that an informed choice takes more into account than just product price and quality.
- The media are also taking an ever more active part in establishing an agenda of relevant social issues.
- Socially responsible investments are also increasingly important, and new indexes are providing a more complex valuation of corporate performance.

I believe that these demands should not simply be seen as a change in trends but should also form part of the debate on the role that companies play in configuring the new world society. Given this situation, new demands set new challenges in terms of CSR. However, we should not forget that the way demands are made and the concept of CSR (and with it, accountability) are not univocal but depend on our vision of the relationship between company and society.

1. Perhaps there is a kind of purely reactive CSR that basically responds to a vision of *business without society*. It leads to a reductionism in which everything is seen in market and regulatory terms. Accordingly, social demands are perceived without reference to any evaluation criteria other than their potential impact on profit or market position. So this approach simply assigns economic value to corporate reputation and its associated risks.

2. A different kind of CSR reflects the acceptance that new links should be established with society. The key is to see everything in terms of the relationships between *companies* and *society*. These relationships can be viewed as creating intersections that mutually satisfy the interests of various social and corporate actors and the relationships between them. CSR is therefore a useful tool for establishing relationships with the social setting. This could even lead to creating a particular management area with special responsibilities on this issue, but always based on the idea that relationships between company and society do not affect companies' core business.

3. However, perhaps there is a third kind of CSR that presents a vision that widens the perspective from business and society to *business in society*—a vision that recognizes that globalization is changing companies' roles and contributions and that there can be no "power without accountability."[3] Companies are seen as both social and economic actors, and they therefore need to understand themselves from both market and social viewpoints. Managing this complexity cannot be dealt with by just reacting to events or by making incremental and cosmetic changes. It is not a question of simply doing the same old things in a new socially responsible way. Rather, it is a question of creating multi-stakeholder value, learning to build relationships and partnerships, redefining one's "license to operate," and reflecting deeply on what legitimizes one's roles and actions. In this context, accountability becomes central because it does not show merely a new way of doing business but rather goes to the core of what the business is about. Defining the role of companies from a "business-in-society"

standpoint involves putting vision, understanding, and processes at the core of corporate practices. This is basically a question of learning, innovation, and integration.

In this respect, it is significant that the business input in the process of launching the European Academy on Business in Society stressed the need to underline this change in paradigm. The companies involved proposed the following themes for research: the role of business in a globalized world; the construction of a business model based on sustainable business value; reflection on the leadership model required; and the policy framework for business in society. In my view, matters like these are also symptomatic of a change in vision concerning the relationships between companies and society, which will also affect how we understand accountability.

Simplifying matters, we can visualize this change by the reworking of a table proposed by Habermas (1973) in his analysis of capitalism.

In Figure 9.1, companies contribute to society through their products and services. The only direct relationship of the company with society is in market terms—in the rest, the state plays an intermediate role. Effectively, it is government that articulates companies' contribution to society through regulation and taxation. Society receives the benefits of this process (e.g., social services) and also a certain cohesion and sense of belonging. Nevertheless, the bottom line is that there is not and can never be any direct relationship between companies and society other than through the market.

In Figure 9.2, relationships have become slightly more complex. Looking at the relationships shown in both figures, we now see direct relationships between companies and society in which the latter no longer sees the former as mere providers of products and services, but now also requires information on the social and environmental quality of their output. Society no longer simply rewards companies with profits but also forges relationships based on trust and credibility that either lend or remove legitimacy, as the case may be.[4] This is why I favor understanding proposals like the triple bottom

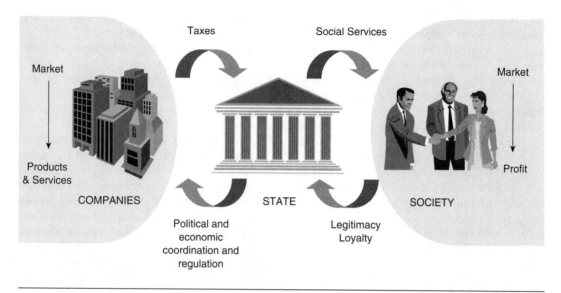

Figure 9.1   A vision of the relationships between companies and society (in a welfare state)

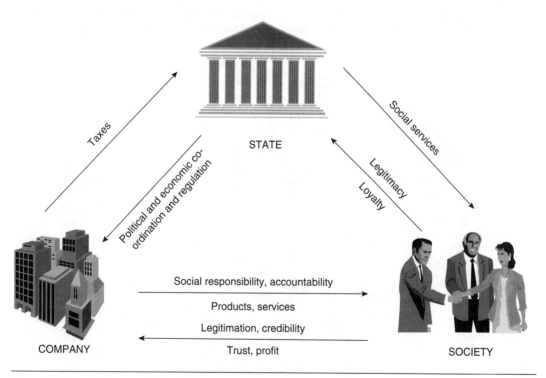

Figure 9.2   A framework for relationships, creating spheres of responsibility and accountability

line (Elkington, 1998) as a more inclusive approximation to business results than the conventional approach. Basically what this highlights is a contrasting view of the issues to be considered when evaluating corporate results.

From a vision that embraces complexity, we create new spheres of responsibility[5] and consequently new spheres of accountability. In much the same way as the different spheres of justice (Walzer, 1983) are created depending on the goods to be shared out, spheres of accountability depend on the relationships that companies establish with the various social actors and the communities to which they belong. Every sphere of accountability therefore sets out how the company focuses its relationship with each of its stakeholders. Viewed from this position, accountability stands within one of the frames of reference[6] used for defining the role of the company in society and, consequently, within one of the various visions that each has of corporate success. How can we bring our understanding of and focus on accountability into sharper relief? The answer is by contrasting rival visions[7]—whether or not

they overlap—concerning corporate success and what constitutes a "good" company.[8]

With the widening of our horizons, accountability is seen not merely as a tool, nor is it confined to certain practices. Accountability also becomes a commitment. It goes to the heart of corporate vision and identity. Its development is therefore intimately related to individual and corporate transformations. In my opinion, it is also intimately related to (a) the transformation of individuals towards greater integrity and personal integration; (b) an organizational transformation towards the building of a shared project capable of creating cohesion and commitment; and (c) an organizational transformation towards greater social legitimacy (this replaces demands for social responsibility with a view of organizations as builders of social relationships). In this respect, I believe that companies today have the opportunity to become reflective value-based spaces that express and reveal themselves in a reflective accountability.[9] Let us briefly examine the relationship between these three points and accountability, as depicted in Figure 9.3.

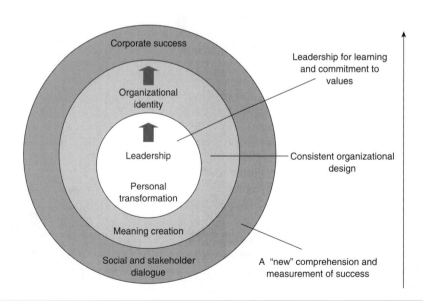

Figure 9.3   Accountability as part of a vision of business innovation
SOURCE: Adapted from CSR Europe

Developing Accountability: From the Corrosion of Character to the Building of Character

When we speak of accountability, we often avoid asking ourselves whether a responsible, accountable company is possible without a staff with these same qualities, given that accountability is as much a question of mindset as of practices and metrics. One must ask oneself whether developing corporate accountability should include corporate work on attitudes, meanings, and understandings, particularly in the context of the *knowledge society.*

The knowledge society is not just a society structured by ICTs (information and communication technologies). It is a society configured by human ability to create, share, and disseminate knowledge. Working with knowledge is not some specialized branch of technology but something that involves people as human beings. And if it involves human beings, this means that organizations need to give direction, purpose, and meaning to their activities, because human life cannot exist without direction, purpose, and meaning. One should therefore not limit oneself to speaking of organizational cultures but also consider how they contribute to building their own identities. Building an identity is a process (Lozano, 2002). In this respect, companies in the knowledge society should constitute reflective value-based spaces (Verstraeten, 2000). No reference can be made to accountability without recognizing its links with processes that include the creation of values that give meaning and purpose; we should be aware that corporate practices can build meaning or destroy it equally well. This is because they have an impact on the life course and personal equilibrium of those who work there.

The use of the term *human resources* is perhaps somewhat unfortunate in this context (Filella, 1994). The problem is that human beings are quite different from other resources, while *human resources* implies that it is legitimate to treat people as mere tools. The term also suggests that staff members are passive objects without any initiative, autonomy, or will of their own. That aside, can a knowledge society be viable with only human resources? What are the chances of creating and disseminating knowledge and generating shared learning processes? What are the possibilities of developing towards reflective accountability and complex responsibility without involving people, treated as persons and recognized as such? It is difficult to imagine accountability really taking root in corporate practices that do not include such an approach. It makes little sense to try to hold a company accountable if the people who work there do not identify with the attitudes that make accountability possible. Nor does it make much sense for a company to proclaim greater transparency and accountability without at least reflecting a little on the values underlying the way it manages its staff.

Sennett (1998) convincingly warned of the risk that certain proposals for change and flexibility can corrode character. This is demonstrated, for example, by that fact that so many professionals are capable only of signing contracts, while proving incapable of forging links. Someone with an outstanding CV is not always capable of narrating his or her career as a meaningful life itinerary. In this respect, it seems that companies are seeking to develop a postmodern version of humanity that lacks any kind of attributes. What they want appears to be rootless individuals who are always on tap and who have no real ties or sense of social, cultural, or national belonging. Such individuals are prized simply for their dedication to the company while the distinction between their personal identities and their professional profiles is often deliberately blurred for the basest of reasons.

It is difficult to have companies that are accountable without their staff also being accountable—hence the need for corporate accountability to embrace developing personal accountability. Corporate accountability is difficult to achieve without staff who are capable of forging relationships and taking on commitments. This poses a new challenge for companies: the development of a corporate capability for working with values. Put in another way, if a company wishes to come to grips with the issue of accountability, it needs to find a framework that makes this focus credible.

Managing and working with people within the framework of the knowledge society is not simply a question of incentives and motivation but also involves their values and beliefs. Managing people within the framework of a globalized world requires not only a model of a company but also a model of and project for the individual within the company. I believe that a serious discussion of accountability leads us to questions such as the following: What kind of people do we want in our companies, and what should we do to get them? What kind of person or personality is being created in our companies?

Does working with people also mean helping build their characters? The answer to this question is probably "yes." And this is so, paradoxically, because currently one's professional life is neither stable nor permanent. The individualization of work seems to be an irreversible trend. However, this individualization is now linked to functions such as research, creation, and the dissemination and use of knowledge. As Carnoy (2000) indicates, it is difficult to envisage someone carrying out these functions without also developing self-knowledge. If accountability (methodologies and processes apart) is a value that involves commitment, it is difficult to imagine it working without a certain degree of personal transformation, because the processes of change that create commitment and transparency must be both personal and corporate.

Clearly, this is closely linked to the challenges of leadership (Goleman, Boyatzis, & McKee, 2002). As the Aspen Institute has indicated, "'knowing yourself' and 'knowing your work' are fundamental building blocks for leadership development."[10] Leadership does not mean dragging along uncritical, passive followers. Rather, it consists of emphasizing the value aspects and commitments that come into play in all kinds of practices, situations, and decision making. In the final analysis, accountability is also a leadership issue because it rests on human and professional

qualities that need to be strengthened if people are to assume accountability. This involves a process of corporate learning, given that it is unreasonable to passively expect these attitudes and capabilities to be provided by the cultural context and prior education. Such a learning process does not shy away from building character. Instead, it recognizes this as a corporate challenge in a context in which volatility is not always seen as a purely financial phenomenon but rather something that forms part of one's raison d'être.

ACCOUNTABILITY: A CHALLENGE FOR ORGANIZATIONAL INNOVATION

There can be no doubt that one of the problems still to be resolved regarding accountability is the clarification of a wide range of ways and procedures for gathering and presenting relevant information.[11] Deciding what to measure and evaluate is not always a simple task, especially when survival in a competitive world is at stake. Clearly, it makes no sense to indiscriminately increase the complexity of management systems in order to deal with an increasingly complex business environment. The triple bottom line (Elkington, 1998) is an excellent point of reference, but we should not forget that the challenge is to integrate different approaches rather than simply to amass data. Nevertheless, one recognizes that an improvement in accountability systems and models is needed. This is particularly vital if progress is to be made in reaching general agreement on standards and methodologies. But this does not mean that we should make do with bringing in new evaluation procedures and communication frameworks. The real challenge lies in treating accountability as something more than just a management tool for dealing with the pressures of the business environment.

A *network society* (Castells, 1996) is one that comprises complex interrelationships. One can no longer indulge in a company-centered discourse that puts each company at the center of the universe. Likewise, economic, cultural, and social trends can no longer be treated as things that only concern a company for reasons of business efficiency. A discourse that narrowly frames responsibility in cause-effect terms and enables companies to elude involvement is one that has had its day. A network society is one that comprises manifold and multidimensional relationships. And since we cannot conceive of nexus outside the network, responsibility (Jonas, 1979) necessarily becomes a question of co-responsibility (Drucker, 1993). One should note that shared responsibility is not a watered-down version of responsibility but simply one that takes account of the standpoint of global governance. It therefore makes sense to begin to talk about stakeholder dialogue (WBCSD)[12] instead of stakeholder relationships. In the network society, responsibility and dialogue are intrinsically linked (Apel, 1987; Pruzan & Thyssen, 1990).

Accountability is therefore not possible without a careful corporate reflection on the relationship between the corporation and its various stakeholders. In this respect, what is needed is to transform this relationship into an opportunity for learning and innovation. It is not simply an instrument for better management of interactions, negotiations, and public relations with stakeholders. The analysis should therefore go beyond simply identifying who can affect corporate actions and be affected by them. The starting point should be a recognition that the relationships between various actors in a network society are interdependent. From our standpoint, this is the position of the best companies involved in reporting, according to the report *Trust Us*. The report refers to these top companies as "Corporate Supersonics" and describes them in the following terms:

> By breaking through transparency's glass ceiling and other critical barriers, *Corporate Supersonics* move towards the goal of total transparency, operating from state-of-the-art accountability platforms, but still know how to maintain their biggest secrets from competitor's eyes. These companies are smart and highly networked—and will redefine the mainstream. The *Corporate Supersonics* may be a figment of our imagination today, but when

they arrive we will know them. These companies will use their reporting not simply to provide assurance, but also to offer prospectuses for transforming market towards CSR and Sustainable Development objectives—whether or not they use such language.[13]

Accountability thus becomes an expression of the relationship between the company and its stakeholders. Such a relationship is capable of generating knowledge and providing a corporate opportunity for innovation and learning—but only to the extent that it takes into account not just the interests of the company and various stakeholders but also the way the latter value the firm's contribution. This represents an opportunity for improvements insofar as accountability is seen as a chance for dialogue with various stakeholders concerning core company activities. This is because accountability is not a complement with neutral formats but something that takes on meaning and relevance only when it provides the opportunity for contextualized communication.

All this explains my earlier insistence that the need for standardization should not prevent one from speaking of spheres of accountability. As I have already pointed out, in the same way as spheres of justice (Walzer, 1983) depend on the goods distributed, spheres of accountability depend on the relationships and dialogue constructed with various stakeholders (which includes the working through of tensions and disagreements, if necessary). Basically, the idea is that the actors have to participate in establishing their criteria and the measures to be taken because it is the recipient who has to interpret the information. The interpretation will vary according to whether the information is provided in the context of dialogue or is simply a one-way process. Accountability requires not only informing people of what is going on but also knowing what is important to people. A good example of this is the experience of Ethical Accounting at the SBN Bank.[14] This approach involved the various stakeholders both in identifying the values they shared with the bank and the process of converting these values into a series of test statements, and in "dialogue circles" to discuss each year's results.

> It could be said that although Ethical Accounting Statements are important sources of information, the real impact of Ethical Accounting is the learning process it instigates and the significant changes in self-reflection it contributes to. In other words, the "product" (Ethical Accounting Statement) is important as a means of creating and maintaining the "process" (the ongoing stakeholder dialogue) and not vice versa, as is usually the case (Pruzan & Zadek, 1997, p. 71).

This leads us to pose a question. We have already said that accountability is impossible without people who are accountable. Furthermore, society also needs to be based on accountability, if accountability is to work. This presents an opportunity for business leadership. Corporate accountability requires organizational accountability. In other words, it would be lamentable if demands for accountability resulted only in an increase in external regulation (whether formal or informal) of companies. It should be noted that NGOs,[15] public administrations, civil society, and social movements are also subject to demands for accountability. These bodies have to act in a way that takes their specific social responsibilities into account, however laudable their professed aims may be. One cannot create multi-stakeholder value without multi-stakeholder accountability. This is the fundamental reason for insisting that accountability is not simply a relationship between impacts and actions but rather the result of publicly reworking each organization's purpose. The opportunity for business leadership lies in the role the business world can play in furthering progress towards the accountable society. Clearly, only companies committed to such a society can exercise this kind of leadership.

It should be noted that the need to link accountability with purpose and a corporation's raison d'être also has a pragmatic component. A company cannot attend to all the demands and expectations that could arise. Rather, a stakeholder dialogue based on the corporation's core values is essential for integrating significant relationships. Because relationships and accountability must be consistent with overall purpose, rather than being open-ended, we have gone beyond simple management of relationships to speak instead of constructing relationships: CSR should increasingly be seen as building relationships based on dialogue, and this is the context in which accountability acquires meaning. It involves putting corporate raison d'être at the center of things. Inquiry and the clarification of one's raison d'être is what allows us to decide what we want to achieve and what information is required to verify that we are acting in accordance with our objectives. This is what turns clarification of accountability into a deliberation on corporate success. Evidently, a company that defines success in only financial terms will limit itself to working with financial accounting systems.

Speaking of corporate values and of its raison d'être involves building a project and hence a corporate image of success. Without such clarification, no dialogue is possible with stakeholders because each project (and its associated image of success) involves different ways of valuing the company and creating a specific interpretational context for corporate practices. In short, all of our intentions, motivations, and actions are situated within these contexts (Lonergan, 1973). We can recognize what learning and innovation (and above all, success) are within the contextual framework for interpretation we set ourselves.

Perhaps one should really speak about a reflective accountability. This arises when a company creates a narrative that gives purpose to its actions, linking core values with policies and practices and creating a framework for critical dialogue with stakeholders and constructing legitimization of its actions. In this respect, we can say that accountability generates knowledge needed for continually improving and transforming a company's contribution to society.

This contribution, contrary to the assertions of some business ideologies, contains its own ambiguities and ambivalences. Not in vain are companies also among the main actors in the so-called *risk society* (Beck, 1986).

ACCOUNTABILITY: A CONTRIBUTION TO THE ETHICAL WEALTH OF NATIONS

When we speak about a risk society, we are referring to the threats and evils associated with economic development and technology. This is so much so that these risks are sometimes made light of in espousing the need for the very progress they presumably imply. In the risk society, the threats we perceive are not the result of forces of nature but rather the consequence of humanity's deeds. A further consideration is that the evils facing us seem to have grown in scale, to the extent that the risk society has also become the *fear society*, the society of fear management. Consciousness of risk is also undoubtedly a social construct—an amalgam of humanity's deeds and our perception of risk. That is why there is a struggle to foster public debate on defining risks and at the same time to decide whom we should listen to. But this, added to the lack of an institutional framework to tackle these issues, is precisely the reason why companies are under increasing pressure from public opinion and social actors to clarify whether corporations are part of the problem or the solution (though the answer may be both). It is also possible that companies are simply a source of risks that need to be controlled and faced where possible, and borne stoically where not. One should not be surprised at the increasing relevance of the precautionary principle and "moderation" as a component of responsible action.

Consequently, if our point of reference is the role of business in society, questions crop up that are intrinsically linked to reflections on companies. Do companies not also contribute to making the world a place for us? (Barber, 1998). "What kind of society are we creating through this globalization of business, trade, and consumption? What forms of governance are likely to be effective? Who will be responsible, and whose ends will they serve? Specifically, what are the new roles and responsibilities of business itself in this rapidly changing environment?" (Pruzan, 2001a, p. 62). These kinds of questions should not be seen as an unwarranted extension of corporate action. Such issues have to be put in a business-oriented way, but this orientation should also involve clarifying what business is about. In other words, it is not a question of companies turning into NGOs or usurping government functions. Seeing things in this light is sometimes the result of ingenuity and of expecting what should not reasonably be expected. However, such views are sometimes ill intentioned, espoused by those who want things to remain as they are. Just as some have spoken of rival visions in ethics (MacIntyre, 1990), we should not be frightened of putting forward the hypothesis of rival views on business in society (each view pursuing its own view of what legitimizes corporate actions).

> Issues of corporate social responsibility have been debated in the United States for decades, but there is still no commonly accepted answer to the question "To whom is the corporation responsible?" I submit that we haven't answered this question because it is not the right question to ask. Instead, we should be asking, "How can and do corporations contribute to constructing 'the good society'?" (Wood, 1991, p. 66).

This question is relevant for every country in the world.

In this respect, I believe one should ask what contribution companies make towards constructing the ethical wealth of nations (Donaldson, 2001). Clearly, this question could be posed simply from the viewpoint that the viability of companies is linked to the viability of the communities in which they operate. However, this is a far cry from being content with endlessly echoing the slogan "ethics pays." Returning to Donaldson, he stresses three key conclusions in relation to the ethical wealth of nations:

> 1. Morality may create economic advantages for nations in ways that extend beyond the notion of an idealized market; 2. In order for ethics to drive economic advantage, ethical concepts must rise to the status of intrinsic value; and 3. If claims for national ethical success factors are true, then nations should attend to the issue of moral education. (Donaldson, 2001, p. 25)

If companies have something to contribute on these three points (and I believe that they have), firms also have to see themselves as both economic and ethical spaces (Donaldson & Dunfee, 1999; Brytting, 2000). In a highly specific sense (i.e., in relation to corporate practices) and given a pluralist multicultural world, one should consider that companies constitute a moral space. It is precisely for this reason that we need to ask what values are fostered by and underlie corporate practices. From this point of view, accountability is a key element in committing companies to their values. Firms (and their managers) are also responsible for acting consistently with values that make up corporate identity and for rendering account for their actions from this standpoint.

This is why we spoke of reflective accountability. From the corporate point of view, building values is the process by which a company constructs itself as an economic and ethical space. We have already mentioned that such construction is relational rather than self-sufficient and autistic. It is also the result of a relationship with a network of stakeholders, which is possible only if it is based on building corporate core values. This multi-stakeholder relationship involves not only sharing information but also creating trust, comprehension, and knowledge. In a certain sense, one can say that accountability forms part of the process of creating corporate self-awareness. There has to be an intrinsic, operative relationship between accountability and corporate core values.

> An organization's values are not just an aggregation of each stakeholder group's values, even though it is a condition for organizational success that the organization's values respect its stakeholders' values. The organization's shared values are those values that emerge from the organization's ongoing self-reflexive, constitutive dialogue as to its identity, purpose, and relationships to its stakeholders. In other words, these are not just any values, but those values that can take on a socially integrative function and can be employed to justify the establishment of organizational goals. (Pruzan, 2001b, p. 278)

I believe this constitutes precisely the space of personal, professional, and corporate integrity. This space articulates social and corporate values that are internal to business practices. Integrity is therefore not something that is simply tacked on, but is rather the result of a proposal for a corporate vision and a willingness to convert that vision into policies and a management model.

> Corporate integrity means that companies have and maintain strong adherence to constructive core values that inspire value-driven behaviors with respect to stakeholders, along with high principles and standards. [. . .]Corporate integrity means that stakeholders are dealt with holistically and honestly, with their needs fully taken into consideration. Taking stakeholders into consideration does not necessarily mean that their needs and interests are always accommodated but rather that they are fully understood and that mutual accommodation can be achieved, with multiple sets of needs and interests understood and considered. (Waddock, 2001, pp. 34–35)

In a reflective accountability, an economic and ethical values-based identity is the link between integrity and accountability.

CONCLUSIONS

Accountability cannot simply be reduced to the level of a new management tool. Neither should it be considered an answer to the increasing social pressures and demands being made on companies. One cannot speak of CSR, integrity, and accountability without clarifying and explaining what we mean by business success. In turn, business success, rather than simply being a question of results, depends on the vision we have of companies and the role they play in society; accountability can be tackled only if we take this fact on board. The issue for the values contained within our practices is not optional, but rather inescapable and unavoidable; there are no practices that do not consciously or unconsciously bring values into play. That is why we need to face up to the fact that what we understand by success is not simply a question of figures but rather is constructed on our anthropological and social views. In this context, we may also have to face what is today still a paradox: Good financial results should not necessarily be equated with business success.

NOTES

1. "The license to operate is the activities which societies allow a company to undertake as a private, profit making enterprise. A company's license to operate, in other words, defines what it can and cannot do" (Burke, 1999, p. 10).

2. That is made clear by the survey by SustainAbility (2002) when it talks about "corporate nerds": "They risk missing out on the Big Picture—and most often still struggle to catch the attention of their boards. The real question is whether stakeholders can make any sense of all the data they are now being provided with."

3. The remit of the Global Accountability Report (2003). It should be emphasized that this report refers to accountability practices of companies, public institutions, and NGOs. This is not the time to elaborate this point, but I could not let it go by without expressing my conviction that it will be the next item on the agenda: the change from the corporate to the organizational, in other words, moving towards talking about organizational social responsibility and organizational accountability. Why should these demands be addressed only to companies?

4. Here I agree with Barber (1998) on the need to empower three aspects of society: the state, the market, and civil society. I also share his affirmation of their special nature. But I do not share what seems to me to be an exaggerated tendency to pit them against each other; specifically, I believe that "complex responsibility" also brings new ways of creating common and complementary ground between each field's organizations.

5. I have proposed that we use the term *complex responsibility* (Lozano, 2000b) in the same way we use the term *complex equality*.

6. Business without society, business and society, business in society.

7. Here I make use of MacIntyre's title (1990).

8. This reflection outwards from the company set out here is inseparable from a reflection inwards

towards the company. Put another way, I believe that no company can develop CSR without also developing an organizational ethic. I have presented my approximation to organizational ethics (2002).

9. As I will argue later, I feel that if we use the term *reflective practitioners* (Schön, 1987), we can similarly refer to reflective organizations.

10. Aspen ISIB Conference: Developing Balanced Leaders: The Role of Executive Education (http://www.aspeninst.org/isib/).

11. See for instance, GRI (http://www.global reporting.org), SA8000 (http://www.cepaa.org/), WBCSD (http://www.wbcsd.org), and AccountAbility (http://www.accountability.org.uk/).

12. World Business Council for Sustainable Development (http://www.wbcsd.org).

13. SustainAbility, 2002, p. 9. According to the study "The Magnificent Seven," these are The Co-operative Bank, Novo Nordisk, BAA, BT, Rio Tinto, Royal Dutch/Shell Group, and BP.

14. "Compared to an ordinary financial statement the bank's Ethical Accounting Statement includes a multiple of qualitative values while its financial accounting statements only focuses on the measurement of performance and profits, and expresses itself in terms of the narrow language of money. In addition, the bank's Ethical Accounting is not only aimed at its nearly 60.000 shareholders but is also targeted at all its stakeholders" (Pruzan & Zadek, 1997, p. 71).

15. See, for example, http://www.fundacionlealtad.org

REFERENCES

Apel, K. O. (1987). *Teoría de la verdad y ética del discurso*. Barcelona: Paidós.

Barber, B. R. (1998). *A place for us*. New York: Hill and Wang.

Beck, U. (1986). *La sociedad del riesgo*. Madrid: Taurus.

Berger, P. L., & Luckmann, T. (1967). *The social construction of reality*. New York: Doubleday.

Brytting, T. (2000). The preconditions for moral competence: Contemporary rationalization and the creation of moral space. In J. Verstraeten (Ed.), *Business ethics: Broadening the perspectives* (pp. 81–96). Leuven: Peeters.

Burke, E. M. (1999). *Corporate community relations: The principle of the neighbor of choice*. London: Quorum Books.

Carnoy, M. (2000). *Sustaining the new economy: Work, family, and community in the Information Age.* Cambridge: Harvard University Press.

Castells, M. (1996). *The Information Age: Economy, society and culture.* Cambridge: Blackwell.

Donaldson, T. (2001). The ethical wealth of nations. *Journal of Business Ethics, 31*(1): 25–36.

Donaldson, T., & Dunfee, T. W. (1999). *Ties that bind.* Boston: Harvard Business School Press.

Drucker, P. F. (1993). *Post-capitalist society.* Oxford, UK: Butterworth-Heinemann.

Elkington, J. (1998). *Cannibals with forks. The triple bottom line of 21st century business.* Gabriola: New Society Publishers.

Filella, J. (1994). Persona y organización: De estructuras convencionales a formas funcionales. In E. M. Recio & J. M. Lozano (Eds.), *Persona y empresa* (pp. 37–98). Barcelona: Hispano Europea.

Gellerman, S. W. (1986). Why "good" managers make bad ethical choices. *Harvard Business Review,* July/August, 85–90.

Goleman, D., Boyatzis, R., & McKee, A. (2002). *Primal leadership.* Boston: Harvard Business School Press.

Goodpaster, K. E. (1991). Ethical imperatives and corporate leadership. In R. E. Freeman (Ed.), *Business ethics: The state of the art.* Oxford: Oxford University Press. 89–110.

Habermas, J. (1973). *Problemas de legitimación del capitalismo tardío.* Buenos Aires: Amorrortu.

Jonas, H. (1979). *Le principe responsabilité.* Paris: du Cerf.

Levitt, T. (1960). Marketing myopia. *Harvard Business Review,* July/August, 45–56.

Lonergan, B. (1973). *Method in theology.* London: Darton, Longman and Todd.

Lozano, J. M. (2000a). *Ethics and organizations: Understanding business ethics as a learning process.* Dordrecht: Kluwer.

Lozano, J. M. (2000b). Companies and society: Ethical responsibilities. In J. Verstraeten (Ed.), *Business ethics: Broadening the perspectives* (pp. 11–40). Leuven: Peeters.

Lozano, J. M. (2002). Organizational ethics. In L. Zsolnai (Ed.), *Ethics in the economy* (pp. 65–186). Bern: Peter Lang.

MacIntyre, A. (1990). *Three rival versions of moral inquiry: Encyclopaedia, genealogy and tradition.* Notre Dame: University of Notre Dame Press.

Mackenzie, C. (1998). Ethical auditing and ethical knowledge. *Journal of Business Ethics, 7*(13), 1395–1402.

Pruzan, P. (1998). From control to values-based management and accountability. *Journal of Business Ethics, 17*(13), 1379–1394.

Pruzan, P. (2001a). Corporate reputation: Image and identity. *Corporate Reputation Review, 4*(1): 50–64.

Pruzan, P. (2001b). The question of organizational consciousness: Can organizations have values, virtues and visions? *Journal of Business Ethics, 29*(3), 271–284.

Pruzan, P., & Thyssen, O. (1990). Conflict and consensus: Ethics as a shared value horizon for strategic planning. *Human Systems Management, 9,* 135–151.

Pruzan, P., & Zadek, S. (1997). Socially responsible and accountable enterprise. *Journal of Human Values, 3*(1), 59–79.

Schön, D. A. (1987). *Educating the reflective practitioner.* San Francisco: Jossey-Bass.

Sennett, R. (1998). *The corrosion of character: The personal consequences of work in the new capitalism.* New York: W.W. Norton.

SustainAbility. (2002). *Trust us.* London: SustainAbility.

Verstraeten, J. (2000). Business ethics and personal moral responsibility. In J. Verstraeten (Ed.), *Business ethics. Broadening the perspectives* (pp. 97–112). Leuven: Peeters.

Waddock, S. (2001). Integrity and mindfulness: Foundations of corporate citizenship. *Journal of Corporate Citizenship, 1,* 25–37.

Walzer, M. (1983). *Spheres of justice.* Oxford, UK: Blackwell.

Wheeler, D., & Sillanpää, M. (1997). *The stakeholder corporation.* London: Pitman.

Wood, D. J. (1991). Toward improving corporate social performance. *Business Horizons,* July-August, 66–73.

10

SMALL FIRM ACCOUNTABILITY AND INTEGRITY

LAURA J. SPENCE

None of the existing work on integrity and accountability has considered the circumstances of the small firm owner-manager as a contextual example. The purpose of this chapter is to use empirical data on the life of the small firm to reflect on how and whether theory, designed on the whole from the perspective of managers in large firms, links to practice in small firms.

The chapter opens with a brief overview of the importance of small firm research, the difficulties of definition, and the limited existing research. The nature of the small firm is then considered. Some standard theoretical notions of integrity and accountability are briefly outlined prior to consideration of data from two research projects. In the discussion and concluding section, reference is made back to the theoretical work on integrity and accountability, demonstrating how different aspects of the two concepts are most relevant for small firms compared with large corporations.

Studying small firms is highly relevant since by far the majority of firms are small. The proportion of small firms in both the U.K. and the United States is in excess of 95 percent (Department of Trade and Industry, 2001; Small Business Administration, 2003a). Small and medium enterprises (SMEs) are significant to the economy in a variety of ways, accounting, for example, for 50 percent of business turnover in the U.K. (Curran & Blackburn, 2001, p. 2) and 50 percent of employment in the United States (Small Business Administration, 2003a).

Formulating clear pictures of the extent of the small firm population is, however, problematic. Different countries and institutions adopt differing definitions of *small*, *medium*, and *large* firms. Curran and Blackburn (2001, pp. 8–22) detail approaches including number of employees, turnover, sector-specific perspectives, self-definition, and combinations of these measures. Firm size definition is an important issue because, as argued in the next section, it is the nature of the small firm that makes it distinctive from larger counterparts. That nature is more common within firms with low numbers of employees, and an awareness of this in small firm research improves the credibility of the findings.

In this chapter, the official government definitions of *small firm* adopted in the United States and Europe are of most interest. The U.S. standard specifications of a small firm uses the North American Industry Classification system to distinguish between definitions of size, although the most common standard is fewer than 500 employees for small firms, with bigger firms being considered *large* (see Small Business Administration, 2003b). In the U.K. and Europe, the standard definitions by number of employees are below 50 employees (small firm) and 50–249 employees (medium firm) (Small Business Service, 2002).

There has been some previous work on small firms and business ethics–related issues in both the United States and Europe. In the United States, the main sources of relevant publications are the *American Journal of Small Business* (e.g., Chrisman & Archer, 1984) and the *Journal of Small Business Management* (e.g., Brown & King, 1982; Humphreys, Robin, Reidenbach, & Moak, 1993) and in Europe, the European Business Ethics Network conference on "Market Morality and Company Size" (Dunfee, Bowie, Hennessy, Nelson, & Robertson, 1991; Robertson, 1991; Ryan, 1991). In a review article, Thompson and Smith (1991) conclude that it is difficult to draw meaningful conclusions from the work that has been done because of the limited number of studies and "the need for larger sample sizes, more diverse geographic dispersion, and controls for the type of small business studied" (p. 41). Other criticisms could be added, notably the focus on quantitative research, which seems to be a preferred approach in the small business field in the United States. Definitions of small business vary widely in the studies, from fewer than 1,000 employees to fewer than 25.

In Europe, the late '90s and early 2000s saw some publications on ethics and small firms that demonstrated a closer understanding of the distinctive nature of the small firm (Quinn, 1997;

Spence, 1999; Spence, Coles, & Harris, 2001; Observatory of European SMEs, 2002; Department of Trade and Industry, 2002a, 2002b). Some common themes begin to emerge from this data, particularly the influence of differing industrial sectors and the common practice of acting on ethical and social concerns.

In this chapter, we continue previous work on ethics in small firms by focusing on the meaning of integrity and accountability for the small firm owner-manager. Two batches of empirical data are drawn upon in doing this. The first is from a study in the U.K. on ethics issues in small firms (fewer than 50 employees), which included 20 qualitative face-to-face interviews with small firm owner-managers and 100 telephone interviews (50:50 service/manufacturing split in each case).[1] The second study was a German–U.K. comparison of small- and medium-sized enterprises in relation to civic engagement and social capital, with 15 face-to-face qualitative interviews in Bavaria and 15 in West London. In this study, the sector focus was clearer, with equal splits of food processing/manufacturing, marketing services, and garages.[2] Only small firms (rather than medium-sized ones) in the study are drawn upon here.

THE DISTINCTIVE NATURE OF THE SMALL FIRM

Small firms are indeed different in nature, not just in size, from large firms (Holliday, 1995, p. 2). The following idiosyncrasies of small firms have been identified: independent and owner-managed; stretched by a broad range of tasks, limited cash flow, and survival challenges; mistrustful of bureaucracy; built on personal relationships; and controlled by informal mechanisms (Spence, 1999).

Perhaps the most significant perspective from the point of view of business ethics is the role of the owner-manager of a small firm. The normal assumption in business ethics and indeed management studies is that we refer to large multinational firms, with responsibilities to shareholders and the separation of ownership and control. In fact, the most common business form is the small independent trader, who is both owner and controller of the firm as an owner-manager. Lack of separation of ownership and control allows the key organizational decision maker to act as principal, not just agent. Hence the legitimacy of making personal decisions with company money, such as charitable donations, is considerable. Owner-managers, as Friedman (1970) argues, have the right to bring their own ethical attitudes to bear on business-related decisions almost as if they are dealing with their own money (Quinn, 1997, p. 121).

A second critical difference for the small firm is the orientation towards profit. Small firms are not typically seeking profit maximization (see Goffee & Scase, 1995; Spence & Rutherfoord, 2001). In analysis of some of the data from the first study mentioned, social and profit motivations of the owner-managers were mapped to build Table 10.1.[3] It should be noted that an individual owner-manager may adopt different positions in this table over time or in relation to different topics, not necessarily consistently acting only according to any one perspective. The table is simply a way of framing the profit and social orientations available to the owner-manager.

Table 10.1 Social vs. Profit Orientation of the Small Firm Owner-Manager

	Profit Perspective	
Social Practice	*Profit maximizing*	*Profit satisficing*
Socially inactive	1. Profit maximization priority	2. Subsistence priority
Socially active	3. Enlightened self-interest	4. Social priority

All of the owner-managers in the study recognized the need for some profit in order for their business to survive. Of key importance here is the distinction between whether profit earned should be the maximum possible (denoted *profit maximizing*), or whether a self-determined reasonable or satisfactory alternative was acceptable to the owner-manager, or indeed preferable to profit maximization (*profit satisficing*). The distinction between the motives of profit maximization versus profit satisficing is the division represented on the horizontal axis.

On the vertical axis, note was taken of whether the respondents were active in issues not directly related to the commercial success of the business. These activities have been called noncommercial, or social, activities. Where social practice does not occur, the category on the vertical axis is *socially inactive*. Where owner-managers falling into this category are clearly aiming to maximize profit, they would be represented by quadrant 1, *profit maximization priority*. Where the owner-manager is socially inactive and seeking a satisfactory rather than a maximum profit level, they are acting in a manner consistent with quadrant 2, *subsistence priority*.

Where social practice does occur, the vertical axis category is *socially active*. Social practices might include giving time or money from the business to charity, involvement with local schools or community groups, offering work experience opportunities, or contributing to caring for the environment. Each of these things has positive, nonpecuniary effects beyond the boundaries of the commercial operation of the business. A distinction made was whether or not these social activities are pursued because of their positive effects on profitability. This distinction separates quadrant 3 (*enlightened self-interest*) from quadrant 4 (*social priority*). Hence if the perspective on profit is one of maximization, and this includes some self-interested social practices (for example, fostering goodwill in order to cultivate business opportunities or making donations because they are tax-deductible), then the orientation is one of acting on social issues for extrinsic reasons (quadrant 3, *enlightened self-interest*). Alternatively, if social activities are done for intrinsic reasons, that is, for their own sake without pursuit of maximum profit, the orientation is one of prioritizing social issues over profit maximization (quadrant 4, *social priority*).

Very few of the respondents in the study on which this analysis is based showed signs of prioritizing profit maximization. A few, particularly marketing consultancies, were socially active for reasons of enlightened self-interest. Subsistence and social priority were found to be the most commonly represented orientations of small firm owner-managers. In light of these findings, it should be clear that "large firm" profit-maximization-for-shareholder-gain assumptions are inappropriate for the small business.

The Meanings of Accountability and Integrity

As with the existing work on integrity, writings on accountability have followed an overwhelmingly "large firm" perspective. In this section, some ideas are drawn from the work of critical management theorists on theoretical perspectives that may prove to be relevant to small firms.

Prompted by the Enron case, corporate accountability has recently become a critical part of debates on ethics, social issues, and business. At the simplest level, accountability can be seen in terms of reliable financial accounts reporting to appropriate bodies on the financial status of the corporation, that is, giving an economic account (Shearer, 2002, p. 546). Sinclair (1995, pp. 220–221) notes the most basic view that accountability "entails a relationship in which people are required to explain and take responsibility for their actions." Much has been written about the meaning of accountability in the accounting literature (cf. the journal *Accounting, Organizations and Society* published by Elsevier Science). The stakeholder alliance traces the notion of corporate accountability back to the beginning of corporate chartering in 1601 (Estes, 1999). In the latter half of the twentieth century, social and environmental issues were brought by some under the same rubric as financial accountability, i.e., corporations were also responsible for their social and environmental records. Unsurprisingly, these were translated into "corporate speak" by introducing the "triple bottom line" (Roberts, 2001a, p. 123) and using environmental, social, and indeed ethical audits and accounting. Linking accountability to the integration of corporate social responsibility in the business, Business for Social Responsibility (BSR) went to great lengths, ironically, to argue for the "business importance" of accountability, including arguments such as improved financial performance, reduction of costs, improved investor attractiveness, marketplace advantages, and enhanced organizational effectiveness (Business for Social Responsibility, 2002).

In the 1990s and thereafter, accountability has become synonymous with issues around corporate governance. A key point of concern is to "integrate accountability at the board level, leading to changes in who serves on the board, how social and environmental issues are handled by directors, and how the board manages itself and fulfils its responsibilities to investors and other stakeholders" (Business for Social Responsibility, 2002). Indeed in the U.K., the Cadbury Report (1992) and the more recent Hampel Report (1998) go to some lengths to advise on how corporate boards should best be organized for high standards of corporate governance and accountability. In the United States, the Sarbanes-Oxley Act of 2002 intends to protect investors by improving the accuracy and reliability of corporate disclosures. This law also acts as a protection for whistleblowers (Government Accountability Project, 2003), with the Public Interest Disclosure Act of 1998 the U.K. equivalent (see Public Concern at Work, 2003). These acts are in large part directed at ensuring the production of reliable accounting information and what Roberts (adopting Foucault's [1979] discussion of Jeremy Bentham's circular prison panopticon as an analogy) calls a "field of visibility" (Roberts, 2001b, p. 1552). It is the act of publishing accounting information that keeps the organization exposed to surveillance and scrutiny. Roberts notes that beyond formal recipients of information concerning accountability (i.e., shareholders and markets), the media also acts as a body to which corporations are accountable, including issues beyond the financial (Roberts, 2001a, p. 122).

Critical management theorists have taken a notably less "corporate" approach to accountability. Munro (1996, p. 16) considers the central question on the topic to be, "Who is accounting to whom, over what?" Given the less formalized, less public environment of the small firm as described earlier, there are grounds for considering that the approach of looking at account-giving may be a more helpful one than just reviewing the formal accounts familiar in large firms, which are not normally published by small firms anyway. Taking a sociological perspective, and focusing on the self as the "space" in which an account is given, Roberts (1996) goes on to discuss the individual, formal accounts previously discussed versus informal, social accounts. By *individual* he means processes of accountability that "generate a sense of self as essentially independent and autonomous with only an external and instrumental relationship to others" (Roberts, 2001b, p. 1551). The classic formal account would be the annual report. In contrast, informal social accounts are typified by processes of accountability that "confirm the self in ways that enact and reinforce a sense of the interdependence of self and other" (ibid.). This distinction is similarly reflected by Shearer (2002) in terms of accountability "for-itself" and "for-the-other," respectively.

Drawing on Levinas (1991), Roberts (2001a, p. 125) has argued that regimes of accountability (that is, ethical, social, and environmental) simply result in a defensive preoccupation with self, concerned with being seen to be doing the right thing rather than having a concern for others. He claims that the preoccupation becomes "how the self is viewed by others" and can become defensive in character, such that the person is concerned to avoid the shame and humiliation associated with the perception of inadequate performance (Roberts, 2001b). To reiterate, the concern is the effect on the self (shame and humiliation) rather than any impact on the other. Hence, the production of public (individual, formal) accounts previously noted and clearly relevant to large firms is simply a unidirectional delivery of a statement intended to protect the self rather than have any reciprocal element of accounting for oneself in response to the other. In short, it is simply fulfilling an obligation for instrumental reasons. Such approaches are called individualizing processes of accountability by Roberts (2001b, pp. 1551–1554).

An alternative approach is "socializing" processes of accountability, which acknowledge the interdependence of self and other (Roberts, 1996, p. 50). This understanding of accountability goes beyond the instrumental to include a moral perspective in relation to others. Roberts explains the concept in the following way. Socializing processes of accountability "are fostered, firstly, where there is relatively frequent face-to-face contact between people and, secondly, where there is a relative absence of formal power differentials." The possibility of lateral exchanges and two-way communication allows for the "opportunity to challenge, elaborate, clarify and question [and] has the potential to engage more fully the persona and thereby offer a fuller sense of personal recognition and identity. At the same time, such open communication draws people into a deeper sense of their relatedness to each other" (2001b, p. 1554).

Roberts goes on to link these processes closely with the establishment through dialogue of interdependence, reciprocal instrumental interests, reciprocal claims, and reciprocal senses of personal obligation, concern, and friendship. Relationships are thus seen in both instrumental and moral terms. Socializing processes of accountability are a normal feature of working environments and day-to-day life. For example, they may occur between colleagues, neighbors, customers, and employees.

To summarize, the forms of accountability identified in the current theoretical discussion include formal accounts in the shape of financial reports, corporate chartering, social and environmental accounts and audits, corporate governance, and various legal frameworks to protect processes of disclosure of unethical practices. Such formal processes can be called *individualizing processes of accountability*. A different approach is that of socializing processes of accountability, which incorporate a dialogic approach to accountability based on reciprocal relationships of mutual dependency. These are the perspectives that will be drawn on in considering accountability for small firms.

The work on integrity is more firmly embedded within the business ethics field than the discussions on accountability. Lynn Sharp Paine (1998, pp. 335–337) helpfully identifies four characteristics related to integrity: moral accountability (acceptance of personal responsibility), moral commitment (a set of defining beliefs or principles), moral conscientiousness (a desire to do what is right), and moral coherence (consistency in commitments, judgments, beliefs, and expression). Paine does not argue that integrity requires all of these aspects to be present, but suggests that integrity is generally identified with one or more of these characteristics (ibid., p. 335).

Paine's notion of moral accountability is consistent with the view of De George on integrity. De George defines *acting with integrity* as "acting in accordance with one's highest self-accepted norms of behavior and imposing on oneself the norms demanded by ethics and morality" (1993, p. 6). He emphasizes the autonomy that this allows since standards are self-imposed, and he links this to responsibility. He comments, however, that although "integrity requires norms to be self-imposed and self-accepted, they cannot be entirely arbitrary and self-serving" (De George, 1993, p. 6); they should be ethically justifiable. This is coherent with Paine's category of moral conscientiousness and possibly moral commitment, where the norms are also a clear set of defining beliefs or principles.

Moral courage is mentioned as an element of integrity by both Solomon (1992, p. 170) and De George (1993, p. 22). Reflecting further on Paine's notion of moral conscientiousness, Solomon defines *moral courage* as the will and willingness to do what one knows one ought to do (Solomon, 1992, p. 170).

The question of whether integrity is an individual characteristic or something that can be held by a group is a recurring one. Solomon sees *integrity* as a "complex of virtues" (1992, p. 168) that a person accordingly either has or lacks (p. 170). Paine has written on "organizational integrity," identifying hallmarks of an effective integrity strategy (1994). She does comment, however, that it is a matter of debate whether "moral integrity can be properly ascribed to entities other than individuals" (1998, p. 336). Since in the research presented in this chapter we are considering integrity of the owner-manager rather than the firm as the unit of analysis, this potential problem is not evident. Nevertheless, as the number of members of each firm is small, there may be some grounds to argue that any perspective exhibited by the dominant owner-manager could influence those around him or her, which is normally the whole firm, that is, the summation of people in the organization.

The definitions arrived at by De George, Solomon, and Paine draw either implicitly or explicitly on an assumption of *integrity* as a feature of concern for managers of large organizations. Paine, for example, cites Sears, Roebuck and Company, Martin Marietta Corporation, and Novacare in her discussion of how organizations can influence individual integrity (1998). In view of the fact that so little work has been done on ethics or indeed integrity in small firms, the four aspects of integrity identified by Paine and supported by the work of De George and Solomon will be used as an initial lens for looking at small firm data.

EMPIRICAL EVIDENCE ON SMALL FIRM ACCOUNTABILITY AND INTEGRITY

In this section, data are presented that suggest that employees are the key group to which small firm owner-managers are accountable. Integrity is considered in terms of the client and competitor relationships. While these elements may also be present in the large firm scenario, they are, it is argued, the dominant locus of concern in terms of accountability and integrity for the small firm.

As is normal with qualitative research, it would be inappropriate to make generalized claims from the small samples researched. However, the citations presented illustrate how patterns of behavior have been discerned for these contextualized samples. It would be fitting and desirable for these findings to be tested further in future research.

Accountability: Employees

In the research data gathered, a strong feeling of accountability to employees was detected. Small firm owner-managers often describe the close relationship that they feel they have with their employees and the associated obligations. It is employees to whom the owner-manager has to be answerable on a day-to-day, indeed face-to-face, basis.

For example, owner-managers often cite their employees as one of the key reasons for staying in business.

Respondent: How come I am still in it, what motivates me these days? One wife, three children, a house, thirty-eight members of staff and the fact that there is still a challenge there. (BE9S, service, computer supplier, 38 employees)

This can be seen, quite explicitly, in terms of a responsibility, as demonstrated by this owner-manager:

Respondent: I have a responsibility to see that this company is profitable, to ensure that they (the employees) have got continuity of income and work and that's my responsibility. (BE15M, manufacturer, adhesives and tapes, 11 employees)

Another employer suggested that he would have liked to shut down the business but kept it going, even though times were very difficult, in part because of the employees. He puts his obligation to the employees in moral terms. The second respondent cited here suggests that he could not just shut down the business if he "won the lottery"; the motivation is clearly neither personal nor shareholder gain, but continuity for employees.

Respondent: I have always been in business and it would have been easy for me to shut the business down over the years when you get bad debts but you sit there and you say . . . to yourself it is not only going to be your family that has been affected but you are going to affect ten other people's lives as well. So if there is a way forward then there is a way forward. . . . Morally I have an obligation and I hope that the people who work for you appreciate what you are trying to do. (BE6M, manufacturer, precision engineers, 6 employees)

Respondent: They are my friends. I don't socialize with them outside work but I consider them to be my friends. . . . In the remote circumstances that I win the lottery on Saturday, not very likely, I couldn't just stop and go away, they are people. (BE19M, rubber parts manufacturer, 12 employees)

The form that this feeling of responsibility can take, right down to ensuring that employees keep a roof over their heads, is spelled out by two employers thus:

Respondent: When members of my family say, "Why do you work so hard?" I say it is because other people's mortgages depend on me and it is a tremendous burden. I really feel this. I really feel desperately responsible. (BE2S, service, performance improvement consultancy, 4 employees)

Respondent: It is not only the fact that you thought it was just your house on the line and your own future, it is actually theirs as well and that's a big responsibility when you are making decisions. . . . I think honesty (with your employees) is the best policy in life. (BE20M, manufacturer, interiors, 10 employees)

This perspective is featured not only in U.K. small firms. In the German sample, when asked about his relationship with the employees, an example response was the following:

Respondent: Yes, we are very friendly. It is simple really, since we are so small, and we put an awful lot of value on a good working atmosphere. We [the owner-managers] also work out there [in the garage]; I am normally in overalls too. (SCD2G, garage owner, 4 employees)[4]

In the studies drawn on for this research, no other single group was referred to so consistently as a body with which the owner-manager held a dialogue and which the owner-manager felt responsible for and accountable to. The descriptions seem to be more in keeping with a "socializing" than an "individualizing" interpretation of accountability. There is no reason to suspect that this was an interview bias; the interviews were not directly orientated towards an employee perspective, but rather consisted of prompted discussions around relationships with different stakeholder groups. Small firm owner-managers consistently prioritized accountability to employees over other relationships. Nevertheless, as with much interview-based research, no verification was sought through triangulation or observation.

Integrity: Clients and Competitors

From studies done on small firm owner-managers, the key partners (in terms of integrity) would often be cited as clients and, contrary to the usual appreciation by firms of important relationships, competitors.

Demonstrating integrity in terms of moral coherence and consistency is an important element of the client relationship for small firms. The following owner-manager makes an explicit link to trust and ethics and describes how mutual trust is a necessity in the client relationship. She also illustrates a "desire to do what is right," linking to Paine's notion of moral conscientiousness,

which the owner-manager refers to as an inner faith not to exploit clients.

Respondent: Trust is also a part of business, and I link it with ethics. There are times when we say we can't do a job—it doesn't happen very often—but it is very important that all clients trust us. It is very important that the people we work with within an organization, not only that they trust us but, interestingly enough, that we trust them and that we feel that they are not involved in doing something that we wouldn't believe in as to how a company should run. We have not had to test that out very much but it is an inner faith that it is important that we don't go in there to screw people for the sake of it. It is important that our clients trust us. (BE2S, service, performance improvement consultancy, 4 employees)

Moral coherence was formulated as an instrumental necessity for survival and growth by the following architect.

Respondent: Most of them are quite fussy who they go to. You can't afford to upset them. They go to people they can trust because they haven't got time to be leaning over your shoulder all the time. ... I think that to survive and grow you have to have a good reputation. (BE11S, service, architects, 5 employees)

Similarly, the following respondent notes that you can get business in the longer term by being honest with people.

Respondent: You can often pick up business by being honest with people; sometimes people come back to me [because of this]. (BE4S, service, fluid power services, 1 employee)

As client relationships develop and clients are assured of the small firm's integrity, the relationship with the owner-manager has been "tested" and can be deepened, as in the following case.

Respondent: It is important that the customers can trust you because sometimes, where you are working on projects, there is an element of secrecy in some firms. A couple of companies I work with are developing new products or developing completely new ideas, and it takes time and it took me two years before one customers would let me see exactly what he was doing. (BE6M, component manufacture, 6 employees)

In some sectors, the relationship with competitors is key for the small firm and is one in which they must ensure that integrity is maintained, particularly in terms of consistency in commitments (moral coherence), as in the following example:

Respondent: You have got to be honest with how you deal with your competitors, because it is very incestuous, this marketplace. You might give business to me as an external consultant today and be my competitor tomorrow, and good consultants who are freelance will understand that and they will go for it because it is a job and they will do the job well. It is very hard to hide anything. (BE7S, marketing, 7 employees)

One respondent explained why he wouldn't poach customers:

Respondent: It's a small world, engineering, certainly around here, and if I found out that one particular company has got half a dozen customers and I start knocking on their doors you quickly get a bad name. (BE6M, component engineering, 6 employees)

Integrity in relation to clients and competitors was illustrated by the overriding trajectory of moral conscientiousness and coherence in the research data gathered. As with the previous section on employees and accountability, this conclusion was arrived at from reflection on data gathered in interviews with the owner-managers

only. Encouragingly, there was no indication that the respondents suspected that the data would be used for anything other than academic research purposes, and they did not question the promised protection of individual firms through confidentiality. Hence the respondents were not motivated to speak of their integrity in relation to customers and competitors. It is concluded that customers and competitors were identified openly by the owner-managers, from among other stakeholders, as a key focus of integrity issues.

DISCUSSION

While other notions of accountability and integrity have not been ruled out, here the relevance of accountability to employees and of integrity in relation to clients and competitors has been illustrated. It is important to note that these observations would not be surprising to academic commentators on small enterprises, since they draw out well-known characteristics. In this final section of the chapter, the empirical perspectives are put in the context of the theoretical standpoints presented earlier and the broader milieu of small firm research.

From the small firm research presented here, there are indications that the form of accountability to employees might be quite different from that in large organizations. Accountability is not about the competence of monitoring and auditing procedures in the small firm, which would reflect Roberts' notion of individualizing effects of processes of accountability (2001b). Formalized procedures are unlikely to be found in organizations of fewer than 50 people, where there is no real need for bureaucratic procedures to achieve daily tasks. Accountability takes place in a face-to-face environment with processes of accountability resulting in socializing effects. As noted previously, Roberts linked socializing processes of accountability through dialogue to interdependence, reciprocal instrumental interests, reciprocal claims, and reciprocal senses of personal obligation, concern, and friendship. We see many of these aspects reflected here, for example the interdependence of employee and employer in order to provide stable employment and to keep the business running successfully. These factors are of reciprocal instrumental interest to both parties. The mutual obligation is also personal, in that there is a basis of friendliness. It should be noted, however, that there were hints at other groups such as the family. This could be an area of further research. The findings are consistent with Table 10.1, which illustrates the role that subsistence, and ultimately ongoing survival, has for the small firm owner-managers.

Accountability to employees can perhaps be attributed to the overwhelmingly social nature of employment in the small firm. Typically there is an emphasis on informal rules and social control coupled with an absence of formal control of employment relations (for corroboration of this, see Ram, 1994; Holliday, 1995; Benmore & Palmer, 1996). Work is seen as being "both a technical and a social activity" (Kitching, 1994, p. 115). Ram suggests that "inherent in the employment relationship is a basic antagonism between capital and labour [*sic*]. Together with this basic antagonism, however, are elements of co-operation since employers need to secure workers' willingness to work while workers rely on the firms for their livelihoods" (Ram, 1999, p. 15). It is perhaps the keen awareness of the employees' reliance on the employer for their livelihood that is different from the larger firm, where decision makers will not normally have personal contact with the individuals who are affected. For example, in the large organization, the director of human resource management is unlikely to be familiar with the family members of all the employees, or aware of the personal living arrangements of those who might lose their jobs if a downsizing program is entered into. In the small firm, as one of the owner-managers pointed out previously, personal friendship between the owner-manager and employees can exist. Jeopardizing the employment relationship is much more like letting down a friend than in the larger organization. Unsurprisingly, the feeling of responsibility to "friends" is an

enormous burden. It is in this respect that we can talk of owner-managers being accountable through socializing processes to employees.

In short, in small firms there is usually a physical proximity, which may be commensurate with moral proximity. Jones (1991) argues that proximity is one of the factors that increase the likelihood of moral behavior. Whereas in the large, depersonalized firm, a decision to downsize might mean little more for a senior manager than delegating the task of reducing staffing costs by 30 percent, in a small firm the owner-manager making an equivalent decision has a much more personalized process to confront. The owner-manager will invariably be well aware of the implications for each employee of a job loss, giving them the resources to take into account not only those most suitable to keep for survival of the business, but also the personal cost to the employees of job loss. This might encompass knowing which ones have just bought a new house, which have elderly parents who need special care, or indeed which could easily get a job elsewhere or have no dependents. The practical working proximity of the small firm brings with it information and familiarity that potentially humanize the workplace resulting, it is proposed, in a moral proximity not pervasive in the large firm, although it may be re-created at department level. Departments, however, do not have the autonomy that an independent firm does, since there is always a higher authority that can be "blamed" for any difficult decisions that may have to be taken.

The notion of accountability to employees may take a more instrumental form in small firms than has been indicated thus far. It is possible that for the small firm owner-manager the most fundamental form of accountability is the act of the regular weekly or monthly payment of wages. This is hinted at in some of the aforementioned quotations. In this respect, perhaps there are similarities between delivering a regular favorable dividend to shareholders for the large firm and delivering a regular favorable salary to employees. The distinction of the lack of formal procedures remains, however.

Whatever channels of accountability there are in the small firm to the employees, they are most likely to be on a face-to-face informal basis without third-party scrutiny beyond the need for basic accounting regularity. From this research, it seems that Roberts' notion of individualizing forms of documented accountability to shareholders, financiers, and the media are unlikely to be customary in small firms. In contrast, socializing forms of accountability, particularly in relation to employees through dialogue and continuity of employment, look to be the main locus of accountability due to the physical and moral proximity of employer and employee.

The integrity of the small firm owner-manager has been identified, in this chapter, as particularly important with respect to clients and competitors. As with close relationships to employees, the connection between members of the small firm and clients is often on a first-name basis. According to the evidence in the research presented here, owner-managers acknowledge that they are too small to do anything but be honest and act with integrity; there are no hiding places in the small firm. This key finding should be researched further—perhaps with a data-gathering technique, such as participant observation, that is more suited to eliciting sensitive information regarding, for example, instances of poor practice.

Returning to Paine's characterization of integrity in terms of moral accountability, moral commitment, moral conscientiousness, and moral coherence, the small firm case seems to be reflected in some of these traits more than others.

First, since there are no systems, rules, or nameless colleagues to hide behind, integrity in the small firm requires a high degree of moral accountability in terms of personal acceptance of responsibility by the owner-manager. This may in some cases extend to personal financial responsibility if the firm has not been incorporated with limited liability. If we accept this, it remains unclear whether being a small firm owner-manager requires one to act with integrity or whether the type of people who run their own firm have more integrity than corporate managers.

These questions need further investigation. What is clear, however, is that small firm owner-managers can gain goodwill and hence improved trading conditions with customers by acting with personal integrity.

A second of Paine's characteristics of integrity that seems to be relevant is that of moral conscientiousness, namely, the desire to "do the right thing." As indicated earlier, commentators on integrity have highlighted its personal nature and its reliance on the autonomy of the individual. Independence and autonomy of action are very important motivators for the small firm owner-manager (Goffee & Scase, 1995, pp. 3–5). Hence in making decisions about how to behave with customers, competitors, employees, and other stakeholders, owner-managers go through their own reflections and awareness of what they are doing. Owner-managers were quite explicit about this in the research done, as shown in the following two citations:

Respondent: What I care about is whether I feel that I have done what is right for me, and that's what it is about. I can't tell you what guides those things. It could be parents, it could be schools, it could be religious teachings when you were a lot, lot younger, who knows, but that's what it is. I know for one thing I don't want to get to the top by treading on people on the way and I know by that I am never going to be a multi-multi-millionaire. (BE9S, computer supply and training, 38 employees)

Respondent: We don't fiddle our expenses with our clients—I suppose everybody would say that—but it is open because I wouldn't know how to live with it if I found out we had fiddled them. (BE2S, service, performance improvement consultancy, 4 employees)

Personal autonomy and moral conscientiousness, the old test of being able to sleep at night with a clear conscience, is highly relevant to the small firm owner-managers in this study. This perspective of integrity, one would hope, is also available to directors and managers of large firms. Further research could usefully investigate the extent to which members of different-sized organizations feel these emotions at a personal level.

Paine's remaining two characteristics of integrity seem less clearly relevant to the small firm. Moral commitment, having a set of defining beliefs or principles, is unlikely to be registered in any formalized sense. Of course, the owner-manager may follow a particular religious perspective, industry code, or personal belief system, but it does not seem necessarily to be the case. In large firms, it is invariably a requirement that stated missions and codes of conduct be approved by the organization's leaders. This may take the form of a requirement to sign a document stating this fact. At least this indicates a coherent system of beliefs. Small firms are extremely unlikely to have any kind of written code. The situation is similar in terms of moral coherence, that is, consistency in commitments, judgments, beliefs, and expression. While a small firm owner-manager may demonstrate these aspects of integrity, a key characteristic of the modus operandi is the individualized service and relationship offered. It may be true that consistency is required in the owner-manager's relationship with one particular client, but there seems to be no compelling reason why that should be standard to all clients, since this would work against an individual service. Nevertheless, there could be consistency in beliefs and judgment even if these are applied differently in differing contexts and according to the owner-manager's assessment of different relationships.

Integrity towards competitors is an aspect that is counterintuitive to those familiar with the sometimes-aggressive competitive environment of large corporations. It is worth adding an additional note about the competitor relationship. It has been argued elsewhere that competitors are important stakeholders for small firms in many sectors where there is a relationship of mutual support (Spence et al., 2001). It was found that we "should not be surprised by competitors who talk of each other as friends" (ibid.). This comes about because for the small firm competitors are often seen as colleagues in the same sector rather than organizations to fight against and ideally conquer. The situation can be different when the competitor is a large, powerful firm. Small firm colleagues are seen as comrades with whom a fight against a more powerful external threat can more efficiently be waged. Furthermore, competitors in a local area are often literally made up of ex-colleagues, perhaps ex-apprentices, who were trained by the owner-manager and have now opened up their own business but regularly return to the former boss for advice. Like employees, competitors are very much humans with faces and names and a common bond of camaraderie.

The picture of the world of the small firm owner-manager has been painted rather rosily in this chapter. The full situation is naturally somewhat more complex. Further research is needed which distinguishes with greater clarity between sectors, size, geographical location, gender, history of the owner-manager, etc. The reliance on data gathered from the owner-manager is also a potential weakness, with owner-manager perspectives being readily conflated with the "small firm." It would be useful to understand whether employees, clients, competitors, and family agree that the owner-manager is accountable to them and acts with integrity. Comparisons to medium and large firms may demonstrate a less distinct difference between small firms and their larger counterparts. For example, many large firms are divided into branches and divisions that may well have the face-to-face relationships of the small firm, albeit with externally imposed structures, controls, and reporting procedures. The research reported on here was not gathered specifically for the purpose of improving understanding of integrity and accountability. This had the advantage of allowing reflection on secondary data without the potential pollution of leading questions, but data commissioned with the objective of unraveling the world of integrity and accountability in small firms would certainly add helpfully to the discussion.[5]

NOTES

1. Thank you to the Institute of Business Ethics and Kingston University for funding this project. For detailed results of the study, see Spence (2000) and Spence and Rutherfoord (2001). Data taken from this study is denoted *BE*.

2. Thank you to the Anglo-German Foundation and Brunel University for funding this project. My gratitude to my colleagues at the Center for Corporate Citizenship at the Catholic University of Eichstaett for permission to use our joint data in this chapter. The project team members were René Schmidpeter, Andrea Werner, André Habisch, and Keith Dickson. Data taken from this study is denoted *SC*.

3. Further details on the identification of the categories in this table are in Spence and Rutherfoord (2001).

4. Original German: Doch sehr freundlich. Das ist einfach, dadurch dass man so klein ist, ähm, und wir sehr großen Wert auf ein gutes Arbeitsklima legen, dadurch dass wir auch draußen arbeiten, also normalerweise bin ich auch im Overall.

5. Thank you to George Brenkert for his helpful comments and useful suggestions in the editing of this chapter.

REFERENCES

Benmore, G., & Palmer, A. (1996). Human resource management in small firms: Keeping it strictly informal. *Small Business and Enterprise Development, 3*,109–118.

Brown, D., & King, J. (1982). Small business ethics: Influences and perceptions. *Journal of Small Business Management, 20*(1), 11–18.

Business for Social Responsibility. (2002). Accountability. *BSR White Papers*. Retrieved March 4, 2003, from http://www.bsr.org/BSRResources/WhitePaperDetail.cfm?DocumentID=259

Cadbury, A. (1992). *Report of the Committee on the Financial Aspects of Corporate Governance.* London: Gee Publishing.

Chrisman, J., & Archer, R. (1984). Small business responsibility: Some perceptions and insights. *American Journal of Small Business, 9*(2), 46–58.

Curran, J., & Blackburn, R. (2001). *Researching the small enterprise.* London: Sage.

De George, R. (1993). *Competing with integrity in international business.* Oxford, UK: Oxford University Press.

Department of Trade and Industry. (2001). *Small and medium sized enterprises (SME) statistics for the UK, 2000.* Retrieved April 19, 2002, from http://www.sbs.gov.uk/statistics

Department of Trade and Industry. (2002a). *Engaging SMEs in community and social issues.* London: Department of Trade and Industry.

Department of Trade and Industry. (2002b). *Business and society: Corporate social responsibility report 2002.* London: Department of Trade and Industry.

Dunfee, T., Bowie, N., Hennessy, J., Nelson, K., & Robertson, D. (1991). Firm size and employees' attitudes about ethics: Some preliminary empirical evidence. In B. Harvey, H. van Luijk, & G. Corbetta (Eds.), *Market morality and company size* (pp. 103–117). London: Kluwer.

Estes, R. (1999). *A brief history of corporate accountability.* Retrieved March 4, 2003, from http://www.stakeholderalliance.org/history.html

Foucault, M. (1979). *Discipline and punish.* Harmondsworth, U.K.: Penguin.

Friedman, M. (1970, September 13). The social responsibility of business is to increase its profits. *New York Times Magazine*, pp. 32–33, 122–126.

Goffee, R., & Scase, R. (1995). *Corporate realities: The dynamics of large and small organisations.* London: International Thomson Business Press.

Government Accountability Project. (2003). *Corporate accountability.* Retrieved March 4, 2003, from http://www.whistleblower.org/getcat.php?cid=23

Hampel, R. (1998). *Committee on Corporate Governance.* London: Gee Publishing.

Holliday, R. (1995). *Investigating small firms: Nice work?* London: Routledge.

Humphreys, N., Robin, D., Reidenbach, E., & Moak, D. (1993). The ethical decision making process of small business owner/managers and their customers. *Journal of Small Business Management, 31*(3), 9–34.

Jones, T. (1991). Ethical decision making by individuals in organizations: An issue-contingent model. *Academy of Management Review, 16*(2), 366–395.

Kitching, J. (1994). Employer's work-force construction policies in the small service sector enterprise. In D. Storey & J. Atkinson (Eds.),

Employment, the small firm, and the labour market (pp. 103–146). London: Routledge.

Levinas, E. (1991). *Otherwise than being or beyond essence.* Dordrecht: Kluwer.

Munro, R. (1996). Alignment and identity work: The study of accounts and accountability. In R. Munro & J. Mouritsen (Eds.), *Accountability: Power, ethos & the technologies of managing* (pp. 1–19). London: Thomson Business Press.

Observatory of European SMEs. (2002). *European SMEs and social and environmental responsibility.* European Commission, 2002/No. 4: Enterprise Publications.

Paine, L. S. (1994). Managing for organizational integrity. *Harvard Business Review,* March-April, 106–117.

Paine, L. S. (1998). Integrity. In P. Werhane & R. E. Freeman (Eds.), *Blackwell encyclopaedic dictionary of business ethics* (pp. 335–337). Oxford, UK: Blackwell.

Public concern at work. (2003). *UK Public Interest Disclosure Act.* Retrieved March 10, 2003, from http://www.pcaw.co.uk/legislation/legislation.html

Quinn, J. J. (1997). Personal ethics and business ethics: The ethical attitudes of owner/managers of small business. *Journal of Business Ethics, 16*(2), 119–127.

Ram, M. (1994). *Managing to survive—Working lives in small firms.* Oxford, UK: Blackwell.

Ram, M. (1999). Managing autonomy: Employment relations in small professional service firms. *International Small Business Journal,* January-March, 13–30.

Roberts, J. (1996). From discipline to dialogue: Individualizing and socializing forms of accountability. In R. Munro & J. Mouritsen (Eds.), *Accountability: Power, ethos & the technologies of managing* (pp. 40–61). London: Thomson Business Press.

Roberts, J. (2001a). Corporate governance and the ethics of Narcissus. *Business Ethics Quarterly, 11*(1), 109–128.

Roberts, J. (2001b). Trust and control in Anglo-American systems of corporate governance: The individualizing and socializing effects of processes of accountability. *Human Relations, 54*(12), 1547–1572.

Robertson, D. (1991). Corporate ethics programs: The impact of firm size. In B. Harvey, H. van Luijk, & G. Corbetta (Eds.), *Market morality and company size* (pp. 119–136). London: Kluwer.

Ryan, L. (1991). The ethics and social responsibility of U.S. small business: The "overlooked" research agenda. In B. Harvey, H. van Luijk, & G. Corbetta (Eds.), *Market morality and company size* (pp. 89–102). London: Kluwer.

Shearer, T. (2002). Ethics and accountability: From the for-itself to the for-the-other. *Accounting, Organizations and Society, 17,* 541–573.

Sinclair, A. (1995). The chameleon of accountability: Forms and discourses. *Accounting, Organizations and Society, 20*(2–3), 219–237.

Small Business Administration. (2003a). *Office of advocacy.* Retrieved March 10, 2003, from http://www.sba.gov/advo/stats/

Small Business Administration. (2003b). *Table of size standards.* Retrieved March 10, 2003, from http://www.sba.gov/size/sizetable2002.html

Small Business Service. (2002). *Small and medium enterprise (SME)—Definitions.* Retrieved April 19, 2002, from http://www.sbs.gov.uk/statistics/smedefs.asp

Solomon, R. (1992). *Ethics and excellence: Cooperation and integrity in business.* The Ruffin Series in Business Ethics. Oxford, UK: Oxford University Press.

Spence, L. J. (1999). Does size matter? The state of the art in small business ethics. *Business Ethics: A European Review, 8*(3), 163–174.

Spence, L. J. (2000). *Priorities, practice and ethics in small firms.* London: Institute of Business Ethics.

Spence, L. J., Coles, A.-M., & Harris, L. (2001). The forgotten stakeholder? Ethics and social responsibility in relation to competitors. *Business and Society Review, 106*(4), 331–352.

Spence, L. J., & Rutherfoord, R. (2001). Social responsibility, profit maximisation and the small firm owner-manager. *Small Business and Enterprise Development* (Summer), 8(2), 126–139.

Thompson, J., & Smith, H. (1991). Social responsibility and small business: Suggestions for research. *Journal of Small Business Management, 29*(1), 30–44.

PART III

Integrity and Accountability of Global Business

I t is quite understandable that one major approach to the topic of corporate integrity derives from the perspective of the accounting and auditing scandals that occurred at the turn of the millennium. These discussions lead to the examination of the appropriate procedures for accounting and auditing, as well as financial reporting. But problems in these areas do not exhaust the ways in which corporations may lack integrity. Bribery, the use of gifts and entertainment to influence business decisions, payoffs, and so on are additional forms of discreditable activities in which some businesses have engaged, both in their home countries and in other countries throughout the world. As forms of corruption, these are other significant ways in which businesses may lack integrity.

In Part III, **Frank Vogl** leads off with an unflinching portrayal of the ethical (and legal) charges in the past several years against many U.S. corporations. These types of charges have resulted in far-ranging cynicism regarding corporate activities and the belief, by some, that corruption is pervasive across American (and Western) business. For much of this time, leading CEOs have been extremely quiet (at least publicly) regarding the reforms needed to correct these problems. Vogl takes this silence to indicate a sense of denial regarding the problems these CEOs and corporate America face. Agreeing with Berenbeim's views, Vogl argues that changes are needed in corporate governance. They also agree that the changes needed are not simply legal ones, but ethical ones that will place corporate integrity back at the center of corporate behavior. Vogl emphasizes, however, that these changes are required not merely in their activities in the United States but throughout the world.

Unfortunately, too many business leaders in the United States have turned a blind eye to important developments in Europe and other parts of the world that might suggest better methods of corporate governance, accounting, and auditing, as well as ways of determining executive compensation. One of the reasons for this corporate provincialism, Vogl suggests, is the belief by U.S. executives that American corporations operate by higher corporate governance and ethical standards than the rest of the world. And though the recent scandals weaken this claim, many corporate leaders in the United States continue to hold this view. This is especially true when it comes to questions of bribery and corruption.

Drawing upon studies by Transparency International, Vogl rejects the view that cultural factors are crucial in the views of people around the world regarding corruption. Universally it is regarded as wrong. The importance of this is twofold. First, there can be no excuses for behavior that involves bribery or corruption in other countries, because "that is just how they go about business." And second, "corruption is the starting point in many countries for discussions about corporate behavior." This second point is crucial because American corporations are also judged by how they are perceived to respond to corruption, and the perception of many outside the United States is that American corporations engage in a number of different forms of corruption, including not merely bribery, but also "speed money" (facilitating payments) and relying on the pressure from the U.S. federal government to help win them contracts.

The response to these charges, Vogl urges, is for corporate America to change its ways. Corporate leaders must speak out against bribery and corruption, as well as against the willingness to compromise ethical standards for profit. They must also speak out for ethical business reform and the exercise of corporate responsibility. Such actions will go a long way toward restoring the integrity and reputation of American business.

In sharp contrast with the stance taken by Frank Vogl, **Manuel Velasquez** argues that in too many instances people have seen corruption where corruption doesn't exist. Instead, something else is going on that is much more closely bound up with the cultures of the societies in which business takes place. In short, context matters, and it matters very much. The upshot is that corruption is not so easy to identify as many have contended. Indeed, in some cases, practices that Westerners have called corruption are seen as morally benign exchanges from the perspective of members of the local culture.

Velasquez's argument for this view involves several steps. First, he focuses on corruption as it occurs between political or administrative officials and business. He excludes from his discussion cases in which a business interferes with the judicial system. Second, Velasquez contends that the reason behind why it is wrong to corrupt a public official might be based on either an internal evaluation or an external one. External evaluations appeal to some moral standards outside that office and its activities and generally refer to the bad consequences of engaging in corruption. On the other hand, some have claimed that such acts may also have good consequences. Velasquez does not focus on this kind of evaluation. Instead he trains his argument on internal evaluations, which appeal to rules that are viewed as legitimately part of the office or activity engaged in by the public official.

The reason why corruption should be seen as wrong from this perspective is that the behavior violates some normatively viewed proper form of governance in which the officials should engage. But since such views may differ from society to society, there cannot be a single, universal view of what is unethical (and hence corrupt) in these situations. To develop this answer, Velasquez portrays three different normative conceptions of government—the competitive state, the patrimonial state, and the personalized state.

In each of these cases, Velasquez contends that certain features of the state and actions condoned by it that are essential for corruption to be said to take place (at least in certain Western countries) may be missing in other countries. The upshot is that in looking at instances of corruption, our evaluations must be relativized to the participants' conceptions of the state. This leaves us with many other questions to answer, including how businesspeople are to respond when they must invoke both internal and external perspectives. The aim of Velasquez's chapter, however, is to enrich our understanding of this discussion by filling in some of the daunting challenges that will arise from the internal perspective. In doing so, he provides a forceful case that context matters a great deal in considering issues of corruption or, indeed, of corporate integrity. Viewed from the internal perspective, Velasquez has argued, multinational corporations (MNCs) may not always be guilty of the corrupt practices they are accused of in the West, because the contexts in which they operate do not support that interpretation.

Richard De George also holds that MNCs are not responsible for many of the ethical problems in developing countries that are attributed to them. However, he takes a rather different line of argument to reach this conclusion. Instead of relying on the conceptual and/or ethical relativist implications of the Velasquez chapter, De George appeals to the importance of the law and other background institutions. Though he acknowledges the distinction between law and ethics, he is nevertheless at pains to argue that the law has played a crucial role in protecting moral companies and in ensuring a minimal level of corporate moral behavior in others. However, when it comes to international business, the background of laws and institutions that businesses rely on is no longer present. And though nongovernmental organizations (NGOs) may play important roles here, there is a need for adequate background institutions in order to foster responsibility and accountability.

Accordingly, when it comes to developing countries, the development of corporations of integrity that may be held accountable requires that those countries pass and enforce appropriate legislation, give people a voice in their country, and acknowledge deficient conditions within their borders that need to be changed. In addition, international legal coordination is needed to outlaw problems that are generally recognized (e.g., computer virus programs, working conditions, child labor) but which lack a coordinated response. Because these conditions are frequently absent, De George concludes that MNCs are not responsible for many of the problems in developing countries that are attributed to them.

International agreements may serve as a kind of surrogate for international legislation fulfilling some of the functions of background institutions on a worldwide level, absent global legislature. For example, the World Trade Organization (WTO) could coordinate legislation. Still, De George acknowledges several weaknesses in the WTO that render it less effective and legitimate than is desirable.

Finally, De George argues that the audited implementation of international codes for corporations should also play a role in developing global corporations of integrity. Not all corporations have codes of ethics. Some of those that do may have codes that are simply ideal statements, not sufficient for accountability. Apart from these problems, there needs to be agreement on, and monitoring systems of, general standards and codes. Corporations of integrity also require external, independent, and public audits, as well as openness regarding the nature of and adherence to relevant codes. In short, though ethics is important in the development of corporate integrity, it cannot bring about changes by itself.

Bruce Moats offers yet a different approach to the concern that each of the authors in Part III share, namely, how to address the effects of globalization in a manner compatible with corporate integrity. Still, he shares a number of important views with De George. In this chapter, Moats focuses on the need to better manage those effects of globalization that result in worker exploitation and mistreatment, the abuse of rights, and economic growth at the cost of economic equity. Increasingly, businesses have taken on greater responsibilities in these areas. In particular, Moats notes, Levi Strauss and Company's (LS&CO's) commitment to integrity (as a form of ethical conduct and social responsibility) resulted in LS&CO's first comprehensive code of conduct, as well as its Global Sourcing and Operating Guidelines. Acting upon these standards has meant that, on occasion, LS&CO

has had to forgo the lowest-cost sourcing options, as well as terminate business with some companies.

The development of such codes by corporations and by international organizations is an ongoing, ever-evolving process. Some may involve rather specific standards, while others may include more aspirational objectives. A legalistic approach, such as that which characterizes U.S.-based codes of conduct, tends to delineate standards that are practical, measurable, and enforceable. European codes tend to include goals and broad global initiatives that companies should strive to attain. Moats concedes that there are benefits and limitations to each approach. Questions of implementation are more easily answered by legalistic codes. On the other hand, aspirational codes provide more ready incentives for continual improvement and progress.

Lacking an international authority to enforce codes, MNCs have turned to their own internal monitoring systems, as well as to third-party monitors and coalitions that focus on monitoring. Both of these may be effective, but they have important limitations. For lasting, positive change, stakeholders at different levels need to be involved, including governments, NGOs, employees, and suppliers. A commitment and partnership among these multiple stakeholders is central in the development of the next frontier for codes of conduct. These codes will involve a shift from monitoring (policing) or aspirational models to those in which the capacity for continuous compliance and improvement of businesses (and communities) is expanded and realized.

Finally, **John Dienhart** focuses on the joint efforts that Moats discusses that are required for the development of global corporations of integrity. He argues that business ethics, far from being the endeavor of some academic specialty or even of businesspeople, is a multi-institutional endeavor of which those two groups are only a part. In addition, civil society organizations (CSOs), NGOs, and governments must also be involved in this project to bring about a (global) business ethics. Beyond this, however, he perceives that these various disparate groups are increasingly coalescing around a broad view of sustainability that includes social justice, economic health, and environmental integrity. Both this view of CSR and the multiple institutions that are part of this endeavor are captured, Dienhart contends, in the UN Global Compact, which involves both a research and an action network. In the last part of his chapter, Dienhart examines a number of conceptual, normative, and practical issues that must be answered for this multi-institutional Sustainability Project itself to be sustainable. Though they are not a focus of Dienhart's chapter, the views he presents here nevertheless provide a theoretical opening for the development of the many different kinds of partnerships between businesses and NGOs, CSOs, and international governmental organizations (IGOs) that are presently taking place. It is ironic that one of the criticisms of the UN Global Compact (one that it is in the process of correcting) is that it did not include, at its creation, a principle against corruption. But this brings us full circle, since the problem of corruption is at the center of Vogl's chapter that begins Part III.

11

THE U.S. BUSINESS SCANDALS

Perspectives on Ethics and Cultures at Home and Abroad

FRANK VOGL[1]

M any U.S. business leaders respect the highest standards of integrity and would agree with the view expressed by James F. Parker, CEO of Southwest Airlines, who told *BusinessWeek*, "I think it's unfortunate that the misdeeds of a few have had the effect of creating questions and undermining confidence of business in general" (Byrne, 2002, p. 31). But this perspective needs to be weighed against another, which Paul Volcker, a former Chairman of the Federal Reserve Board, voiced in the same magazine: "Corporate responsibility is mainly a matter of attitudes, and the attitudes got corrupted . . . in the 1990s. We went from 'greed is good' being said as a joke to people thinking 'greed is good' was a fundamental fact" (Byrne, 2002, p. 31).

"What happened?" asks William J. McDonough, president of the Federal Reserve Bank of New York. Speaking at Trinity Church in New York on September 11, 2002, he said,

Sadly, all too many members of the inner circle of the business elite participated in the over-expansion of executive compensation. It was justified by a claimed identity between the motivation of the executives and shareholder value. It is reasonably clear now that this theory has left a large number of poorer stockholders, especially including employee stockholders, not only unconvinced, but understandably disillusioned and angry. The policy of vastly increasing executive compensation was also, at least with the brilliant vision of hindsight, terribly bad social policy and perhaps even bad morals. (McDonough, 2002)

The public mood in the United States since Enron's collapse in late 2001 is so distrusting of business that even corporations that consistently seek to demonstrate ethical leadership have found themselves vilified. Merck and Coca-Cola, for example, were both featured in prominent articles that erroneously suggested that their accounting practices have fallen foul of the Securities and Exchange Commission (SEC). The SEC approved their accounts, but the negative articles challenged their reputations.

Corruption[2] at the helm of American business leadership will take time to erase. It calls for recognition by CEOs of the need to reexamine the full panoply of corporate activities, in their domestic and their foreign operations, to ensure against corrupt practices. This reexamination has barely started, and this should be a matter of public concern.

In the first 12 months after the bankruptcy of the Enron Corporation in December 2002, the focus of business was almost exclusively on legal issues—companies faced official investigations, civil suits, new requirements as a result of the Sarbanes-Oxley Act, new regulations by the SEC and other authorities, including the National Association of Securities Dealers (NASD) and the New York Stock Exchange (NYSE). But restoring trust in Corporate America will require more than legal compliance by chief executive officers and boards of directors. It will require a major effort to place sound business ethics at the center of corporate operations, at home and abroad.

Numerous corporate leaders appear to be in denial as to what is required, or unconvinced that they need to do more than comply with new legal requirements. Calls by organizations, such as the Ethics Resource Center (ERC), for a heightened focus on corporate ethics have largely fallen, it appears, on deaf ears (Ethics Resource Center, 2003). Suggestions from abroad that U.S. business adopt governance approaches that strengthen management accountability have so far attracted little attention on this side of the Atlantic. Awareness that the scandals have added ammunition to foreign antiglobalization organizations, who accuse U.S. firms of ignoring their international social responsibilities, appears so far to have cut little ice in Corporate America. Recognition that reform at home must be visibly undertaken in tandem with reforms in the ways U.S. companies operate overseas is, so far, minimal among the major institutions representing U.S. business, such as the Business Roundtable and the U.S. Chamber of Commerce.

Neither American business leaders nor politicians have given any indication of recognizing the damage that has been done to America's standing in the world by the corporate scandals. Negative perceptions of the behavior of U.S. multinational corporations have contributed to rising anti-American sentiments abroad. The scandals have provided ammunition to foreign critics who have long depicted U.S. firms as giant leviathans striving to exploit the poorer countries of the world. France's *Le Monde Diplomatique,* for example, published an article in March 2002 under the headline "Enron, symbole d'un système" (Enron—symbol of a system) that argued, "The extraordinary aspect of the Enron affair is that it is not extraordinary at all." It then suggested that corruption is pervasive across American business and politics. Similar views have been widely expressed in influential publications across the globe.

The negative international perceptions may damage the ability of U.S. business leaders to influence debates and agreements in official multilateral organizations, from the World Trade Organization to the United Nations, which will influence the shape of globalization in the years to come. As Jeffrey E. Garten, Dean of the Yale School of Management, has noted, "Unless they [CEOs] attempt to dig themselves out of the reputational black hole that they are in, they cannot be major players on the national and international stage in the way they should be" (Garten, 2002, p. 30).

The scandals opened the doors to investigations by the attorney generals of various states, by the SEC, by the Internal Revenue Service, by Congressional committees, and by other official bodies. The findings have combined to yield an unacceptable face of capitalism—a business landscape where concerns about ethical actions and doing the right thing are absent. Business leaders took risks on compliance with laws, rules, and regulations when they thought U.S. enforcement was weak. They adopted an "it's just about in accord with compliance requirements" approach and aggressively exploited legal and regulatory loopholes, with the assistance of lawyers and accountants more concerned with their own profits than with conflicts of interest and integrity.

A catalog of actions has soiled the reputation of American business leadership. How wretched corporate values have become when

- Boards of directors grant executives multimillion-dollar loans that they know will never be repaid, while simultaneously agreeing to plans to lay off thousands of employees (for example, WorldCom, Enron, and Tyco).
- Securities firms advise customers to buy junk so that these firms can make quick profits at the expense of the customers who trust them (for example, prosecutions of numerous New York investment firms by New York AG Eliot Spitzer).
- Some firms pay foreign bribes because they see little risk of being prosecuted under the Foreign Corrupt Practices Act (FCPA), while many firms use a clause in this law to make extensive modest payments to foreign government officials, while never considering that this is unethical (see subsequent sections of this chapter).
- Major American companies that seek to dodge U.S. taxes by finding a legal loophole that enables them to place their corporate "legal" headquarters in an offshore tax haven (for example, Tyco registered in Bermuda, and "Enron created 881 offshore subsidiaries, 692 of them in the Cayman Islands, as part of its strategy to avoid taxes," according to a report by U.S. Congress experts) ("Tax Moves by Enron . . . ," 2003, p. C1).
- Corporate executives make vast fortunes through convincing their boards of directors to grant them vast stock option allocations, which are not expensed on the balance sheet, then find ways for their corporations to pay vast fees to accountants so that they can assist the executives to develop offshore tax shelters to avoid paying U.S. income tax (for example, top executives at Sprint who were forced to leave the company in January, 2003) (Lublin, 2003).

While corporate lawyers and accountants may justify moving a corporate headquarters under law from the United States to Bermuda by arguing that such a move is in line with maximizing value for shareholders, it serves as a blunt example of placing profits above integrity. Justice Oliver Wendell Holmes said, "Taxes are what we pay for a civilized society."

Decency and business ethics, relative to taxes and every other aspect of corporate behavior, are what a civilized society requires. While numerous U.S. business leaders have been publicly forthright about the need for far-reaching reforms, many have been silent. This attitude by CEOs may indicate caution prompted both by the advice of their lawyers to keep their heads down for fear of potential litigation and by the advice of their public relations staff to avoid becoming embroiled in controversy. Then again, numerous CEOs may still be in denial.

DOMESTIC CHALLENGES

Denial

> Do many CEOs still believe that being in compliance and having expensive legal counsel on hand is an adequate response to today's pressures?

> Do they believe that the reforms and the public outrage are excessive?

> Do they consider that these scandals are merely the loud bangs of burst bubbles and that when stability returns to the stock markets and the U.S. economy it will be back to business as usual?

There is a broad sense that, as *The Economist* magazine put it, "there is corruption without contrition" ("Corruption without Contrition," 2002, p. 59).[3] The silence by many corporate leaders indicates a sense of denial, which is compounded by abundant evidence that, despite all of the scandals and investigations, companies can continue to operate in the manner seen in the pre-Enron crisis days. Top executives can continue to demonstrate extraordinary greed, corporate lobbyists can continue to work to dilute regulations designed to make corporate leaders more accountable to shareholders, and consulting firms can continue to engage in conflict of interest situations and in false advertising with abandon.

- For example, there are numerous instances of CEOs winning large increases in compensation as their corporations have suffered profit declines. Just to illustrate, on the very day that Bernard Ebbers was fired as CEO of WorldCom, the E*Trade Group, the online brokerage firm, which had a $241 million loss in 2001, announced that it was awarding its (now former) chief executive, Christos M. Cotsakos, $77 million in total compensation. It was business as usual.

- In August 2002, as an increasing number of banking scandals were being revealed by New York State Attorney General Eliot Spitzer, a senior Citigroup executive, Jack Grubman, who was in the midst of the investigations, was granted a $32 million severance pay award. It was business as usual.

- Mr. Grubman, as well as Citigroup, retained the services of the same law firm (Wilmer, Cutler & Pickering). So too did the board of directors of WorldCom, which asked the law firm to pursue an investigation of the company's scandal (Weil, 2003). The firm did so, but despite a host of business transactions between Citigroup involving Mr. Grubman, WorldCom, and Mr. Ebbers, the law firm determined not to include these banking ties in its investigation. It was business as usual.

- In early August 2002, *The Financial Times* ran a series of articles under the title "Barons of Bankruptcy," which noted that the 200 top executives of the 25 largest corporations that went bankrupt in previous months in the United States had together taken home compensation of at least $3.3 billion (Cheng, 2002, p. B6; Hill, 2002, p. B5). As they prospered, tens of thousands of American workers lost their jobs and their retirement funds. It was business as usual.

- Prominent in many of the scandals that have emerged are the world's leading auditing firms. Arthur Andersen expired and KPMG was prosecuted by the SEC for knowingly agreeing to the publication of false earnings statements by Xerox. The head of KPMG had at one point privately discussed the Xerox situation with SEC Chairman Harvey Pitt (a former lawyer to KPMG), and he made no public apology when this was revealed in the press.[4] Coincidental with these press disclosures, KPMG ran major newspaper advertisements where the message was, "We believe integrity is a constant. That the process of maintaining it is never ending. That getting there requires foresight and vigilance. And that with integrity and objectivity comes greater strength and freedom for our capital markets. Over the years we have committed ourselves to upholding integrity and objectivity. . . ." (KPMG, 2002).

The Ethical Challenge in U.S. Business

Corporate denial and business-as-usual attitudes need to be replaced by broader willingness on the part of business leaders to introduce meaningful corporate governance reforms. Continuing disclosures of scandals and the heavy press reporting of investigations is generating exceptional pressures on business leaders to pay more attention to business ethics.

The challenge to CEOs starts at home, but they dare not ignore global operations. So far, the responses to the crisis by U.S. CEOs are narrow and limited to compliance with the main provisions of the Sarbanes-Oxley Act of 2002 and the SEC's approaches. These compliance actions, on their own, may not strengthen corporate ethical cultures. But, while the SEC may be looking more closely at firms for legal violations, there will be others who will be looking at business behavior more broadly. The combination of zealous journalists, aggressive civil society organizations, and the Internet means that major firms have nowhere to hide and, as Walter van de Vijthe, a member of the Management Committee of Royal Dutch Shell, noted in the 2001 Shell Report, "the eyes of the world are on us." The accuracy of this phase was proven in March 2003 when this top Shell executive and Shell Chief Executive Officer Sir Philip Watts were both forced to resign in a major public scandal, when it was revealed that they had persistently failed to report vital negative information on Shell's proven oil reserves.

Restoring public trust will demand that CEOs move beyond compliance. The public is fully aware that, as noted by Stuart Gilman, former president of the Ethics Resource Center (ERC), "You cannot legislate ethical behavior" (Gilman, 2002). Many experts are now promoting a host of actions that corporations should be taking in addition to the new laws and regulations. There is no single formula that can be applied to all companies, but there is a strong sense among corporate chief ethics officers that a series of basic measures are imperative for many companies now to strengthen a fundamental corporate ethical culture. Following a mid-2002 meeting of the ERC's Fellows Program, which brought together a number of chief ethics officers from large corporations, Mr. Gilman suggested that there was consensus, for example, around a set of actions, including the following:

- Rules and regulations will not yield change without corporate leaders who shape a company culture that has an unwavering commitment to ethical behavior in all aspects of the business.
- Ethics officers must be significant members of a corporation's governance process. Boards of directors should demand that the ethics officers have direct access to them as well as to senior management. This would include regular meetings with the audit committee of the board.
- Under no circumstances should a company's code of conduct be waived.
- Leadership's commitment to ethical behavior must be backed by a solid ethics program with appropriate communication and training mechanisms to build a foundation of integrity.
- Business leaders must set a clear example of ethical behavior and establish "doing right" as a business priority, not merely meeting the minimum required standards.

The press has not only highlighted the hard facts of the scandals but has also contributed to public education on leadership ethics. *BusinessWeek*, for example, has asserted that the CEO must set the company's moral tone by being forthright and by taking responsibility for any shortcomings. Not only has it devoted many cover stories to business ethics, it has also opined that if the challenge for executives in the '90s was to transform corporate behemoths into nimble competitors, then the challenge in coming years will be to create corporate cultures that encourage and reward integrity as much as creativity and entrepreneurship.

The slow progress in placing integrity back at the center of the domestic corporate governance system, however, is in accord with scant evidence that U.S. business leaders even recognize that they need to pursue reforms that strengthen confidence abroad—confidence of foreign investors, business partners, foreign customers and suppliers, and host governments in countries where they trade and invest.

INTERNATIONAL PRESSURES AND ISSUES

American business appears to be largely blind to foreign concerns and pressures, such as

1. pressures by foreign business leaders to secure greater understanding by their U.S. peers of European corporate governance and accounting approaches;

2. pressures by international organizations, such as the United Nations, together with civil society organizations, to convince leading U.S. corporations to become more proactive on global social responsibility issues;

3. pressures to convince U.S. business leaders that it is no longer viable (even if it once was) to pursue a high ethical standard at home while applying lower ethical standards abroad.

Corporate Governance

Representatives of U.S. business have consistently promoted the U.S. system of corporate governance across the world as the gold-plate model. Today, that system is tarnished as television shows the financial chiefs of Enron and WorldCom in handcuffs, as it describes the lavish multimillion-dollar lifetime retirement benefits of Jack Welch, the former CEO of

General Electric, and as it highlights greed at the top of business. America's system of good corporate governance may, as a result, sound to many American and foreign ears like an oxymoron.

While in many respects the U.S. system of corporate governance, with its myriad rules designed to make officers accountable to shareholders and to protect the rights of shareholders, is superior to those that exist in most other countries, the scandals have shown that there is scope for improvement. However, so far, there has been little evident interest on this side of the Atlantic about learning, for example, from intense debates on corporate governance in Germany and in Japan. In both countries, top executives earn a fraction of the amounts regularly given their U.S. peers. In Europe and in Japan, "American-style" remuneration is widely reported in the press as obscene.

Recent years have seen substantial corporate governance discussions in Europe where shareholder groups have set their sights on curbing "American-style" compensation.[5] There has been a widespread rejection of the kind of lavish stock option schemes that exist in the United States and of mechanisms that permit top executives to borrow vast sums from their corporations (Bernard Ebbers of WorldCom borrowed more than $350 million, while Ken Lay of Enron borrowed over $70 million).

American business leaders have mostly dismissed European arrangements designed to curb the powers of the CEO and management by ensuring that two individuals, not one, hold the offices of corporate chairman and CEO. Paul Volcker has been a vocal advocate of the U.K. system where major corporations have an "independent" nonexecutive chairman alongside a full-time corporate CEO. The division reduces the ability of just one person to dominate the corporation. There are very few major U.S. multinational corporations that have a split system at the top, such as The Charles Schwab Corporation, where founder Charles Schwab is the chairman and David S. Pottruck is the CEO. Another example at one time was AOL Time Warner, where due to a merger, Steven Case (formerly of AOL) was

chairman and Richard Parsons (formerly of Time Warner) was CEO. But no sooner did Mr. Case retire in January 2003 than the board of directors consolidated power in the hands of Mr. Parsons and made him CEO and chairman. Then, at Lucent Technologies, when former company veteran Henry Schact announced that he would be retiring as chairman, the board of directors moved swiftly to give this title to Lucent President and CEO Patricia Russo and thus consolidate her power.

In Germany, major corporations have two-tier board systems, where a supervisory board of nonexecutive directors has the responsibility to oversee a management board of full-time executives. Again, the system aims to ensure clear control over managers and accountability. There is no current consideration of this approach in the United States, despite the absolute failure of controls in numerous enterprises.

Another area of corporate governance relates to accounting approaches. The Europeans embrace a system of international standards that, above all, establish very clear broad principles that set the approaches that auditors need to follow. The U.S. system, by contrast, pays scant attention to broad principles and is a vast mass of detailed rules. The leaders of the International Accounting Standards Board, the Bank for International Settlements, and other European experts have argued that had the principles-based approach been in place in the United States, some of the balance sheet scandals here would have been avoided. Leaders of the U.S. auditing profession are reviewing this with European counterparts, but so far there is scant evidence that U.S. business leaders are interested in fundamental change on this front.

In sum, despite the scandals, U.S. business leaders do not appear to be studying approaches tried and tested abroad that ensure heightened control and accountability at the top of business. A record of abuse, starting with Enron, does not seem to have stimulated initiatives over and above new laws and regulations to ensure greater control over powerful full-time corporate executives. This situation is evident abroad amid building skepticism about whether the greed creed will ever be replaced by a system that places value on corporate accountability.

Corporate Social Responsibility

Negative foreign perceptions of U.S. corporate values easily spill into social responsibility areas. The scandals have added fuel to the fire of civil society organizations that have long attacked companies like Nike (over labor conditions in Asia), Exxon (over oil spills going back to the Valdez), Monsanto (over genetically modified foods), Enron before it went bankrupt (over corruption in India), and numerous others. Radical antiglobalization organizations have gained strength by mounting campaigns that depict all U.S. multinational corporations as unethical (McDonalds, for example, has been a prominent target). More mainstream civil society organizations—be they related to organized labor, to development groups such as Global Witness, or to environmentalists such as Friends of the Earth—have been more focused but no less scathing of some U.S. enterprises.

Charges by radical antiglobalization organizations of irresponsible social actions by U.S. corporations abroad may not be balanced, but they have had a public impact across Europe and have influenced leading media there. Many U.S. executives have been deaf to the foreign charges, dismissive of the civil society monitoring organizations, and ignorant of the degree to which the ethics of U.S. business leadership is questioned abroad. Today, the questioning is not only by radicals but also by respected politicians, academic institutions, and social responsibility–oriented investment funds.

Numerous U.S. corporations, such as Ford and General Motors, have long taken pride in their global environmental approaches, their policies on workforce diversity, their workplace health and safety conditions, and their philanthropic contributions to multiple communities. Some companies, such as Merck and DuPont, have demonstrated exceptional leadership. But, overall, U.S. corporations have been less visible

than their European rivals in responding to public calls for evidence of their commitment to global social responsibility.

- European firms, for example, have shown greater interest than their U.S. competitors in participating in and learning from the UN Global Compact, established by UN Secretary-General Kofi Annan to strengthen global corporate social responsibility.
- European CEOs provided the leadership in seeking business involvement and promoting business positions at the Summit on Sustainable Development in Johannesburg in August 2002.
- European firms have been in the forefront of pushing for an upgrading of systematic business reporting on environmental actions, while most U.S. major multinational corporations have been relatively slow in this area. A key corporate reporting program is that developed by the Global Reporting Initiative (GRI), which has attracted far more European companies than U.S. ones (www.GRI.org).
- European firms have been far more active than their U.S. counterparts in developing Web sites to demonstrate to the public their detailed approaches to social responsibility. Few, if any, U.S. firms can match the Web sites of such U.K. companies as ICI, Prudential, Tesco, Shell, Tate and Lyle, BP, and many others.

Many European firms have specifically assigned responsibilities for social responsibility issues, and for communicating with external civil society and other groups on these issues, to senior executives. This is rarely the case in large U.S. multinational enterprises. The comparatively low priority assigned to global social responsibility issues in leading U.S. companies can undermine their influence in international discussions to set standards in such fields as the environment and labor conditions through the GRI, the UN Global Compact, and other bodies. And the corporate malfeasance that has come to light has further weakened potential U.S. corporate influence in these forums. So far, there appears to be little evidence that U.S. business leaders are aware of these consequences, let alone doing much to remedy the situation.

Values and Cultural Perspectives

One of the reasons why the international implications of the U.S. corporate scandals may not have fully registered here at home may rest in the continuing belief in some business leadership circles that U.S. corporate governance standards and ethics are superior to those abroad.

This is a sweeping assertion that is difficult to prove. It is based in part on anecdote. Sometimes, businesspeople point to suggestions that European corporate leaders use secret Swiss bank accounts to hide income and/or obtain far greater corporate benefits, rarely fully reported to shareholders, than their American counterparts.[6] But such assertions, even if valid, now tend to be undermined by the evidence that has come to light of massive self-enrichment schemes by top executives at such companies as Tyco, Adelphia, and WorldCom, as well as reports of hundreds of top U.S. corporate executives using questionable tax shelter schemes to evade large-scale U.S. tax liabilities.

Leaders in corporate governance on this side of the Atlantic, such as Ira Millstein, the senior partner at the law firm of Weil, Gotshal, and Manges, have been forceful advocates of U.S. approaches in international forums by striving to demonstrate, for example, that U.S. shareholders demand greater transparency and accountability from publicly listed corporations than do their foreign counterparts. The malfeasance in the United States that came to light in 2002 weakens this line of argument.

On the issue of international bribery, many U.S. business executives and corporate lawyers engaged in international commerce are swift to suggest that foreign firms, foreign government officials, and the broad public in foreign countries in general (and thus foreign cultures) are willing to accept lower ethical standards than exist in the United States. For a long time, this assertion was based on the fact that the United States was the only country that made it a criminal offense for its enterprises to bribe foreign government officials (FCPA).[7]

The perception in U.S. business that foreign countries and peoples are more accepting of bribery easily translates into assertions that the standards of U.S. business ethics are higher than those existing in foreign corporations. This notion may continue to lead U.S. business leaders to be complacent about reviewing the practices of the foreign operations of their companies, despite the lapses in domestic corporate behavior highlighted by the post-Enron investigations.

The question of whether some peoples are more tolerant of lower ethical standards than are others has concerned Transparency International, the leading global anticorruption nongovernmental organization, as it publishes an annual Corruption Perceptions Index. There has been interest in determining whether respondents to a broad range of surveys around the world on corruption have similar perspectives and attitudes with regard to the bribery of public officials. Dr. Johann Graf Lambsdorff of the University of Passau, Germany, who serves as a senior advisor to Transparency International and originated the index, has researched these issues.

Lambsdorff concludes,

> Some societies are characterized by a high level of trust among their peoples, while others may lack this, and investigations suggest this has an impact on levels of corruption. However . . . , on exploring cultural roots for perceptions of corruption we find, at least from the data for the CPI, that there is convergence, irrespective of whether locals or expatriates have been surveyed. We take this as an indicator that cultural factors do not seem to be crucial to the outcome. To put it more cautiously, up to now there is no evidence that cultural factors as they relate to samples of local or expatriate business people play an important role when it comes to assessing levels of corruption.[8]

An array of opinion polls and analyses by Lambsdorff[9] and others suggest that across the world, the general public is outraged by corruption as defined as the abuse of public office for personal gain. At the broad public level in country after country, there appears to be very little public tolerance for bribery, and in many countries there is clear frustration that governing elites are failing to enforce antibribery laws. Admiral Ram Tahiliani, chairman of Transparency International–India (a country where he is the first to admit there are major corruption problems today), stated, "There is nothing in our culture which condones bribery, grand larceny or petty facilitating payments. Old customs in India during the days of Maharajas or Moghuls dictated that you took a gift when you went to see the monarch. This was offered publicly and an enlightened monarch ensured that you went back with a bigger gift."[10]

The Corruption Example

Corruption is the starting point in many countries for discussions about corporate behavior. It is the key concern of people in developing countries and in Central and Eastern Europe in relation to business integrity. The broad publics in these countries understand that bribe-taking by their government officials undermines social welfare systems, increases poverty, destabilizes the economy, and can wreck hopes for building democracy and an efficient economy. Corruption plays a major role in public debates in many developing countries and in those in Central and Eastern Europe, especially around elections. The election campaign in late 2002 in Brazil and the one in early 2003 in Kenya are excellent examples of this.

This is not always well understood in major U.S. corporations, and many in U.S. business may underestimate the reputational damage done abroad by perceptions of the willingness of U.S. firms to bribe officials. This underestimation starts with the perception by numerous leaders of large U.S. enterprises that there is very widespread adherence in the United States to the FCPA. This view contrasts with data evident in the Transparency International Bribe Payers Index (BPI) (see http://www. Transparency.org) that shows that senior business executives (including foreign nationals) in numerous emerging market economies perceive U.S. companies as having a high propensity to pay bribes.

This assertion has been widely disputed by some U.S. businesspeople with expertise in international corruption. They suggested that general jealousy of the United States' dominant place in global affairs might have influenced survey respondents to be especially negative about U.S. multinationals. There is no evidence that this did influence survey respondents. At the same time, the BPI study revealed that perceptions are widespread in numerous leading emerging market countries that U.S. corporations use exceptional political and diplomatic pressure, taking advantage of the U.S. status as the sole superpower, to convince foreign governments to "buy American" and that this is seen as a form of corruption and unfair business practice.

Concern about the behavior of multinational corporations abroad may be due to perceptions in developing countries that corruption has been introduced to developing countries by multinational firms. "Bribery and corruption in all their forms are as repugnant to ordinary Botswana as they are in Western Europe and North America . . . most Botswana tend to regard corruption as something which 'foreigners' initiate, if reports and editorials in the newspapers are any indication of local sentiment," noted H. L. C. (Quill) Hermans, chairman of Transparency International–Botswana.

Shaukat Omari, who heads TI–Pakistan, added, "The multinationals are probably a cause for most of the corruption or the 'culture of corruption' that now exists in Pakistan. It seems harsh and this is not to deny that the Pakistani companies do not indulge in bribery, I am sure that they do, but the culture of 'Baksheesh' has been definitely supported on its way by the multinational corporations."[11]

This view may rest, in part, on the scale of overseas bribery by U.S. firms. Many U.S. corporate executives argue that this is a false charge and note that there have been relatively few prosecutions under the FCPA. However, this may be explained by a lack of resources at the Justice Department and the intense difficulty of finding sufficient evidence in international corruption cases to bring successful prosecutions. There is no documented information on the actual scale of bribery by U.S. enterprises around the world, and thus the Transparency International surveys are especially important, even if they are based on perceptions, rather than hard evidence.

The U.S. score in the 2002 BPI at 5.3 (a score of 10.0 represents public perceptions of virtually zero bribery) is down from the 6.2 score in the first BPI in 1999. In both surveys the United States performed worse than a number of countries that until recently provided tax rebates for firms that paid bribes abroad. The U.S. score compared poorly with countries that have not made visible efforts to enforce the OECD Anti-Bribery Convention.

It is possible that the high level of global publicity associated with the Enron bankruptcy may have influenced some survey respondents to be more negative overall about U.S. corporations. More generally, the scandals have almost certainly deepened negative perceptions in many developing countries about the behavior of multinational enterprises.

But even if these opinion poll findings (developed for Transparency International by Gallup International) are contested by U.S. business leaders, there is acceptance by U.S. business executives that many U.S. firms do use facilitating payments abroad, and they note that these are allowed under the FCPA.[12] While U.S. executives argue that these are not bribes, this view is not shared in developing countries where these payments are made.

Payments under the table, of any amount, to a government official are bribes. Officials may extort such payments and may make demands in ways and at times that make refusal by foreign businesspeople very difficult, but they are still abuses of public office for personal gain. Across the developing world there is a uniform view on this, as expressed, for example, by Claudio Weber Abramo, managing director of TI-Brazil, who stated, "There's no country in the world that accepts bribery ('facilitating payments') in its laws. Here the matter is reinforcing the state in order to guarantee the rule of law."[13]

Shaukat Omari suggested that many U.S. corporations have come to depend on using "speed money" (a widely used term for *facilitating payments*) to obtain all kinds of permits from officials (licenses, adjustments in tariffs, the processing of papers) and that the amounts paid can be substantial. Many representatives of national chapters of Transparency International from developing countries and Central and Eastern Europe equated the use of facilitating payments with standard bribery in a debate at the organization's annual meeting in Casablanca in October 2002. They argued that the allowance of facilitating payments under the FCPA, and under the OECD Anti-Bribery Convention, encourages U.S. corporate representatives abroad, and those of other Western enterprises, to grease the palms of foreign officials without seeking alternative ways to pursue their business. Facilitating payments to government officials are not legal in developing countries and in Central and Eastern Europe.

U.S. multinational corporations do not make facilitating payments in the United States, despite facing long delays from U.S. authorities to secure work permits for nonresidents and to build new factories and shopping centers, let alone open land for mining. In the United States, the corporations hire specialist lawyers and lobbyists to assist in their quests for permits, while in emerging market economies where they may also face permitting delays they may resort to "grease" and "speed" payments to attain their goals. U.S. firms do not use facilitating payments in Canada and in the U.K., France, Germany, and Australia, but they do use these payments in countries such as Brazil, Bangladesh, South Korea, and South Africa.

U.S. advocates of the current system often suggest that it is unrealistic to ask U.S. firms not to use facilitating payments so long as small-scale bribery is commonplace in developing countries, enforcement of laws to prevent this form of payment is weak, and efforts by public officials to extort payments are widespread. Do such practical considerations justify breaking foreign laws? Is it somehow ethically acceptable for U.S. firms to break laws in countries where law enforcement is weak? Should corporate business ethics codes permit U.S. corporate executives to make facilitating payments in poor countries but refrain from doing so in rich countries?

The advocates of current U.S. practice sometimes suggest that there is no real harm in making facilitating payments. However, Alexandra Wrage, president of TRACE: Transparent Agents and Contracting Entities, which works with multinational corporations to curb corruption among international business intermediaries, argued, "No form of corruption is victimless. Widespread petty bribes set a permissive tone, which breeds more and greater demands." Ms. Wrage added that the FCPA should be changed to curb the use of facilitating payments, and she noted that the U.K. antibribery law, enacted in February 2002, does not provide for these payments.

The issue of facilitating payments illustrates what is widely perceived in developing countries as a double standard deployed by U.S. multinational corporations—an anticorruption ethic in their operations in the United States and in other OECD countries, and a lower ethic, which permits bribery of public officials, in the rest of the world.

Dr. Sini'a Petroviæ, president of TI–Croatia, stated,

It is well known that corporations from some countries are ready and others are not to "ease" their investments by, as you say, "facilitating payments." I do not believe that corruption can be easily or fully overcome. Nevertheless, I also do not think that the solution is in stating simply that many cultures and nations consider it normal or usual or common to accept money to "facilitate payments." If the countries and stakeholders in the countries of Western civilization really want to change things, they should themselves follow the procedures they stand for.[14]

Inese Voika, chairperson of Transparency International–Latvia, noted that it has been difficult in her country to convince multinational companies to speak publicly about their opposition to bribery and facilitating payments. This reluctance can lead to the conclusion that these corporations take the position that "the most important thing for us is profit, and we will never risk profit to ethics standards. . . . Western businesses in many cases talk about integrity, but in so general terms, that it shows they are ready for compromises if needed for their profits."[15]

The ardent anticorruption assertions by U.S. corporate representatives at the OECD and in the International Chamber of Commerce are widely seen as hypocritical. They are contrasted with the use of facilitating payments, with the widely reported high level of corporate contributions made to political campaigns in the United States, and with the practices that Enron and others engaged in. Jacques Dinan of TI–Mauritius noted,

The most important issue with regard to corporate social responsibility is the ability for a corporation to be trusted by all its stakeholders, internally and externally. This implies that the corporation must behave as perfectly as possible making sure that everything it does helps to build up its credibility and reputation. Corruption, influence peddling, half-truths, distorted facts and made-up stories have almost become a way of life and corporations have to be really daring to avoid being identified with such malpractices. Their irreproachable behavior must single them out.[16]

CONCLUSION

For a long time, America's 80 million shareowners believed they could trust the U.S. corporate brand. They believed U.S. corporations pursued irreproachable behavior that singled them out in the world. Now, their confidence is in tatters.

There have been many scandals in the past that have shaken public confidence in business ethical leadership, most notably in recent years the savings and loan crisis. But rarely before have reported scandals appeared to cast such a wide net across huge U.S. corporations, revealing conflicts of interest within the nation's most powerful financial institutions and involving the pocketing by top CEOs, in several cases, not of tens of millions of dollars, but of hundreds of millions of dollars. Now, it is imperative for all associated with U.S. business leadership to recognize that the crisis impacts everyone and that just being in compliance with the newest strictures and rules set by the U.S. Congress and the SEC is not enough to restore public trust.

U.S. corporate leaders need to start making substantial public efforts to be seen as acting beyond legal compliance and moving the behavioral approaches of their enterprises onto a higher plain. CEOs and boards of directors need to do far more to place the corporate culture on the moral high ground. There is a need to establish transparent reporting systems that demonstrate that doing the right thing in their operations, at all levels of management, is not a matter of choice, but a fundamental requirement.

CEOs should understand that they will start to win respect only when they begin to speak forcefully about the need for ethical business reform and act to demonstrate that this is not just public relations and mere rhetoric. They will start to regain public trust only when they declare to the lawyers and the auditors that while they may see the technical merits of the latest minuscule legal loopholes and tax avoidance opportunities that have been discovered, these are not opportunities that the firm's ethical culture can embrace.

Just as America's CEOs must open their eyes to the breadth of criticism at home, so too should they use this opportunity to attain a new sense of reality regarding how they are seen abroad. And they should listen to foreign expert views and learn from the experiences abroad with different systems of governance. For example, they should give greater consideration to European approaches that strengthen board control over corporate managements and enhance accountability.

CEOs will foster greater public understanding when they demonstrate that corporate social responsibility, which demands respecting human and labor rights and the globe's delicate environment, is not a course one pursues only when there is a short-term compelling business imperative to act. They will also enhance their image by addressing the ethical issues associated with

facilitating payments in foreign business and by introducing programs to end this practice.

The propensity of some U.S. firms and senior corporate executives to take advantage of legal loopholes to evade U.S. taxes in the extreme is an apt symbol of the attitudes that should be changed. How can CEOs, who wear the U.S. flag in their lapels and who use the flag in their corporate advertisements, consider it ethical to enter into dubious complex schemes to massively evade their U.S. tax liabilities? How can companies that proudly declare to the public that they are American even contemplate establishing their "legal" corporate head office in an offshore tax haven? New York District Attorney Robert M. Morgethau has noted that the pursuit of such practices by business "undermines respect for government and the rule of law."[17]

Greed and the constant willingness to sacrifice ethical standards to increase profits, at home and abroad, by numerous U.S. corporations damage our society and endanger the substantial progress in recent years to establish an open, liberal global economic system that can foster development and cross-border investment. Importantly, the lack of ethics has done, and is doing, immense damage to the prime asset of corporate America—its reputation.

NOTES

1. The author wishes to acknowledge the insights that shaped perspectives in this essay and statements that influenced conclusions highlighted in this essay from Admiral Tahiliani, Chairman, Transparency International–India; H. C. L. (Quill) Hermans, Chairman, Transparency International–Botswana; Claudio Weber Abramo, Executive Secretary, Transparency International–Brazil; Professor Laura Pincus Hartman, Wicklander Chair in Professional Ethics, DePaul University, Illinois, U.S.; Dr. Sini'a Petrovi, President, Transparency Interational–Croatia; Shaukat Omari, Managing Director, Transparency International–Pakistan; Alexandra Wrage, President, TRACE: Transparent Agents and Contracting Entities; Jacques Dinan, member of the board of directors of Transparency International–Mauritius and president of the

International Public Relations Association; Inese Voika, Chairperson, Transparency International– Latvia; Peter Rooke, Chief Executive, Transparency International– Australia and member TI board of directors; Dr. Johann Graf Lambsdorff, Professor, University of Passau, Germany, and Senior Research Adviser, Transparency International; Bronwyn Best, National Coordinator, Transparency International–Canada; Huguette Labelle, member Transparency International Advisory Council, former president of the Canadian International Development Agency; Jermyn Brooks, TI Executive Director; Professor Wesley Cragg, George R. Gardiner Program in Business Ethics at the Schulich School of Business, York University, Ontario, and chair of Transparency International–Canada; Professor George Brenkert, McDonough School of Business at Georgetown University and director of the Georgetown Business Ethics Institute; Stuart C. Gilman, Ph.D., President, the Ethics Resource Center, Washington, DC.

2. In this context, *corruption* is used broadly to describe practices at Enron, WorldCom, Adelphia, and numerous other companies. Thus, *corruption* is defined in terms of the abuse of position of corporate trust by business leaders who enriched themselves at the expense of the stakeholders in the companies that they directed: employees, pensioners, shareholders, customers, creditors, and other business partners. To illustrate international perspectives, the latter section of this chapter deals with corruption more narrowly defined in terms of bribery by multinational corporations of foreign government officials, who abused their public offices for personal benefit.

3. An article in *The Economist* (July 6, 2002) suggested that Xerox repeatedly restated its earnings without ever admitting to any wrongdoing and that, as the saga continues, its share price has slumped below book value. The article mentioned Xerox's "fiddles" and noted, "The restated accounts which the company filed on June 28th, show that this 'misapplication of GAAP,' as Xerox calls it, overstated profits by $1.4 billion between 1997 and 2001."

4. *The Wall Street Journal*, May 6, 2002, story under the headline "SEC's Pitt Met With Head of KPMG Raising New Questions About Ethics."

5. The Cadbury Commission and a series of other high-profile reviews in the U.K. of corporate governance have stimulated considerable debate. Activist shareholder groups in Germany have mounted effective programs against major stock option allocations to CEOs.

6. For example, February 10, 2003, *The Guardian* in the U.K. reported that Marks & Spencer is paying for its chairman, Luc Vandevelde, to live at

London's luxurious Claridge's hotel in Mayfair as part of a pay package worth nearly £1 million a year (about $1.6 million) for a three-day-a-week job.

7. U.S. corporations lobbied for many years for a "level playing field" on this issue. In early 2001, the OECD approved the OECD Anti-Bribery Convention, which led to more than 30 countries approving national legislation similar to the U.S. FCPA of 1977, while several governments at the same time ended the practice of making foreign bribes tax deductible.

8. Comments by Professor Lambsdorff to the author.

9. Reports by the World Bank Institute (WBI), Dr. Daniel Kaufman of WBI, Transparency International, and the 2001 and 2003 editions of the Global Corruption Report published by Transparency International.

10. E-mail comment to the author.

11. E-mail comment to the author.

12. The U.S. Department of Justice explains that FCPA contains an explicit exception to the bribery prohibition for "facilitating payments" for "routine governmental action" and provides affirmative defenses, which can be used to defend against alleged violations of the FCPA. There is an exception to the antibribery prohibition for payments to facilitate or expedite performance of a "routine governmental action." The statute lists the following examples: obtaining permits, licenses, or other official documents; processing governmental papers, such as visas and work orders; providing police protection and mail pickup and delivery; providing phone service, power, and water supply; loading and unloading cargo or protecting perishable products; and scheduling inspections associated with contract performance or transit of goods across country. (www.usdoj.gov/criminal/fraud/fcpa/fcpa.html)

13. E-mail comment to the author.

14. E-mail comment to the author.

15. E-mail comment to the author.

16. E-mail comment to the author.

17. New York District Attorney Robert M. Morgethau spoke about offshore tax havens at a seminar at the Brookings Institution on June 5, 2002.

REFERENCES

Byrne, J. A. (2002, June 24). Restoring trust in corporate America. *BusinessWeek*.

California Public Employees' Retirement System. (2003, March 27). CalPERS 2003 focus list at-a-glance. *Corporate Governance*. Retrieved from http://www.calpers-governance.org

Cheng, I. (2002, July 31). Barons of bankruptcy (Part 1). *The Financial Times*.

Clark, A. (2003, February 10). It's a flat-out life of luxury for M&S chair. *The Guardian*.

Conference Board. (2003, January). *Findings of the Commission on Public Trust and Private Enterprise*. Retrieved from http://www.conference-board.org/pdf_free/758.pdf

Conflict and corruption. (2002, October). Global Witness. Retrieved from http://www.global witness.org

Control Risks. (2003). See Annual corruption survey and facing up to corruption: http://www.crg.com/html/service_level2.php?area=publication&id=71

Corruption without contrition. (2002, July 6). *The Economist*.

Enron, symbole d'un système. (2002, March). *Le Monde Diplomatique*.

Ethics Resource Center. (2003, February 6). *ERC advises companies to reach beyond SEC requirements*. Retrieved from http://www.ethics.org/releases/nr_20030206_sec.html

Ethics Resource Center. (2003, February 7). *Ethics today*. Retrieved from http://www.ethics.org

Garten, J. (2002, May 13). Corporate standards: Raise the bar around the world. *BusinessWeek*.

Garten, J. (2003). *The politics of fortune*. Cambridge: Harvard University Press.

Gilman, S. C. (2002, November 18). *Testimony to the Advisory Group on Federal Sentencing Guidelines for Organizations*. Retrieved from http://www.ethics.org/resources/article_detail.cfm?ID=765

Group of Thirty. (2002, May). *Enron et al: Market forces in disarray*. Occasional Paper 66. Retrieved from http://www.group30.org/pubs.php?page-pubs2002.html

Higgs, D. (2003, January). *Higgs Report: Review of the role and effectiveness of non-executive directors*. The UK Department of Trade and Industry, UK The Stationery Office 19585 809438. Retrieved from http://www.dti.gov.uk/cld/non_exec_review

Hill, A. (2002, August 2). Barons of bankruptcy (Part 1). *The Financial Times*.

KPMG. (2002, May 7). We believe integrity is a constant (KPMG advertisement). *The Wall Street Journal*.

Lambsdorff, J. G. (n.d.). *Internet Center for Corruption Research*. Retrieved from http://wwwuser.gwdg.de/~uwvw/

Levine, S. (2003a, April 8). Ex-Mobil officer pleads not guilty to accepting $2 million kickback. *The Wall Street Journal*.

Levine, S. (2003b, April 23). Exxon Mobil's role in payment to officials under investigation. *The Wall Street Journal*.

Lublin, J. S. (2003, February 13). Spring president LeMay seeks more exit pay. *The Wall Street Journal*.

McDonough, W. J. (2002, September 11). *Federal Reserve Bank of New York (Speeches 2002)*. Retrieved from http:// www.newyorkfed.org/newsevents/speeches/2002/mcd020911.html

Morgenthau, R. (2002, June). Speech delivered at the Brookings Institution, Washington, DC.

National Association of Securities Dealers. (2003, April 28). *Global settlement of conflicts of interest between research and investment banking information*. Retrieved from http://www.nasd.com/global_settlement.asp

New York Stock Exchange. (2002, August 1). *NYSE measures to strengthen corporate accountability*. Retrieved from http://www.nyse.com

New York Stock Exchange. (2003, November). *Final rules*. Retrieved from http://www.nyse.com/pdfs/finalcorpgovrules.pdf

OECD Principles of Corporate Governance. (1999, May). Retrieved from http://www.oecd.org/dataoecd/47/50/4347646.pdf

Royal Dutch Shell. (2002). *Shell Report*. Retrieved from http://www.shell.com/home/Framework?siteId=shellreport2002-en

$77 million for E*Trade chief. (2002, May 1). *Bloomberg News*.

Smith, R. (2003). *Smith report: Audit committees combined code guidance*. Financial Reporting Council. Retrieved from http://www.frc.org.uk/publications

Tax moves by Enron mystify the IRS. (2003, February 13). *The New York Times*, p. C1.

TRACE: Transparent Agents and Contracting Entities. (2003, February). *The high cost of small bribes*. Retrieved from http://www.traceinternational.org

Transparency International. (2002). *Bribe payers index*. Retrieved from http://www.transparency org/pressreleases_archive/2002/2002.05.14.bpi.en.html

Transparency International. (2003a). *Corruption perceptions index.* Retrieved from http://www.transparency.org/cpi/index.html#cpi

Transparency International. (2003b, June). *Business principles for countering bribery.* Retrieved from http://www.transparency.org/building_coalitions/private_sector/business_principles/dnld/business_principles2.doc

United Nations Global Compact. (2003, July 21). *Report on Advisory Council meeting.* Retrieved from http://www.unglobalcompact.org

U.S. Sentencing Commission. (2003, October 7). *Report of the ad hoc advisory group on the organizational sentencing guidelines.* Retrieved from http://ww.ussc.gov/corp/advgrprpt/advgrprpt.htm

Weil, J. (2003, January 29). WorldCom's fall. *The Wall Street Journal.*

World Bank and World Bank Institute. (n.d.). Extensive research retrieved from http:// www1.worldbank.org/publicsector/anticorrupt/index.cfm

12

IS CORRUPTION ALWAYS CORRUPT?

MANUEL VELASQUEZ

A tremendous amount of attention has been paid during this past decade to the topic of corruption and to the role that businesses play in corruption (Naim, 1995). The United States in 1977, of course, was the first major nation to make it illegal for a business to bribe foreign officials. But the member countries of the OECD recently pledged to enact legislation that similarly makes it a crime for a business to pay a bribe to a foreign official. Other regional groups of countries have adopted similar resolutions. In addition, both the World Bank and the International Monetary Fund, as well as several other regional financial institutions, have adopted regulations that prohibit companies that pay bribes from participating in projects they fund.

This flurry of legislation and regulations against businesses that participate in corruption is, obviously, based on the assumption that it is wrong for businesses to engage in corruption. Businesspeople have protested that it is a mistake to make such blanket condemnations of corruption because, in many cultures, exchanges that Westerners condemn as unethical corruption are seen by locals as morally acceptable and are widely practiced. Ethicists and other writers have generally discounted such protests of businesspeople as self-serving. Virtually everything that has been written on corruption during the last decade, including the countless articles, books, symposia, and research studies on corruption that have appeared in this period, almost unanimously take the stand that corruption is an unmitigated social evil. Businesses that engage in corruption are characterized as engaging in deviant and socially harmful behavior. Indeed, the very term *corruption* connotes degenerate and pathological behavior.

I want in this chapter to examine the assumption that it is universally wrong for businesses to engage in corruption—so wrong, in fact, that it should be made a crime everywhere. I want to show that it is not an easy matter to identify corruption to begin with, and that in many cases what appear to be clear cases of unethical corrupt exchanges turn out to be morally benign when seen from the perspective of participants in the local culture. In fact, I will try to show that the moral absolutism that afflicts our views on corruption is based on a kind of ethnocentrism characterized by an inability to recognize the moral legitimacy of forms of government that are quite different from ours and, consequently, by an inability to see social exchanges from the perspective of participants to these exchanges. We should, I believe, abandon an absolute and universal condemnation of corruption in favor of a more relativistic and particularistic understanding of the conceptions that underlie our views of the ethics of corruption, a view that would be more tolerant of what we are so ready to condemn as immoral.

Lest I be misunderstood, I must hasten to add right at the beginning that I do not hold that corruption is always blameless. On the contrary, I believe that there is a great deal of evidence that many, perhaps most, corrupt exchanges are among elites who are conscious of the wrongfulness of their actions and who make these exchanges in contexts that by no means absolve them from blame. However, I will argue, there are also many cases of exchanges that we Westerners would see as instances of unethical corruption but that when seen from the perspective of a local culture cannot be judged to be wrong. And these cases, I believe, should instill in us a greater caution when we are tempted to issue universal and absolute moral condemnations of corruption.

Before embarking on my discussion of corruption, I need first to indicate the kinds of corrupt exchanges that I will be discussing and distinguish these from the forms of corruption that I am not discussing in this chapter.

Let me begin, then, by pointing out that corruption, at least as I will be using the term in this chapter, is primarily a concept of politics. That is, corruption refers essentially to the abuse of public office (Beattie & Barbour, 2000, p. 138), such as the extortion or acceptance of bribes by government officials, nepotism or favoritism by government officials, influence peddling, or misappropriation of government funds. An act of corruption or a corrupt exchange must involve a government official as one of the parties to the exchange, so that there can be no corruption without the involvement of a government official. Clearly, therefore, corruption need

not involve a business. Of course, businesses are often involved as parties to a corrupt exchange, such as when a business bribes a government minister or a customs official. But corruption can occur without the involvement of a business, such as when a government official misappropriates government property for her own benefit or when a government official defrauds his own government. Strictly speaking, then, corruption is not essentially a business ethics issue, so much as an issue in government ethics.

However, in this discussion I want to address the issue of corruption only insofar as it is an issue for business and so for business ethics. The Foreign Corrupt Practices Act and the OECD convention are focused on businesses and on criminalizing the giving of bribes by businesses, not the taking of bribes by government officials (although each government, of course, prohibits its own officials from engaging in corrupt exchanges). Consequently, in this chapter I will restrict the kind of corrupt exchanges I will be taking about. In what follows, the kind of corruption that I am interested in is corruption that involves a private commercial party, either an individual person engaged in business or a firm, as one of the parties to a corrupt exchange and that has a government official as the other party. This means that I will be discussing only a limited range of kinds of corruption; in particular I exclude discussion of abuse of office that does not involve a private business party, such as government fraud and misrepresentation, embezzlement and theft, graft, and many other kinds of wrongdoing that are often included under the umbrella of corruption. The only forms of corruption that I am interested in are those in which a private party engages in a corrupt exchange with a public official.

Second, I also want to limit my discussion to what is generally called political corruption. Political corruption is the kind of corruption that occurs when a business attempts to get a political official or an administrative official to favor the business in some way—for example, by facilitating an administrative process, by exempting the business from payment of taxes or other fees, by granting the business a contract, by purchasing services from a business, and so on. I am therefore explicitly excluding business interference in the judicial system, the kind of interference that occurs when, say, a business bribes a judge to get the judge to render a favorable opinion in a judicial proceeding. The flurry of attention that has been paid to business involvement in corruption recently has been focused, for the most part, on business attempts to corrupt political or administrative officials so as to get business or facilitate a business activity (see, for example, Transparency International, 2002). It is this kind of corruption that I am interested in discussing and not judicial corruption, which, I believe, raises special issues that I do not want to address.

EVALUATING CORRUPTION: INTERNAL AND EXTERNAL EVALUATIONS

Let me begin with a simple question: Why is it wrong for a business to engage in a corrupt exchange with a political or administrative official? Suppose, for the sake of argument, that it is wrong for government officials to engage in corruption. After all, there are usually clear rules stipulating that the government official may not take bribes, and so the official who takes a bribe violates the rules of his office. But why is it wrong for the other party, the party supplying the bribe, to give a benefit to a government official? Why should the activity of the other party be criminalized? The standard argument, and the argument that I think is fundamentally correct, is that it is wrong for a person to bribe a government official because by doing so he or she is causing, helping, or participating in the wrongful act of that other person. The giving of a bribe is wrong because it causes the official to violate the moral standards that govern his office: The briber does wrong because he causes someone else to do wrong. Thus, the wrongfulness of the act of bribing depends on—is parasitic on—the wrongfulness of the act of being bribed. If this is correct, then only if it is wrong for a government

official to engage in a corrupt exchange will it be wrong for a businessperson to engage in that same exchange.

Why then is it ethically wrong for a government official to engage in corruption?

When government corruption is condemned as immoral, the complaint can be based on two different kinds of moral evaluation: an internal evaluation of the activity or an external evaluation. It is important to keep these two different kinds of evaluation distinct. An internal evaluation of the morality of an activity judges the activity in terms of whether or not it violates a rule or a system of rules that is accepted as legitimate by an individual or a community. It evaluates the activity from the internal perspective of an individual or a member of a community that accepts a rule or system of rules that stipulates that activity of that kind is morally prohibited or morally permitted. An external evaluation of an activity judges the rule or system of rules themselves that require or prohibit the activity, in terms of whether or not the rule or system meets certain standards that are held to be standards that moralities should meet. Thus, an external evaluation primarily judges the adequacy of a moral rule or system of moral rules and secondarily judges the activity as justified or not according to whether the rule or system of rules prohibiting (or permitting) the act is itself judged adequate.

I make the distinction between internal and external evaluations because the moral arguments that have been given for the ethics of corruption fall into these two categories, and I believe it is important that they be kept separate.

First, there are a number of external arguments that have recently been proposed against corruption. (See Rose-Ackerman, 1999, for a summary.) External arguments claim that corruption is wrong because corruption, as a practice, has bad consequences. External arguments do not imply that each and every act of corruption has bad consequences, and so all must be condemned. Instead, external arguments against corruption claim that the practice of corruption generally has bad consequences. For example, recent empirical research on corruption indicates that corruption has a negative impact on the ratio of (domestic and foreign) investment to a country's gross domestic product, so that the more corruption a country exhibits, the lower its investment rate and consequently its economic growth rate (Brunetti, & Weder, 1997; Keefer & Knack, 1996; Kisunko, Mauro, 1995). Others have found evidence that corruption drives away foreign direct investment and that increases in a country's level of corruption function much like increases in its tax rates, except that the negative effects of corruption are worse than those of taxes because corruption is more arbitrary and unpredictable (Wei, 2000). On the other hand, some economists have claimed that corruption has beneficial consequences. Leff, for example, famously argued that bureaucratic corruption can facilitate economic development by reducing risk for investors and by inducing government officials to relax costly regulations; furthermore, since the most efficient firms can pay the highest bribes, corruption may also encourage efficiency (Leff, 1964). Bayley, Nye, and Lui have also argued that corruption can encourage economic development by assisting the development of an entrepreneurial class, or by reducing red tape and excessive bureaucratic rules (Bayley, 1966; Lui, 1985; Nye, 1989). All of these arguments, both pro and con, are examples of what I mean by external evaluations of corruption because they are designed to show that a rule that allows corruption will have significant costs or benefits. These arguments do not show that there is something about corruption itself that is wrong or unethical (or right and ethical) or that each act of corruption necessarily has bad consequences. Instead, they show that the cumulative effects of a rule or system of rules that allows corruption are bad (or good), even if the effects of a particular corrupt act may not be bad (or good).

I mention these external arguments simply to set them aside. I am not interested here in discussing the admittedly important question of whether corrupt exchanges, if generally practiced, would have consequences that entitle us to condemn the practice as inefficient, unproductive, or otherwise dysfunctional. In order to adequately

evaluate such arguments we would have to inquire into the costs and benefits involved in changing such practices, and this would take us in directions I do not want to go in this chapter. For example, as I will soon argue, some systems that permit "corrupt" exchanges do so because such exchanges are embedded in cultural practices (e.g., gift exchanges) that participants value; suggestions that these exchanges should be eliminated must address the question of how much weight should be given to the desires of locals who want to retain these familiar and valued cultural practices, and how much weight should be given to the potential benefits of life in the absence of those cultural practices. These are very difficult questions involving contested cultural values that, I believe, are extremely difficult to settle. I suspect, in fact, that in many cases there is no rational way of resolving such controversies. (For example, Titmuss has argued that replacing "gift relationships" with the impersonal relationships of the market imposes cultural losses whose value is impossible to adequately assess.) I therefore set aside these external evaluations of corruption that, I believe, would require comparisons of incommensurable values and that, I believe, also raise methodological questions that they do not adequately address. (For example, these studies rely on surveys that allow respondents to decide what constitutes corruption, so it is not clear that all respondents are using the same concept of corruption; for other criticisms, see Qizilbash, 2001.) I want to concentrate here, instead, on the arguments that evaluate corruption from an internal perspective, that is, on arguments that attempt to show that there is something about corruption itself that is bad, some feature that each and every act of corruption carries and that renders each and every act of corruption wrongful. Why, I want to ask, would one think that a corrupt exchange is wrong from an internal perspective, a perspective that relates corruption to some accepted ethical norm that implies that corruption has features that render it wrongful?

To answer this question, I think that we need to have before us an understanding of what corruption is since internal evaluations of corruption necessarily appeal to the features of corrupt exchanges. One traditional way of defining corruption has its roots in a conception of what healthy or just governance is. In its historical meaning, corruption implies a falling away from a good or healthy condition to a state of decay or perversion. As applied to government, corruption implies an unjust state or perverse condition of governance. The government official who engages in corruption, then, behaves immorally because his action constitutes or causes unjust governance. Plato and Aristotle, writing in the fifth century B.C., were among the first to explicitly use the term in this way to refer to an unjust condition of governance, and they condemned those who engaged in corruption on the grounds that their actions constituted or brought about such an unjust state. Discussions of corruption as an unjust form of governance can be found in other classical authors such as Thucydides and Machiavelli as well as in some contemporary authors (Dobel, 1978). A corrupt government on this view is one that has been "perverted from uprightness," and a corrupt action is one that brings about such a perversion from uprightness (*Oxford English Dictionary*, online edition).

Obviously, then, the notion of corruption implies that there is a normatively proper form of governance, a just form of governance, and corruption is defined as a deviation from this morally preferred state. What counts as an act of corruption, then, will necessarily depend on what one believes morally appropriate governance is, so different cultural conceptions of normal or morally appropriate governance will yield different moral evaluations of corruption. Now notions of normal or appropriate governance differ from one locality to another and may even differ in the same locality. As there is no single universally accepted and uncontested view of what morally appropriate governance is, there also can be no single universally accepted and uncontested view of what constitutes unethical corruption and so no single absolute view of when exchanges between government officials and businesses are wrong (or so I will argue).

If this analysis is correct, then evaluations of corruption are necessarily relativistic: It is not possible to say, in any absolute or universalistic way, that corruption is unethical or that it is always wrong for businesses to engage in corruption. It all depends. An exchange between a business and a government official may be corrupt and unethical relative to one conception of government, yet may be morally benign relative to another competing conception of government. It is not possible, then, to condemn corruption in any absolute sense, that is, in a sense that assumes that corruption can be condemned independently of one's conception of appropriate government. Or, at any rate, that is what I will now try to show. I will describe and discuss three conceptions of government—the competitive state, the patrimonial state, and the personalized state—and argue that what we would characterize as unethical corruption relative to our own ideas of normal or appropriate government can constitute morally acceptable exchanges relative to these competing conceptions of government.

CORRUPTION AND THE COMPETITIVE STATE

Let me begin by considering the current case of Methanex and Archer Daniels Midland. An analysis of this case, I believe, will quickly show that whether a certain exchange between a business and a political official is judged to be unethical depends on one's conception of just or appropriate governance.

Methanex, a Canadian company, is the world's leading producer of MTBE, an oxygenate that reduces air pollution when added to gasoline. In October 1997, California required that MTBE be added to all gasoline sold in the state. However, in March 1999, the newly elected governor of California, Gray Davis, issued an order banning the use of MTBE (to take effect on December 31, 2002, and later delayed to January 1, 2004). Davis cited a University of California study that concluded that MTBE was contaminating California's water supplies. (The additive, which has been found to produce certain cancers in rats, is also a possible carcinogen, although no studies have yet demonstrated that it causes cancer in humans.) Methanex immediately brought a complaint against the U.S. government before a commission (the Commission for Environmental Cooperation) established by the North American Free Trade Agreement (NAFTA) to adjudicate such complaints. Methanex alleged that the California governor's ban of MTBE, one of the company's key products, constituted an unfair and inequitable expropriation of its investment in the United States and demanded $907 million in compensation from the U.S. government. (Expropriation occurs when government action interferes with or removes an alien's ability to use or enjoy his property, and under NAFTA, expropriation can include not only the taking of property but also the taking of market share and market access. Under the rules of NAFTA, a government of a NAFTA member country that unfairly and inequitably expropriates the investment of a company from another NAFTA country must compensate that company for its investment.) In a March 2001 amendment to its original claim, Methanex stated that Governor Davis's ban on MTBE constituted an unfair and inequitable expropriation because the governor's decision was influenced by corruption (Methanex, 2001). Methanex alleged that in August 1998, before his election, but while he was campaigning for governor, Gray Davis flew to Decatur, Illinois, where he "secretly" met with personnel of the Archer Daniels Midland Corporation (ADM). ADM is an American company that manufactures ethanol, a gasoline additive that is the main competitor to the MTBE additive manufactured by Methanex, and ADM is the main beneficiary of Gray Davis' decision to ban MTBE. Two weeks after the meeting, ADM officials donated $100,000 to Davis's election committee and another $55,000 in donations over the next four months. Two weeks after Governor Gray Davis banned MTBE, ADM gave Davis's election committee another $50,000. Davis's action gave a significant advantage to ADM's ethanol business in California while undercutting the market for Methanex's MTBE within the state. In its amended claim, Methanex argued that

when a state official, acting in an ostensibly neutral fashion, discriminates in favor of a protected domestic industry that has given the official substantial political contributions, his actions are not independent, but instead improperly influenced by political and pecuniary considerations. . . . Consequently, they violate international law because they are unfair, inequitable, and not in accord with the duty of independence. (Methanex, 2001, p. 50)

The contribution that ADM made to Governor Davis during his campaign was perfectly legal, and neither the contribution nor Davis's subsequent ban of MTBE would be counted as corruption under any American laws. However, Davis's action favoring ADM would be considered corruption in various countries. V. V. Veeder, a British attorney chairing the NAFTA panel hearing the Methanex complaint, said of Davis's action, "It would be the tort of malfeasance in my land and it would not be lawful. It would be an abuse of power" (Nissenbaum, 2002). Methanex, in its complaint, approvingly quoted several observers of the American political system who labeled as "corruption" the kind of campaign contribution that Davis accepted and that is common in American politics. Methanex, for example, quoted Yale Law Professor George L. Priest, who stated, "The central organizing thought of the reform tradition [of U.S. campaign finance] is that money, whether in the form of a contribution to a campaign or an expenditure on behalf of a candidate, corrupts the electoral system" (Methanex, 2001, p. 51-2).

Was Gray Davis' act a corrupt exchange and was ADM's contribution of $200,000 to the governor's election campaign a form of corruption? The answer to that question depends, I believe, on whether one believes that their exchange constituted a departure from the way government ought to be carried on. On one view of governance that is widespread in the United States and that underlies much of our conception of legitimate and just political activity, neither Davis nor ADM was involved in the corruption of government. Dennis Thompson has suggested the term *competitive politics theory* for the common view that acts such as Davis's are not corrupt because "the conduct was part of a normal competitive process, in which all politicians are encouraged by the political system to solicit support and bestow favors to win elections.... [On this view] the quest for campaign contributions and the provision of services to influential contributors are necessary features of a healthy competitive politics" (Thompson, 1993, p. 370). Obviously, from the perspective of this conception of normal and legitimate government, the ADM/Davis incident was not a case of genuine corruption. On the other hand, from the perspective of a conception of government that rejects the competitive politics theory, the ADM/Davis incident may be seen as a clear instance of the corruption of government. Dennis Thompson, for example, uses the term *mediated corruption* for those cases where politicians receive benefits that are not personal but political (such as campaign contributions) and where the benefit is given in a way that "damages the democratic process" (Thompson, 1993, p. 369). In the case before us, in Mr. Veeder's conception of British government and in the conception of proper government that is accepted by the reformers Methanex quoted in its complaint, the ADM/Davis incident is a clear example of political corruption.

The Davis/ADM incident, then, shows that judgments about the wrongfulness of corruption will depend on one's conception of whether or not it is appropriate that government should be the subject of a competitive process in which candidates and parties compete for election with the understanding that they will favor their supporters if they win—to the victor belong the spoils. It should not be thought that the incident is concerned with mere superficial differences over campaign laws that are not fundamental features of government; on the contrary, the incident highlights differences over the fundamental question of whether, in return for a monetary gift that helped place him in office, a politician can justly use the public resources of his newly acquired office to grant favors to his benefactor, a question that is at the very heart of our understanding of what the corruption of government is all about. One's view of the legitimacy of such exchanges depends on one's conception of proper governance, and, as

the Davis/ADM incident demonstrates, such judgments are subject to moral relativity even when they are viewed from the perspective of cultures that are quite similar to each other, such as, in this case, Canada, the United States, and Great Britain. We would expect that when countries differ from each other to an even greater extent, even a greater degree of relativity will afflict their respective judgments of the wrongfulness of corruption. I will now try to argue this.

CORRUPTION AND THE PATRIMONIAL STATE

I have so far discussed corruption as a perverse form of governance in order to emphasize the extent to which the idea of corruption, in its root meaning, is linked to a conception of normatively appropriate government that necessarily relativizes the concept. However, most contemporary discussions of corruption, particularly discussions of corruption in the social science literature during the past decade, have attempted to provide sharper and more focused definitions of corruption, definitions that, it is felt, would be more amenable to analysis by the analytical methods of the social sciences. Such definitions have not attempted to understand corruption as a general condition of government, but as the behavior of individuals in government. These attempts at definition have resulted in a plethora of divergent and sometimes conflicting characterizations of corruption (Johnston, 1996; Philp, 1997; Qizilbash, 2001; Williams, 1999). Nevertheless, there has been considerable convergence toward and agreement on the view that corruption is best defined as the abuse of public office for private gain (Elliott, 1997; Rose-Ackerman, 1999), and this is the definition that I will discuss in what follows.

Obviously, this definition contains terms that are morally ambiguous, such as *abuse*, *public*, and *private*. What I want to argue now is that this moral ambiguity is so great that much of what counts as corruption under this definition is, in its cultural context, not morally wrong. In particular, I will argue that judgments about the wrongfulness of corruption under this definition are based on a Western conception of government that is not present in some cultural contexts and, as a consequence, there are some cultural contexts where actions that would be counted as "corruption" by a Western understanding of corruption are not ethically wrong relative to competing notions of government.

Corruption, as I noted, is characterized by Westerners as the abuse of public resources or public office for the benefit of private parties. Why is corruption unethical in terms of this definition? The standard argument, which is either explicit or implicit in Western discussions of the wrongfulness of corruption, is based on the idea that the corrupt official appropriates something that is not his. Corruption is thus a form of theft. Contemporary Western discussions of corruption assume that government, government resources, and government services are, in some sense, the property of the public and that any rents accruing to those resources or services also belong to the public. When the government official extracts a fee for providing his services and then pockets this fee, he has taken for his private use what actually belongs to the public, and so his act is unethical. In a similar way, if an official exhibits favoritism or partiality toward a business because of a relationship the business has established with the official, perhaps by giving personal gifts to the official, then the official is using a public resource, his office, to serve his own private interests. Thus, the core argument for the wrongfulness of corruption assumes that there is a distinction between the public and the private; the services the official performs are public, not private, and any rents or benefits accruing to those services belong to the public and so are not the private property of the official.

Now this argument on the wrongfulness of corruption depends on a distinction between the public nature of government service and private or personal interests. What is the origin of this distinction? Historically, the distinction is a relatively recent one, having originated in the nineteenth century with the development of modern ideals of public service, ideals that were most

clearly described in the work of Max Weber on bureaucracy. Weber describes bureaucracy as a "rational" form of "domination," as opposed to patrimonialism, which he calls a "traditional" form of domination. A bureaucracy is a hierarchical system of offices, each of which is associated with (a) a precise and detailed set of official duties, (b) the nonpersonal authority and jurisdiction to give the commands required to discharge those duties, and (c) a set of formal qualifications that persons employed to hold the offices must meet (Weber, 1956, p. 956). A key characteristic of a bureaucracy is that

> legally and actually, office holding is not considered ownership of a course of income, to be exploited for rents or emoluments in exchange for the rendering of certain services.... Rather, entrance into an office ... is considered an acceptance of a specific duty of fealty to the purpose of the office in return for the grant of a secure existence. It is decisive for the modern loyalty to an office that, in the pure type, it does not establish a relationship to a person, like the vassal's or disciple's faith under feudal or patrimonial authority, but rather is devoted to impersonal and functional purposes. (Weber, 1956, p. 959)

Weber contrasts this modern ideal of bureaucratic administration with patriarchalism and patrimonialism, both of which he characterizes as "pre-bureaucratic types of domination." The wider term is *patriarchal authority*, of which patrimonial authority is a special case. Patriarchal authority is the personal authority exercised by the master of a household and is based on a "strictly personal loyalty" to the master and to tradition. It thus contrasts with the impersonal relationships and the distinction between the public and the private realms that characterize bureaucratic authority. Weber holds that patriarchal authority is the form of authority characteristic of earlier societies that organized themselves on the basis of an extended household ruled over by the master. The medieval manor is one example, where the master of the manor assigns land to his dependents, with the understanding that the land still belongs to the master and that his dependents are obligated to support and serve the master "with all available means" since the land, literally, belongs to the master.

The patrimonial state arises when one master establishes domination over other masters who previously were not subject to his patriarchal power, through their forced or voluntary submission, and the ruling master then organizes his domination "just like the exercise of his patriarchal power" (Weber, 1956, p. 1013), that is, the authority of the ruler is modeled on the authority a master exercises over his household. According to Weber, "In the patrimonial state the most fundamental obligation of the subjects is the material maintenance of the ruler, just as is the case of a patrimonial household" (Weber, 1956, p. 1014). Administering the complexity and extent of the ruler's domains, Weber notes, requires a division of labor and "in this fashion, the patrimonial offices come into being." The offices characteristic of patrimonial states, however, differ significantly from the offices characteristic of the bureaucratic state. According to Weber, "The patrimonial office lacks above all the bureaucratic separation of the private and the official sphere. For the political administration, too, is treated as a purely personal affair of the ruler, and political power is considered part of his personal property, which can be exploited by means of contributions and fees" (Weber, 1956, pp. 1028–1029).

Because the state and its administration were considered to be the personal property of the ruler, the ruler could, of course, give or sell to a subject the right to keep the rents that derive from an administrative office. In medieval Europe an office that the ruler thus gave or sold to an official as the official's own personal property was termed a "fee benefice" (Weber, 1956, p. 1031ff.). Both the office and the rents that accrued to it were then considered the private property of the official occupying the office.

Government offices in the patrimonial state, therefore, had, for Weber, two broad characteristics that distinguished them from government office in the modern bureaucratic state. First, the patrimonial state conceives of the state and its administration as the private property of the ruler or of the government official to whom the ruler has granted an office, while the modern state is based on the idea that the state and its administration belong to the public. Second, the patrimonial state is based on personal relationships, primarily the relationship of the ruler to his subjects but also the relationship between an official and his clients, and not on the impersonal and impartial fidelity to rules that characterizes the modern bureaucratic administration of the state. I will, in what follows, consider the first of these features (the view of government as private property) as the essential feature of the patrimonial state and consider the second feature (the personalized nature of relationships with government officials) as an associated but not necessarily essential feature of the patrimonial state. Although this is a departure from Weber's original conception of the patrimonial state, this will enable me to focus on the first feature in this section and to set aside discussion of the second feature for the next section of this chapter.

Weber's idealized description of the patrimonial state is important for our purposes because it describes a regime in which the concept of corruption in the sense of the abuse of public office for private interests makes little sense. It makes little sense because offices in the patrimonial state are not the property of the public but are, instead, considered to be the private property of the ruler or of the administrator to whom the ruler has given the office. Of course, the official in the patrimonial state can engage in an attenuated form of corruption when, not having been given the office, he nevertheless diverts into his own pocket the rents that belong to the ruler or otherwise fails to administer the office as the monarch has requested. But the official in the patrimonial state cannot engage in the kind of corruption that we have in mind when we speak of corruption as the abuse of public office for private interests because in the patrimonial state the public, as such, does not own the state or its administration. Moreover, when the ruler gives or sells an office and its rents to an official, even the attenuated sense of corruption will not apply because, having been given to the official, the office itself and its rents have become the private property of the official and the official therefore does not abuse his office when he pockets these rents and fails to pass them on to the ruler. The ruler may, of course, require the official to continue to turn over a percentage of the rents, or a fixed regular fee taken from the rents, and the official may be said to engage in a form of corruption if he fails to provide these payments to the ruler from the rents. But there can be no corruption when the official, having given the ruler his share, then requires clients to pay him for his services and then keeps those payments. Moreover, because it is not immoral for the official in the patrimonial state to do these things, it is also not immoral for a merchant—a businessperson—to induce the official to take a payment in return for showing him favoritism in the performance of the official's services, nor is it immoral for an official to show favoritism to the merchant simply because of a relationship the two have established between themselves. What we moderns would see as corruption in such contexts is not corrupt.

This Weberian notion of a patrimonial state has clear applications, of course, to premodern states. During and prior to the seventeenth century, virtually all states were considered the private property of the ruler, and government offices were given or sold to individuals to be exploited for their private benefit. These states included the monarchies ruled by kings in England and most European states from the Middle Ages to the seventeenth century, the Mogul empires of the seventeenth and eighteen centuries, the dynastic kingdoms of China from the Chin dynasty to the fall of the empire in the twentieth century, and the great Egyptian kingdoms. In all these patrimonial regimes, the administration of the state was indistinguishable from the administration of the royal household, and no distinction was made between the private business of the royal family and the administration of the government (Theobald, 1990, pp. 19–20; Weber, 1956, p. 956). Government officials in such states are considered servants of the royal household, and to secure their loyalty and service the monarch often gave them a fee benefice, which is the right to whatever fees, taxes, or gifts

the official can extract from his clients in exchange for providing the services of his office. Such arrangements are clearly evident in England in the thirteenth, fourteenth, fifteenth, and sixteenth centuries, when a complex network of offices, manors, wardships, titles, keeperships, and other forms of patronage permeated English society and continued to do so right up to the eve of the industrial revolution. They are evident, also, in the absolute monarchy that ruled France until the revolution.

In such a society, where the modern distinction between public office and private interests does not exist, there can be no corruption in the modern sense. Edward Gibbon, considered a morally upright gentleman, declared without the slightest embarrassment that men should seek government office "to employ the weight and consideration it gives, in the service of one's friends" (Theobald, 1990, p. 25).

The objection may be raised against my account that throughout the early and late medieval ages, when the patrimonial state was the rule in Europe, moral condemnations of corruption were common. In fact, throughout history, and in virtually every part of the world, one encounters condemnations of the abuse of government office. How can this be, if, as I have argued, moral condemnations of bribery make sense only within a cultural context that distinguishes the public from the private?

If we look carefully at the condemnations of corruption that are to be found in medieval European writings, it turns out that they are fairly easy to reconcile with the view that in medieval Europe our modern notion of corruption was absent. First, medieval condemnations of corruption are against two particular kinds of corruption that are distinct from the kind of administrative corruption that we have been discussing: the corruption of judges and the corruption of churchmen (Noonan, 1984). Judges are condemned when they show favoritism or take bribes, because they have been established to judge disputes between the ruler's subjects and, as such, they are required by the ruler to judge fairly and justly without being influenced by bribes or favoritism. As late as 1765,

Blackstone defined bribery in a way that excluded administrative bribery: in his *Commentaries on the Laws of England*, he wrote that bribery was a crime committed by "a judge or other person concerned in the administration of justice" (quoted in Noonan, 1984, p. 399). On this definition, neither the ruler of the state nor any of his ministers or administrators could be guilty of the modern crime of corruption; judges could, however, commit a crime against the ruler when by accepting bribes they failed to carry out the task entrusted to them by the ruler; their crime consisted of disobedience to their personal master and was not perceived as a theft of public resources. The condemnations of corrupt churchmen also have nothing to do with what we today understand by political corruption. Churchmen were condemned for engaging in corruption because they sold spiritual benefits for material goods; in short, they engaged in simony. The sale of masses, indulgences, baptisms, absolutions, marriages, and funerals; the demand for money before confessing penitents; and the sale of parishes and bishoprics were all condemned as wrongful because, ultimately belonging to God, such spiritual goods should not be sold by churchmen for money.

Second, premodern writings also contain moral condemnations of administrative corruption, but these are cases where a minister attempts to cheat the king out of money that rightfully belongs to the king or when a minister serving the king takes a bribe against the express or implied wishes of the king (see, for example, the discussion of Samuel Pepys in Noonan, 1984, p. 378). Such condemnations of administrative corruption as are to be found in premodern writings, then, condemn as corrupt those actions wherein the king, not the public, is seen as being cheated by his ministers. This is quite different from the modern understanding of corruption as the abuse of public office for private gain.

In the many historical examples of patrimonial states, then, actions that we today would see as corrupt could not have been perceived as wrongful abuse of public office for private gain. This feature of the Weberian model of the patrimonial state is not a mere historical oddity, as it would be if the patrimonial state were a thing of the past. The patrimonial state, if we may accept the judgment of ethnographers and sociologists, is alive and well in several parts of the world.

Several noted observers of underdeveloped societies have argued that many are patrimonial or "neo-patrimonial" states. In 1966 Aristide Zolberg (Zolberg, 1966) argued that the single-party regimes of West Africa are patrimonial states whose rulers have appropriated the state and now are allowed to administer it as private property. Gunther Roth made a similar claim about the traditional regimes of Morocco and sheikhdoms of the Gulf, as well as the administration of Thailand (Roth, 1968). Others have made similar claims about other developing nations including Indonesia, Brazil, and, especially, the nations of sub-Saharan Africa.

There is a key difference, however, between the contemporary patrimonial state and the patrimonial states of sixteenth- and seventeenth-century Europe. Those modern nations that sociologists have characterized as patrimonial states were once colonized by European powers. During the colonial period, Europeans installed in these nations the kind of bureaucratic structures that Western political regimes developed during the nineteenth and twentieth centuries. But while these colonized nations adopted the external forms of Western administrative practices, they did not necessarily adopt the conceptions and values of public service that, for various reasons, developed in the West, after the long and often violent history of reform and transition that marked the change from the patrimonial politics of the sixteenth, seventeenth, and eighteenth centuries to the democratic and bureaucratic forms of Western public administration that developed in the nineteenth and twentieth centuries (Theobald, 1990). Although the colonized nations adopted the organizational forms of Western bureaucratic states, they retained a conception of political office as the private property of the officeholder, a conception that, as we saw earlier, was once also characteristic of European administrative systems (Sissener, 2001). The result was a "mixed" system in which the values of patrimonialism now exist side by side with the formal structures of rational bureaucracy. Jean-Francois Medard has labeled this kind of mixed system as "neo-patrimonialism"—"a kind of hybrid of patrimonialism and bureaucracy" (Medard, 1996). Neo-patrimonialism, he notes, "has to be defined not only as the lack of distinguishing between the public and private domains, but also as the non respect of this distinction when it is made. In the pure patrimonial situation, the distinction does not exist, in the neo-patrimonial situation the distinction is made, but rarely internalized, and even when it is, it is not respected" (Medard, 1996, p. 85).

Corruption, traditionally defined as the abuse of public office for private interests, is a concept that is, strictly speaking, alien to these neo-patrimonial states, and it is particularly alien to the consciousness of the great masses of people who have not been schooled in Western ways and who daily participate in exchanges that we would characterize as "corrupt." J. P. Olivier de Sardan (Sardan, 1999), while granting the "widespread stigmatization of corruption" in African societies, nevertheless notes that practices that observers might condemn as corruption "are nonetheless considered by their perpetrators as being legitimate, and often as not being corruption at all" (Sardan, 1999, p. 34). Consistent with the blurring of the public/private distinction, Sardan points out that office holders in African states, for a number of traditional and historical reasons, understand their office as carrying with it "the right to levy tribute" (Sardan, 1999, p. 42) as well as the obligation to distribute their takings among relatives and friends through "ostentation" and "largesse." Sardan notes that a number of other cultural practices or "logics" encourage this understanding of government office, including the intense negotiation and bargaining that affects every social exchange and thus all exchanges with government officials; the obligation to provide gifts to those who are helpful to one's cause and hence to officials who legitimately remind clients of their obligations; and the networks of social relationships that create solidarities and pressures to extend favoritism toward other members of one's network and thereby pressure officials to show favoritism toward friends and relatives. The effect of these practices, he notes, is to "dissolve juridically reprehensible practices into the fabric of familiar and socially commonplace practices, which happen to be accepted and even esteemed." These practices, "while exerting continuous pressure on social actors, help to accord a cultural acceptability to corruption" (Sardan, 1999, p. 44). Yet another factor that facilitates the perception that a government office is the private property of the officeholder is the practice of buying and selling government positions. The practice is common in patrimonial states, particularly in those of central Africa. Once a person has paid good money for an office, it is inevitable that he will think of the office and its rents not as belonging to the public but as his own property, to be used as he chooses.

It is not only in the patrimonial states of Africa that the distinction between the public and private makes little sense. Ethnographers report, for example, that in Indian villages, the government officials operate in a manner that also makes no distinction between their private lives and their public office. Consider, for example, Akhil Gupta's description of Sharmaji, an Indian government official who recorded and kept records of who owned the land in five to six villages (Gupta, 1995). He carried out his official functions in a room in his own house, surrounded by clients and assistants. His job was to add or delete names on land titles, to settle disputes over ownership, and, when necessary, to physically measure and survey land to settle disputes over boundaries. His clients came to him aware that having him perform these tasks "cost money," and the rates were well known and fixed. The process of giving bribes was therefore open and unconcealed. Two young men approached him one day saying they wanted to add a name to the record of the land the two of them owned so that the land could be used for collateral for a loan to purchase fertilizer. Several farmers and assistants were present.

> Sharmaji announced loudly that they would have to "pay for it." The young men immediately wanted to know how much would be required. [His assistant] said "Give as much as you like." The two clients then whispered to each other. Finally, one of them

broke the impasse by reaching into his shirt pocket and carefully taking out a few folded bills. He handed 10 rupees to [the assistant]. Sharmaji responded by bursting into raucous laughter. . . . Sharmaji told them that they didn't know anything about the law, that it took more than 14 rupees just for the cost of the application because in order to add a name to a plot, the application would have to be backdated by a few months. . . . Sharmaji then told the young men that they should have first found out "what it cost" to "get a name added to the register" these days. "Go and find out the cost of putting your name in the land register," he told them. . . . He immediately turned to one of the farmers present and asked him how much he had paid ten years ago. The man said it had been something like 150 rupees. . . . The young men turned to the other people and asked them if they knew what the appropriate sum was. All of them gave figures ranging from 130–150 rupees, but said that their information was dated because that is how much it had cost ten or more years ago. The young men tried to put a good face on the bungled negotiation by suggesting that it would not be a big loss if they did not succeed in their efforts. (Gupta, 1995, pp. 380–381)

The events in Sharmaji's home office are interesting for a several reasons. First, his administrative functions are carried on in his private home so that the distinction between the private and the public is dissolved; his administrative activities are part of his private household (Sissener, 2001). Second, he requires and takes payments from clients for performing his administrative duties. Third, these transactions are open and unconcealed; they are, as it were, transparent. And fourth, related to this transparency, there is no evident sense of shame, remorse, or guilt for what he does; it is an ordinary and accepted part of his administrative activities.

Do his activities constitute corruption? By Western standards they do. Yet from the perspective of the participants involved in this incident—Sharmaji, his assistants, and his farmer clients—there is nothing wrong with the fact that he charges the fees he charges, because they perceive his office as belonging to him and not to an abstract public. He expends his personal energies to accomplish the tasks his clients ask of him, and he is compensated for his efforts through the fees that he charges. He receives, of course, a small salary from the local government for the work he does. But the salary is not enough for him to live on, and it is understood that he will charge clients for his services in order to make enough for him to support himself and his family and assistants. From the internal perspective of those who participate in these exchanges, their activities are morally legitimate, even if from an external perspective they may complain about the high levels of corruption that afflict Indian life (Sissener, 2001).

Corruption and the Personalized State

I have concentrated so far on the extent to which patrimonial and neo-patrimonial states provide examples of cultural contexts in which what we Westerners would call corruption is not perceived as corrupt because the public/private distinction required for corruption is absent. But the Weberian conception of the bureaucratic state also assumes that government must be impersonal and impartial. The government official, in particular, must not exhibit partiality or favoritism toward parties with whom the official has emotional ties or a personal relationship. To exhibit such favoritism is to become corrupt. I want to turn now to examine cultural contexts where the impersonal and impartial fidelity to rules that is characteristic of modern public administration is replaced by favoritism and partiality. I will argue that what we perceive as corruption in such cultures is in fact morally acceptable relative to local conceptions of government and social exchanges, and I will refer to a state in which dealings with government officials are based on such favoritism and partiality as a *personalized state*.

I need to say something here about the fact that I am distinguishing between the patrimonial state as a state in which the public/private distinction does not hold, and the personalized state as a state in which dealings with government officials are not impersonal and impartial. I make this distinction mainly because I want to discuss these two features of states separately. In reality, states in which the public/private distinction is not made— i.e., patrimonial states—usually are states in which governance is based on personal relationships and favoritism and so are usually also personalized states. In fact, Weber himself defines the patrimonial state as one in which both the public/private distinction is not made and in which government dealings are not impersonal and impartial. Nevertheless, it is possible for a state that lacks the public/private distinction (e.g., a state in which the king is the owner of the state and all its resources) to be administered by ministers who carry out their duties for the king in an impersonal and impartial manner. So one can distinguish between the patrimonial state as a state whose essential feature is the absence of the public/private distinction and the personalized state as a state whose essential feature is that dealings with officials are neither impersonal nor impartial, even though Weber himself does not make such a distinction and even though these two features are usually found together. However, although I here distinguish the personalized state from the patrimonial state, I do not place a great deal of weight on the distinction. I simply use the terms here to highlight two different ways in which distinct conceptions of the state can lead to distinct moral views on corruption. If the reader wishes to see my discussion in this section as nothing more than a continuing discussion of another aspect of the patrimonial state, that will not affect the substance of my argument in any way.

Ethnographers report that in a number of cultures, the administrative decisions of officials are commonly based on the obligations created by personal relationships. In the cultural contexts I have in mind, the obligations created by personal relationships are given much greater moral weight than the moral weight given to the impersonal rules of administrative structures.

Drawing on his own ethnographic studies of the practice of "favoritism" in Nepal, Alex Kondos, for example, reports the following:

One of the first things Nepalis do whenever they have to negotiate with a government or state office, is to ask themselves and their families, "Whom do we know, who works there?" The question signposts the fundamental Nepalese belief that having a contact, preferably a relative or close friend in public office with power to render favors is a legitimate avenue or right and proper way of getting things done. (Kondos, 1987, p. 17)

In most cultures, of course, even highly bureaucratic ones like our own, we sometimes ask ourselves whom we know before we try to deal with the bureaucracy; nevertheless, we expect the bureaucrat to adhere to impersonal rules and to be impartial in his dealings with us in a way that rules out overt favoritism. Kondos makes the point, however, that in the Nepali context, dealings with administrators are always personalized and are always considered interpersonal meetings—not bureaucratic interactions based on impartiality—where overt favoritism and partiality are expected and which regularly call on the obligations of kinship, friendship, or other special relationships. Kondos notes that often, in order to establish the contacts and relationships that supplicants can rely on to gain political favors, Nepalis use the Hindu institution of *chakari*, a prolonged and elaborate process of bestowing flattery, praise, obsequiousness, and gifts upon public officials. Western intellectuals, she argues (including Nepalese intellectuals schooled in the West), interpret this institution and the favoritism or partiality that it engenders as "corruption" and conclude that Nepalese bureaucracies are "riddled with corruption." But, Kondos notes, "From its very inception as a nation just over 200 years ago, Nepal has been a Hindu kingdom ruled in accordance with Hindu principles of statecraft, principles popularized among its subjects through great epics like the Ramayama. . . . Whatever else is involved, the traditional mode of Nepalese statecraft is not one characterized by 'impartiality.'"

A similar acceptance of the legitimacy of relying on personal relationships and favoritism in dealing with government officials can be found in

West Bengal (India). Ruud notes in her study of the formation of networks of relationships among Bengali citizens that such relationships, and the favoritism and obligations of partiality that such relationships give rise to in exchanges with government administrators, are "culturally acceptable and saturated with cultural meaning" (Ruud, 1998). Relationships form the basis of exchanges between citizens and government officials that Westerners would characterize as "corruption" but that Bengalis see as a morally acceptable and ordinary practice because they conceive of interactions with government as legitimately infused with personalistic partiality.

Another example of a cultural context in which bureaucratic impartiality is overridden by partiality and favoritism is, of course, modern-day China. The practices associated with the institution of "guanxi," or what Yang refers to as "the gift economy," are prevalent and widespread in China. The word *guanxi* in Chinese means "social relationships" or "social connections" and refers more generally to the obligations associated with one's social relationships (Yang, 1989). The obligations that constitute guanxi can be based on friendship; on family relationships; on membership in the same social group; on attending the same school; on having lived in the same city or region of the country; on having a mutual friend, acquaintance, or other intermediary; or on the giving and acceptance of gifts or assistance. Unlike the impersonal obligations that, say, a Western bureaucrat has to be impartial toward all clients, the obligations created by guanxi require that one exhibit partiality and favoritism toward those with whom one has the obligations of guanxi. The Chinese practice of giving gifts to administrators or of invoking relationships of kinship, friendship, or other connections and of thereby creating in the administrator the obligations of guanxi will appear to the Westerner as bribery or as unethical favoritism and therefore as corruption. But to the Chinese, the institution of guanxi is a morally acceptable form of human exchange that "cannot be confused with bribery" (Yang, p. 46).

It is important to see that I am here considering guanxi from what I earlier called an "internal" perspective and not from what I have termed an "external" evaluation of the practice—e.g., an evaluation of guanxi in terms of its consequences. Dunfee and Warren (2001), among others, for example, have argued that guanxi is unethical because it has bad consequences, such as "reducing societal wealth." But these arguments do not show that guanxi is in itself unethical or that it has features that make it inherently wrong to the Chinese. An utterly benign cultural practice may sometimes have social costs that outweigh its social benefits, but this would not show that the practice is in itself conceived as evil. From an internal moral perspective, I am here arguing, guanxi is considered morally acceptable to the Chinese even when it is used in dealings with government officials.

China's is not the only culture in which it is morally acceptable to invoke social relationships and gift giving to create the obligations of partiality in interactions with government officials. Similar practices exist in Hungary (Kenedi, 1981), Bangladesh (Andvig, Fjeldstad, Amundsen, Sissener, & Søreide, 2000, pp. 75–77), and Russia (Ledeneva, 1998). In all of these cases, the state is not conceptualized as an impersonal and impartial institution, but as an institution that is legitimately and rightfully infused with the partiality and favoritism that arise from the obligations created by personal relationships. The state, in short, is seen as a personalized state, and relative to this conception of the state, what appears to us as unethical corruption is in fact locally accepted as morally legitimate by participants (Ledeneva, 1998, pp. 83–87).

It is important to acknowledge that citizens of personalistic states often criticize the intrusion of partiality into their government. China's citizens, for example, often lament the high levels of corruption. As several researchers have pointed out, however, the very actors who criticize government as unethical when they observe government being partial to others see no moral infraction when they themselves participate in a transaction in which government administrators are partial to them or to others to whom they feel closely related (Ledeneva, 1998, p. 60; Sardan, 1999). Indeed, because they interpret their transaction in morally benign terms, they willingly participate in the transaction with no feeling of having done anything wrong. The perspectives of observer and of participant yield distinct moral judgments so that the cultural practice that a person will characterize as unethical when she approaches it as an external observer will be characterized by that same person as morally innocent when she is a participant in the social practice. My suggestion is that when a person looks at the personalistic state from an external perspective, he or she will often judge it as objectionable in terms that are very similar to the way that Western external observers would judge it. It is only from the genuinely internal perspective of the participant in the practice that the personalized state and its favoritisms are accepted as morally legitimate. And that is what I have been trying to argue.

CONCLUSION

Let me conclude this overly long discussion. I have tried to defend the beleaguered businessman who protests that in many cultures what Westerners perceive as unethical corruption is not seen as unethical by members of those cultures, and whose protests have been discounted as self-serving. It is true that many of the members of virtually every country and culture condemn corruption as evil. Nevertheless, I have claimed, one needs to look closely at how participants within the culture understand so-called corrupt exchanges, because participants may understand their behaviors in terms of an understanding of the state that renders their exchanges morally acceptable. I have tried, that is, to show that moral evaluations of corrupt exchanges between government officials and private parties must be relativized to participants' conceptions of the state. Different conceptions of the state—in particular of the competitive state, the patrimonial state, or the personalized state—grant moral legitimacy to exchanges between businesses and officials that our own local conceptions of governance would condemn as unethical.

Let me end with a brief quote from John Noonan's massive work on the history of bribery, where he examines bribery from a natural law

approach (an approach which I myself favor) that sees ethical notions as fluid and changing from one cultural context to another and from one temporal period to another. Noonan perceptively writes,

> Bribes are a species of reciprocity. Human life is full of reciprocities. The particular reciprocities that count as bribes in particular cultures are distinguished by intentionality, form, and context. What is a bribe depends on the cultural treatment of the constituent elements. The observer outside the culture, like the cynic or rigorist within it, is inclined to see the conventional differences as arbitrary and to reduce all reciprocities of a given kind to bribes, to treat, say, any gift to an officeholder as a bribe. Doing so, the outsider imposes his own standard and reaches a judgment that is unreasonable if the culture's own norms are used. (Noonan, 1984, p. xiv)

REFERENCES

Andvig, J. C., Fjeldstad, O.-H., Amundsen, I., Sissener, T., & Søreide, T. (2000, December). *Research on corruption: A policy oriented survey.* Report commissioned by NORAD. Chr. Michelsen Institute, Bergen, Norway. Retrieved November 2003 from http://www.uv.no/documents/showdoc.cfm?id=26

Bayley, D. H. (1966). The effects of corruption in a developing nation. *Western Political Quarterly, 19,* 719–732.

Beattie, A., & Barbour, J. (2000). Sunshine: The best disinfectant. In *No longer business as usual: Fighting bribery and corruption* (pp. 137–146). Paris: OECD.

Crouch, H. (1979). Patrimonialism and military rule in Indonesia. *World Politics, 31*(4), 571–587.

Dobel, P. J. (1978, September). The corruption of a state. *American Political Science Review, 72*(3), 958–973.

Dunfee, T. W., & Warren, D. E. (2001). Is guanxi ethical? A normative analysis of doing business in China. *Journal of Business Ethics, 32,* 191–204.

Eisenstadt, S. N. (1973). *Traditional patrimonialism and modern neo-patrimonialism.* London: Sage.

Elliott, K. A. (1997). Introduction. In K. A. Elliott (Ed.), *Corruption and the global economy* (pp. 1–5). Washington, DC: Institute for International Economics.

Gupta, A. (1995). Blurred boundaries: The discourse of corruption, the culture of politics, and the imagined state. *American Ethnologist, 22*(2), 375–402.

Johnston, M. (1996, September). The search for definitions: The vitality of politics and the issue of corruption. *International Social Science Journal, 149*, 321–336.

Keefer, P., & Knack, S. (1996, November). Institutions and economic performance: Cross-country tests using alternative institutional measures. *Economics and Politics, 7*, 207–227.

Kenedi, J. (1981). *Do it yourself: Hungary's hidden economy.* New York: Pluto Press.

Kisunko, A., Brunetti, G., & Weder, B. (1997). Credibility of rules and economic growth: Evidence from a worldwide private sector survey. Background paper for *The World Development Report.* Washington: The World Bank.

Kondos, A. (1987). The question of "corruption" in Nepal. *Mankind, 17*(1), 15–29.

Ledeneva, A. V. (1998). *Russia's economy of favours: Blat, networking and informal exchange.* Cambridge: Cambridge University Press.

Leff, N. H. (1964, November). Economic development through bureaucratic corruption. *American Behavioural Scientist,* 8–14.

LeVine, V. (1980). African patrimonial regimes in comparative perspective. *Journal of Modern African Studies, 18*(4), 657–673.

Lui, F. (1985). An equilibrium queuing model of bribery. *Journal of Political Economy, 93*(4), 760–781.

Mauro, P. (1995). Corruption and growth. *Quarterly Journal of Economics, 110*(3), 681–712.

Medard, J.-F. (1996). Patrimonialism, neo-patrimonialism, and the study of the post-colonial state in sub-Saharan Africa. In H. S. Marcussen (Ed.), *Improved natural resource management: The role of formal organizations and informal networks and institutions* (pp. 76–97). Occasional Paper no. 17. Denmark: International Development Studies, Roskilde University.

Methanex. (2001). *Claimant Methanex Corporation's amended claim.* In the arbitration under Chapter 11 of the North American Free Trade Agreement and under the UNCITRAL arbitration rules between Methanex Corporation, Claimant/Investor, and The United States of America, Respondent/Party. Retrieved August 2001 from http://www.methanex.com/investorcentre/mtbe/draft_ amended_claim.pdf

Naim, M. (1995). The corruption eruption. *The Brown Journal of World Affairs, 2*(2).

Nissenbaum, D. (2002, June 29). Davis at center of international treaty dispute. *Mercury News.*

Noonan, J. (1984). *Bribes.* New York: Macmillan.

Nye, J. S. (1989). Corruption and political development: A cost-benefit analysis. In A. J. Heidenheimer (Ed.), *Political corruption: Readings in comparative analysis* (pp. 564–557). New Brunswick: Transaction Books.

Philp, M. (1997). Defining political corruption. *Political Studies, 45*, 436–462.

Qizilbash, M. (2001). Corruption and human development: A conceptual discussion. *Oxford Development Studies, 29*(3), 265–278.

Roett, R. (1972). *Brazil: Politics in a patrimonial society.* New York: Praeger.

Rose-Ackerman, S. (1999). *Corruption and government: Causes, consequences, and reform.* London: Cambridge University Press.

Roth, G. (1968). Personal rulership, patrimonialism and empire-building in the new states. *World Politics, 20*, 194–206.

Ruud, A. E. (1998). *Corruption as everyday practice: Rules and rule-bending in local Indian society* (Working Paper 1998.4). Centre for Development and the Environment, University of Oslo.

Sardan, J. P .O. de. (1999). A moral economy of corruption. *The Journal of Modern African Studies, 37*(1), 25–52.

Sissener, T. K. (2001). *Anthropological perspectives on corruption* (Working Paper 2001:5). Chr. Michelsen Institute, Bergen, Norway. Retrieved November 2003 from http://www.cmi.no/publications/2001%5Cwp%5Cwp2001-5.pdf

Theobald, R. (1990). *Corruption, development and underdevelopment.* London: The Macmillan Press, Ltd.

Thompson, D. F. (1993). Mediated corruption: The case of the Keating Five. *American Political Science Review, 87*(2), 369–381.

Transparency International. (2002). *Business principles for countering bribery.* Berlin: Transparency International. Retrieved from http://www.transparency.org/building_coalitions/private_sector/business_principles.html

Weber, M. (1956). *Economy and society: An outline of interpretive sociology* (G. Roth & C. Wittich, Eds.). Berkeley: University of California Press.

Wei, S.-J. (2000, February). How taxing is corruption on international investors? *Review of Economics and Statistics, 82,* 1–11.

Willame, J.-C. (1972). *Patrimonialism and political change in the Congo.* Stanford: Stanford University Press.

Williams, R. (1999). New concepts for old? *Third World Quarterly, 20*(3), 503–513.

Yang, Mayfair Mei-Hut. (1989). The gift economy and state power in China. *Comparative Studies in Society and History, 31*(1), 25–54.

Zolberg, A. (1966). *Creating political order: The party-states of West Africa.* Chicago: Chicago University Press.

13

LAW, ACCOUNTABILITY, AND GLOBALIZATION

RICHARD DE GEORGE

I n the United States, business ethics as a field began when the focus of concern shifted from the individual person in business to the corporation (see De George, 1987).[1] By the '80s, when corporations on a large scale started to adopt codes of corporate conduct, it was important for those interested in ethical issues and in the incorporation of ethics in firms to distinguish legal compliance from moral requirements and ideals. The emphasis at the time was necessary to prevent a simple equation by many firms of the ethical with the legal. But in the process the close relation between law and ethics was more or less ignored by those in business ethics in favor of a concentration on the ethical norms and issues. In fact, law often represents the moral minimum required of a corporation, and that minimum has been raised as more and more people have come to see that certain practices are unfair or injurious to people, that moral argument and suasion have less than sufficient impact, and that law is necessary to bring about the morally desirable changes.

If we look back at the early period of the industrial revolution, we see many of the ills of unrestrained market forces in a stark light. Moral condemnation did not do much to change the sweatshops, to prevent the child labor described in England in the *Sadler Report*, to improve working conditions for workers, to establish the right to strike and other workers' rights, or to control pollution. In each case, vested business interests for the most part first shrugged off moral criticism and then fought any restrictive legislation. Moralizing and moral argumentation were necessary to raise the consciousness of the general population, to articulate the justified moral requirements that decent societies should recognize, and to prepare the way for appropriate legislation. But it was only the passage of legislation that brought about the needed changes on a national scale and that forced all businesses to abide by what even in the nineteenth century were morally mandatory ways of conducting business. As a result of the legislation, those companies that in fact had been acting as morality demands were no longer at a competitive disadvantage because they paid a living wage or provided decent working conditions. Legislation both raised the acknowledged moral minimum and leveled the playing field for all firms. The important point to notice is that although raising moral consciousness was necessary, it was not sufficient to effectively end ethical abuses. Enforced legislation was also necessary.

In more recent times, the story has been the same. Despite the criticism of environmentalists and others, many companies did not control noxious pollution until forced to by legislation. The automakers did not willingly lower pollution emissions on their own, in part because lowering pollution emissions was not seen as a marketable competitive strategy. It took legislation. Nor in the very recent past have we found corporations voluntarily making their accounting procedures and decisions more transparent, despite widespread popular moral indignation at the abuses that took place in companies such as Enron and WorldCom. It is unlikely many will do so without legislation.

Beyond controlling harmful practices, however, legislation is also necessary for the market to work efficiently and for the benefit of all. Legislation protects property rights, guarantees contracts, prevents unfair monopolies and other predatory business practices, regulates financial markets, and in general makes possible fair competition. The brief history of Russia since 1991 shows the very negative consequences of attempting to have a market economy without adequate legislative rules and protections in place.

Business ethics, then, in the developed countries operates with a background of laws and institutions—ranging from a free investigative press and media to labor unions and consumer groups to NGOs such as Amnesty International and the Audubon Society. The latter—to the extent that they spotlight ethical issues—help articulate the perspective of different groups whose interests are frequently overlooked or given insufficient attention; raise public consciousness about issues the groups in question feel are morally important; shine a light on practices the groups consider

unethical; and investigate cases and practices they believe involve morally questionable behavior. All of these feed into what is called *business ethics*, which has its role to play in raising the ethical dimension of new practices, analyzing complex issues, uncovering presuppositions, and focusing attention on wrongdoings and harms to people.

When we turn to the phenomenon of globalization of markets and production, however, the striking contrast with the national scenario of industrialized countries is the lack of significant adequate background institutions both in the developing countries and on the international and global arenas. The ills that early industrialization brought with it in England, France, and Germany, and later in the United States and other countries, have been transported, together with incipient industrialization, to the developing countries. As a result, globalization has often become the object of condemnation and of moral invective, which is more properly directed against its negative effects rather than against the process itself. Sometimes the solution to the problems found in less developed countries is sought through cajoling multinational corporations to act ethically and with integrity (see De George, 1993). But this can at best be only part of the solution, just as it was only part of the solution during the nineteenth century. Adequate background institutions must be developed, responsibility correctly placed, and accountability properly demanded.

I shall suggest four areas that relate to responsibility and accountability in the current period of globalization. The first is the need for legislation that is both passed and enforced in the developing countries, and the concomitant need for the development of the infrastructure necessary to make it possible to get such legislation both adopted and effectively enforced. The second is the need for international legal coordination. The third is the development of international agreements that serve some of the functions of background institutions on a worldwide level, absent any global legislature. The fourth is the audited implementation of international codes for corporations. The third and fourth are surrogates for international law.

When it comes to responsibility and accountability, we have to get the causes of ills correct if we are to find effective remedies.

DEVELOPING COUNTRY
LEGISLATION AND INFRASTRUCTURE

Although the general public as well as those in business ethics have focused attention on the ethics of multinational corporations (MNCs), the ills we find in business in less developed countries (LDCs) can ultimately be solved only by those countries changing local conditions, enforcing existing legislation, and passing and enforcing additional restrictive legislation. If we look at the major ethical issues in globalization, we can usefully divide the kinds of harm with which MNCs are charged into three categories: those in which they do direct harm, those in which they take advantage of corrupt conditions, and those in which they are instruments of changes that undermine the local culture.

Examples of the first would be an agricultural MNC that buys up the best land in a less developed country, turns it into producing export crops, and leaves those who formerly lived off the land with poorer land or no land, leading to malnutrition or worse. Another example would be establishing polluting industries in countries with no or little control and polluting land, air, and water. The second category includes bribery, the use of child labor, the transfer of dangerous industries and productive processes, and so on. The third comes about as a result of organizing production and marketing goods that change or undermine the local culture.

In all cases, the MNCs do not bear all the blame, and the solutions lie not only in preaching to the MNCs but in the LDCs passing appropriate legislation. In order to achieve that result, the consciousness of the people has to be raised, and they have to have an effective voice in the running of the government and hence in the

legislation passed. Preaching to the MNCs will not accomplish this, even though the MNCs, by acting ethically, might set an example that helps raise consciousness of what ethics demands in business and might even take an active role in supporting activities that raise consciousness and encourage appropriate legislation.

In the first set of cases, the MNCs bear a giant share of blame. In those cases, the practices do more harm than good to the host country, and for this the companies can be morally faulted (see De George, 1993, chap. 3). Even here, however, one can ask where the host country government is, whether it is corrupt and benefits from the actions of the MNCs, whether it is the rich members of the society that benefit. Where are those who represent and speak for the interests and benefits of the people of the society? Even usually well informed critics are sometimes not clear about the proper remedy.[2] If the system being changed is feudalistic, then the claim that feudalism—with all its ills, oppression, and quasi-slavery—deserves defense against change is at least questionable, even if it allows people to live at a subsistence level. That some slaves after the Civil War were in some ways worse off than they had been previously did not justify the continuance of slavery in the American South. There are better and worse ways to replace feudalism, and multinationals that dispossess farmers may well be open to censure for doing so, but not simply because they undermine a feudal system. The important point is that the changes must come from those in the country, who can effectively raise the aforementioned questions and possibly can do something about them. Outsiders raising them will not change the conditions.

In the second category, American and Western European multinationals do not impose market economies on host countries. They find restricted, incipient, and distorted markets there, which vary from country to country. The ethical issues of business from the nineteenth and the first half of the twentieth century in the United States and Western Europe are now found in developing countries. That is where we find sweatshops, gross exploitation, bribery, high unemployment, and mass migration from the countryside to the cities. These are not conditions that multinationals bring with them and impose on developing countries. They are not the result of an incipient free market introduced by MNCs. They existed and would exist without the presence of MNCs. That they are evils that should be corrected is evident. That the MNCs have either the primary responsibility or the capability of changing the conditions is far from evident. Going back to the history of the developed countries, as we noted earlier, these ills were eliminated only after public consciousness had been raised and popular support managed to promote effective new legislation.

Multinationals do not typically lower wages in developing countries. The wages are low before they arrive, and they sometimes raise them. Although countries may lower taxes to attract multinationals, they do not lower wages. The fact that many less developed countries attempt to attract multinational corporations seems to be a fairly clear indication that the LDCs believe they benefit from the presence of the MNCs. The multinationals do not start sweatshops even when they take advantage of their existence and use by their contractors. These practices are not the result of an imposed Western market but the result of incipient industrialization or of local traditions.

It is difficult to blame multinational corporations for seeking cheaper sources of labor in less developed countries than they have in their own countries. There is no moral requirement that they should employ only workers in their own countries. It may be said that they take advantage of the low wages elsewhere. But they did not introduce them or cause them. And they are in a position to help the less developed country and its workers not only by supplying work but also by raising wages, as some do. On the other hand, they cannot raise wages too much without skewing the labor market in those countries and being open to the charge that they attract all the best workers and undercut the local enterprises that cannot afford to pay comparable wages.

In looking at child labor as a case in point, multinationals do not introduce child labor. They find it the local practice, and many multinationals have become sensitive to the problem of child labor and have adopted policies against using suppliers who employ child labor. High-profile cases, such as Nike and Wal-Mart,[3] have brought the issue to the attention of both American MNCs and many American consumers. Starting in 1999, some American students became concerned about the sweatshop conditions in which collegiate licensed apparel is made and demanded that their universities use only sources that do not use child labor and do not have sweatshop conditions.[4] But critics often present the problem as one that multinationals have introduced, instead of one that they have sometimes exploited. According to a 1997 UNICEF report, probably less than 5 percent of the children involved in child labor work in production for international export (UNICEF, 1997, p. 21). The other 95 percent are involved in farming, in local production, or in the informal economy.

Not only do enlightened multinationals require that their suppliers not use child labor, but they also worry about what happens to those children who are fired so the supplier can meet the multinational's standards. The Swedish-based apparel company Hennes and Mauritz tries to find an alternative approach to simply dismissing the children, such as making some provision for them once dismissed.[5] Levi Strauss in one case in Bangladesh not only continued to pay the small salary the children had previously received but also built a school for them to attend.[6] Requiring that multinationals have "clean hands" with respect to child labor sells well in developed countries and is an ethically proper stance for MNCs to adopt. But it ignores the reality of child labor in the developing countries and in some cases exacerbates it. Multinationals cannot solve the problem of child labor, and it requires too much of them to expect that they do. The society in question must address the issue and take steps to eradicate it. Most countries have laws prohibiting it, but they are often ignored and not enforced. This policy of benign neglect in this area exacerbates the plight of the country. One result is that the children receive little if any education and so, since they cannot take part in the country's development, they eventually contribute to high unemployment, low wages, and the cycle of child labor.

The same kind of story is true with respect to working conditions. If the multinationals build their own facilities, they are often the envy of local companies. Those MNCs that use suppliers frequently require that certain minimum conditions be met, such as having fire doors and adequate ventilation. But although these are only appropriate, they do not touch the conditions in which most of the population that is not involved in supplying the multinationals works. Enforced legislation is necessary for that.

Local- and national-level corruption often accompanies development. It is necessary to spotlight this. The use by U.S. multinationals of suppliers who use child labor is a legitimate target of ethical critics. But these critics rarely blame the local suppliers who employ the child labor with or without the multinational buyer. The critics seldom blame the governments of the countries that allow these conditions, and they offer no solutions to changing conditions other than controlling the behavior of the multinationals. The multinationals have the obligation not to use such suppliers and to pay enough so that suppliers who do not use child labor can produce for them. Multinationals also have a role to play in fighting corruption. They should not oppose legislation that seeks to remedy the ills we have described, and to the extent possible should encourage such legislation. It is difficult to see how opposing unethical practices can be held to be unethical.[7] But we cannot and should not expect multinationals to do more than they can and should with respect to developing nations. Such nations must also take responsibility for their bribery, corruption, child labor, and conditions of labor. To focus exclusively on multinationals is to miss an important cause of the problem.

The basic problem is not the way most multinational companies treat workers or suppliers, but the conditions that they find and either accept and exploit or in part remedy. By providing work in countries with high unemployment rates and by bringing with them higher standards, MNCs can be an important part of the solution to some of the problems faced by less developed countries.

Critics in the developed nations may feel more comfortable in condemning multinationals for child labor and sweatshop conditions than in criticizing local governments and entrepreneurs, because their criticism often has some effect on the actions of the corporations in question. Critics may also often feel that as outsiders they have no right to criticize the local perpetrators or the local elite that profit from the practices. Moreover, if an outside critic does condemn the local practitioners, that person is often labeled as someone who blames the victim. Despite the good intentions of critics, the basic problems ultimately cannot be solved solely from outside but must be solved from within—even though outsiders can cajole, encourage, and supply help, both monetary and other, as appropriate.

In the third category, the MNCs find a market for products that change the local culture rather than create it. In China, millions of pirated copies of American movies, such as *The Grinch Who Stole Christmas*, are sold within a week of their opening in U.S. movie houses. It is not the MNCs that create that demand or, in this case, that benefit from it.

To the extent that the culture does not violate ethical norms, multinationals should respect the local culture and work with and not against it (see De George, 1993). But this should not be taken to mean that multinationals necessarily act unethically if they bring about change.

Exactly what critics complain about when they charge multinationals with undermining local culture is often not clear. Multinationals are ethically required not to discriminate against women or minorities, for instance. And if they do not so discriminate, even when it is the local custom to do so, they should not be ethically faulted for failing to follow the local custom. Nor should they be faulted if they indirectly help undermine a feudal society as it enters the stage of industrialization. As we have already noted, there are better and worse ways of doing this, and the ethical obligation is to minimize the harm done to people. But to expect multinationals not to impact local culture at all is to ask more than any company can legitimately be asked to do.

If an industrial society develops anywhere, it changes the agricultural culture from which it springs. It does not matter whether the system is capitalist or socialist, whether there is government control or free enterprise. An industrialized country is different from its agricultural antecedent. And the change produces a change in culture, broadly conceived.

The introduction of TV, cell phones, and the Internet into rural communities in poor countries will change them. This is all part of globalization. If the people of Moscow or Beijing like McDonald's and Coke, as they do, that is their choice. Nor is it all bad. MNCs are transferring knowledge and know-how as well as international standards—technical and ethical. The stories of abuse should be weighed against such stories as those of the companies that fought apartheid in South Africa by following the Sullivan Principles; of McDonald's in Guatemala raising standards for bread as well as for cleanliness and working conditions; of Unilever in India introducing its policy of protecting the environment and developing products for the poor; and of companies that adopt and follow the Caux and other international principles.

As in the other cases, the host country has responsibility for its culture and it should assume that responsibility, passing appropriate legislation restricting multinational corporations that it feels are affecting it adversely.[8]

In placing some of the onus for solving their problems on the less developed countries, I am not claiming that they must do so either entirely on their own or without outside help. Governments of developed countries, international organizations, multinationals, NGOs, and others all have a positive role to play. But the central actors are the country itself and its people. The basic responsibility and accountability lie there, and the need for enforced legislation is paramount.

In England, Germany, the United States, and other developed countries, we have seen that legislation was necessary to end child labor and control other harmful tendencies of unrestricted capitalism. Restrictive legislation was passed despite the opposition of business interests. This was possible only because of the existence of democratic governments that were and are at least to some extent responsive to the people. And central to responsive democracy are an opposition party, the plethora of groups that make up civil society, trade unions, environmental and consumer groups, a free press and media, investigative reporters, and government representatives who are held accountable by the people in regular elections.

Authoritarian regimes in less developed countries typically serve the elite and the leaders of the country. They do not have to consider the welfare of the general population, and frequently do not. They have little incentive to do so, since they are not accountable to the people. Tradition supports acquiescence on the part of people, and the absence of a free press keeps dissent from becoming organized. Nonetheless, we have seen the power of the people in overthrowing the socialist regimes of Eastern Europe and the USSR, and we have seen the people in countries such as South Korea force leaders from power when their large-scale bribery became public.

Free markets and democracy have tended to develop together.[9] This is no coincidence, for both markets and democracy process information better and more efficiently than can or does any centralized command economy or any other type of controlled economy or any type of authoritarian government. Free markets, among other things, establish many sources of economic power, which seek a voice in the government and a hand in running the country. If the market is truly free and not kept under the control of a small number of families or oligarchs, it allows entry and new entrepreneurs. India in recent years provides an example of the rise of computer-based software and programming industries that presage a wave of the future. Modern technology, the Internet, and cell phones have all made it possible for people anywhere not only to become informed about what is happening elsewhere but also to enter areas in which to compete that do not require large plants and large initial capital investments. Multinationals and globalization can help spread democracy as well as free markets to the benefit of the people of developing countries.

To unleash the potential of the Information Age and reap the benefits of globalization requires the freedom to experiment and take risks and to try new approaches that are not allowed under strict authoritarian control. To some extent, China is allowing a limited free market in certain areas, while keeping political power in the hands of the leadership. Whether it will be able to sustain the uneasy relation between free markets and lack of political freedom in the form of democracy still remains to be seen. History tends to indicate that the two do not fit well together, although usually a strong government, such as those in China and Singapore, can foster business better than a weak one, such as those in Russia and in many of the African nations. Although authoritarian regimes can institute development and bring countries to a certain level of productivity, they typically—as we saw with the USSR—can go only so far. Moreover, authoritarian governments tend to support corruption at the top more than do democratic governments that are responsive to the people.

Ultimately, the people must change their country. Freedom, democracy, and development cannot be given to people or brought to them. The people must seize them. Governments should be responsive to their people. Yet, responsive governments cannot be dictated from without or imposed on countries. They must be formed from within. Changing the conditions of labor will not result simply from outsiders, such as MNCs, making changes but requires the conditions being changed internally. The people must demand protective legislation, which must be passed and enforced by their governments.

INTERNATIONAL LEGAL COORDINATION

There are two senses in which international legal coordination is necessary. One involves all or most nations coordinating laws that outlaw what at least most see as problems to be so controlled, but on which laws differ or do not exist. One example was provided by the "I Love You"

computer worm/virus that caused billions of dollars of damage to computers throughout the world. The program was released by Onel de Gusman, a student in the Philippines (see De George, 2003, p. 243). At the time, there was no Philippine law that made his action illegal. Although the Philippine government wished to prosecute him, there was no legal way to do so. Since then, the government has passed appropriate legislation. Such legislation is needed in all countries, lest malicious computer hackers find a safe haven from which to wreak destruction. Clearly, all countries should have similar laws sufficient for the task of preventing such programs from being distributed. Countries that refuse to pass such legislation should be kept, to the extent possible, from taking part in the Internet by screens, by Internet Service Providers refusing access, or by other appropriate means.

A second example is the U.S. Foreign Corrupt Practices Act, which was passed in 1977 and which made it a criminal offense for U.S.-based companies to pay bribes to high-level government officials of other countries. This was the first instance of extraterritorial legislation in which a country forbade a company from engaging in certain practices in another country. The United States sought to have other countries follow its example and so level the playing field for all. It was not until 1998 that the OECD countries finally agreed to adopt similar legislation with respect to their home-based companies. Such legal coordination clearly makes the restraint on U.S. companies more palatable, since they know that companies from Germany, France, Great Britain, Japan, and so on are similarly restrained. It also puts pressure on less developed countries, where the practice is most blatant and injurious, to pass legislation making bribery illegal or to enforce such laws already on their books. Wiping out bribery requires international legal coordination.

The second way in which international legal coordination is required concerns the legislation in less developed countries, which I referred to in relation to suggestions in the previous section of this chapter. There I argued that it is up to each country to pass and enforce legislation outlawing child labor, to set minimally acceptable conditions of health and sanitation for workers, and to set minimal limits of acceptable pollution. The reply of many less developed nations is that the international system does not allow them to do this. If they were to set such standards, then multinationals would move their investments to countries with lower standards, and they would be left worse off than they presently are. So the system requires them to lower, rather than raise, standards if they are to attract outside investment and multinationals. The solution, if it cannot be expected to come from the self-restraint of multinationals, is for all less developed countries to pass similar legislation with respect to these issues, in effect taking child labor, sweatshops, and unrestricted pollution out of the marketplace. In this way, countries cannot be pitted against each other on the basis of such considerations. This will require international legal coordination among the less developed countries. But this action can be supported and promoted by the developed countries and international organizations such as the UN, as well as by NGOs and even by multinational corporations, as we have already indicated.

INTERNATIONAL LEGISLATION

The third proposal is a surrogate for international legislation, since there is no world government that can pass global laws. There are good reasons why any such global government is not an acceptable development. Yet the absence of such legislation does not preclude multinational agreements. I have already referred to legal coordination, and a good example of that is the European Union, which proposes to its member nations legislation that each passes with its own specific conditions entering into the final laws that are passed in each country.

The WTO is another example of a mechanism to coordinate legislation. But the WTO as presently constituted suffers from at least three drawbacks, which have drawn considerable protest. The first is that it is not democratic in its operation and so is neither clearly representative of the people of the countries involved nor clearly responsive to them. The second is that there is a tendency to adopt the least stringent policies that affect trade, without adequate consideration of the moral desirability of more stringent conditions. The third is that the developed nations get to set the rules, and the smaller, less powerful, less developed nations are frequently the ones who have to accept unequal and unfair conditions of trade (e.g., with respect to agricultural products). Nonetheless, we have an example of how in the absence of an international legislature predatory and harmful practices can be tamed.

In protests in Seattle and Genoa against the WTO and other international organizations, activists have demanded, among other things, more transparency and a democratization of these institutions. Exactly what the latter means and who is supposed to have a say in their policies is not clear. But it is noteworthy that the protests are part of the democratic process, that they take place in democratic countries, and that the protestors see democracy and democratic processes as important. They correctly expect their protests to be heard, be considered, and possibly have an effect on the way their governments conduct business. This expectation and the possibility of protest are often absent in developing countries.

International agreements have an important role to play in providing something on the international level akin to the necessary laws on the national level. But just as the national governments should be held accountable by the people for the justice of the laws they adopt and the system they support and implement, so should the groups that arrive at and implement international agreements. The demand for democracy by protestors, while often confused in what the acceptable alternative might be, correctly focuses on the need for such groups and agreements to be ethically defensible, to be as transparent in their operations as possible, and to be accountable not only to the member countries but also to the people affected by the agreements, wherever they may be.

AUDITED IMPLEMENTATION OF INTERNATIONAL CODES FOR CORPORATIONS

The fourth proposal is to hold corporations accountable to a greater extent than they presently are. Not everything can or should be legislated, either on a national or on an international level. I have argued so far for legislation to handle harmful aspects of industrialization and globalization that have not been corrected by the market and that seem amenable to no other solution. But there is ample room for corporate free enterprise and initiative without restrictive legislation but with greater accountability of corporations to their shareholders, workers, customers, and the general public whom they affect. It has become almost a cliché that some large corporations control more financial assets, and in that respect are more powerful, than many small nations. That is not a problem if they are held accountable for their actions.

Codes of conduct are the surrogate in this case for legislation. However, not all companies have codes, some companies have codes that simply state ideals or values, many codes are not publicized, many do not address the really difficult ethical issues a company faces, and many are not implemented and have no teeth to them. Hence codes by themselves are certainly not sufficient for accountability. Nonetheless, they provide a good starting point.

I shall briefly address three issues. One is the development and content of codes. Second is the possible coordination of codes or the creation of codes for groups of corporations or industries rather than simply individual corporate codes. The third is implementation and accountability.

An example of the sort of code I am arguing in favor of is supplied by the Sullivan Principles. They were a set of principles intended to justify the presence of multinationals in South Africa during the apartheid period. They prohibited signatory companies from obeying the South African apartheid laws and specified certain practices that companies could not engage in—such as segregation and racial discrimination—and certain affirmative practice that they were to engage in. Companies voluntarily subscribed to the principles, and the principles were the same for all signatories. What made the situation unique was that each signatory was audited for compliance and the audits were publicly available. Those U.S. companies that did not sign were known and could be targeted for adverse publicity in the United States as well as being held accountable for their nonparticipation by their shareholders and customers.

There are many international codes from UN and ILO conventions to the Caux Round Table and other sets of principles generated by private groups, in addition to individual corporate codes (see Williams, 2000, appendices). In some cases, they help guide a company and inform its employees of the ethical standards they are expected to adhere to. They are sometimes monitored for compliance in accordance with the requirements necessary to satisfy the Federal Sentencing Guidelines. But they are rarely publicized or audited, with the results made public. Prakash Sethi outlines the independent monitoring system adopted by Mattel, Inc. (see Sethi, 2002) and notes, "To the best of my knowledge, there is at present only one company, i.e., Mattel, Inc., that has opted for a full-fledged external monitoring system." Clearly one company is not enough and the vast majority of companies have to adopt monitoring systems whose results are available to workers, shareholders, customers, and the general public. But, as the Sullivan Principles demonstrate, it is not necessary that each company has to or should, in Sethi's words, "go it alone." There is no reason why there cannot be general standards agreed upon by corporations but formed with the input of workers, shareholders, customers, nongovernmental organizations, and other related parties. There may also be codes that are specific to a particular industry, such as the industry-wide guiding principles of the "Responsible Care" program adopted in 1988 by over 170 members of the Chemical Manufacturers Association (CMA) of the United States. The guiding principles of the program were published in full-page ads in the *New York Times* and the *Wall Street Journal* (April 11, 1990), and the signatories committed themselves not only to implement the principles but also to apply peer pressure to help ensure compliance by other companies. The publication of the principles and of the signatories was an important first step. Peer pressure to comply is appropriate. But any annual publicly disclosed audit of the companies to verify compliance has been lacking. Accountability requires such audits. Any implementation that is effective must be audited internally by a company that takes a code seriously to see if it is working at all and then to see if it is working as intended. If it is not, then the company should take appropriate measures to change the situation so that it does work as intended. But an internal audit will not satisfy either external critics or watchdogs or even stockholders and others who have a direct relation to the company and deserve documented assurance that the code is being followed. That requires an objective and independent audit, preferably by a firm that is not hired by the company itself, although that might be a first step. The Enron/Andersen episode has made the public skeptical about companies that are paid by the entity being audited. Eventually, to be maximally effective, audits of compliance with codes should be routine for every company, the results should be part of the public record, and the audits should be conducted by independent auditors whose services, although paid for by the company, are carried out by a regional, national, or global accrediting and auditing group.

The conclusion to which I come is that although globalization raises new issues, the history of the development of capitalism in the industrialized world provides us with important lessons that we can and should apply. The first

is that the market is not self-correcting in many areas and that although ethics is required at the personal, organizational, systemic, and international levels, ethical people and moral exhortation are insufficient to adequately restrain the market. Legislation is also necessary. In countries such as those in much of the developing world, appropriate legislation must be passed and enforced. In the absence of worldwide legislation, international legal coordination of various types is necessary and should be pursued. In addition to legislation, international agreements and coordinating groups—which must be ethically justifiable, transparent in their processes and decisions, and responsive to the people affected—should be developed. In addition, corporations should both hold themselves accountable and be held accountable by the general public for their actions. Codes or sets of standards can help in this respect, but only if they are both enforced and publicly audited. Ethics, although important in all four areas, cannot by itself bring about the needed changes. It is important for both those in business ethics and vocal critics of business, who often speak and act as if it could, to keep this in mind.

NOTES

1. This marked the shift from ethics in business to business ethics.

2. Patricia Werhane, for example, seems to defend the existing system she identifies as feudalism in the Philippines (see Werhane, 2000).

3. Nike was found using subcontractors who employed children in making soccer balls for Nike in Pakistan in 1996. Since then, Nike has been accused of a variety of exploitative labor practices in sweatshops in Indonesia and other labor violations in Vietnam and China. From 1995 to 1998, Wal-Mart was accused of using child labor in Bangladesh and Guatemala and of sweatshop abuses in China, Indonesia, Pakistan, and other countries. After boycotts and public protests, both companies claimed they no longer use suppliers engaged in the use of child labor and other substandard labor practices.

4. University officials formed the Collegiate Licensing Company to arrive at standards to be applied, and the Fair Labor Association monitors compliance with its code of conduct. A Workers Rights Consortium was also formed by labor and student activists to monitor for sweatshop conditions, a University Consortium Against Sweatshops was established, and other groups have been appearing.

5. See its code of conduct (http://www.somo. nl.monitoring/reports/handm-coc.htm), article 2.3, which requires the company to make sure that the situation of any child dismissed from a factory be improved and not worsened.

6. Levi Strauss first adopted this practice in 1993. See Smith (1999).

7. Hence those who argue that MNCs should not interfere in the governance of host countries should not complain about MNCs supporting legislation that makes unethical practices illegal. One of the requirements for American companies in South Africa that signed the Sullivan Principles was to lobby the South African government to abolish the apartheid laws. The lobbying was done not by open campaigning but by bringing what collective pressure the companies could on the government.

8. This does not mean that any country has the right to defend its culture in ways that violate the human rights of its citizens or that harm rather than protect them.

9. Sen (1999) defends the thesis that from an economic point of view, capitalism in a democratic society is the most productive form of social system.

REFERENCES

De George, R. T. (1987). The status of business ethics: Past and future. *Journal of Business Ethics, 6,* 201–211.

De George, R. T. (1993). *Competing with integrity in international business.* New York: Oxford University Press.

De George, R. T. (2003). *The ethics of information technology and business.* Oxford, UK: Blackwell.

Hennes & Mauritz. *Code of conduct* (article 2.3). Retrieved from http://www.somo.nl.monitoring/reports/handm-coc.htm

Sen, A. (1999). *Development as freedom.* New York: Alfred Knopf.

Sethi, S. P. (2002). Standards for corporate conduct in the international arena: Challenges and opportunities for multinational corporations. *Business and Society Review, 107*(1), 20–40.

Smith, Gare A. (1999). *A trade policy that works for everyone.* Remarks at the UN Association forum: Globalization with a human face. Retrieved from http://www.tradeobservatory.org/library.cfm?filename=Trade_Policy_that_Works_for_Everyone_Why_It_Ma.htm

UNICEF. (1997). *The state of the world's children.* New York: Oxford University Press.

Werhane, P. (2000). Exporting mental models: Global capitalism in the 21st century. *Business Ethics Quarterly, 10*(1), 354–355.

Williams, O. (Ed.). (2000). *Global codes of conduct.* Notre Dame: University of Notre Dame Press.

14

THE NEXT GENERATION OF CODES OF CONDUCT

BRUCE MOATS

Although there is much debate regarding globalization and whether or not it is good or bad, it is a reality of the world in which we live. Moreover, the opening of markets, the global expansion of business investment, and the resulting economic interdependency between countries will likely progress more and more quickly as economic benefits are realized by both developed and developing countries.

However, we—governments, corporations, nongovernmental organizations, and citizens—need to do a better job of managing the effects of globalization. As economic bases shift from agricultural to industrial and workforces move from villages to cities, there often is a great risk of worker exploitation and abuse. Just as these changes occurred in the United States in the early 1900s, we are witnessing the same dynamics today in developing countries, with countries at different stages in their evolution.

Although applying new technologies and eliminating trade barriers spur economic growth, they don't guarantee greater economic equity among all citizens or resolve exploitative workplace practices, such as discrimination or the suppression of migrant worker rights. Multiple stakeholders, including governments, multinational corporations, and nongovernmental organizations, must work together to ensure acceptable labor standards, respect for worker rights, and a broad distribution of benefits. The alternative is increased potential for worldwide social unrest and instability.

BUSINESSES' RESPONSIBILITY

As businesses have expanded globally, they have taken on more and more responsibility for righting the wrongs of globalization. Increasingly, multinationals are being held accountable for resolving issues that are traditionally the responsibility of governments, particularly in the area of labor and environmental practices. Consumers, nongovernmental organizations, government agencies, community activists, and others expect corporations to conduct their business in socially responsible ways and to contribute positively to the communities in which they operate.

It is incumbent upon business to help shape societal norms by modeling ethical conduct and enabling positive change in both the workplace and the broader community. While public pressure can be one motivating factor for prompting corporations to accept such responsibilities, the more enduring and sustainable motivator is embedded within a company's culture—the intrinsic belief in "doing the right thing" as a crucial component of commercial success.

Many companies have mounted corporate social responsibility programs voluntarily because they are conscious of not only their public accountability but also their moral responsibility. They also recognize the positive impact adhering to such programs can have on their business.

While there may be short-term costs associated with doing the right thing, when corporate social responsibility is an integral part of a company's business strategy, it contributes to achieving long-term financial success within a morally defensible operating framework.

The concern for socially responsible corporate action has been rooted in Levi Strauss & Co.'s culture since Bavarian immigrant Levi Strauss founded his company 150 years ago and began donating money to a San Francisco orphanage. Integrity, demonstrated through ethical conduct and social responsibility, is a core value that characterizes the company's way of doing business. Even when personal, professional, and social risks or economic pressures confront the company, its leaders have demonstrated the willingness to do the right thing for employees, the company, and society as a whole.

The Emergence of Codes of Conduct

In the context of globalization and businesses' responsibilities, Levi Strauss & Co.'s commitment to ethical conduct resulted in the development in 1991 of the first comprehensive code of conduct setting standards for working conditions in contract manufacturing and finishing facilities. Since then, such codes have emerged as a significant tool for multinationals to use to address labor standards and worker rights issues they encounter in their suppliers' factories in developing countries.

Historically, LS&CO. had relied on owned-and-operated plants to produce its world-famous jeans. But as the company grew, it started outsourcing more of its manufacturing to overseas contractors. Some of the company's managers and employees began raising concerns about questionable working conditions in those facilities and the apparent disconnect between such conditions and the values and high standards the company had always held.

A cross-functional task force was formed to create the company's Global Sourcing and Operating Guidelines—a two-part document that helps LS&CO. select the countries and the contractors with whom it will do business. Part one, the Country Assessment Guidelines, identifies the political and socioeconomic risks of doing business in specific countries that are generally beyond the control of any single firm. Such issues include economic stability, the adequacy of the legal system to protect commercial interests, the human rights environment, and health and safety conditions. Using these guidelines, the company is able to evaluate whether to do business in a specific country and, if so, how to do it responsibly. It is a holistic approach to market entry into new countries whereby issues and risks are identified, and remediation programs are developed that not only are aimed at mitigating potential risks to the business but also take into account how to address significant community needs that may impact the business.

The second part of LS&CO.'s Global Sourcing and Operating Guidelines is the Terms of Engagement (TOE), which help the company select business partners who follow workplace standards and practices consistent with the company's values and policies. Underpinning the TOE, as well as most codes of conduct adopted by multinational companies, are the *UN Universal Declaration of Human Rights,* which addresses basic human rights and freedoms, and the *International Labor Organization Conventions,* which establish core labor rights, including freedom of association, minimum working age, and nondiscrimination.

As the first company to institute guidelines governing workplace practices and conditions in overseas contractor factories, LS&CO. faced tremendous skepticism and implementation challenges. Contractors had to be convinced of the need for meeting new labor and environmental standards; to abide by such standards often meant they had to invest in physical improvements in the factory and systemic improvements in management and personnel (human resources) practices. Seeking out contractors willing and able to work with LS&CO. typically meant forgoing the lowest-cost sourcing options. Additionally, the company needed to build the internal infrastructure to implement TOE, develop training, educate contractors, and monitor compliance.

Over time, many contractors began realizing that embracing the standards set by a code of conduct would actually help them attract new customers and grow their business, while simultaneously improving the lives of their employees. In recent years, a willingness to try to meet the conditions set forth by codes of conduct has become the price of entry for contractors who want to do business with major branded companies. Numerous multinationals, both within and outside the apparel industry, have utilized codes of conduct as a mechanism to raise the bar for workplace practices and help mitigate the risks of worker exploitation and abuse. However, although codes and their associated monitoring and compliance programs have become almost commonplace for major companies, there is still much work to be done to achieve consistent, sustainable, and continuous improvements at the factory level in developing countries.

EVOLUTION OF CODES OF CONDUCT

The development and implementation of corporate codes of conduct and compliance programs is not a singular event, but an ever-evolving and dynamic process. Corporations and other stakeholders, including nongovernmental organizations and companies who provide monitoring services, are continuously learning how to improve their efforts to bring about better conditions for workers.

Since 1991, Levi Strauss & Co. has updated its Terms of Engagement several times and expanded and deepened its training and monitoring program, drawing upon practical learnings from the field, as well as input from stakeholders. For example, a project in the late '90s involving local NGOs which assessed the company's TOE implementation process led to a more complete definition of *freedom of association* in the Terms themselves (among a number of other improvements to the process). From a simple phrase stating that workers should be "allowed the right of free association" that appeared in the company's initial TOE document, the current version elaborates upon this concept. The company's expectations around respecting the right of workers to form and join organizations of their choice and bargain collectively are more clearly spelled out for the contractors who must honor this right.

As individual companies have developed codes of conduct, global initiatives also have emerged to provide a platform of socially responsible standards and guidelines applicable to multiple industries and business practices. Companies can choose to subscribe to and incorporate into their social responsibility programs the guidelines set forth by such initiatives as the *Global Sullivan Principles,* the *OECD Guidelines for Multinational Enterprises,* the *United Nations Global Compact,* the *Global Reporting Initiative,* and the *Ethical Trading Initiative.*

Such global initiatives often encompass a broad spectrum of principles promoting political, social, and economic justice. They may incorporate specific labor standards, as well as more aspirational objectives, and include elements of transparency whereby corporations publicly demonstrate their commitment to the principles.

The aspirational aspects of these initiatives are particularly noteworthy in the ongoing evolution of corporate codes of conduct.

LEGALISTIC AND
ASPIRATIONAL APPROACHES

Most, if not all, codes of conduct delineate specific standards that are practical, measurable, and enforceable. Such codes represent a legalistic approach to addressing the issue of worker exploitation arising from globalization. This approach characterizes in particular U.S.-based corporations' codes of conduct. In a culture that looks to the legal system to remedy all manner of transgressions, it is not surprising that U.S.-based companies emphasize immediate supplier compliance with specific code of conduct requirements. For example, suppliers are expected to pay workers at least the minimum wage as required by local laws or the prevailing industry wage. During the monitoring process, a review of payroll records can determine whether a supplier is in compliance with such a requirement.

However, some codes of conduct, especially those of European-based companies as well as the broad global initiatives, include goals that companies should strive to attain. These efforts involve a more aspirational and normative approach to resolving the challenges of globalization. In such cases the language around wages, for example, may include the concept of meeting employees' *basic needs*, a more aspirational but less well-defined goal than paying the legal minimum wage.

Each approach has its benefits and limitations. The legalistic approach to codes of conduct sets a high expectation for compliance. There is a narrow, laserlike focus on specific performance criteria that a supplier is expected to abide by—meeting certain safety standards, limiting the number of hours worked, having written policies in place. Multinational companies employ internal and external monitoring systems to oversee and enforce compliance. However, this legalistic approach offers a relatively weak vehicle for continuous improvement of social conditions over the long-term. The requirement for quick compliance with precise performance criteria does not create an incentive for the multinational company, the supplier, the industry, or the developing country to progress beyond the scope of these criteria.

The aspirational components in codes of conduct supply such an incentive. They help to set a direction and model for the future, beyond the standards of today, which companies and other stakeholders can strive to achieve. The aspirational approach will be weaker than the legalistic approach in terms of implementation; when a code's guidelines describe the conditions that should prevail in some future world, corporate managers have fewer guideposts for conducting business operations in the present world.

The aspirational component of codes and global initiatives help to shape the public debate around the role of corporations not only within the four walls of the factory but also in the greater society. The *Global Sullivan Principles* urges companies to "work with governments and communities in which we do business to improve the quality of life in those communities—their educational, cultural, economic and social well-being—and seek to provide training and opportunities for workers from disadvantaged backgrounds."

Clearly, codes of conduct and global initiatives that encompass both legalistic and aspirational elements can be both practical and motivational tools for fulfilling businesses' responsibility to effect positive change. The specific standards set forth in a corporation's code of conduct should be considered a floor, not a ceiling. A code's aspirational goals can then provide the impetus for expanding a company's focus from today's workplace improvements to tomorrow's societal advancements.

COMPLIANCE AND ACCOUNTABILITY

As codes of conduct evolve, so too do the programs established to ensure compliance with those codes—at least for the legalistic components. Because there is no international authority empowered to enforce codes of conduct, multinational businesses are being held accountable. Most major corporations with codes of conduct have established internal monitoring systems and many also utilize third-party monitors and/or participate in coalitions that focus on monitoring. Such groups include the following:

- The Fair Labor Association (FLA)—A partnership of consumer groups, human rights organizations, U.S. universities, and apparel and footwear companies. The FLA accredits and oversees third-party monitors and determines whether member companies are in compliance with the FLA's code of conduct.
- The Worldwide Responsible Apparel Partnership (WRAP)—An initiative of the American Apparel and Footwear Association developed to address labor practices, factory conditions, and environmental and customs compliance issues. WRAP focuses on certifying the compliance of factories rather than of the member companies.
- Social Accreditation (SA) 8000—A factory-based certification program launched by the nonprofit group Social Accountability International and modeled after its 9000 quality auditing process. This program covers multiple industries.

Over the years, Levi Strauss & Co. has developed a comprehensive internal compliance program, supplemented by third-party monitoring using skilled and experienced outside firms or nonprofit organizations. Every manufacturing and finishing contractor utilized by the company is thoroughly assessed at least annually for compliance with the Terms of Engagement. LS&CO.'s compliance staff works with contractors to develop corrective action plans to remediate problems. Follow-up visits between annual assessments are conducted to verify the factory's progress in implementing improvements. If improvements fail to materialize, the company will end its business relationship with the contractor.

Although partnering with factory management to correct problems is the preferred course of action, the termination of business is sometimes necessary to demonstrate how serious LS&CO. views compliance with the Terms of Engagement. In one instance, the company withdrew production from a contractor in Mexico that did not implement changes to working conditions, although they had been given several months to make improvements. The contractor quickly realized that by not adhering to a key customer's code of conduct there would be both a short-term financial impact to its business and a detrimental effect on its ability to attract new business over the long-term. Within a year and a half, LS&CO. reestablished its business relationship with the contractor, which had made substantial improvements in its business operations and treatment of workers.

Internal and third-party monitoring can be effective in measuring factory compliance with specific requirements of codes of conduct; however, these systems are not foolproof and are limited in their ability to drive long-term sustainable change in factory working conditions. The goal of such systems is to ensure acceptable working conditions at all times, but the enforcement mechanism gauges compliance at just a single point in time. Additionally, the myriad of codes, monitors, and improvement plans result in duplicative efforts and inefficient uses of time and resources by both the supplier and the multinational companies.

PARTNERSHIPS—BUILDING GOVERNMENT CAPACITY

To a great extent, globalization has pushed multinational businesses into adopting the role of global policemen, enforcing the rules laid out in their codes of conduct, which often reflect the actual laws of the communities and countries where they are conducting business. Corporations guided by a strong moral compass accept and embrace their responsibility as a matter of integrity, but they do not relish the need to be constant enforcers of the law, a role more suited to governments and their enforcement agencies.

In order to achieve lasting positive economic and social change, multiple stakeholders must engage together at several levels—at the national or governmental level, within communities, and in cooperation with local factories and workers. Each participant on the globalization stage plays a role in promoting social justice and greater economic equity.

Ultimately, the establishment and enforcement of social laws are inherently governmental functions. They cannot be privatized. However, in the area of labor standards and worker rights, the private sector and the international community can assist governments in this regard through programs to build governmental capacity. For example, governments of developing countries need help to improve their labor regimes, establish effective monitoring systems, and enforce labor laws. To date, one of the most effective ways of doing this is to work with governments to teach the economics of good labor laws and respect for human rights. Laws that promote worker rights and social justice can serve as incentives to attract foreign investments.

LS&CO. has already seen positive results in this area in Guatemala, where the company leveraged its trade relationship to encourage the government to pass more stringent ILO-consistent labor laws. In another instance, when violations of LS&CO.'s code of conduct were found in a factory in Mauritius, arising from discrimination against migrant workers, the company intervened with the Mauritian government and advocated for change. Consequently, the government created a cabinet-level committee to look at labor conditions for migrant workers, resulting in strengthened labor laws.

LS&CO. also actively engages with government and public policy leaders to advocate for labor standards and worker rights to be a part of trade negotiations and final agreements. The company supports incorporating key workplace standards and worker rights provisions within the context of bilateral, regional, or multilateral trade agreements. For example, in 2001 LS&CO. was the first and only company to advocate for the linkage of trade and labor policies during the Congressional Trade Promotion Authority debate.

PARTNERSHIPS—BUILDING FACTORY CAPACITY

Hand in hand with stronger laws and enforcement at the governmental level is the need for local factories to take ownership and accountability for complying with local laws and their customers' codes of conduct. The next frontier for codes of conduct programs is a shift from the monitoring or "policing" model to one in which a factory's capacity and capability for continuous compliance and improvement are developed, with the help of multiple stakeholders. Multinationals, NGOs, labor unions, and human rights organizations must be engaged in educating, encouraging, and rewarding local factories that will embrace the responsibility of "owning" code of conduct compliance.

Since the inception of its Terms of Engagement, LS&CO. has found that a philosophy of partnership and continuous improvement is key in driving long-lasting positive results. The company maintains and cultivates relationships with the NGO community, including human rights, labor, and other international and local institutions. These strategic partnerships provide LS&CO. with information on local factory conditions, including instances of alleged noncompliance. They also generate specific recommendations on ways to improve the TOE process. Finally, since these groups play a critical role in influencing public opinion, they assist LS&CO. in shaping public policy so that it can make a greater impact on workers' rights and factory conditions worldwide.

LS&CO. is also engaging in conversations with other brands and key suppliers on ways to more effectively tackle these issues together. In fact, one of the next steps may well be to merge multiple codes into a single strong global code. There is much commonality among current codes of conduct, and the company is seeing a growing consensus among stakeholders that a common code is important. LS&CO. is pursuing this idea through participating in efforts such as the Ethical Trading Initiative and through quiet dialogue with other brands, NGOs, governments, and multilateral organizations.

Additionally, the company has found a high degree of agreement among brands and suppliers on the workplace issues that need to be corrected, as well as on the specific corrective actions that should be taken. When multiple "customers" of a factory are able to send a consistent message on code requirements and remediation steps, the supplier responds more quickly and effectively and appreciates the coordinated approach.

For code of conduct programs to evolve to the next level requires the cooperation of these many stakeholders. All must work together to help build the capacity of suppliers to develop and implement progressive management and human resources systems, which promote a culture of respect for workers' rights and a commitment to safe and humane working conditions. Programs to educate workers about their labor rights should supplement these efforts. Compliance monitoring programs are often ineffective for the very reasons that they are necessary: the absence of an informed, empowered workforce.

When factory owners and management adopt a "corporate social responsibility" mindset toward business operations, they can reap rewards through increased productivity, lower worker absenteeism, fewer labor disputes, and increased business. True sustainability of codes of conduct will happen only with such factory self-sufficiency.

Engaging multiple stakeholders to increase institutional capacity and educate workers will enable individual factories to adhere more rigorously and consistently to the legalistic components of codes of conduct. At the same time, multinationals, in cooperation with other stakeholders, can begin to shift their attention from policing duties to pursuing the more aspirational goals that will benefit the lives of workers and the communities in which they live.

FOCUS ON RESOLUTION OF SPECIFIC ISSUES

Through joint cooperative efforts, corporations, governments, NGOs, and suppliers can tackle and begin to resolve some of the most high-profile and damaging issues facing workers today. One of the most significant challenges confronting global companies is the issue of migrant worker rights. Just as multiple stakeholders came together over the past decade to address child labor, we once again must rally to ensure that migrant workers' rights are respected in a fair and nondiscriminatory way.

Migrant labor is occurring at many different levels, making this a complex issue. In some instances, workers migrate from one country to another, often to developing countries where labor standards are lower and less well enforced. Worker migration also occurs within a single country as laborers from rural areas flood into cities seeking jobs in growing industries. Furthermore, some factory owners and managers migrate into regions outside their own countries, bringing with them little understanding of and sensitivity to local culture and customs.

Migrant workers face a multitude of problems—different culture, new language, and too often discriminatory rules and policies. Migrant workers may be obligated to pay fees for obtaining their new jobs, may be paid less and have fewer benefits than local workers, and may be subject to harassment and humiliation.

To remedy such issues, multinationals must work closely with their suppliers to enforce the standards of their code of conduct, but such efforts also need to go beyond ensuring that legal wages are paid or benefits are equitably provided to the workforce. Governments and the NGO community can partner with corporations to seek appropriate changes to local laws and social welfare policies and provide educational programs for factory management and workers.

For several years, LS&CO. and the Levi Strauss Foundation have supported an Asia Foundation project dedicated to helping migrant women factory workers in Guangdong Province, China. The Social Justice for Working Women Program has provided thousands of women with valuable information and access to services through legal aid centers, mobile health care providers, and education and counseling centers. Local government service providers have been encouraged to expand their programs to this underserved population, and some local factories have begun to allow project teams on site to give lectures. As a result, these women workers are learning about their legal and worker rights, gaining knowledge on how to protect their health, and developing interpersonal skills and more confidence to deal with personal and workplace issues.

Another critical issue that we must address is HIV/AIDS in the workplace and in society. The consequences of the HIV/AIDS pandemic reach far beyond the four walls of the factory. With the continued proliferation of this disease worldwide, particularly in key sourcing geographies of Africa and Asia, whole populations are either infected or affected. The impact to communities and to the available workforce can be devastating. It is essential that all stakeholders work in partnership to eliminate discrimination faced by individuals infected or affected by HIV/AIDS, to increase awareness of the issues, and to find innovative and effective ways to reach at-risk populations with prevention programs.

LS&CO. and the Levi Strauss Foundation have been deeply involved with promoting and supporting HIV/AIDS awareness and prevention programs for more than 20 years. Additionally, nondiscrimination is a key element of the company's Terms of Engagement. HIV/AIDS prevention is one of the global issues that multinationals can incorporate into their social responsibility programs that will have far-reaching benefits for their suppliers and workers.

THE ROAD AHEAD

The active engagement of multiple stakeholders to address the effects of globalization will continue to intensify throughout the world. Change begins with a single step by a single entity. It takes root and flourishes with the nourishment of many individuals and organizations. When LS&CO. created an unheard-of code of conduct a dozen years ago, little did it know that working conditions would begin to improve for hundreds of thousands of workers around the world as many other companies implemented similar programs.

Yet there is so much more to accomplish.

Both governments and businesses worldwide are just beginning to recognize the importance of incorporating social responsibility into their operating model and economic value equations, not only because it is the right thing to do, but also as a means to create a competitive edge. While initial efforts by corporations to integrate social responsibility programs, such as codes of conduct, into the fabric of their operations carry economic commitments, not to do so costs even more in the long run. The progress in this arena represents a significant milestone—one that reflects how far we have come in the past decade and how far we have to go.

Although codes of conduct have begun to help alleviate worker exploitation, there is no simple way to ensure long-term, sustainable compliance. This is a complex, sophisticated subject that requires sophisticated solutions.

The first codes of conduct focused on the adoption, refinement, and implementation by multinationals of the legalistic requirements spelled out in such codes. Later, aspirational components were incorporated into some codes. As corporations strive to enforce their own codes and governments struggle to create and enforce laws consistent with international expectations, the NGO community advocates for better methods of monitoring, more accountability, and higher workplace standards. All parties look to create a better and more promising future for workers.

The next generation of codes of conduct requires the commitment and partnership of these multiple stakeholders to ensure that long-term sustainable changes are made in factories and communities. Building the capacity for governments, communities, and suppliers to tackle difficult issues, enforce needed labor laws, and bring about enduring positive changes in the workplace and the lives of workers is key to smoothing out the inequities of globalization. As factory self-sufficiency is developed, the pursuit of aspirational goals by all stakeholders can then provide a framework for the continuous improvement of social conditions.

Continued progress in this area will become even more critical when textile and clothing trade quotas are eliminated for WTO member countries on January 1, 2005. As we enter a quota-free environment, arguably many companies will move quickly and deeply into some of the lowest-cost countries of the world, countries where the enactment and enforcement of labor laws and respect for human rights are inadequate to protect workers from exploitative practices. There is a growing sense of urgency for all of us—governments, multinationals, nongovernmental organizations, suppliers, and citizens—to act with integrity and join forces in tackling the ongoing issues of globalization.

Levi Strauss & Co. is committed to playing a leadership role in bringing about positive societal change through the continued evolution of a code of conduct program, through public policy advocacy, and by working in partnership with multiple stakeholders.

REFERENCE

The Global Sullivan Principles. (n.d.). Retrieved August 21, 2002, from http://www.globalsulli vanprinciples.org/principles.htm

15

GLOBAL BUSINESS ETHICS AND SUSTAINABILITY

A Multi-Institutional Approach

JOHN W. DIENHART

THE ROAD TO SUSTAINABILITY

Issues we now include under the rubric of business ethics, such as labor and corporate governance, have been discussed since the beginning of the industrial revolution. In the '50s, corporate social responsibility arose as a topic in business schools (Bowen, 1953). In the '70s, in the wake of domestic and international scandals involving business and government, there was a growing demand for business ethics education. Philosophy was the home department of ethics courses and had been prominent in medical ethics and bioethics. This made philosophy departments a natural home for business ethics.

Philosophy's approach to business ethics differed from earlier discussions by being primarily normative and having a broader scope. Normatively, a wide range of ethical theories, from egoism to utilitarianism to eco-feminism, were covered in philosophy. Regarding scope, the philosophical approach to business ethics included all the functional areas and professions involved with business, as well as the relationships between business and the environment, government, civil society organizations, and society at large. Perhaps the most important contribution of the philosophical approach to business ethics was to discuss topics in business within the larger normative debate about how to construct a good

AUTHOR'S NOTE: I want to thank George Brenkert, who commented on several drafts of this chapter. Also, thanks go to Renee Gastineau, who helped with technical details.

society, the role of business organizations within such a society, and the roles of individuals as citizens and employees, friends and family members.

The audience for philosophical business ethics consists mainly of undergraduates, MBAs, and business people in executive education. The hope is that those in the audience will operationalize ethical principles in business. To operationalize these principles, people need more than tools of normative philosophy. This is not a criticism of philosophy. There are other academic disciplines that examine how to operationalize goals. The social science and business disciplines that study moral reasoning, organizational behavior, finance, and economics, for example, provide descriptive and instrumental research needed to operationalize normative insights.

People and organizations in nonacademic social institutions also work on business ethics, although they may not characterize their work in this way. Civil society organizations (CSOs) promote environmental causes and human rights issues that are topics within business ethics.[1] Governments and intergovernmental organizations, some more than others, pass laws or regulations or urge policies to protect the environment and promote human rights. Many businesses have ethical value statements, codes, and programs. Several issue audited reports on how well they abide by their value statements and codes. In sum, there are at least four institutional sectors involved in business ethics:

- Academia
- CSOs
- Government and intergovernmental organizations
- Business and industry

One might expect that business ethics would mean different things in different institutions. However, this is not the case. The diversity of views about business ethics occurs within institutions, and the diversity in one institution is similar to the diversity in other institutions. For example, in academia we have people who think business should only be about profits, those who

see it only as a social engine for group well-being, and many shades in between. We find the same diversity in the other three institutions, although the proportions of those who hold these diverse views may be different. Amidst this diversity, however, we find a growing consensus that business ethics, as Rushton has argued, should be understood in the broad sense of sustainability: social justice, economic health, and environmental integrity (Rushton, 2002).

The Brundtland report (World Commission on Environment and Development, 1987) defined sustainable development as follows:

> Sustainable Development should meet the needs of the present without compromising the ability of future generations to meet their own needs.

While the original concept of sustainability focused on the environment, it soon grew to include larger economic and social justice issues (Nemetz, 2003). The reasoning was that environmental issues were linked to economic and social justice issues. These three elements, sometimes thought of as three legs of a stool (Ibid., p. 4), are understood as an integrated system. Problems with one leg threaten the integrity of the other two and the stability of the entire system.

In a speech to the World Economic Forum in 1999, Kofi Annan proposed the creation of the UN Global Compact to promote the tripartite goal of sustainability (Annan, 1999). The Global Compact (GC), inaugurated the next year, is a network organized by an office at the UN. The GC includes people and organizations from academia; CSOs; governments and intergovernmental organizations; and business and industry groups. As such, it integrates the aforementioned institutions under the shared goal of sustainability.

In this chapter, I provide evidence that there is an emerging multi-institutional global business ethics project that is focused on sustainability in the broad sense, what I refer to as the Sustainability Project or sometimes as the Project. The key word in the preceding sentence is *emerging*. I do not argue that sustainability was ever formally planned or initiated as a global project.

Nor do I argue that the Project is the only business ethics project. People and organizations will continue to work on discrete issues in business ethics without reference to, and perhaps in opposition to, the Project. However, the Sustainability Project is pervasive, and we need to take it into account if we are to understand other developments in business ethics. For example, the Project can provide a context to understand corporate integrity, an issue that has received a great deal of attention since the recent financial frauds at large U.S. companies.

Corporate integrity can mean different things.[2] It could mean that a corporation knows what its values are and acts consistently in accord with those values (White, 2003). But what if those values are cheating, lying, and corruption? Perhaps what we need is an ethical standard for company behavior that grounds consistent behavior. If this is the way we understand corporate integrity, then sustainability, as described in this chapter, can guide companies who want to develop or refine their quest for corporate integrity.

In the conclusion, I argue that the Sustainability Project has significant obstacles. First, the idea of sustainability has conceptual and normative difficulties. Second, multi-institutional cooperation is difficult, as illustrated by the problems with the Chad–Cameroon pipeline project. Despite these problems, I argue that historical trends in democracy and intergovernmental cooperation show that these difficulties can be overcome.

The chapter is unashamedly speculative. It is similar, I think, to writing about the possibility and nature of democratic nation-states in the late 1700s. Something is going on, but no one can be sure just what.

INSTITUTIONAL APPROACHES TO BUSINESS ETHICS

Academia

The primary role of academia is education, which we can understand as teaching and research. While there are many academic disciplines that participate in the Project, in this section I discuss three. I first discuss philosophy, which takes a descriptive-normative approach to business ethics. By saying that philosophy is descriptive and normative, I mean two things. First, the philosophical approach to business ethics is based on what business does. Business actions and decision making are described, and normative analyses are prescribed and defended. Second, as social science research reveals, the ethical principles on which the philosophical approach to business ethics relies are used by most adults in decision making. I then discuss social science and business disciplines that take a descriptive-instrumental approach to business ethics. Descriptions in the social sciences have different foci and are sometimes more fine-grained than those found in the philosophical approach.

Philosophy: A Descriptive-Normative Study of Business Ethics

The domestic and international business scandals of the '60s and '70s gave birth to the philosophical approach to normative business ethics. Teaching students about the ethical aspects of business was proffered as a way to help prevent such scandals in the future. Business ethics texts began with theories of ethics and discussions of different social and political systems. Ethical theories included egoism, care, utility, and human dignity; religious views; and postmodern approaches such as deconstruction and eco-feminism. Capitalism, Marxism, and socialism were discussed as ways to organize a political economy. Typically, these texts then turned to a set of cases and problems: environmental pollution, bribery, misleading marketing, and a variety of other issues.

The specific problems of business ethics were often framed as a conflict between making a profit and being ethical. It was widely assumed that business and ethics were radically different and that ethical behavior had little or no return on investment. The first assumption is based on a conceptual and normative analysis of business and ethics. The second is an empirical claim that I discuss in the following section under the topic of social science.

Ironically, the view that ethics has no place in business is itself an ethical view. Those who argued that ethics and business were incompatible, such as is sometimes alleged in the case of Milton Friedman, generally meant that a particular ethic—such as one that dictated corporate giving to the poor or the ballet—was, in fact, unethical because it violated the rights of shareholders.

A major goal of the philosophical approach is to help individuals understand the way in which ethical assumptions ground much of our reasoning and to provide resources to evaluate these assumptions so that individuals can make their own informed decisions. This is why philosophical approaches cover many different and conflicting ethical theories. The goal is to inform, not indoctrinate. Two people could take the same business ethics class and come out with very different ideas about what ethical business is. For example, one successful student could come out believing that business should focus on the Sustainability Project, while another successful student could come out holding a narrow stockholder view. What they should have in common, however, is a critical understanding of the assumptions underlying their views and implications of these assumptions for how society and organizations should be constructed. By understanding their assumptions, they have the conceptual resources to discuss their views in ways that can lead to reconciliation.

If philosophical business ethics helps inspire individuals to change business for the better, however they interpret that, they have several options. They could join a civil society organization that promotes causes they value. They could work with government or intergovernmental organizations that shape policy. Or they could join a business or industry group that is committed to the values they care about. We will discuss hereafter these different institutional sectors. However, it would help if those who want to make changes— or resist them, for that matter—have information about how individuals, organizations, and social systems interact and respond to influence. This is the subject of the social sciences.

Social Science: A Descriptive-Instrumental Approach to Business Ethics

Social and Organizational Psychology

Social scientists, and management scholars using the tools of social science, examine, among other things, how individuals make decisions and use this information to design organizations and groups so that individuals are more likely to make some kinds of decisions rather than others.

One branch of this research, cognitive moral development (CMD) theory, examines how individuals develop moral reasoning. Another branch of this research examines how an individual's moral reasoning interacts with the individual's personality and organization to influence decisions. I discuss these in order.

According to cognitive moral development theory, moral reasoning develops in predictable cognitive and affective ways (Dienhart, 2000; Duska & Whelan, 1979; Kohlberg, 1984). In what follows, I describe moral development in terms of *stakeholder recognition*.

There are three levels of moral reasoning through which we can progress. In the first level of moral reasoning, a person is concerned with only one stakeholder, her- or himself. The good of the self is understood in terms of immediate desires. In the second level of moral reasoning, the person expands his or her stakeholder horizon by identifying with a *referent* group. The self is still important, but the person now interprets the good of self in terms of the good of the referent group. CMD theorists speculate that a majority of adults are in this stage (Treviño & Nelson, 1995). In the third level of reasoning, people make reflective decisions about their own ethical standards. They do not invent new ethical principles but choose one or two from those they have learned, such as justice, fairness, utility, care, or universalized self-interest (Dienhart, 2000) and use those to guide their ethical decision making.

CMD focuses on reasoning, not behavior. Does our level of moral reasoning affect the way we behave? For example, does someone who chooses justice as his or her dominant moral principle always act on it?

According to research by Treviño, the level of moral reasoning is one of three factors that affect behavior in organizations. The other two factors are personality traits such as risk aversion and locus of control, and organizational attributes such as incentive systems and time pressures (Treviño, 1986). Depending on how these three factors fit together, an organization can get ethical behavior from low-level moral reasoners focused on their own desires and unethical behavior from high-level moral reasoners focused on justice. By ethical behavior, Treviño means such things as "it is wrong to steal company property, lie to customers, dump cancerous chemicals in the local stream. . . ." (Treviño & Nelson, 1995).

Research on moral development shows that ethical principles discussed in philosophical ethics are present, in basic form, in everyday adult decision making. Research on organizations makes a good case that business can influence the ethical decisions employees make. If an organization wants to commit itself to the Sustainability Project, this research suggests it can do so, even if employees and managers do not have preexisting commitments to it.

Financial Performance

Do companies that incorporate ethics perform well financially? For this discussion, I will focus on ethics as sustainability. Regarding the relationship between ethics and performance, I discuss the weaker claim that ethics and financial performance are correlated, not the stronger claim that ethics plays a causal role in financial performance. To review the literature on this topic is beyond the scope of this chapter. I will cite a few studies where these two indicators are positively correlated.

One of the best-known research projects about the relationship between ethics and financial performance is the *Business Ethics Magazine* "100 Best Corporate Citizens," which began in 2000. This list evaluates companies by how they treat seven stakeholder groups, including stockholders (Kelley & Asmus, 2003). While not using the term *sustainability*, these seven stakeholders are related to issues that can be sorted into the categories of social justice, economic health, and environmental

integrity. The conclusion is that sustainability and profits are not inconsistent. In 2002, Verschoor and Murphy used publicly available data that support the conclusions of the *Business Ethics Magazine* list (Verschoor & Murphy, 2002). Two other ways to approach this are through evaluating financial risk and employee attractiveness. Orlitzky and Benjamin argue that firms that treat stakeholders well have lower financial risk (Orlitzky & Benjamin, 2001). Backhaus, Stone, and Heiner argue that firms that score well in their attention to social justice, economic health, and environmental integrity are more attractive to potential employees (Backhaus, Stone, & Heiner, 2002).

According to Rushton, writing in 2002, the Dow Jones Corporate Sustainability Index significantly outperformed the Dow Jones 30 Industrials in the previous five years (Rushton, 2002). The Corporate Sustainability Index defines sustainability in the broad sense (Corporate Sustainability, 2003).

The Interdisciplinary Trend in Academic Research and the Multi-Institutional Sustainability Project

Research in business ethics in the past 10 years has become strikingly interdisciplinary. The reason, I suggest, is that social justice, economic development, and the environment are tightly related, and it takes several disciplines to address them adequately. For example, the *Business Ethics Quarterly* of April 2002 is devoted to "The Stakeholder Revolution and the Clarkson Principles." Authors are leading scholars from philosophy, management (social sciences), law, and finance. Max Clarkson was a businessperson who became passionate about business ethics and, in particular, stakeholder theory because it spoke the language of business. A major theme of the collection is how to integrate the fiduciary obligations management has to owners (economic issues) with ethical obligations to other stakeholders (social justice issues). One article criticizes the stakeholder approach because it does not accord direct value to the environment, the third leg of sustainability. *The Journal of Corporate Citizenship*, which is interdisciplinary, has one or two articles per issue that deal with sustainability in the broad sense and how CSOs, government, and business, individually or together, should strive for it. In 2003, *Corporate Citizenship* devoted an entire issue to the Global Compact and its efforts to promote the Sustainability Project.

Civil Society Organizations

Civil society organizations (CSOs) are voluntary organizations that promulgate a particular vision of the world. They do so by trying to influence business, government, and their stakeholders. I discuss three kinds of CSOs: those that focus on specific outcomes, those that focus on changing the principles and procedures businesses use to make decisions, and those that seek to change the social and political environment in which business operates.

Outcome-Oriented CSOs

Outcome-oriented CSOs have very definite ideas about what actions are right and wrong. This kind of CSO does not usually work directly with business to foster change. The most common strategies are protesting to influence public opinion, working with legislative or executive branches of government, and appealing to courts. In some instances, as we will see later, they exert direct (not definitive) influence through working with particular businesses. Let's look at Greenpeace as an example. According to their Web site,

> Greenpeace is an independent, campaigning organisation that uses non-violent, creative confrontation to *expose* global environmental problems, and *force* solutions for a green and peaceful future [emphasis mine]. Greenpeace's goal is to ensure the ability of the Earth to nurture life in all its diversity. (Our Mission, 2003)

In 1995, Greenpeace boarded Brent Spar, an aging oil platform in the North Sea. Royal Dutch Shell, which owned the platform, was planning to dispose of it by towing it into deep water and sinking it. According to Greenpeace, sinking Brent Spar would be an environmental disaster.

As Greenpeace activists tried to board the platform, Shell security tried to fend them off with fire hoses. Greenpeace had alerted the press about the attack. As Europeans were watching the evening news, the stunning events were broadcast live from circling helicopters. Public outrage was swift and widespread. In Germany, two Shell gas stations were firebombed, and Shell's retail revenues fell by 50 percent. In Europe, Shell retail receipts fell by 20 percent (Paine & Moldoveanu, 1999).

Greenpeace is only one of many CSOs. There are other outcome-based CSOs that are devoted to the environment and other causes such as labor, HIV/AIDS, and abortion.

Process- and Principle-Oriented CSOs

Process- and principle-based CSOs have definite ideas about *how* business decisions should be made but do not try to force companies to act in specific ways in specific situations. They work with business to have them sign on to principles that will govern their decision making. Typically, this type of CSO does not protest or appeal to courts. CERES and the Caux Round Table are examples of this kind of CSO.

CERES is a nonprofit organization devoted to protecting the environment. It has ten principles to which companies can subscribe (Our Work: The CERES Principles, 2003). CERES describes itself as a coalition between environmental and public interest groups on the one hand and investors and foundations on the other. While CERES counts many environmental groups as members, Greenpeace is not one of them.

To improve its effectiveness, CERES sponsors a Sustainable (in the broad sense discussed in this chapter) Governance Project to urge "investors, public pension funds, labor, environmental, religious, and other public interest groups . . . to increase the accountability of corporate directors and executives for the 'triple bottom line' of corporate social, economic, and environmental performance" (Our Work: Sustainable Governance Project, 2003). Finally, CERES sponsors the Global Reporting Initiative (GRI), which provides standards for corporate and organizational accountability. While CERES started out with an environmental focus, they are moving to sustainability in the broad sense.

The Caux Round Table is a CSO that wants to influence business culture and, through that, influence decision making towards sustainability. The Round Table also has a set of principles, which they divide between General Principles and Stakeholder Principles. The Caux Round Table is presently field-testing a reporting mechanism, the Self Assessment and Improvement Process, which an organization can use to determine whether its culture is one that promotes sustainable decisions (Goodpaster, Maines, & Rovang, 2002).

System-Oriented CSOs

System-oriented CSOs use journals, press releases, and policy statements to directly influence government to alter the basic social structure in which business operates. Hence, these CSOs, if successful, will have indirect but potentially powerful effects on business. Consider two such organizations, the Economic Policy Institute and the Cato Institute.

The Economic Policy Institute (EPI) was established to give "people who work for a living . . . a voice in the economic debate" (EPI Web site). Robert Reich and Lester Thurow are founding members. The mission of the Economic Policy Institute is "to provide high-quality research and education in order to promote a prosperous, fair, and sustainable economy. The Institute stresses real world analysis and a concern for the living standards of working people, and it makes its findings accessible to the general public, the media, and policy makers" (About EPI: Frequently Asked Questions, 2003).

EPI uses a variety of means to get its ideas into the public realm, including its own journal, books, conferences and seminars, helping other CSOs with technical information, testifying before Congress, and supplying information and background to the press. The EPI receives most of its funding from foundations, with the rest

coming from individuals, business, labor unions, and government.

The mission of the Cato Institute is "to broaden the parameters of public policy debate to allow consideration of the traditional American principles of limited government, individual liberty, free markets and peace. Toward that goal, the Institute strives to achieve greater involvement of the intelligent, concerned lay public in questions of policy and the proper role of government" (About Cato, 2003).

The Cato Institute uses the same methods for distributing information as EPI, including a journal and a newsletter. It is funded by foundations, corporations, and individuals; it receives no government funding.

CSOs and the Multi-Institutional Sustainability Project

From a normative standpoint, CSOs represent the wide spectrum of ethical views covered in philosophical approaches to business ethics. Taken together, they cover the three legs of the Sustainability Project. However, of the CSOs we looked at, it was only the process- and principle-oriented CSOs that focused on the Project itself.

As CSOs are private, voluntary associations, the question of legitimacy arises. For example, what gives them the right to challenge policies, as Greenpeace does, to block implementation of governmental polices of representative democracies? These governments, we may assume, were elected by the people. No one elected those in the CSOs. First, it should be noted that the legitimacy question applies most strongly to outcome-oriented CSOs that use protest to stop otherwise legal procedures. Process- and principle-oriented CSOs work with businesses that are willing work with them. System-oriented CSOs add their voices to the many voices arguing that society should be organized in better ways (NGO Legitimacy—Voice or Vote?, 2003). Second, when protest is involved, there is a long history of legitimate civil and even armed disobedience—for example, the American colonies' War of Independence.

Governments and Intergovernmental Organizations

Governments enforce different normative systems. Cuba has a command-and-control economy with all business functions controlled by the state. It is one of the most regulated countries in the world, reflecting the view that the common good is too important to be left to impersonal market forces. The United States has a market economy in which individuals can incorporate with little expense or expertise. It is one of the least-regulated countries in the developed world, reflecting the intersecting values of individual autonomy and private property rights. Finland, with much higher tax rates than the United States, has a free market integrated with a socialized system of welfare and health care. This approach tries to integrate the views that there are basic rights to some human goods but that market forces are necessary for production of wealth. Governments express much of the normative diversity we find in the CSO community and in philosophical ethics.[3]

Intergovernmental organizations (IGOs) coordinate behavior between nations. Insofar as their members have different normative systems, IGOs have to reflect this, at least in practice. The goal of IGOs is to help nations attain benefits they could not get by themselves or through direct nation-to-nation negotiation and treaties. The first IGO was the League of Nations, created after World War I to prevent future world wars. The League failed, but after World War II, four IGOs were formed that still have considerable influence today: the United Nations, the World Trade Organization (WTO) (formerly GATT), the International Monetary Fund (IMF), and the World Bank. Each group was created to serve a specific function. The UN is a forum for coordinating government action, the WTO's role is to create wealth around the globe by increasing trade, the IMF's role is to promote financial stability in countries through loans and consultation, and the World Bank's role is to promote development, especially infrastructure, in developing countries. These IGOs were created after World War II to provide the basis for a prosperous and peaceful world (Lenway, 1985).

Government

By shaping and enforcing macroeconomic systems, governments provide some opportunities and restrict others. At the industry and organizational level, governments can impose laws and regulations that protect the environment, increase workplace safety, prevent discrimination in hiring, reduce taxes, and a myriad of other things. They can also leave business alone to do what it wants in these areas. These laws reflect the diversity of ethical views we find in philosophy and in the CSO community.

The United States has a history of laws that try to make business more ethical. These can be broken down into three areas: laws protecting the environment, laws affecting labor, and laws affecting commerce. In this section, I focus on the environment, and specifically on how the Environmental Protection Agency (EPA) grew from a narrow focus on the environment to a commitment to endorsing the Sustainability Project. The EPA was inaugurated in 1970. It was born from a public demand for clean air, water, and land. The EPA was charged to coordinate the diverse laws that existed at the federal, state, and local levels and to help set new standards to protect the environment (Our History, 2003). For the first 20 years, the EPA focused on the environment per se. During that time, however, the agency recognized that environmental dangers affected the poor more than other economic classes. In 1992, the agency issued an Environmental Equity Report that confirmed the inequity of pollution distribution (Release of Environmental Equity Report, 1992). In 1994, President Clinton issued Executive Order 12898, which stated that "each Federal agency shall make achieving environmental justice part of its mission by identifying and addressing, as appropriate, disproportionately high and adverse human health or environmental effects of its programs, policies, and activities on minority populations and low-income populations. . . ." (Federal Actions to Address

Environmental Justice in Minority Populations and Low-Income Populations, 2003).

The EPA was in charge of coordinating the execution of this order, which integrates two legs of the sustainability stool: social justice and environmental integrity. In 1996, the EPA issued a report that added the third leg, economic health. The report was prompted in part by the Report of the President's Council on Sustainable Development, issued in the same year. The EPA report stated that "sustainable development focuses on economic development that goes hand-in-hand with ecological integrity and social equity" (Zieba, 1996). One of the results of the EPA focus on sustainability is the EPA's Smart Growth program. Smart Growth promotes "development that serves the economy, the community, and the environment" (Encouraging Smart Growth, 2003), the tripartite goal of the Sustainability Project.

Intergovernmental Organizations

After the end of World War II, four IGOs were created to promote world peace: the United Nations, the World Bank, the IMF, and GATT, which became the WTO. In this section I will discuss the UN efforts to protect the environment and show how these efforts evolved into a commitment to sustainability in the broad sense. Following this, I will make some brief remarks on how the other three IGOs and the European Union are promoting the Sustainability Project.

There are several milestones in the UN's efforts to protect the environment (UNEP Milestones, 2003). The 1972 Stockholm Declaration stated that a clean environment was dictated by human rights and specifically the right to life (Declaration of the United Nations Conference on the Human Environment, 1972). That same document linked the environment with economic development and human well-being (Ibid., Section 2, 1972). While the term *sustainability* was not used, its components were present. In 1992, the Rio Declaration on Environment and Development reaffirmed the Stockholm Declaration and officially adopted the term *sustainability* in the broad sense (Rio Declaration on Environment and Development, 1992). The

Rio Declaration argues that social justice, economic development, and environmental integrity cannot be promoted independently of each other. The Nairobi Declaration of 1997 states the UN's intention of being the global leader in setting the environmental agenda, under the banner of sustainable development (Nairobi Declaration, 1997). Finally, the World Summit on Sustainable Development in 2002 takes the broad sense of sustainability as its theme. The UN Division for Sustainable Development is charged with pursuing the resolutions of the 2002 summit (United Nations Division for Sustainable Development, 2003).

The World Bank Group emphasizes the importance of integrating social, environmental, and business needs (What is the World Bank, 2003). This is clearly articulated in their Millennium Development Goals, which aim at sustainability in the broad sense (Strategic Direction, 2003). The IMF argues for a close connection between macroeconomic policy, environmental integrity, and poverty reduction, thus embracing the sustainability triad. The IMF argues that these elements form a "virtuous circle, where gains are mutually reinforcing" (The IMF and the Environment: A Factsheet, 2003). In 1999, the WTO had a meeting on "Trade and the Environment." The vice president of the European Commission argued for a close link between trade (economic development) and the environment. The connection, however, was based on the fact that outcome-based CSOs would try to hinder trade policy that did not take environmental concerns seriously (Brittan, 1999). The WTO riots in Seattle later that same year seemed to confirm his worries. The speech did not suggest that the environment was valuable in itself. The EU states its commitment to sustainability in the broad sense in its Four Objectives, which include fundamental rights, economic progress, and environmental protection (The European Union at a Glance, 2003).

IGOs, Governments, and the Multi-Institutional Sustainability Project

Governmental and intergovernmental organizations are endorsing the Sustainability Project.

However, the extent to which governments actually pursue and enforce sustainable practices is questionable at best. IGOs committed to the Sustainability Project have some power to influence member nations to act on it. Still, their power lies primarily in forcing governments to adopt certain fiscal policies. It is very difficult, as we will see in the Chad–Cameroon pipeline project, to enforce the broad elements of sustainability. While these are serious concerns, they are not uncommon when there are large shifts in ideology, as we will see in the conclusion. We turn now to how business and industry are pursuing the Project.

Business and Industry

One of the primary roles of business is to create wealth through the production and distribution of goods and services. There is a growing belief in business that sustainability is the way to understand business's economic role. In this brief overview, I will look at some companies and industries that use sustainability to understand their economic role in society.

Business

Businesses are beginning to embrace the broad use of sustainability. Here is a brief recap of one company's journey.

In 1993, Royal Dutch Shell began restructuring the corporation because of weakening financial returns. In 1995, the company experienced two major problems. In spring, Greenpeace and other groups protested the sinking of Brent Spar, an aging oil holding platform (described previously). This incident cost Shell a great deal of money and generated months of bad publicity. In autumn of the same year, Shell was implicated in the hanging of nine dissidents in Nigeria. These dissidents and MOSOP, the CSO/political party they represented, argued that Shell was destroying the environment of their homelands and working with the corrupt Nigerian government to drain money out of Nigeria. Using the sustainability triad to analyze this problem, Shell was focusing on its own economic well-being to the exclusion of social and environmental issues and was paying an economic price. This irony was not lost on Shell.

Phil Mirvis was a consultant for Shell when these crises occurred. According to Mirvis, two things happened that resulted in changes at Shell. First, the company saw its narrow focus on profits put that goal at risk. Second, it gave people in leadership, especially Mark Moody-Stewart, a member of the Committee of Managing Directors, strong reasons for pushing the company to recognize the importance of social and environmental issues. As a result of the efforts of Moody-Stewart and others, the new Shell added an organizational component to its corporate structure to promote a broad sense of sustainability.

Shell's commitment took many forms, including working directly with Greenpeace and issuing an audited report on Shell's impact on civil society and the environment. The first report, *Profits and Principles—Does There Have to Be a Choice?*, covered the year 1998. This report was organized around Shell's business principles. In 1999, Shell renamed the report *People, Planet, and Profits*. This report was based on "the triple bottom line," which focuses on social, environmental, and economic concerns. *People, Planet, and Profits* was published for the next two years. In 2002, the report was renamed again, becoming *The Energy Challenge*. This report contains substantial sections devoted to sustainability in the broad sense. Whether the most recent name change of the report signals a retreat from sustainability is yet to be seen.

British Petroleum (BP) also has programs and reports devoted to a broad view of sustainability. BP states, "Our goal is to be a positive force in all of our operations. We want to help the world meet its needs for energy at the same time as minimizing the environmental impact of fossil fuel consumption and maximizing the social and economic benefits of our activities" (Sustainable Development, 2003). BP explains this goal in more detail: "The challenge of sustainable development in the 21st century is to strike a balance—to sustain economic growth and reduce the income gap between rich and poor, while preserving the resource base and avoiding damage to the environment" (Ibid.).

Shell and BP both see their role in the Project in terms of a broad view of sustainability. Cummins Engine (Who We Are, 2003), Hewlett Packard (Our Commitment to Global Citizenship, 2003), Alcoa (Sustainable Development: The basis for Alcoa's future, 2003), and Nokia (About Nokia, 2003) are just a few of the many companies that state a commitment explicitly to sustainability or to the three components that constitute sustainability.

Industry

Several industries urge policies that promote the Sustainability Project. In what follows, I discuss briefly the petroleum, aluminum, and chemical industries.

According to a joint report of the American Petroleum Institute and the International Petroleum Industry Environmental Conservation Association (IPIECA), 75 percent of the companies they surveyed "issue external reports that include measurements of environmental and safety performance relative to specific indicators, and many are now publicly reporting and setting targets for performance related to social as well as traditional environmental and safety indicators" (Compendium of Sustainability Reporting Practices and Trends for the Oil and Gas Industry, 2003).

This statement reflects sustainability in the broad sense. The membership of IPIECA includes all major petroleum companies.

According to the Aluminum Industry,

A company's approach to sustainable development could affect share value and a company's standing. For example the Dow Jones Sustainability Group Index measures the performance of industrial companies according to criteria for social responsibility and sustainable development. They assert that companies which are conscious of sustainability not only manage the standard economic factors affecting their business, but also the environmental and social factors as well. There is mounting

evidence that their financial performance is superior to that of companies that do not adequately, correctly and optimally manage these important factors. (The Aluminum Industry's Sustainable Development Report, 2003)

This statement illustrates the industry's view that the three aspects of sustainability are connected. This was certainly Shell's experience.

The European Chemical Industry Council supports the Brundtland report's conception of sustainability previously discussed. Specifically, the Council states that sustainable development balances three principal requirements:

1. The needs of society (the social objective)

2. The efficient management of scarce resources (the economic objective)

3. The need to reduce the load on the ecosystem in order to maintain the natural basis for life (the environmental objective) (Sustainable Development, 2003)

Business, Industry, and the Multi-Institutional Sustainability Project

Many business and industry groups are advocating policies that promote the Sustainability Project. However, this commitment is not always reflected in behavior, as environmental problems and extreme poverty across the world demonstrate. In the conclusion, I will discuss the extent to which these problems show the Project to be ineffectual or, at worst, a sham.

The UN Global Compact: A Multi-Institutional Network

In a speech to business and government leaders at the World Economic Forum in February 1999, Kofi Annan argued that the social justice and environmental issues pursued by the UN could not be achieved without forming strong partnerships with businesses and the market forces within which they work. These partnerships will also be good for business. The global economic system, he argued, is threatened by social injustice and environmental degradation. The solution, he argued, is not to limit or halt globalization but to engage businesses and those from other institutions to promote what we are calling the Sustainability Project.

The Global Compact (GC) was launched in 2000. The GC is network of companies (now numbering over 1,000), governments, labor groups, civil society organizations, academics, and the United Nations. The mission of the GC is to promote sustainable globalization, paying special attention to the poorest peoples. According to the GC, unless the poorest are part of economic development, the social stability required for economic growth will deteriorate. The GC's mission is promoted in two ways. First, for companies to join the network, they must endorse the GC's nine principles covering human rights, labor, and the environment. Once in the network, the GC offers companies three mechanisms for using the network to learn how to grow their business in sustainable ways.

Dialogue Meetings convene high-level representatives from different institutions to identify problems and develop workable solutions. The GC sponsored five Dialogue Meetings in 2002 and 2003. In February 2002, for example, the Dialogue on Business and Sustainable Development was initiated. Several months later, a follow-up meeting focused on sustainability in least-developed countries. This meeting "was attended by British Prime Minister Tony Blair, French President Jacques Chirac and other heads of state and government; ministers; UN officials; representatives from labour and non governmental organizations; and the chief executive officers of such companies as Hewlett-Packard and Shell International" (Initiative to Grow Sustainable Business in World's Poorest Countries, 2002). Participants agreed to identify specific least-developed countries and to help businesses forge partnerships with members of other institutional sectors to promote sustainable development. Other topics in this Dialogue stream included financing entrepreneurship, financial markets and sustainability, and a performance model for sustainability (Dialogue, 2003).

Learning Forums provide for the exchange of best practices and sharing of fundamental research. There are two kinds of forums. *Actual* forums occur in conferences, which are typically attended by representatives from business, government, and CSOs. There are also *virtual* forums, which are searchable databases available on the Internet. Some of the areas the forums cover are corporate experiences in implementing the nine principles, case studies of corporate experiences, description of partnership projects, research matching database, and Learning Forum publications. According to the GC, "The Learning Forum is particularly interested in co-operating with networks worldwide that engage in knowledge development and training and dissemination" (Learning Forum, 2003). These include academic, CSR, and HR networks.

Outreach/Networks (O/N) are created to achieve country, regional, or sectoral goals. At present there are Outreach/Networks in Chile, South Africa, and Sri Lanka. The Sri Lanka O/N was formed because participants believed that government is not equipped to provide jobs and economic wealth. This O/N seeks to bring businesses together with organizations from other institutions to address the need for sustainable wealth creation.

Is the Multi-Institutional Sustainability Project Sustainable?

I have cited evidence that individuals and organizations from four different institutional sectors are promoting the Sustainability Project. The GC can be seen as recognizing and attempting to promote this converging view by networking these institutional players. But is the ideal of sustainability itself sustainable? To answer this question, we need to address several problems with the Project. Some of these problems are conceptual, some normative, and some practical.

There are three conceptual issues with sustainability that I will discuss here. The first concerns the time frame. How long must a solution be sustained to count as sustainable? For example, if we are trying to preserve oil supplies, but the fuel cell and other alternatives are on the horizon, how long should we preserve oil to ensure, in the words of the Brundtland report, "the ability of future generations to meet their . . . needs," in this case, petroleum-based energy needs? Second, what is the scope of sustainable development? Is it the town, the nation, the region, or the entire globe? Some issues, such as global warming, are, of course, global. However, what if towns, nations, or even regions must implement solutions that are not sustainable for them in order to solve the global problem? Finally, the economic aspect of sustainability can be understood at the organizational and systemic levels. General Secretary Anan is correct when he says that business interests are served by sustainable economic development, but that does not mean that the interests of all businesses are so served. Some businesses will lose in the move toward sustainability.

The normative challenges are daunting. What does *social justice* mean in Israel and Palestine, the United States and China, China and Tibet? Is there a normative approach that can explain and reconcile these differences, as much of classical, modern, and Western philosophy assumes? Perhaps the normative approach of Isaiah Berlin, who argued that there is a plurality of irreconcilable ethical views that must be held in tension, is a plausible option (Berlin, 1998). Of course, the only way to hold these in tension without crippling violence is to make sure that extremists do not have enough power to harm their opponents. And that is not the world in which we live.

These conceptual and normative problems with sustainability do not show that it cannot work for specific projects. Unfortunately, one of the most ambitious projects using sustainability as its goal, the Chad–Cameroon oil pipeline project, has run into trouble.

The Chad–Cameroon oil pipeline project is a $4 billion project that involves the World Bank, the governments of Chad and Cameroon, NGOs, ExxonMobil, Petronas, and ChevronTexaco. The goal is economic development, a fair distribution of wealth to companies and to the peoples in the

two countries, and environmental integrity (The Chad-Cameroon Petroleum Development and Pipeline Project, 2003). To achieve these goals, the World Bank has set up the International Advisory Group to monitor the social and ecological impacts of the project. A Special Oil Revenue Account was set up so that no one group would have the power to abuse the revenues from this project.

When this project was set up, there was much hope that this was the right way to pursue the tripartite goal of sustainability. However, as the project progressed and the oil started to flow, problems began to appear. Although the workers were receiving higher wages than they could from local employment, this appears to have driven inflation, making food too expensive for many (Bretton Woods Project, 2003). Also, prostitution, including children, flourished at construction sites, with the concomitant rise of HIV/AIDS (Ibid., 2003). A coalition of CSOs has issued two reports citing damage to water supplies, lost hunting grounds for Pygmies, and a reduction in land available for agriculture (Brown, 2002). The pipeline runs over several rivers and extends into the ocean to the tanker platform. The ability to control leaks is a matter of contention between supporter and detractors of the pipeline (Grossman, 2001).

In one of the most embarrassing episodes, Chad spent $15 million of pipeline funds earmarked for education and development on the military (Brown, 2002). How did this happen when the funds are supposed to be disbursed by a multi-institutional committee to ensure the correct use of funds? According to human rights groups, "[Chad] President Idriss Deby effectively controls the committee, which includes representatives of the judiciary, legislature, human rights and religious groups (Gupta D'Souza, 2003).

Do these conceptual, normative, and practical problems mean that the multi-institutional sustainability project is doomed to failure? I don't think so. Neither democratic nation-states nor IGOs were very promising when they began. Yet, they both led to practices and institutions that are still with us today. When the 13 colonies joined together to create the United States of America, they did so under the banner of inalienable rights of the individual to "life, liberty, and the pursuit of happiness." However, it was a country that had a huge slave population and in which only landed, white adult males could vote. Over the next 200 years, slavery was abolished and voting rights were gradually extended to all adults. While voting problems still exist, as the Florida voting problems in the 2000 election showed, no one can gainsay the progress we have made since 1776.

The progress democracy has made in the United States seems to be happening globally. However, as Fareed Zakaria has argued in "The Rise of Illiberal Democracy," many of these democracies are, in John Stuart Mill's phrase, tyrannies of the majority (*Foreign Affairs*, 1997). Does that mean that democracy will fail in these countries? We do not know, of course, but what we do know is that countries can move toward their official ideals even if they do not practice them at the time of their inception.

There is also progress in the scope and effectiveness of intergovernmental organizations. The League of Nations, the first large-scale IGO, was created after World War I to prevent future wars. It soon failed. However, this failure provided several lessons that helped the UN, the WTO, the IMF, and the World Bank to be much more long-lived and more effective than the League of Nations (League of Nations Photo Archive: Introduction, 2003). The UN itself was severely challenged by the United States' decision to go ahead with the war in Iraq without its clear approval. Will the UN fail like the League of Nations? We don't know yet. Even if the UN is disbanded, it may merely be the second step in the process that teaches how to construct better IGOs.

I have argued that there is an emerging consensus across institutions about the Sustainability Project. The Global Compact builds on and tries to further this threefold goal though a multi-institutional network focused on learning, cooperation, and action. The difficulties that the GC, governments, and business have in implementing sustainable projects say much about the problems the Project faces. However, history shows that such problems are not insurmountable.

History also shows that the success of such large ideological shifts, if achieved, is not seen by those who are present at its early stages.

NOTES

1. CSO replaces NGO as a broader and more descriptive term.

2. A recent Google search for the phrase *corporate integrity* yielded over 13,000 hits.

3. This is true of state and local governments, too.

REFERENCES

About Cato. (n.d.). Retrieved 2003 from Cato Institute Web site: http://www.cato.org/about/about.html

About Nokia. (n.d.). Retrieved 2003 from Nokia Web site: http://www.nokia.com/nokia/0,8764,72,00.html

The Aluminum Industry's Sustainable Development Report. (n.d.). *International Aluminum Institute, 2.* Retrieved 2003 from http://www.world-aluminium.org/iai/publications/documents/sustainable.pdf

Annan, K. (1999, January 31). *Address to the World Economic Forum.* Retrieved 2003 from http://www.weforum.org/pdf/AnnualMeeting/kofi_annan_speech_1999AM.pdf

Backhaus, K., Stone, B., & Heiner, K. (2002). Exploring the relationship between corporate social performance and employer attractiveness. *Business & Society, 41*(3), 27, 292.

Berlin, I. (1998). The hedgehog and the fox. In H. Hardy & R. Hausheer (Eds.), *Isaiah Berlin: The proper study of mankind.* New York: Farrar, Straus, and Giroux. (Original work published 1978)

Bowen, H. R. (1953). *Social responsibilities of the businessman.* New York: Harper.

Bretton Woods Project. (2003). *Chad-Cameroon: Oil and poverty reduction don't mix.* Retrieved 2003 from Global Policy Forum Web site: http://www.globalpolicy.org/security/natres/oil/2003/0503mix.htm

Brittan, L. (1999). *Speech to World Trade Organization High Level Symposium on Trade and Environment.* Retrieved 2003 from http://www.wto.org/english/tratop_e/envir_e/lbenv.htm

Brown, P. (2002, September 27). Chad oil pipeline condemned for harming the poor. *The Guardian,* 15.

The Chad-Cameroon petroleum development and pipeline project. (2003). Retrieved 2003 from World Bank Web site: http://www.worldbank.org/afr/ccproj/project/pro_overview.htm

Compendium of sustainability reporting practices and trends for the oil and gas industry. (2003). Retrieved 2003 from American Petroleum Institute Web site: http://api-ec.api.org/environ/index.cfm?objectid=E7E783EA-06AD-45D4-A23FF688389DFAAB&method=display_body&er=1&bitmask=001003000000000000

Corporate Sustainability. (2003). *Dow Jones Sustainability Indexes.* Retrieved 2003 from http://www.sustainability-index.com/htmle/sustainability/corpsustainability. html

Declaration of the United Nations Conference on the Human Environment. (1972). Retrieved 2003 from United Nations Environment Programme Web site, Section 1: http://www.unep.org/Documents/Default.asp?DocumentID=97&ArticleID=1503

Dialogue. (n.d.). Retrieved 2003 from United Nations Global Compact Web site: http://www.unglobal-compact.org/Portal

Dienhart, J. (1982). *A cognitive approach to counseling psychology.* Lanham, MD: University Press of America.

Dienhart, J. (2000). *Business, institutions, and ethics* (pp. 39–56). New York: Oxford University Press.

Duska, R., & Whelan, M. (1979). *Moral development.* New York: Paulist Press.

Encouraging smart growth. (n.d.). Retrieved 2003 from U.S. Environmental Protection Agency Web site: http://www.epa.gov/livability/index.htm

About EPI: Frequently asked questions. (n.d.). Retrieved 2003 from Economic Policy Institute Web site: http://www.epinet.org/content.cfm/ about

The European Union at a glance. (n.d.). Europa: The European Union online. Retrieved 2003 from http://europa.eu.int/abc/index_en.htm

Federal actions to address environmental justice in minority populations and low-income populations. (n.d.). Retrieved 2003 from U.S. Environmental Protection Agency Web site: http://www.epa.gov/history/ topics/justice/02. htm

Foreign Affairs. (1997). Nov/Dec, 76(6), 22.

Goodpaster, K., Maines, T., & Rovang, M. (2002). Stakeholder thinking: Beyond paradox to practicality. *Journal of Corporate Responsibility,* 7.

Grossman, J. (2001, November 7). Blue planet: Africa oil project draws fire. *UPI Science News.*

Gupta D'Souza, V. (2003). Which way will Chad's oil money flow? *Inter Press Service.*

The IMF and the environment: A factsheet. (n.d.). Retrieved 2003 from International Monetary Fund Web site: http://www.imf.org/external/np/exr/facts/enviro.htm

Initiative to grow sustainable business in world's poorest countries. (2002, September 2). Retrieved 2003 from United National Global Compact Web site:http://www.unglobalcompact.org/content/NewsEvents/NewsArchive/joburgpress.htm

Kelley, M., & Asmus, P. (2003). 100 best corporate citizens of 2003. *Business Ethics.* Retrieved 2003 from http://www.business-ethics.com/100best.htm

Kohlberg, L. (1984). *The psychology of moral development: The nature and validity of moral stages.* San Francisco: Harper & Row. (Secondary sources on Kohlberg include Dienhart, 1982; Dienhart, 2000; Duska & Whelan, 1979)

The League of Nations. (n.d.). Retrieved 2003 from History Learning Web site: http://www.historylearningsite.co.uk/leagueofnations.htm

League of Nations photo archive: Introduction. (n.d.). Retrieved 2003 from Indiana University Web site: http://www.indiana.edu/~league/intro.htm

Learning forum. (n.d.). Retrieved 2003 from United Nations Global Compact Web site: http://www.unglobalcompact.org/Portal/

Lenway, S. (1985). *The politics of U.S. international trade.* Marshfield, MA: Pitman.

Mirvis, P. H. (2000). Transformation at Shell: Commerce *and* citizenship. *Business and Society Review,* 105(1), 63–84.

Nairobi Declaration. (1997). Retrieved 2003 from United Nations Environment Programme Web site (para. 2): http://www.unep.org/Documents/Default.asp?DocumentID=287&ArticleID=1728

Nemetz, P. N. (2003). Basic concepts of sustainable development for students. *Journal of International Business Education,* 2. Retrieved 2003 from http://www.senatehall.com/ international_business/pdfs/sNemetz.pdf

NGO legitimacy—Voice or vote? (n.d.) *Global Policy Forum.* Retrieved 2003 from http://www.globalpolicy.org/ngos/credib/2003/0202rep.htm

Orlitzky, M., & Benjamin, J. (2001). Corporate social performance and firm risk: A meta-analytic review. *Business & Society,* 40(4), 28, 369.

Our commitment to global citizenship. (n.d.). Retrieved 2003 from HP Web site: http://www. hp.com/hpinfo/globalcitizenship/commitment. html

Our history. (n.d.). Retrieved 2003 from U.S. Environmental Protection Agency Web site: http:// www.epa.gov/epahome/aboutepa.htm#history

Our mission. (n.d.). Retrieved 2003 from Greenpeace Web site: http://www.greenpeace.org/extra/? item_id=4265&language_id=en

Our work: Sustainable Governance Project. (n.d.). Retrieved 2003 from CERES Web site: http:// www.ceres.org/our_work/sgp.htm

Our work: The CERES Principles. (n.d.). Retrieved 2003 from CERES Web site: http://www. ceres.org/our_work/principles.htm

Paine, L., & Moldoveanu, M. (1999). *Royal Dutch Shell in transition (A and B).* Cambridge: Harvard Business School Press. (See also Mirvis, 2000)

Release of Environmental Equity Report. (1992). Retrieved 2003 from U.S. Environmental Protection Agency Web site: http://www.epa.gov/ history/topics/justice/01.htm

Rio Declaration on Environment and Development. (1992). Retrieved 2003 from United Nations Environment Programme Web site (Principle 1): http://www.unep.org/Documents/Default.asp? DocumentID=78&ArticleID=1163

Rushton, K. (2002). Business ethics: A sustainable approach. *Business Ethics: A European Review, 11*(2), 137.

Strategic direction. (2003). Retrieved 2003 from World Bank Group Web site: http:// web.worldbank.org/ WBSITE/EXTERNAL/EXTABOUTUS/0,contentMDK:20103831~menuPK:250985~pagePK: 43912~piPK:44037~theSitePK:29708,00.html

Sustainable development. (n.d.). Retrieved 2003 from BP Web site: http://www.bp.com/environ_social/ sus_dev.asp

Sustainable development. (2002). Retrieved 2003 from European Chemical Industry Council Web site: http://www.cefic.be/Templates/shwStory .asp?NID=10&HID=53

Sustainable development: The basis for Alcoa's future. (n.d.). Retrieved 2003 from Alcoa Worldwide Web site: http://www.alcoa.com/global/en/ environment/goals.asp

Treviño, L. (1986). Ethical decision making in organizations: A person-situation interactionist model. *Academy of Management Review, 11*(3).

Treviño, L., & Nelson, K. (1995). *Managing business ethics* (p. 89). New York: John Wiley & Sons, Inc.

UNEP milestones. (n.d.). Retrieved 2003 from United Nations Environment Programme Web site: http://www.unep.org/Documents/Default.asp?Do cumentID=287

United Nations Division for Sustainable Development. (n.d.). Retrieved 2003 from United Nations Web site: http://www.un.org/esa/sustdev/index.html

Verschoor, C., & Murphy, E. (2002). The financial performance of large U.S. firms and those with global prominence: How do the best corporate citizens rate? *Business & Society Review,* 107.

What is the World Bank? (n.d.). Retrieved 2003 from World Bank Group Web site: http://web.world-bank.org/WBSITE/EXTERNAL/EXTABOU-TUS/0,contentMDK:20040558~menuPK:34559 ~pagePK:34542~piPK:36600,00.html

White, D. (n.d.). *Corporate integrity development program.* Retrieved 2003 from David White Education and Coaching Web site: http:// white. com.au/corporate_integrity/program.html

Who we are. (n.d.). Retrieved 2003 from Cummins Web site: http://www.cummins.com/na/pages/ en/whoweare/vision_mission.cfm

World Commission on Environment and Development. (1987). *Our common future.* New York: Oxford University Press.

Zieba, K. (1996). What is sustainable development? *US EPA Region III Center for Sustainability.* Retrieved 2003 from http://www.epa.gov/ r3chespk/whatissd.PDF

PART IV

FOSTERING CORPORATE INTEGRITY

T he last part of this book looks at the challenge of fostering corporate integrity. What obstacles stand in the way of promoting corporate integrity and what measures can be taken to promote corporate integrity? These are issues that have vexed businesses and business ethicists for as long as these issues have been raised. The answers remain highly contentious even if there are prominent contributions both by businesses and by organizations outside of business of the kinds of arguments and mechanisms whereby these questions may be answered.

At the outset, **Steven Rochlin** notes the increased pressures for corporations to demonstrate both corporate integrity and accountability. He examines these issues under the rubric of "good corporate citizenship." He argues that to respond to these pressures corporations must develop a practical understanding of corporate citizenship and of the ways to integrate a strategic vision of it in their organizations. Corporate citizenship, in Rochlin's view, can be used to subsume the various terms in which business's ethical, social, and environmental obligations are currently discussed. As such, in his interpretation, corporate citizenship includes both business ethics and corporate social responsibility. So understood, corporate citizenship is a process in which organizations (a) create policies and processes to make ethical decisions; (b) anticipate social issues and stakeholder concerns, and create strategies to respond; and (c) assess business decisions and operations in the context of a broader social environment. Unfortunately, few corporations have explicitly undertaken efforts to develop and integrate such activities in a formal manner within themselves.

Nevertheless, there have been many efforts outside of corporations to address these problems. The result is a multitude of codes, standards, and metrics being developed by nongovernmental organizations (NGOs) and other international organizations to help provide guidance to management regarding corporate citizenship. Some of these efforts are compliance based, others principle based, and still others process based.

The driving motives that lead companies to adopt these different systems include soft social expectations of the public and the members of individual businesses, formal and informal regulatory systems, concern about corporate reputation, and new views regarding the value-creating nature of business ethics and corporate social responsibility (CSR) mechanisms for corporations. Rochlin acknowledges that many of these drivers work concurrently, though they may also result in conflicting and unaligned programs. Far too often the failure to address this situation adequately is due to the fact that many of the fundamentals of sound management are lacking not only in the business itself but also in the design and implementation of corporate citizenship processes. Beyond remedying such basic management inadequacies, Rochlin urges that businesses must also institute systems "to monitor, analyze, anticipate, and respond to critical ethical, social, and environmental issues." To the extent that they integrate these systems within sound management systems, they will find that their driving motives may be aligned with their constructive purposes and that both integrity and profits are prioritized at the same level.

But what, more particularly, can be said to accomplish these aims and procedures that Rochlin has identified? The chapter by **Eleanor O'Higgins** gives a partial response through her discussion of CEO compensation, a topic that has occasioned considerable outrage on both sides of the Atlantic.

Boards of directors tend to appeal to one (or more) of three different criteria: fairness, the free market, or pay for performance in their determination of CEO compensation packages. Ideally, these three would have the same result, but O'Higgins notes they rarely do. Consequently, she examines each of these criteria for how they are currently being implemented and the difficulties each criterion occasions. For example, fairness or equity criteria seem to be violated by the extreme differences not only between CEO compensation packages in different countries but also between the compensation that CEOs receive and that which lower-level employees receive in the organizations the CEOs run. The free market criterion runs up against the dubious existence of "a true open market for CEOs." And the performance-related pay criterion crashes headlong into questions such as the following: How are the relevant criteria to be determined and measured? How lengthy a perspective should be taken? What should be the form of the reward? Who is to make these decisions? Each one of these questions and the answers they receive is discussed by O'Higgins. The last question receives a particularly lengthy consideration by O'Higgins as she reviews the various stakeholders who might step up and claim to have a voice in answering the questions related to CEO compensation. The aim of this discussion is to reveal the complexities, the different stakes and cross-purposes, and the strengths and weaknesses of the positions that these various stakeholders occupy in this process. The upshot is a richer understanding of the "dynamic interplay of power differentials, social processes and individual values, motives, and personality traits" that play a role in the determination of CEO compensation.

In tendering her own views on this issue, O'Higgins' notes the additional role that the opposing views of the corporation and its relation to society play on the two different sides of the Atlantic. In place of an answer that looks to agency theory as its basis, O'Higgins suggests that we must move closer to a "stewardship model" or a "trusteeship model" if we are satisfactorily to address the issue of CEO compensation. Central to such an approach are values grounded in accountability, probity, and transparency. These values and characteristics, she insists, "should be applicable across all systems in all regions."

Though O'Higgins chapter looks at an issue that is generally viewed as one that exists within corporations, she ends up discussing at considerable length the role that stakeholders outside a corporation may play in arriving at an answer to CEO compensation. The next chapter looks at the role that the owners or the stockholders of a corporation may play in affecting its behavior in the area of social responsibility.

Jane Collier focuses on the role that socially responsible investing (SRI) may play in the effort to foster corporate integrity. SRI is of increasing importance these days as a way to promote this aim. Changes in the legislation and regulations of a country may foster or retard SRI practices. In the case of Great Britain, regulatory changes have been seen as encouraging SRI. Yet, since tensions supposedly remain between SRI and the fiduciary interests that the executives of a corporation are supposed to fulfill, how are we to understand the rationale for such changes?

To grapple with these issues, Collier first looks at the rationale behind institutional investors as corporate stakeholders. Whether SRI includes negative or positive screens, Collier views SRI as the effort, by major investors, "to optimize returns on portfolios by investing across the market, [and] then engaging companies to encourage them to improve their CSR performance." As such, SRI is a form of engagement based on voice and loyalty, rather than exit. It targets corporate governance as well as CSR policy and practices.

Next, Collier places this engagement of investors within the context of stakeholder theory and agency theory. Stakeholder theory portrays the different risks that shareholders, suppliers, employees, and customers experience. Good governance requires establishing equitable distribution between different risk bearers. But stakeholder theory tells us very little about how we are to arrive at equity of treatment. More generally, Collier claims, stakeholder theory provides few guidelines by which investor engagement may be understood and directed.

Similarly, agency theory is of little help when it comes to investor stakeholders and the organizations they engage. What we do know is that investor engagement works only if accountability is embedded in corporate practices and procedures. But in traditional agency theory views of accountability, these relationships are competitive and instrumental. Stakeholder interests are unimportant. Collier suggests that a more realistic view may be one where processes of accountability are designed "not as a constraint on the powerful, but as an organic feature of organizational life." In the resulting kinds of relationships, a different form of management can develop in which managers may enter into transparent relationships that involve openness and mutual loyalty. These processes of accountability may be the basis on which SRI investors can build.

For processes of accountability to work in a situation of engagement requires critical cooperation where there are both conflicting and converging interests. To examine the criteria for successful investor engagement, Collier surveys an example of low-profile investor engagements and two examples of high-profile investor engagement, that of a company selling anti-AIDS drugs and of EasyJet. These cases represent different engagement dynamics. Through her study of these cases, she claims that there are four necessary conditions for successful engagement: (a) the balancing of power asymmetries; (b) an acknowledgment of rights and responsibilities; (c) communication and relationship building; and (d) management of relations with stakeholders.

Collier ends on a cautionary note. Though there is a great deal of current fascination with SRI and the countervailing power it offers to various corporate practices, it is less easy to say, she maintains, whether it actually improves CSR. It is possible that changes in corporate behavior that SRI advocates seek might happen otherwise. Further, because there is no one model of investor engagement, any determination of the effectiveness of SRI would have to focus on the particular model in question. Still, Collier believes that these different approaches will coalesce in the future. This may, in itself, give the SRI movement greater countervailing power and effectiveness when it comes to fostering corporate integrity and social responsibility.

The final chapter, by **Catherine Smith** and **Pieter Kroon,** draws on their experiences with ING Group. Here we learn about what an actual corporation has done and how it has sought to answer some of the challenges discussed early in this part (and other parts) of the book.

Smith and Kroon begin by noting the different terms that have been used to discuss business ethics over the past several decades, as well as the recent ascendancy of the notion of "sustainability." Though many treat sustainability as the equivalent of being ethical, ING does not accept this equivalence. It is possible, they argue, for a company to engage in sustainable activities but not be moral, and (conversely) to be moral but not engage in sustainable activities. In place of the sustainability, or "triple bottom line" model, ING prefers to use a model of stakeholder dialogue.

The four most important stakeholder groups that ING deals with are its customers, shareholders, employees, and society in general. In making business decisions, ING seeks to forge an equitable treatment of each of these groups. In this way, it seeks to be an ethical leader, which is something that goes beyond sustainability and doing good in a society to questions of doing the right thing in a wide variety of social contexts. For this, moral competence is needed.

Moral competence is exercised within the "shell" of corporate policies, codes of conduct, risk management systems, and the like, but it is not reducible to these various items. The nature of this "technical" competence is captured, they suggest, in the notion of an Aristotelian mean in which the various stakes involved are weighed, the company's own values engaged, and the risks analyzed and assessed on a case-by-case basis. ING's decisions to withdraw from Burma but to remain in China are provided as examples of such moral competence in action. With training, such moral competence should ultimately become a form of "technical" decision making, "removed from personal conscience."

Moral competence does not simply happen. Its development cannot be left to personal conscience, but must be fostered through a "company conscience." This involves articulating a company's business principles, which include integrity and responsiveness to clients. These principles go beyond the bare minimum of the law and regulations. They provide guidelines for all staff around the world. At ING Group, Inc., they are spread using a "cascade approach" that begins with the executive board and flows down to all employees. It involves training that incorporates everyday dilemmas, as well as common questions employees should ask themselves regarding the actions they are considering. Finally, the results of this process are monitored on a structural basis. Such monitoring takes place on the two levels of compliance and risk management. In this way, Smith and Kroon argue, ING Group instills its values in its operations, creates moral competence in its employees, and endeavors to do the right thing.

It is through these efforts that ING Group has sought to make itself a corporation with integrity.

16

PRINCIPLES WITH PROCESS

Corporate Integrity Within a Corporate Citizenship Framework

STEVEN A. ROCHLIN

Businesses face intensifying pressures to demonstrate integrity and accountability. With better-informed and discerning customers and employees, and growing activism from civil society, there are heightened expectations on companies to behave with the highest ethical standards and contribute to social and environmental development. Even equity markets—through the growth of the socially responsible investment community—are joining in. More and more investors include ethics and social responsibility among the major criteria in selecting investments. Corporate integrity and accountability, which are often brought under the rubric of "good corporate citizenship," are increasingly seen by many progressive companies as having a direct bearing on economic success. The complementarities of financial, environmental, and social objectives of enterprises are increasingly appreciated.

Resistance to these ideas persists, however. Industries are hesitant to invest the time, resources, and research and development (R&D) to establish more sophisticated and professional approaches to managing corporate citizenship. There exist few leaders in the art and practice of comprehensive corporate citizenship. The current landscape includes far more examples of false starts, spinning wheels, or highly uneven performance than of sophisticated, professional, and effective approaches to corporate citizenship management.

Understanding and then managing the scale and scope of ethical, environmental, social, operational, and financial issues and opportunities confronting contemporary businesses represents an intimidatingly complex challenge. Nevertheless, the success of private sector organizations rests to a large degree in their ability to tackle a range of complex tasks and problems. In this regard, there is value in working with companies to overcome inadequacies in existing definitional constructs of corporate citizenship. This can be done by investing in the development of more sophisticated approaches to weigh difficult choices and build "citizenship systems" that enable companies to anticipate, diagnose, and respond to issues in an integrated and seamless way into typical operations and standard decision-making processes. Doing so means overcoming the confusing and competing intellectual underpinnings for the field. It also means overcoming the traditional internal drivers motivating corporate citizenship that often yield inefficient, ineffective, and unaligned corporate citizenship operating systems.

This chapter, therefore, addresses the following three issues:

1. The need to develop a practical understanding of corporate citizenship

2. The problems raised with the ways in which corporate citizenship concepts have been previously developed

3. The need for an integrated, strategic vision of corporate citizenship

With so many competing terms and definitions, the scope, focus, and boundaries of corporate citizenship are both vague and unwieldy. This chapter argues that focusing on a systems approach to understanding and managing corporate citizenship will better enable corporate managers to find balance among the ethical challenges they (and their business) confront, their principles, and the processes necessary to make principles real.

A Thousand Flowers Are Blooming

It is an exciting time to be a part of the evolving field of corporate citizenship. The ethical, environmental, and social role of business is receiving attention from the highest levels of governments, multilaterals, NGOs, academia, and even business itself (although this attention is far greater outside the United States than within it).

Currently, a growing number of representatives from civil society, the public sector, academia, and even the private sector are joining the battle to fully integrate corporate citizenship as a business fundamental. This evolving agenda takes both an internal and external view. Constituencies that champion the internal view focus on enhancing the core dynamics of accountability and integrity. In this regard, corporate citizenship is designed to reduce (if not eliminate) "harms" and, as much as possible, distribute broad benefits from a range of business practices including purchasing, marketing, manufacturing, and selling. The principles underlying what constitutes harms and who we should be concerned about harming constitute a significant range of options and opinions (two of the leading frameworks involve social contract theory and stakeholder management; see Donaldson & Dunfee, 1999; Freeman, 1984). In contrast, champions of the external agenda focus on developing an approach to citizenship in which companies become explicit leaders in working to solve challenging problems of social and environmental justice and equity. This view asks corporate "citizen-statesmen" to devote their considerable resources toward promoting a vision of the common good. The characteristics of such a vision vary as well. Both views require business decision-makers to lead their organizations into unmapped territory and untraditional roles. Current business leaders adopting a corporate citizenship mandate have the formidable agenda of redefining the concept of "business as usual."

Therefore, it is important for business decision makers to understand what corporate citizenship means. This is no simple task. The fertile thought behind corporate citizenship is yielding a thousand conceptual flowers. Defining *corporate citizenship* or its namesakes in a way that a broad number of people can agree on is an especially difficult problem to tame. The problem starts with the fundamentals: What term is the most appropriate?

Today there exists a panoply of terms that describe the ethical, social, and environmental obligations of business. There is a fair amount of debate regarding the merits of terms such as corporate citizenship, corporate social responsibility (CSR), business ethics, sustainable development, sustainability, corporate social performance, corporate responsibility, corporate social accountability, triple bottom line, community relations, corporate community involvement, social investment, external relations, public affairs, corporate reputation management, social risk management, and others.

Most of these terms possess significant conceptual and operational overlap. However, there are important distinctions among the terms and conflicting ideas and prescriptions within the terms that do not lend themselves well to framing and guiding the choices of decision makers. For example, to operationalize a program of corporate commitment to sustainable development typically (but not always) emphasizes the prominence of environmental stewardship over a concept of business ethics (narrowly defined by practitioners as compliance with laws and regulations) or community support (to name two such distinctions). In Europe, a commitment to CSR has recently prescribed a different set of priorities (supply chain, labor, human rights) than a similar commitment among most U.S. firms, which are more largely focused on community development and charitable giving (Googins, 2002; Mohan, 2001).

Further complicating the issue is that few companies have explicitly chosen to pursue a unified concept of their engagement in the triple bottom line (or as Emerson counters, an approach to "blended value" of financial, environmental, and broader social outcomes).

For the sake of argument, this chapter proposes *corporate citizenship* as the unifying term to describe the overarching relationship of business to ethical decision making, environmental stewardship, and social performance. Adapting the work of Epstein, corporate citizenship is composed of business ethics and CSR. This is an important claim. The terms defined in practice typically are seen to possess strong boundaries that reflect separate disciplines. However, within the practical context of organizational management and decision making, Epstein argues the following:

> [O]ften . . . scholars have tended . . . to focus conceptually on either business ethics or corporate social responsibility with little apparent recognition of conceptual complementarities or mutual practical concerns. This intellectual dualism is somewhat ironic. During any given time, the business ethics and corporate social responsibility literatures have been mirror images with regard to specific issues and concerns. (Epstein, 1987, p. 103)

Figure 16.1 portrays the definition of corporate citizenship used for this discussion.

First, as Epstein argues, it is important to remove the "dualism" creating artificial conceptual boundaries between the concepts of corporate citizenship and ethics, or between corporate citizenship, integrity, and accountability. Corporate citizenship encompasses both business ethics and CSR. Adapting Epstein's views, business ethics concerns the systematic, value-based reflection by managers and employees on the moral significance of personal and organizational business action and its consequences for societal stakeholders (Epstein, 1987, p. 104).

In practice, CSR has related primarily to minimizing harms caused by organizational behavior and decisions on both broader social and environmental interests. In addition, it seeks to promote as much as possible maximum beneficial outcomes from organizational behavior, decisions, and specific programs designed to support social and environmental goals.

For the purpose of this discussion, corporate citizenship is used as an overarching, integrative concept, representing a place of intersection for business ethics and CSR. Corporate citizenship thus becomes the process by which organizations do the following:

- Create policies and processes to make ethical decisions.
- Anticipate social issues and stakeholder concerns and create strategies to respond.

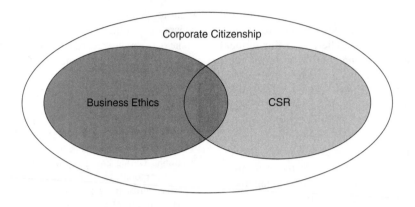

Figure 16.1 Corporate citizenship

- Assess business decisions and operations in the context of a broader social environment and make plans to adapt continuously to changing circumstances.

In our work and association with several thousand companies over the years, those of us at The Center for Corporate Citizenship at Boston College (The Center) have observed that few businesses have developed an approach to these processes that is codified in formal strategies and policies, with corresponding operating procedures, guidelines, action plans, incentives, and review. There is little to no interaction among decision makers, their business units, and their departments on issues related to corporate citizenship. As but one example of the commitment of organizations to integrate corporate citizenship, few companies possess formal incentive systems for executives, midlevel managers, or employees for their performance in this arena. One may find isolated examples of successful practices in this area. Executives, for example, may accept responsibility to particular stakeholders, such as shareholders or employees; however, few possess incentives that cut across the elements of the "triple bottom line." For those that do, anecdotal evidence suggests that such incentive systems typically lack real teeth

and conceptual underpinnings that direct action to support the broader and deeper application of the normative expectations of corporate citizenship systems.

This problem has not gone unnoticed. Currently, the field is producing flowers of a different sort. These are the emergence of codes, standards, metrics, and management principles. This is summed up by some in the field as "code-mania." Notable examples include the following: the Global Reporting Initiative (GRI); SAI8000; AA1000s; the UN Global Compact; the Global Sullivan Principles; OECD guidelines for multinational corporations; the UK CSR Index; The Center for Corporate Citizenship at Boston College's *Standards of Excellence*; Kinder, Lynderburg, and Domini indicators; the Dow Jones Sustainability Index; the *Financial Times* FTSE4Good ratings; the Conference Board of Canada and Imagine Campaign's CSR performance guidelines; ILO's Total Responsibility Management system; and ISO 14000 (and a new initiative of the ISO concerning business ethics).

These codes reflect a wide range of approaches, frames, and incentive systems. Some exist as guidelines, others as compliance systems. Some are normative, defining either explicitly or implicitly a concept of the harms to avoid and the appropriate benefits to engineer. As an example, the Global Reporting Initiative (www.globalreporting.org) lists among its indicators a report on political contributions, arguably implying a presumption of an ethical quandary created by corporate participation in financing political campaigns. Others are process based; these tend to focus on a systems level, looking for the evidence of leadership, written strategy, budgets, and evaluation of corporate citizenship practices. Some, such as the growing social investing equity market, rely on third-party influence. Others rely on public reputation through published awards and rankings. Others pursue agendas for formal policy change to require greater transparency and reporting along the practice dimensions they define.

Despite the diversity of tactics, they share a common characteristic. They all seek to create—through different mechanisms, to be sure—a set of guiding management principles for corporate citizenship. A rough typology sorts the mechanisms into the following categories:

• *Compliance based.* These systems attempt to build from normative foundations a set of formal prescriptive policies around a range of dimensions, from environment to labor and a variety of issues in between. Corporations are expected to adhere to the policies and to produce (eventually) public reports audited by objective third parties cataloging the level of compliance. A notable aspect of these systems is that they rely on voluntary, rather than legal, compliance. While their design is legalistic, they depend on a mix of carrot and stick to encourage corporate adoption.

• *Principle based.* These, like the UN Global Compact, define a set of normative principles—for example around human rights, labor, and the environment—and seek corporate endorsement. As with compliance systems, these often possess weak enforcement mechanisms. They rely on exposure to the court of public opinion to encourage companies to commit and stay the course.

• *Process based.* These are arguably the least developed. These make no explicit normative claims. Rather, they establish a set of operating strategies and process guidelines to assist in the structure and implementation of effective corporate citizenship management practices.

What is the result of such systems and the expectations for corporate behavior and action that undergird them? Before discussing, it is useful to identify the driving motives that are inspiring companies to entertain, if not adopt, these systems. In the United States, where the shareholder value model of capitalism dominates, there remains a very real debate that questions both the utility and obligation of a company's investments in corporate citizenship performance. If the Friedman view of the business obligation merely to deliver shareholder value and to obey the law reigns paramount, why are companies compelled at all to broaden their horizons?

MOTIVATIONAL SILOS

In research conducted with the support of the Ford Foundation, The Center identified a consistent set of motivational drivers that influence the voluntary adoption of corporate citizenship programs by business decision makers and suggest both the character and intensity of a company's commitment. These are identified in Figure 16.2.

The first driver described is *soft social expectations.* These generally reflect the expectations perceived by top management. The expectations may come from peers in other businesses or other major social institutions. Some expectations may arise from other voices in the broader community. Wherever they come from, they are typically understood to reflect a demand for business organizations and their leaders to participate at some level in promoting the commonweal. These expectations will typically translate into norms that relate to the traditional virtues of "giving something back" or similar aphorisms such as "From whom much is given, much is expected." They are manifested in the form of

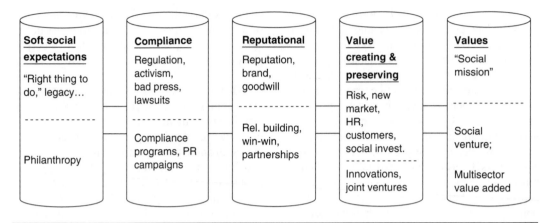

Figure 16.2   The motivational silos

charitable contributions and volunteerism. The dominant organizational outcome of this motive is the formation of a corporate giving function.

The response of managers to these expectations plays an important role in establishing and strengthening stocks of social capital that are particularly useful, at senior executive levels, for inspiring trust and bonds that yield more efficient economic transactions (Fukuyama, 1996; Putnam, Leonardi, & Nanetti, 1994). In companies that become more attuned to the expectations of employees as well as external communities, the individual employee's role in determining philanthropic and volunteerism choices becomes more central.

The second driver in the figure is *compliance based*. Whereas compliance is typically seen as being limited to laws and regulations for which business must comply, the term as used here reflects a mix of formal and informal regulatory systems that govern and constrain corporate operations. Some of the most common formal systems include environmental and worker safety, to name but two. Well-known industry specific compliance systems include the Community Reinvestment Act (CRA) for banking institutions.

However, compliance-based drivers are not limited to formal regulation. The court of public opinion plays an important role as well, driving companies to respond to pressures to comply with expectations that often exceed existing regulation (e.g., diversity and discrimination in the workplace) or fill gaps where no regulation exists (e.g., worker rights and global sourcing).

The dominant organizational response to compliance drivers is to define a concentrated "fix" for the problem. This results in the formation of a related function designed to ensure compliance (such as the environment, health, and safety department) or an increase in staffing and responsibility in functions with internal policing authority such as legal, accounting/ auditing, and HR. Often, compliance motives create organizational systems designed to adhere to the letter of the law. There is little incentive to consider strategic or innovative approaches to the compliance issue in question.

The third driver is *reputational*. This reflects the growing attention to reputation as a valuable "intangible asset" for the business (Boulton, Libert, & Samek, 2000; Fombrun, 1996). The visible commitment to corporate citizenship behaviors enhances corporate brand, goodwill, trust, and overall favorability among key stakeholders such as customers, employees, suppliers, and even investors. In a sense, this represents a more holistic argument than that posed for the soft social norms driver. Corporate citizenship becomes more strongly integrated within the organization as a whole as a tool to create system-wide social capital.

Building reputational benefits requires more visible displays of corporate citizenship. This requires organizational responses that lend themselves to public relations and communications efforts. However, the tricky expectations and issues raised by corporate citizenship create incentives for innovation, experimentation, and generally deeper commitments to citizenship than those found for soft norms and compliance. Where compliance drivers exist with strong reputational drivers, companies will find powerful incentives to move beyond adherence to the letter of the law and will seek innovative approaches that reduce compliance costs and enhance effectiveness. Strong examples of this are the movements of well-known corporate brands such as DuPont, 3M, and BP to set aggressive environmental waste and emission-reduction targets. Reputational drivers are liable to create a mix of programs, from high-glitz philanthropy to high-impact partnerships and proactive commitments to self-regulate.

The fourth driver is *value creating and preserving*. This represents a stream of maturing thinking regarding the "business case" for corporate citizenship, buttressed by a growing volume of research and anecdotal evidence that good corporate citizenship practices create premium returns (for a survey of scholarly research on the topic, see Margolis & Walsh, 2001). Corporate citizenship practice is seen as creating bottom-line benefits by saving costs and enhancing profits. With respect to cost savings, corporate citizenship becomes a central facet of risk management and risk analysis. Among the more popular ideas is the ability of corporate citizenship to protect the corporate "license to operate" (Burke, 1999; Googins, 1997; Nelson, 1998). In addition, corporate citizenship programs along the component dimensions of business ethics and CSR lead to a variety of cost savings from reduced employee turnover, increased customer loyalty, goodwill during times of crisis, and favorable treatment by public officials and regulatory bodies.

As far as profits are concerned, more attention has been focused on the opportunity to use corporate citizenship as a competitive advantage. Programs can be used to attract customers, to innovate, and to build new markets (Environics, 2003; Margolis & Walsh, 2001; Moss Kanter, 1999; Rochlin, Coutsoukis, & Carbone, 2000; Weiser & Zadek, 2000).

The fifth and final driver is *values based*. This driver relates to core philosophical values of ethical and socially responsible behavior as defined by corporate founders, senior executives, and/or employees. Notable examples include the Johnson & Johnson (J&J) credo (see David Collins in this book), the founders' mission for Ben & Jerry's, and the mission of the Body Shop.

The values define in clear terms an organizational mission beyond shareholder value. They often, but not always, define clear goals to deliver value to society and the environment and to "do the right thing." The successes of Ben & Jerry's Homemade, the Body Shop, Tom's of Maine, Whole Foods, Paul Newman's Foods, and numerous others have spawned greater attention and interest in "social ventures." These organizations use market-based approaches to pursue a greater agenda of support, reform, or social and ethical leadership. Other examples in this category, such as J&J, may not be driven to reform social institutions. However, its credo provides equal footing to values other than profit maximization.

THE MOTIVATIONAL "SILOS"

The motives presented in Figure 16.2 drive decisions, strategies, resource allocations, and system development around corporate citizenship. Many businesses, and many industries, find several if not all of the drivers at work concurrently. However, more often than not, the influence these drivers possess over organizational behavior is discrete. Rather than working in concert, the outcomes of multiple drivers yield disconnected, divergent, and unaligned programs.

Figure 16.3   Organizational Outcomes

Even companies that take corporate citizenship seriously find that conflicting motives, combined with the competing frameworks described previously, yield organizational outcomes such as that diagrammed in Figure 16.3.

The figure describes an energy company with whom The Center at Boston College is currently working. This "corporate citizenship map" illustrates the best of intentions gone awry in implementation. Sixteen largely discrete corporate citizenship programs and initiatives exist. For the most part, each possesses its own set of champions, managers, goals, objectives, success measures, resources, and agendas. While many overlap in mission and content, few connect to explore potential synergies. Most operate in isolation. Philanthropy and foundation systems exist to respond to the social norms of the energy company's contributions to civic life. Numerous compliance-based systems exist. Several make the effort to respond to more sophisticated and globally based codes of conduct currently in vogue. A reputation management

committee has formed to take better advantage of the links between citizenship practice and reputational "equity." Several programs such as stakeholder engagement and total loss management exist to support risk management and enhance project rates of return.

The other notable quality of this diagram is the absence of a unifying leadership presence. In this company, the top management team and board lead through a process of what might be described as benign neglect. The midlevel managers that report to top management are permitted to design and develop these systems to respond to any of the driving motives they experience.

In our observation, the experience of this company is shared by numerous others, across industries. The Center is currently working on a two-year initiative with a group of companies from the financial, consumer manufacturing, information technology, and communication, energy, and telecommunications industries seeking to better align, integrate, and manage their manifestations of Figure 16.3.

Managing Corporate Citizenship

Epstein (1987) argues that most business organizations are inadequately equipped to manage corporate citizenship concerns in a strategic, integrative fashion. More recent work by David Baron on the nonmarket strategy system (1995), Roger Martin's "virtue matrix" process to manage social risk and opportunity (2002), and Waddock and Bodwell's (2002) views on "Total Responsibility Management" (TRM) make similar claims. All, in their fashion, suggest that process-based approaches to addressing corporate citizenship have not kept pace with the compliance- and principle-based models. As a consequence, we are left with the lament of business decision makers commonly heard at The Center's conferences and training sessions: "How do you manage corporate citizenship day-to-day?" A common result in the *best of cases* is the company portrayed in Figure 16.3—disparate programs, ill-defined objectives, haphazard resource allocation, nonexistent performance metrics, and no formal accountability at the top.

In complex business organizations, process must stand eye-to-eye with principles. While principles should guide process, unless effective delivery systems exist, the promise of principles will go unrealized. If, as noted earlier, corporate citizenship is the process of

> creating policies and processes to make ethical decisions,

> anticipating social issues and stakeholder concerns and creating strategies to respond, and

> assessing business decisions and operations in the context of a broader social environment and making plans to adapt continuously to changing circumstances,

then it calls for efforts to more rapidly mature the operational systems that together form the engine that drives corporate citizenship outcomes. The challenge is not necessarily to innovate new management processes but rather to adapt tested and accepted management practices to the new management discipline of corporate citizenship.

These performance elements are shown in Figure 16.4.

The figure provides the systemic "building blocks" to effective corporate citizenship management. They are not organized into an elegant presentation of a dynamic management system. Instead the building block representation is meant to signify the essential elements of effective corporate citizenship management. The tactics, and even the progression by which they are applied, are open to question. Instead, their fundamental value resides in their application, through whatever particular process representation is most salient for the operating culture of a unique organization.

It is important to note that the elements in this figure are for the most part familiar. The majority of these managerial processes are fundamental to effective operations in general. Vision and values, strategies, goals, etc., are all part of the basics of effective organizations (see Collins & Porras, 2002, among others). The issue for the topic of corporate citizenship is how often these fundamentals are lacking in the design and implementation of corporate citizenship processes. Visions are lacking—or lack teeth. The role of leadership is unclear or nonexistent. To wit, a recent assessment by a Swiss-based financial services company reports that 16 percent of the 1,336 companies assessed in 2002 have established specific board committees on CSR and sustainability (see http://www.sam-group.com/). Observers will be hard-pressed to find notable instances of organization-wide corporate citizenship strategy, communication plans, accountability systems, and least of all measurement. In a survey of its members, The Center finds that only 14 percent of its members possess a system to measure their corporate citizenship performance and only 7.3 percent feel they are doing an adequate job measuring corporate citizenship.

While many of these steps can be categorized as "Management 101," two dimensions in particular are distinctive. These are issues of management and relationship building. Effective corporate citizenship management calls for systems to monitor, analyze, anticipate, and respond to

Measurement	Feedback
Communication	Innovation
Infrastructure	Accountability
Relationship	Strategy
Leadership	Issue
Values & Vision	

Figure 16.4   Corporate Citizenship Processes

critical ethical, social, and environmental issues. These issues typically will pose threats to the company and its stakeholders. However, there are instances when they will present opportunities. Similarly, corporate citizenship rests on negotiating effectively the interests, concerns, and needs of a variety of both competing and complementary stakeholder interests. Identifying, understanding, and responding to these stakeholders are fundamental aspects of citizenship practice.

The challenge for companies is to apply these processes in an integrated and aligned manner across the business and across the pertinent ethical, social, and environmental issues confronting the company. While there will be significant overlap of key issues both within and across industries, it is also the case that each organization will have unique contexts requiring distinct applications, choices, and resource allocations. Few, if any, companies are leaders in each of the dimensions outlined in Figure 16.4. However, there are examples of promising practices in developing integrative corporate citizenship management processes.

Conclusion

The intent of this discussion is not to suggest that core principles and values are not central to corporate citizenship. To the contrary, as Figure 16.4 shows, vision and values are the foundational building blocks of effective corporate citizenship management.

Peter Drucker famously observed that, in the end, the best and most creative strategy eventually degenerates into work. This is also true in the case of the principled and responsible management of a company's ethical, social, and environmental obligations.

The field has evolved whereby principle-based and compliance-based approaches to managing corporate citizenship exist at a higher level of maturity than strategic management approaches. However, the development of management skills and expertise in this arena can create interesting tensions. Strategic process management approaches will typically seek a happy medium among the priorities of profit maximization and the objectives of social and environmental sustainability and ethical behavior. While there are many instances where such dynamics can relate synergistically, such an approach also leads to compromise and "satisficing."

An emphasis on management also suggests an approach that relies on situational leadership. When applied, companies and their decision makers will often find that the decision (for example) to cease manufacturing in Burma will not necessarily make clear a decision to leave China. Context, nuance, and vagaries all contribute to a management system that is, at core, flexible and adaptive.

In short, corporate citizenship and its founding principles and values are messy when applied to day-to-day situations. Only through the design of formal management processes and the commitment to continuous improvement will companies succeed at meeting the competing claims and demands of various stakeholders. Only by committing to manage corporate citizenship in a professional manner will companies be able to use their driving motives to constructive purpose, and only then will we find businesses prioritizing integrity at the same level as profits.

References

Baron, D. (1995). The nonmarket strategy system. *Sloan Management Review, Fall.*

Boulton, R. E. S., Libert, B., & Samek, S. M. (2000). *Cracking the value code: How successful businesses are creating wealth in the new economy.* New York: HarperCollins.

Burke, E. M. (1999). *Corporate community relations: The principle of the neighbor of choice.* Praeger Trade.

Collins, J., & Porras, J. I. (2002). *Built to last: Successful habits of visionary companies.* New York: HarperCollins.

Donaldson, T., & Dunfee, T. W. (1999). *Ties that bind: A social contracts approach to business ethics.* Boston: Harvard Business School Press.

Emerson, J. (2000). *The nature of returns: A social capital markets inquiry into the elements of investment and the blended value proposition* (Harvard Business School Social Enterprise Working Paper). Retrieved from http://www.redf.org/download/other/emerson1.pdf

Emerson, J., & Gertner, J. (2002, October 29). A new world order: Jed Emerson's capitalist utopia. *Money Magazine.*

Environics. (2003). *Corporate Social Responsibility Monitor.*

Epstein, E. (1987). The corporate social policy process: Beyond business ethics, corporate social responsibility, and corporate social responsiveness. *California Management Review, Spring.*

Fombrun, C. J. (1996). *Reputation: Realizing value from the corporate image.* Cambridge, MA: Harvard Business School Press.

Freeman, R. E. (1984). *Strategic management: A stakeholder approach.* Boston: Pitman.

Fukuyama, F. (1996). *Trust: Human nature and the reconstitution of social order.* New York: Free Press Paperbacks.

Googins, B. (1997). Why community relations is a strategic imperative. *Strategy and Business, 3rd quarter.*

Googins, B. (2002). The journey towards corporate citizenship in the United States: Leader or laggard? *Journal of Corporate Citizenship, Spring*(5), 85–101.

Margolis, J. D., & Walsh, J. P. (2001). *People and profits: The search for link between a company's social and financial performance.* Mahwah, NJ: Lawrence Erlbaum.

Martin, R. (2002, December 1). The virtue matrix: Calculating the return on corporate responsibility. *Harvard Business Review.*

Mohan, A. (2001, March). Corporate citizenship: Perspectives from India. *The Corporate Citizenship Journal, II.*

Moss Kanter, R. (1999). From spare change to real change. *Harvard Business Review, 77*(3), 122–133.

Nelson, J. (1998). *Building competitiveness and communities: How world class companies are creating shareholder value and societal value.* London: Prince of Wales Business Leaders Forum.

Putnam, R. D., Leonardi, R., & Nanetti, R. Y. (1994). *Making democracy work.* Princeton University Press.

Rochlin, S. A., & Christoffer, B. (2000). *Making the business case for corporate community involvement.* The Center for Corporate Citizenship at Boston College.

Rochlin, S. A., Coutsoukis, P., & Carbone, L. (2001). *Measurement demystified.* The Center for Corporate Citizenship at Boston College and the American Productivity and Quality Center.

Waddock, S., & Bodwell, C. (2002). Total responsibility management. *Journal of Corporate Citizenship, 7*, 113–126.

Weiser, J., & Zadek, S. (2001). *Conversations with disbelievers.* AccountAbility and The Center for Corporate Citizenship at Boston College.

17

CEO COMPENSATION

Parameters, Paradigms, and Paradoxes

ELEANOR R. E. O'HIGGINS

In May 2003, faced with outrage from corporate governance advisors and trade unions, HSBC, a U.K.-based global banking group, issued a defense of its remuneration package to Bill Aldinger, head of its U.S. operations. Mr. Aldinger had been chief executive of Household, a U.S. company bought by HSBC for $14 billion earlier in the year. On the takeover, Mr. Aldinger received $20.3 million and stands to receive a further $37 million over a three-year period, together with the use of a company jet for personal holidays, free dental care for life, and a multimillion-dollar payoff if he is dismissed from his job. HBSC stressed that the payment reflected exceptional one-off arrangements under Mr. Aldinger's previous contract, the desirability of retaining Mr. Aldinger and his team with their special skills in and experience of consumer finance, and company policy of paying staff at a level that reflects local market practice (Croft, 2003).

This episode encapsulates many issues of accountability, probity, and transparency in corporate governance and CEO compensation. Bob Garratt (2003) maintains that for over 400 years, good governance, public and private, has been built on core values of accountability, probity, and transparency. He believes that a return to these values is imperative to restore public confidence in business after the scandals of the "celebrity CEO" era. In fact, the core values of an organization may be reflected in its treatment of executive compensation. "The acid test for reform," wrote Warren Buffett, "will be CEO compensation" (Useem, 2003, p. 24).

THREE COMPENSATION PARAMETERS

The HSBC vignette, and public and media indignation at the apparently undeservedly exorbitant pay packages granted to some CEOs, serve to remind us how difficult it is to find a justifiable basis on which to reasonably reward senior management. Boards of directors that set CEO pay generally fall back on a combination of three parameters:

1. Fairness in the distribution of rewards

2. The free market supply and demand for CEOs

3. Performance-related pay

Ethically, fairness is an ideal to be achieved as an end in its own right, while resorting to the free market or pay-for-performance are lower-order means toward an end. In fact, the latter two are often used to justify the fairness of awards to CEOs. Thus, the fairness parameter should take priority. In a perfect world, the three parameters would produce the same result. Yet, in reality, attempts to meet the criteria of one of the parameters may violate the satisfaction of the others. For example, HSBC concentrates on the "free market" argument. However, when the head of the U.S. subsidiary receives greater rewards than the CEO of the whole company, equity seems to be violated. As will be demonstrated, the three parameters cannot be implemented precisely anyway. Distortions occur due to imperfect information, bounded rationality of decision makers, power differentials among key stakeholders, and lack of agreement about criteria and measures.

Equity, Fairness, and Distributive Justice

The first rationale of reward is that of equity or fairness. Relativity may be more important than absolute figures; some people should not be unduly rewarded compared with others. One form of comparison is among CEOs internationally. The average CEO compensation in industrial companies with revenues of $500 million in the United States is higher than all others at $1.93 million per annum, taking salary, bonus, benefits, and long-term incentives such as stock options into account. Next in line with less than half the U.S. figure are Mexico, Argentina, and Canada, averaging $879,068, $866,831, and $787,000, respectively. In Europe, Belgium is first with $696,697, followed by the U.K. with $668,526. By comparison, in other major European economies, the average

CEO would make $519,060 in France, $454,974 in Germany, and $413,860 in Sweden (Towers Perrin, 2003). It is difficult to reconcile the huge disparities in these figures on the basis of cost-of-living differences or job demands, given the similarity in company size. Monks (2002/03) has declared executive compensation in the United States in the last decade "an atrocity," with regard to historical precedent, comparison with other countries, and especially value to shareholders (p. 165).

Equity calls for a reasonable sharing of rewards and pain among all levels in companies. The difficulty is deciding what is a reasonable distribution. For example, Ben & Jerry, the founders of the eponymous U.S. ice cream company, were initially determined that the chief executive should earn no more than seven times the average worker's salary. On an aggregate basis, in the United States, CEOs earn between 200 and 475 times as much as the average worker (estimates vary). In the U.K., a Trades Union Congress study showed that the salary of the top director equates to 16 times the salary of the average worker, the highest in Europe. However, in FTSE 100 companies, the CEO's salary is 48 times that of the average worker. The figures for Germany and Japan are 13:1 and 15:1, respectively (Kakabadse & Kakabadse, 2001). Another recognized form of comparison is that between the CEO and other senior executives. Again, the United States stands apart in the relatively larger gap. For example, the ratio of CEO to human resource director compensation in the United States is 4.3:1, compared with 2.4:1 in France, 2:1 in Germany, 2.4:1 in Japan, and 2.2:1 in the U.K. (Cheffins, 2003). The total compensation of management other than the CEO is similar across OECD countries, and higher in Italy than in the United States (Becht, Bolton, & Roell, 2002). It is suggested that U.S. executives are readier to tolerate greater differentials, in the hope and anticipation of themselves achieving CEO status and its associated riches someday—the "tournament model." The highly competitive "survival of the fittest" corporate culture breeds this attitude (Bebchuk,

Fried, & Walker, 2002; Main, O'Reilly, & Wade, 1993). This is consistent with research that shows how systems that distribute outcomes unequally among their members depend on both the winners and losers to legitimize the system. Losers may perceive speaking out against the system as socially undesirable (Jost & Major, 2001). Thus, in a milieu where the winner takes all and gets adulation for doing so, it would be self-defeating to go around whining about being a loser and blaming the system.

Relative contribution to civil society may also be a yardstick to determine CEO compensation. Martin Simons, a former investment banker turned shareholder activist, asked how the chief executive of Barclays Bank could possibly be worth more than 10 U.K. High Court judges. Barclays' CEO package for 2002 was £1.7 million, compared with £147,198 for High Court judges (Gimbel, 2003).

Reward may be motivational in the symbolic as well as the material sense (Zajac & Westphal, 1995). A CEO may assess the value of a package, not in absolute terms, but relative to those of comparable peers, leading to an upward spiraling effect. Convinced that they must keep up with the market rate in their industry, firms seek to match or exceed it and a general ratcheting up occurs (Cheffins, 2003). Moreover, strong associations have been found between CEO and outside director compensation levels, explained in part by the influence of comparisons (O'Reilly, Main, & Crystal, 1988). Again, in the United States, typically higher remuneration is perpetuated by the comparison system. However, even in the United States, what is regarded as greedy excess in CEO compensation is under attack. The traditionally pro-business *Fortune* magazine ran a story in April 2003 entitled "Oink! CEO Pay in the US is Still Out of Control" featuring a pig in a pinstriped suit on the cover and decrying U.S. excess versus relative European moderation.

The Free Market

The "free market" argument claims that talent is a rare commodity, with global competition for a small talent pool. Is this conviction a myth? The question is not easily answered, since there is not a true open market for CEOs, with perfect information and mobility. Potential and actual CEOs proclaim their own indispensability, while boards that appoint CEOs are risk averse and tend to go for established names with high price tags, without really testing the market.

Testing the market might show that the global demand for costly U.S.-style executives is not so strong as to outpace supply. Outside the U.K., there is little demand for U.S.-sourced CEOs in Europe. Those European CEOs who have awarded themselves U.S.-type compensation and lifestyles have received short shrift from the body politic where there is a more egalitarian ethic and less tolerance for conspicuous consumption (Useem, 2003). When U.S. companies transfer their own executives to run their foreign subsidiaries, these expatriates do not always succeed. An example is Wal-Mart in Germany, which has been a loss-making market laggard. In the wake of company failures and scandals perpetrated by handsomely paid CEOs in the United States, many people are rethinking the supposed efficiency of the free market and superiority of U.S. CEO talent.

One might have thought that there are always queues of people for leadership jobs and that supply outstrips demand, rather than the other way around. To quote one jaundiced observer, "Whenever I hear that a chief executive post is difficult to fill, I think they cannot be looking very hard" (Fuller, 2003, p. M2). In fact, in May 2003, shareholders voted down the pay package of the U.S. resident CEO of a U.K.-headquartered company, GlaxoSmithKline. This was a watershed; the bluff had been called, and the free market argument blown out of the water. Shareholders were quite willing to risk the departure of the CEO if he was not satisfied with a reduced package and to take their chances on finding a better-value successor.

Performance-Related Pay

The question of "who deserves what" is relevant to the third parameter, performance-related pay. While seemingly obvious, the notion is based on some dubious psychological precepts. It suggests that chief executives will not do their best in the long-term interests of their enterprises unless they are given special rewards, over and above an agreed salary. This implies that the commitment of the CEO to optimize performance cannot be depended upon unless s/he is "bribed" into it. To say the least, this is the most naïve and fallacious view of human motivation and behavior. Research has demonstrated that material reward is only one dimension of inducing commitment to contribute in a meaningful way to one's organization (Morse, 2003). Anyway, who wants a CEO, or any employee, whose entire interest in and loyalty to the company rests on something as impersonal as monetary reward? To quote Martin Simons, "We want a civilised [sic] society . . . if you are the head of Lloyds Bank or ICI or BP, you shouldn't be there if you've got to be motivated to perform" (Gimbel, 2003, p. 5). Furthermore, even if there were a proportionate link between reward and motivated effort, results are not inevitably produced by effort.

Finally, in terms of fairness, how much pay for how much performance? Research studies with aggregated data have failed to demonstrate any clear relationship between pay and performance (Barkema & Gomez-Mejia, 1998; Bebchuk, Fried, & Walker, 2002). Anecdotal evidence suggests that pay and performance do not influence each other. For instance, *Business Week* magazine annually publishes trends in CEO compensation. There is never any shortage of counterintuitive examples of the highest-paid CEOs' companies reporting huge drops in shareholder value, while their lower-paid counterparts reaped benefits for their shareholders. In June 2003, the *Financial Times* published a U.K. "thin cats versus fat cats" list (Rigby, 2003). If there were a pay-performance relationship, it should show up as a virtuous cycle, whereby the promise of huge rewards for exceptional performance incentivizes superior performance, which keeps improving, thanks to the prospect of further rewards. Where does it all end? Is there a satiation point? Is an Enron or WorldCom the inevitable result?

Implementing Performance-Related Pay

In addition to the spurious and simplistic motivational assumptions at the heart of performance-related pay, dissection of the pay/performance relationship shows why it is so problematic to implement effectively and fairly. Five interrelated issues impact on the implementation of performance-related pay:

Why? The performance criteria

How? How will the criteria be measured?

When? A short- or long-term perspective?

What? What form of reward?

Who? Who decides and on whose behalf?

On the *why* question, a key performance indicator centers on shareholder value. Capitalism proposes shareholder value as an anchor indicator for other types of performance measures, especially potential profitability. Profitability, in turn, is deemed to result from excellent executive decisions and practices. If share price is a good proxy for performance, it should be tightly related to profitability and behavior, as follows:

CEO Behavior $\Rightarrow$ Profit $\Rightarrow$ Share Price

The connection between CEO behavior and firm profitability is far from clear. The disproportion in CEO pay and the celebrity-cum-guru CEO cult in the United States suggest that CEOs are deemed to be directly responsible for the fortunes of the company. Apart from ignoring other influences, some outside the control of the CEO, and even chance, success cannot be attributed to one person alone. In fact, the best, longest-lasting companies have been those with robust organizations and values that have transcended any one star CEO (Collins & Porras, 1994; De Geus, 1997).

If the link between CEO behavior and profit is not clear, that between profit and share price is also tenuous. We need look no further than the dot.com bubble for evidence. The flourishing discipline of behavioral finance has been very convincing in its description of irrational decision making in wild share price fluctuations (Nicol-Maveyraud, 2003). Apart from irrationality, companies are often regarded not for their intrinsic value creation through products and services to customers, but on the fervent hope that an attractive takeover bid will drive up the share price.

Turning to the *how*—performance measurement—prevailing common wisdom suggests quantifiable objective outcome measures, such as share price, return on investment (ROI), or economic value added (EVA = after tax profits minus the cost of capital), are best. This simplistic view fails to recognize the complexity of performance. How can it be captured in one statistic, especially at senior levels, where complex issues of leadership, vision, values, and strategic direction are involved? How can we be sure that what gets measured is the correct basis for building a successful company? Outcome measures may actually distort behavior, so people spend more time and energy trying to make the scoreboard look good, rather than playing the game by the rules.

Even if CEO motivation and behavior influence performance, it is not clear what constitutes a good performance. In an adverse economic or industry climate, declining numbers may actually reflect superior performance relative to rising numbers in buoyant market conditions. Many companies lowered their targets in the face of a worsening economic outlook, enabling executives to receive substantial bonuses anyway, while shareholders still suffered. Often bonuses do not decline with deteriorating performance, as over time they come to be an expected entitlement, decoupled from real performance—the "anchoring-and-adjustment heuristic" (Bender, 2003, p. 208). Some U.S. CEOs actually have a "guaranteed bonus" written into their contracts (Useem, 2003). Similarly, some companies have repriced stock option exercise targets downwards since they were underwater in the bear market that emerged after they were granted. Perhaps moving the goalposts is sometimes justifiable on relative performance grounds, but equity may not be served if shareholders and employees are still adversely affected by exogenous factors.

The *when* question falls naturally out of the *what* and *how* questions. Are we interested in present performance, or are we discounting the present for the future? Time frames vary between industries—for example, the seasonal fashion industry versus pharmaceuticals where a new drug takes more than a decade to develop. If it is difficult to measure present performance, anticipating future performance is even harder. Companies are often accused of denominator management, that is, starving the business of long-term investment to massage current returns on investment, frequently in response to impatient investors. "Managers that always promise to 'make the numbers' will, at some point, be tempted to *make up* the numbers" (Buffett, 2002).

An attempt to shift attention to the future has resulted in the popularity of stock options, one of the responses to the *what* question of what is an appropriate reward for performance. Stock options are meant to align the interests of managers and shareholders. But do they? Consistent linkages between firm performance and executive equity ownership have not been demonstrated (Dalton, Daily, Certo, & Roengpitya, 2003). As already mentioned, share price may not reflect performance, and misguided efforts may be expended in raising share price without improving underlying fundamental business sustainability. Until recently, the actual costs to the shareholders of granting options, in equity outflows to managers and in voting power dilution, were left out of the reckoning. In an examination of the exercise of stock options, McGuire and Matta (2003) found little support that stock options act as an incentive for improved performance. Options just motivate CEOs to hype expectation in ways not built on sustainable earnings, but by convincing analysts (who could be owned by investment bank clients) that the company stock has a great future. Or CEOs use aggressive accounting or engender a rapid but unsustainable rise in short-term earnings, for example, by restructuring. (Martin, 2003).

Warren Buffet (1999), the investment guru, sums up doubts about stock options. He denounces them as "wildly capricious in their distribution of rewards, inefficient as motivators, and inordinately expensive for shareholders." Stock options are seen as a one-way bet favoring managers; the most they can lose is the potential for reward if the shares go down, while the shareholders lose real money (Plender, 2002). Robert Monks (2002/03), a leading shareholder activist, cited the rise in the ratio of option shares to the total outstanding from 2 to 12 percent in the United States in the 1990s and declared this to have been the greatest peaceful transfer of wealth in recorded history. To add insult to injury, top executives were often given free loans to exercise their options and promptly resold them back to the company, realizing a profit without ever putting up any money. Another problem with stock options is the uncertainty about how much they actually cost, and when and at what price they will be exercised. In fact, they might not be exercised for 10 years. Thus, their cost to the company and their value to the executive entail a great deal of speculation, based on assumptions that may be unfounded.

Performance-related bonuses and stock options are meant to be variable performance dependent. Comparative research shows that U.S. executive remuneration packages emphasize pay for performance, especially stock options with a higher lucrative upside, more than other countries (Cheffins, 2003). Indexed options, the earning of which depends on beating some designated index, or the granting of restricted shares are recommended as ways of tying incentives more firmly to performance, ensuring CEO commitment through ownership and guarding against voting dilution. These have not caught on, partly because they are unpopular with CEOs who dislike the greater risk to themselves entailed in these measures. Efforts to make stock options and other rewards more sensitive to performance through indexing and various contingencies in long-term incentive plans (LTIPs) seem to have backfired in a sample of U.K. companies. The plans produced higher absolute levels of executive pay, but lower performance-pay sensitivity. These counterintuitive results are explained by the bureaucracy and power imbalances in the administration of these often-complicated packages (Buck, Bruce, & Main, 2004).

The perquisite component can be significant. Even upon retirement from IBM, CEO Lou Gerstner received a going-away present of 125,000 restricted shares worth approximately $15 million. However, Mr. Gerstner has certainly not gone away. He still has a contract with the company to do consulting work at a daily rate based on his final CEO salary. He will continue to receive "access to company aircraft, cars, office apartment, financial planning, home security services, club expenses, plus usual IBM retiree entitlements to pension, medical benefits for him and his spouse, etc." (Monks, 2002/03). In the U.K., a current bone of contention is the generosity of pension provisions for CEOs, whose funds rose by an average of £1 million, with annual pensions now averaging £550,000. Moreover, the longer an executive stays with the company, and the higher their salaries rise, the bigger their final pension (Connon, 2003).

In the United States, the CEO does not even have to be with the company for any length of time, thanks to supplemental executive retirement plans (SERPS). These credit CEOs and other senior executives with phantom extra years of service to "make whole" their entitlements and compensate them for years of service to previous employers. Clauses are written into contracts guaranteeing their pensions through special company-funded trusts, even in the event of being fired or company bankruptcy. These plans are in contrast to the plight of ordinary employees, as companies seek to curtail traditional pension rights of employees in the face of declining pension fund values. As with other aspects of CEO benefits, shareholders in the United States are less concerned about extravagant retirement arrangements than their European counterparts. The public outcry that greeted the revelation that the board of the Swedish company ABB had awarded its former CEO, Percy Barnevik, a huge pension was quickly followed by Mr. Barnevik's "voluntary" forgoing of half the amount. While Jack Welch was also embarrassed into abstaining from some of his GE retirement benefits, he gave up little more than some extraneous perks, such as club memberships, and kept the main package (Revell, 2003; Useem, 2003).

Nowadays, CEOs do not have to wait for their retirement to collect handsomely. Those who fail to deliver and are forced into an early departure from their company are given golden handshakes, usually under terms stitched into their contracts. Potential payoff is linked to length of notice period. In the U.K., there is an attempt to bring the period down to 12 months maximum, from the usual two years—some are even calling for six months. In the United States, three years is typical. Interestingly, Rick Haythornthwaite, CEO of a troubled U.K. engineering company, Invensys, has voluntarily moved to a one-month contract, as a sign of his commitment to see through the job of rescuing the company. The sad plight of Invensys, due to a badly judged and badly timed series of acquisitions by his predecessor, predates Mr. Haythornthwaite.

It was an implied reward for failure that finally convinced GSK shareholders to vote against the $33 million golden farewell for the CEO, Mr. Garnier, should he be dismissed before the end of his contract. U.K. governance experts and politicians are demanding greater due diligence in writing potential severance arrangements into contracts, reducing the notice period and requiring payoffs to be staggered in case the CEO finds another job. In the United States, CEOs receive an average of $16.5 million severance, and companies that have just paid out to get rid of a failing CEO will then pay an average of $15 million in "hello" money to the successor, would be saviors (Useem, 2003).

The final question is *who* decides on whose behalf. In fact, many stakeholders inside and outside the focal firm have an interest in what eventually turns out to be the outcome remuneration package for any given CEO.

STAKEHOLDERS AND CEO COMPENSATION

The stakeholders with an interest in and/or influence on CEO compensation are portrayed in Figure 17.1.

These stakeholders may call on the various parameters previously outlined to justify their often divergent positions on the CEO's remuneration package—for example, the free market for CEOs, distributive justice, and pay for performance. Many stakeholders are themselves subject to conflicts of interest. The agency approach is the prevailing paradigm in corporate governance literature, whereby the interests of the shareholder-principals and manager-agents are not perfectly convergent, so the pursuit of self-interest by either side could damage the other. As seen in Figure 17.1, the board of directors is perceived as a key element in corporate governance arrangements to solve agency issues, among them compensation arrangements. This optimal contracting approach may minimize but not entirely eliminate agency costs to shareholders because some degree of "managerial hegemony" remains (Bebchuk, Fried, & Walker, 2003). Managers have accumulated so much more power than the board that they can suit themselves in pursuing personal rather than organizational goals. This includes bestowing upon themselves the best possible compensation arrangements (Stiles & Taylor, 2001). The stakeholder analysis that follows will show how the agency approach, with its emphasis on power differentials, is insufficient to arrive at a fair determination of CEO pay.

The CEO—Power and Person

At the center of the compensation jigsaw is the CEO. The CEO's compensation is determined by the interplay between systemic factors, characteristics of the CEO himself/herself, and relative power between the CEO and the board. The U.S. CEO is uniquely placed to be more powerful than his/her European counterpart. The joint role of CEO/chairman that typically prevails in the United States, and a unitary board composed primarily of outside directors, means, in effect, that the CEO enjoys power of appointment over a majority of the board members, precisely the ones who sit on remuneration committees. In the European model, the CEO/chairman roles are usually split, and the chairman's participation in choosing nonexecutive directors somewhat curtails CEO power over outside directors. Moreover, since many boards include more

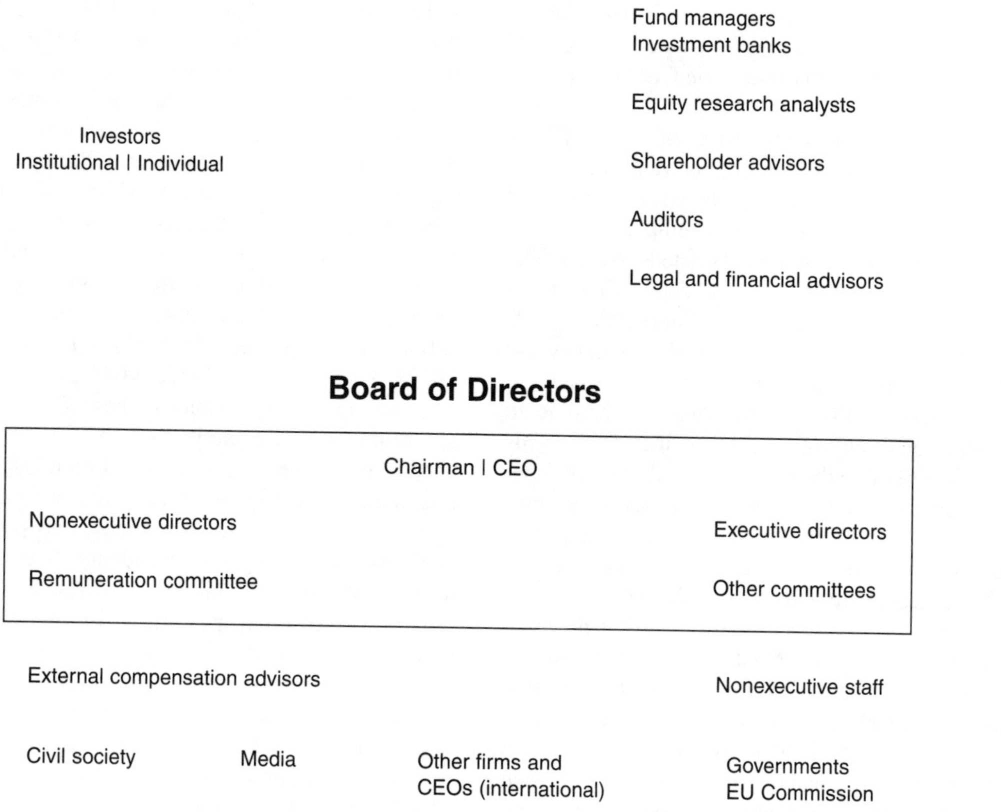

Fund managers
Investment banks

Equity research analysts

Investors
Institutional I Individual

Shareholder advisors

Auditors

Legal and financial advisors

Board of Directors

Chairman I CEO

Nonexecutive directors   Executive directors

Remuneration committee   Other committees

External compensation advisors   Nonexecutive staff

Civil society   Media   Other firms and   Governments
                                      CEOs (international)   EU Commission

Figure 17.1   CEO compensation—stakeholders

executive directors, there is less information asymmetry than in the United States, where the CEO possesses more company details than a wholly outsider board. Some European jurisdictions have a two-tier board system where a supervisory board, consisting entirely of nonexecutive directors, with an outsider chairman, decides CEO pay. The CEO has much less control over the appointment of supervisory board members than that enjoyed by CEOs of unitary boards, and especially U.S. CEOs, over nonexecutive selection (Monks, 2002/03).

The U.S. CEO as chairman has greater control than a CEO who must work together with a chairman. After influencing the composition of the board, the U.S. CEO sets the agenda and controls the meetings, information, and committee appointments and terms, including the remuneration committee (Main, O'Reilly, & Wade, 1995). Hence, in the United States, the CEO is in a very powerful position indeed. This may be the origin of the "star" CEO, since so much apparently rests in the hands of the CEO, who seems to have greater discretion and influence on the fate of a company than his/her European counterpart. Indeed, in a U.S. study, greater CEO discretion, based on strategic contingencies such as demand instability and more investment opportunities, was associated with higher CEO pay. Moreover, firm performance benefited from a closer alignment of CEO discretion and pay (Finkelstein & Boyd, 1998). These results imply that if the impact of CEO behavior on performance were understandable and assessable, it might be possible to tie CEO compensation to performance.

The more inflated role of U.S. CEOs may also epitomize the greater value placed on individual effort and achievement in the United States, compared with a group emphasis, even in other capitalist countries (Hofstede, 1993). The past two decades have seen a "celebritization" of CEOs in the United States (Lucier, Schuyt, & Spiegel, 2003), due partly to the tendency for business media, analysts, and shareholders to attribute causality to individuals rather than to institutional, cultural, or economic forces. This tends to devalue the relative contribution of other executives, not to mention nonexecutive staff, without whose efforts many CEOs arguably could not have achieved their putative results ("The Leadership Challenge," 2003).

Once the business establishment has made up its mind that an individual is a star, extraordinary qualities are ascribed to that person. Even failure might not sink that person's career, because their attributed superior talent is weighted over and above the countervailing evidence of their dismal performance. Such an attitude prevailed in Enron, cheered on by the likes of management gurus because it purportedly signified entrepreneurial flair (Gladwell, 2002). The trappings of power can also act as potent symbols to reinforce an individual's aura. Khurana (2002) points out the destabilizing effect of charismatic leaders. First, in order to make an impression, the charismatic leader will engage in unnecessary discontinuities for their own sake, breaking with the past and creating disorientation that may lead to failure. Jacques Nasser at Ford is given as an example. When the person leaves, there may be a vacuum of authority and direction in the organization—the post-Welch effect in GE. Naturally, such superhumans, regarded as so uniquely irreplaceable, must be awarded superhuman compensation.

The real damage of superstar CEOs becomes most evident when they begin to believe in their own mythology or when they impose that belief on those around them to bolster their self-esteem. The charismatic CEO can easily descend into the destructively narcissistic one (Lubit, 2002). The hallmarks of destructively narcissistic managers are grandiosity, a preoccupation with power, a sense of entitlement to anything they want, alongside a willingness to exploit others to get it, and a lack of concern for other people. Such characteristics can easily result in an ethical deficit not only in the individual but also in the practices that become accepted by acquiescent external associates and internal subordinates (Conger, 1990; Howell & Avolio, 1992). This includes outside advisors, auditors, and members of governance bodies such as audit and remuneration committees.

While Europe is not entirely immune to the charisma phenomenon, many business people prefer to keep a lower, more anonymous profile. With the odd exception, the identities of most leaders of Europe's biggest business empires remain unknown except to those in their immediate business circles or within their own countries. Interestingly, when one French CEO, Jean-Marie Messier, ventured into U.S.-style grandiosity and self-emoluments, this proved to be highly unpopular with the French business establishment. It was not helped when Monsieur Messier wrote a book entitled *J6M*, which stood for "Jean-Marie Messier, *moi-meme, maitre de monde*"—"me, myself, master of the universe."

Khurana (2002) is concerned about the lack of skepticism that has allowed the superstar CEO to flourish, alongside the irrational exuberance of capital markets. Although somewhat contagious, it did not catch on to the same degree in Europe, where generally skepticism tended to temper fervor, other than in the telecommunications industry where exorbitant sums were paid for 3G licensees and to Christopher Gent, CEO of Vodafone, the U.K.-based global operator. In fact, the furor over a £10 million ($16 million) pay award to Mr. Gent proves how exceptional such cases are, compared with the United States, where the same payment in a similarly sized company would hardly have registered.

Excessive reliance on the CEO can rebound when things go wrong. Companies may be inclined to blame the CEO personally for structural company dysfunction and fire the incumbent, seeking an outside savior, often a high-profile individual with an expensive price tag. Outsiders initially perform better than insiders do, but worse over time, as underlying weaknesses of the company kick in. Early outsider success may be due to more latitude by the board to tolerate staff and other cost cuts, which an insider might be more hesitant to force through (Lucier, Schuyt, & Spiegel, 2003). There is evidence that agency issues become more problematic the longer a CEO is on the job (Becht, Bolton, & Roell, 2002; Shen, 2003). At earlier stages, the CEO's desire for implicit incentives that enhance his/her career development drive CEO performance on behalf of the firm, with less emphasis on explicit material rewards that increasingly motivate CEOs over their tenure.

Executive Directors

As previously mentioned, the greater presence of other executive directors on European boards somewhat curtails CEO power compared with U.S. boardrooms. The larger power distance between the CEO and executive team in the United States compared with Europe is echoed in greater compensation differentials (Cheffins, 2003) and acceptance of the "tournament model" (jousting for the top job) rather than the wage compression model. The latter model suggests that greater equality in compensation among executive team members should ensure cooperation and collaboration and reduce competitive and damaging "office politics" (Main, O'Reilly, & Wade, 1993). The tournament model is more associated with performance as measured by stock market returns and return on assets (ROA) than the wage compression model, while the wage compression model is related to lower mean levels of executive pay.

Nonexecutive Directors and the Compensation/Remuneration Committee

Theoretically and legally, the board of directors represents the interests of the owners of the firm and, acting at arm's length, objectively sets executive compensation. Best practice, enshrined in regulations and guidelines on both sides of the Atlantic, now regards only nonexecutive directors as qualified to make an independent judgment on executive pay. It is also recommended that listed companies have a remuneration committee of the board, composed entirely of nonexecutive directors to ensure independence and objectivity.

So, does an entirely nonexecutive remuneration committee guarantee a fair outcome, devoid of self-dealing by the CEO? It may or may not, but certain conditions make it less likely. In a sample of 94 FTSE 100 companies, it was found that top management pay and corporate performance were more aligned when the board and the remuneration committee were dominated by outsiders (Conyon & Peck, 1998). However, being an outsider does not necessarily ensure independence. For example, the outsider may have a link to the local firm through a business relationship that compromises independence and makes the individual beholden to the CEO for continued business. A survey conducted by Towers Perrin in 2001 found that outside directors in the United States were paid three-quarters in stock, much of it in the form of options, and only a quarter in cash, unlike in the U.K. and mainland Europe, where share options are rarely awarded to nonexecutive directors. Thus, in the United States, nonexecutive directors have incentives to massage the share price and to be lax in their monitoring of executives, as long as the executives deliver share price rises, irrespective of the means used to achieve them. Having formerly been an executive in the company may also compromise independence and arm's-length dealing. Even without such relationships, the nonexecutive's inclination to challenge excessive management remuneration may be limited by management's power to select and reappoint nonexecutive directors.

Social dynamics of in-group coziness and the expectation that nonexecutives should act in solidarity with the management team in a unified board system also militate against nonexecutives stepping out of the agreeable comfort zone. There is little to gain and much to lose by rocking the boat. The director might not be reappointed, which could cause reputational damage and the psychological feeling of exclusion from the in-group. The latter consideration is important, because in most countries directors are drawn from the business elite, so ejection from a board would have social overtones (Stiles & Taylor, 2001). It is precisely these social overtones that make it harder to disagree (Main, O'Reilly, & Wade, 1995). There are, nonetheless, individual differences. Some nonexecutives do possess the will, skill, and personal authority to overcome even a lack of structural power (Pettigrew & McNulty, 1998).

Statistics show that 25 percent of compensation committee members are CEOs of other boards, who would be inclined to approve higher compensation to justify, by implication, higher compensation for themselves. This is consistent with research that found similarity in compensation levels between nonexecutive directors on remuneration committees and the CEO of a focal company (O'Reilly, Main, & Crystal, 1988) and that boards with more CEOs among their nonexecutive directors award higher compensation to CEOs (Westphal & Zajac, 1997). Westphal and Zajac (1995) found that compensation increases were higher for relatively powerful incumbent CEOs during whose tenure directors who were demographically similar to the CEO had been appointed.

In both the United States and Europe, there is increasing pressure to make nonexecutive directors more independent and accountable. In the United States, this has been spurred by the obvious dereliction of duties by nonexecutives at scandal-ridden companies like Enron and WorldCom. In Europe, national governments and the European Commission are engaged in initiatives to tighten up corporate governance and strengthen the role of nonexecutive directors. Successive U.K. governments have published a series of reports that have been knitted together into a Combined Code. Although the Code is not legally binding, companies must "comply or explain." In similar fashion, the Bouton Report has been published and endorsed in France, again not written into law. In essence, these reports stress the key role that should be played by independent nonexecutive directors.

However, even where nonexecutive directors are inclined to behave in an independent manner, they may be prevented from doing their homework properly because of an information asymmetry problem. Deference to authority compounds the propensity by nonexecutive directors to yield control over decisions to the CEO, including those on executive compensation (Main, O'Reilly, & Wade, 1995). Current power dynamics may be influenced by past power transactions (Pettigrew & McNulty, 1998). Thus, it is easy to understand how a previous cycle of CEO dominance over the remuneration committee in setting compensation results in an ever-upward spiral as the habit of deference to the CEO becomes increasingly more entrenched.

External Compensation Advisors

To correct the imbalance, remuneration committees often seek advice on devising appropriate pay packages from independent compensation consultants. However, in many cases, the firm (i.e., the executives) has already hired particular remuneration consultants to advise the company, and the same consultants are still retained to advise on CEO pay. Hence, the consultants' independence may be compromised (Bebchuk, Fried, & Walker, 2002). As already mentioned, the use of consultants also has the effect of ratcheting up compensation packages. Research shows that consultants are important transmitters of CEO compensation practices across companies (Bender, 2003).

Investors

Investors stand to lose much from inappropriate CEO remuneration, so they should be intolerant of overpaid executives who do not deliver "shareholder value." One might also have thought that excessively paid CEOs risk offending investors who could withdraw their support for the company, thereby jeopardizing the CEO's job. So why does the market not impose discipline on underperforming, overpaid CEOs?

Explanations are found in asymmetries of power and information and in conflicts of interest.

Small, individual shareholders are usually not privy to the more extensive information available to institutional shareholders, who are briefed regularly by most companies. In fact, leading European fund managers are organizing an education campaign to fill a perceived gap in small investor expertise to help them make more informed decisions (Targett, 2003). These shareholders are too fragmented to have the clout to be heeded by the company. They cannot organize themselves as any forceful opposition, even if they disagree with company policy. Vociferous protests mounted at annual general meetings of both U.S. and European companies, while unpleasant for the directors at the time, are usually ineffectual. The most that small shareholders can do is sell their shares to protect themselves against damage to their assets, but this has no impact on the company.

Fund Managers

Institutional shareholders are in a more powerful position to be heard by the company. So why have they traditionally been so reticent about using their power? One of the answers is that institutional investors such as pension funds, headed by trustees, are not influential parties to CEO pay determination, since they delegate their investment decisions to fund managers. While fund managers owe their reputations over the long-term to how well their funds perform on behalf of their investor clients, they are subject to certain short-term pressures. Many asset management departments are subsidiaries of financial institutions that may themselves not be models of corporate governance and rectitude in CEO pay. Thus, fund managers who protest too loudly about the compensation packages of the companies in their portfolio might be minded to practice the standards they preach in their own companies. In fact, senior fund managers themselves often benefit from overly generous remuneration levels.

Another consideration that might preoccupy fund managers is the corporate business that other divisions of the parent company do with various companies, often in the gift of these companies' CEOs. Even in their own divisions, activism on the part of fund managers might be muted, simply by not wishing to offend companies whose pension fund business they seek or wish to retain. Fund managers defend their independence by stressing the presence of Chinese walls in their firms. However, many observers are concerned that senior fund managers have become part of the executive director class, a proposition in keeping with the class hegemony capitalism model (Riley, 2003; Stiles & Taylor, 2001). The concerns about conflicts of interest are consistent with findings that CEO compensation is lower when there is a powerful institutional blockholder of shares—unless that blockholder is dependent on the firm invested in (Barkema & Gomez-Mejia, 1998). Generally, institutional fund managers who are not subject to conflicts of interest—that is, those who are "pressure-resistant"—are more likely to engage in activism (Daily, Dalton, & Cannella, 2003). Block shareholders, not unusual in many continental European countries, have a vested interest in the company and direct access and influence on it, thereby curtailing excesses that may damage the firm's sustainability. The problem is a potential lack of liquidity and the fact that other shareholders may be ignored ("Corporate Governance," 2002/03).

Due diligence on the corporate governance of companies and remuneration of their CEOs is time consuming and costly, while it is in the interests of fund managers to expend as few resources as possible. An increasing reliance on passive indexing strategies by fund managers suggests that monitoring of firms may not be necessary if, on average, the portfolio will yield returns comparable to the market as a whole. Even if an investor is dissatisfied with the conduct of a firm in his/her portfolio, activism is a far more costly option than exit, and nine times as costly as indexing (Daily, Dalton, & Cannella, 2003). In 2003, fund managers were under pressure, with steep declines in assets under management and poor performance. Boston Consulting Group, analyzing 40 fund management businesses controlling $8000 billion of assets, estimates that one-fifth of fund managers worldwide were loss-making in 2002. A further 20 percent struggled to remain profitable (Gimbel & Targett, 2003). The "free rider" issue discourages activism, since the discipline imposed on a company by the diligence of a fund manager benefits all shareholders, not just the active fund manager who has borne the costs. The forced disclosure of voting records by fund managers could help ensure their independence and that they act on behalf of their investor clients and do not just go along with company management. The United States is further along the road to voting disclosure than Europe, since the SEC is compelling mutual fund managers to reveal their voting records.

The source of analyst research on companies may also affect fund managers. The conflicts of interest of research analysts who worked for the subsidiaries of firms patronized by the very companies they analyzed were notorious. In the U.K., the authorities are urging more arm's-length, transparent transactions between fund managers and brokers and an end to "soft commissions" whereby fund managers direct broking business to dealers who supply them with a bundle of services or goods, including research. Separating broking from research should ensure competition, efficiency, and more transparency in the costs of both, and a choice for investors as to whether they want the research they are paying for, since the costs are passed on to them regardless. It is questionable to what extent fund managers, even those uncompromised by conflicts of interest, heed research indicators anyway, judging from the herd tendency among fund managers during the dot.com bubble. Indeed, those that resisted mindless forays into dot.com investments were often punished with dismissal. The effect was that fund managers got carried away during the boom, turning a blind eye to extravagant remuneration. Even when the bubble bursts, executive compensation is not usually adjusted downward (Haskins, 2003).

It has been suggested that the conflicts of interest that attach to fund managers would be avoided if fund management firms are debarred from obtaining direct listings or being subsidiaries of listed companies and if fund management became professionalized. This would foster independence and an inclination to act in the long-term interests of investor clients. In contrast, financial institution parents of asset managers tend to operate under short-term marketing pressures (Riley, 2003).

Shareholder Activists

To counter the tendencies toward compliance by fund managers to go along with company management, there is growing institutional shareholder activism on both sides of the Atlantic. For example, the International Corporate Governance Network (ICGN), which includes the California Public Employees Retirement System (CALPERS) and ABP, Europe's largest pension fund, has devised a list of shareholder stewardship demands on fund managers. These include allocating resources to corporate governance, voting disclosure, submitting nominees for election to company boards, and listing conflicts of interest. Where conflicts of interest exist, the power to undertake ownership/corporate governance responsibilities should be separated from money management responsibilities.

Governments have encouraged shareholder activism. In the U.K., this stems from the government-commissioned Myners Report, which urges shareholders to exercise their voting rights or face legislation forcing them to do so. So far, the spotlight has been on exorbitant pay packages and risk-free arrangements that protect executives. However, presumably pressure could be brought against the election or reelection of acquiescent nonexecutives and remuneration committee members. After overthrowing the compensation package and golden parachute provision for the CEO at GlaxoSmithKline, further shareholder demands forced the early resignation of the chairman of the remuneration committee and other nonexecutives.

Falling share prices suffered by investors while executives remain immune, some even enjoying rises in compensation at the same companies that have seen dramatic performance declines, have finally awoken affected shareholders out of their slumber. Forced disclosure of executive remuneration in annual reports in the United States and the U.K. has also had the effect of activating shareholders. Votes against the remuneration packages of CEOs are not legally binding. In the United States, binding resolutions require a two-thirds majority of shareholder votes, almost impossible to achieve. In the U.K. and European countries, votes are only advisory. However, it would be injudicious for companies to ignore the disapproval of a majority of shareholders or even a substantial minority.

Shareholder Advisors

Another increasingly important stakeholder in the governance/CEO compensation arena is the investor advisory service. These agencies have emerged on both sides of the Atlantic. They advise shareholders on how to vote on given issues, including executive pay. One of the largest U.S. agencies, Institutional Shareholder Services (ISS), with a database of 22,000 companies worldwide and an electronic voting service, has joined forces with the large U.K. National Association of Pension Funds (NAPF). However, there are concerns that ISS takes an overly quantitative "box-ticking" superficial approach to evaluating companies. Indeed, ISS does have a formula for calculating whether an executive pay package delivers value in monetary terms. However, the formula fails to capture relevant qualitative and strategic considerations other than financial ones. Many of these are not available from quantitative data and require an understanding of the company's internal workings and dynamics (Plender, 2003). In contrast, European shareholder advisors, such as NAPF and Belgium-based Deminor, take a more contextual, multifaceted, holistic view (http://www.issproxy.com; http://www.deminorrating.com).

Corporate executives are not very keen on the perceived interference of these shareholder advisory services. Undoubtedly, they are helpful in raising the rigor of corporate governance, nonexecutive director independence, and monitoring of executive pay. However, once again, the conflict of interest issue arises, as many of these agencies engage in monitoring of companies to whom they simultaneously offer corporate governance advisory services. Like fund managers, they plead the presence of Chinese walls. Another concern is the propensity of fund managers to derogate their duties and their own vigilance by passively outsourcing their company research and voting intentions to the likes of ISS.

External Advisors, Suppliers, Auditors

The potential conflicts of interest of various suppliers and professional advisors to a firm may have the effect of enhancing the positioning, prestige, and perceived performance of the CEO, making him or her appear more deserving of an inflated compensation package. An example is the relationship between McKinsey and Enron. McKinsey conducted 20 separate consulting assignments in Enron, topping $10 million annually in billings. A McKinsey director regularly attended Enron board meetings, where the CEO himself was a former McKinsey director. McKinsey publicly hyped the entrepreneurial Enron culture, celebrating it in a book entitled *Creative Disruption* (Gladwell, 2002).

Enron also provides evidence of how auditors may be suborned into concealing financial deficiencies through aggressive accounting. In the case of Enron and Andersen, the lucrative consulting work that Andersen carried out is given as an important reason for its willingness to indulge in creative accounting. However, Enron's audit work alone was profitable enough for Andersen to compromise its audit standards simply to retain its audit business at any ethical cost. An acknowledged difference between the United States and Europe is the rules-based system of the United States, which emphasizes compliance (encouraging devices like the off-balance sheet entities created by Andersen for Enron to hide its true financial position), versus the European "principles"-based system. The latter concentrates on a "true and fair view" of the financial position of the company. Thus, the auditor is seen to be negligent if s/he has not exposed the true financial state of a company, as blatant dishonesty cannot be rationalized behind a legalistic smokescreen. Auditors differ from other advisors because they are meant to protect the investing public by providing independent verification of financial results, whereas other advisors provide services to the company itself. Nevertheless, even company advisors are ethically liable if they collude with senior officers to the long-term detriment of other stakeholders.

Nonexecutive Staff

Much of the outrage against excessive CEO pay is perceived gross unfairness vis-à-vis employees. Now, in the economic downturn, nonexecutive staff are expected to take the brunt of the pain. Many a company has laid off employees with minimum entitlements, while the CEO, who may have engineered the company's downfall through grandiose, ill-conceived costly projects and acquisitions, even if he loses his job, walks away with a golden handshake and full retirement benefits. Bear in mind that CEOs count their total compensation, including all incentives, as the basis for their pensions ("Wallowing in Wages," 2002). Shortfalls in pension funds are dealt with by curtailing pension benefits to staff or making them work longer to earn pension rights in many companies. On the other hand, the pensions and benefits of CEOs remain intact and are even "topped up" at the expense of shareholders. This egregious type of behavior tends to be most blatant in the United States. A gross example is Delta Airlines, whose remuneration committee, consisting of one current and three retired CEOs of major companies, awarded the airline's CEO a pay raise of 120 percent and topped up his pension fund by 22 years of service, even as shareholder returns declined to minus 58 percent. In the meantime, the company altered the pension terms of its ordinary

employees, moving from a defined benefit to a defined contribution plan, which transfers the risk from company to employees. American Airlines attempted something similar, when the CEO failed to inform the unions about large bonuses and pension protection for top executives while negotiating concessions from the staff to avoid bankruptcy. In this case, when the truth emerged, the CEO resigned—presumably with full pension rights (Useem, 2003).

Ironically, unlike shareholders, who can simply sell their shares, employees cannot disengage so easily by just exiting from their jobs when they are dissatisfied. When employees own shares in the company, their lock-in is even greater. It would probably be self-destructive to publicize their dissatisfaction, thereby deflating the stock. It would also be against their own self-interests to sell off their shares, triggering a lack of confidence in the company and a further drop in the share price, perhaps jeopardizing their jobs.

Civil Society, Governments, Media

Apparent disregard for employees by companies, while looking after those at the top with ultra-generous pay and perks, has created an affront to "ordinary people." It is fueled by the media who report on the lavish lifestyles of existing or departed CEOs, even as their companies implode, people lose their jobs, and pensioners see their savings evaporate. The perks, such as chauffeured limousines and corporate jets, fuel even more resentment, because they isolate their occupants from "the ordinary world of subways and check-in queues" (Kay, 2003, p. 21). Also, by virtue of their power position, CEOs may be recipients of special "favors," such as the awarding of IPOs by investment bank clients at the height of the dot.com era. This allowed CEOs such as Bernie Ebbers of WorldCom to reap millions of dollars in quick profits (Chaffin, 2002). It justifies the animal imagery of "fat cats" gorging on cream in Europe and of pigs at troughs in the United States.

Governments have joined the protest bandwagon, commenting on the excesses and sometimes passing legislation, such as the Sarbanes-Oxley Act. Individual European countries and the EU Commission offer only guidelines, with the implicit threat that if they are not followed, stricter regulation will ensue. Compulsory disclosure of CEO salaries is one regulatory tool that has been applied in the United States and in several European countries, but in others such as Germany, disclosure is not mandatory. Another form of transparency is the trend toward forcing full disclosure by fund managers of their voting intentions and records. The EU Commission is encouraging member states to publish and enforce their own guidelines regarding disclosure of all board processes and decisions and to make arrangements to allow greater shareholder participation through electronic meetings and proxy voting.

Thus, multiple stakeholders are involved in the determination of CEO compensation. These exist at different interrelated levels of organization:

- The macro level, which includes government, the media, and the general public
- The business system level and its institutions, which includes investors, advisors, and industry groups
- The business corporation and its corporate governance arrangements
- Individuals as members of the different stakeholder groups

As seen in the delineation of various stakeholder stances, CEO compensation size comes about through a dynamic interplay of power differentials, social processes and individual values, motives and personality traits.

CONCLUSIONS

Comparisons between the United States and Europe reveal contrasting fundamental features that account for higher CEO compensation and disparities in compensation between the CEO and others in the United States (see Table 17.1).

The very notion of the corporation is differently conceived in the United States and Europe (Kay, 1997). In continental Europe, the corporation is a social institution, encompassing the interests of a wide range of stakeholder groups. In the American model, the corporation is a private body, defined by economic contracts and transactions.

Structural recommendations and legislative initiatives to curb corporate greed and wrongdoing have accelerated in both the United States and Europe in the wake of scandals. Many involve issues of independence and conflicts of interest, for example, of nonexecutive directors, fund managers, and advisors. These are eminently sensible. However, the fundamental rationale underlying them is that people will behave badly unless they are prevented from doing so. Only if it costs more to behave badly than to behave well will they behave well. This is the basic futility of agency theory. Control and monitoring measures always fail to catch up with people who find ways of circumventing them. For example, remuneration committees set up to curb excess have had the opposite effect of actually increasing it, with the added abuse of using the remuneration committee device for self-serving justification (Kay, 1997).

Corporate governance situations that are less dependent on external mechanisms and systemic controls are closer to the "stewardship model" (Davis, Schoorman, & Donaldson, 1997; Stiles & Taylor, 2001). This model provides an alternative to the extreme one of "economic man" underlying agency theory. It accepts that managers and board directors work collaboratively, motivated by the intrinsic satisfaction of doing a good job, to be good stewards of the corporation's assets. John Kay (1997) takes the conception further in his description of the "trusteeship model," where the directors are the trustees of the tangible and intangible assets of the corporation, rather than merely shareholders' agents. The objectives of the managers relate to the broader purposes of the corporation, not simply the financial interests of shareholders. The corporation is treated as a continuous evolutionary entity, with its own

Table 17.1   U.S. and European Comparisons

	U.S.	*Europe*
Average CEO compensation	Approx. $2 million	>$400,000, <$700,000
Sourcing CEOs	Local	Local except U.K.
CEO compensation disparities (average worker)	200–475 times	13–48 times
CEO compensation disparities (other executives)	4-plus:1	2-plus:1
Pay-for-performance emphasis	High; especially stock options	Growing but not as high as U.S.
Severance notice period	3 years	1–2 years, declining
Board leadership	Joint chairman/ CEO	Separate chairman/ CEO
Board composition	Mainly outsiders	Mixed, greater proportion of executive directors than U.S., or two-tier system
Company leadership	CEO discretion and power	Less CEO discretion and power than U.S.
Causality	Individual orientation and charisma	Group and stakeholder orientation
Outside director remuneration	Three-quarters stock option	Director fee
Outside director selection	Mainly by CEO	Chairman and CEO
Accounting	Rules-based	Principles-based
Corporate governance government intervention	Legislation	Recommended guidelines
Shareholder capitalism	Dispersed	Dispersed and/or block shareholders

unique history, skills, and sets of activities—in short, its own personality. This differs from the concept of the firm as a set of financial assets only.

In effect, these beliefs and practices characterize many successful companies in both the United States and Europe. The hallmarks of enduringly successful companies (Collins & Porras, 1994; De Geus, 1997) are the same as those run on stewardship lines. A central feature of corporate longevity is a sense of purpose that concentrates on ensuring the sustainability of the firm's performance and integrity, with due regard to its legitimate stakeholders. Board processes involving all directors in constructive dialogue and teamwork in decision making should facilitate this (Finkelstein & Mooney, 2003).

The stewardship model context attempts to ensure fair play for all stakeholders. This includes the remuneration of the CEO and all others employed by the firm, as well as fair returns to investors. The central tenets of equity and fairness should create an ethos where longer-term firm interests will transcend immediate personal and self-serving ones. This is consistent with an approach that regards the firm as a continuing social entity whose well-being must be protected. The steward CEO obtains an intrinsic sense of achievement from the satisfaction of leading a viable firm with a meaningful purpose, along with fair extrinsic rewards for doing well by the company.

By definition, the stewardship model depends on honorable purposes and a sense of values among those who lead and direct organizations. Garratt (2003) names the human values necessary if corporations are to be grounded in accountability, probity, and transparency. Interestingly, he notes that these necessary human values—humility, honesty, trust, frugality, quality, accountability—are taken from America's founding fathers. Such fundamental characteristics should be applicable across all systems in all regions and should be held by all stakeholders, especially the board of directors and the CEO. The presence of these values should create more profound and lasting benefits than repeated tinkering with external control devices.

REFERENCES

Barkema, H. G., & Gomez-Mejia, L. R. (1998). Managerial compensation and firm performance: A general research framework. *Academy of Management Journal, 41*(2), 135–145.

Bebchuk, L., Fried, J. M., & Walker, D. I. (2002). Managerial power and rent extraction in the design of executive compensation. *University of Chicago Law Review, 69*, 751–846.

Becht, M., Bolton, P., & Roell, A. (2002). *Corporate governance and control.* European Corporate Governance Institute Finance Working Paper No. 02/2002.

Bender, R. (2003). How CEO compensation is determined in two FTSE 350 utilities. *Corporate Governance—An International Review, 11*(3), 206–217.

Buck, T., Bruce, A., & Main, B. G. M. (2004). Long-term incentive plans, executive pay and UK company performance. *Journal of Management Studies.*

Buffett, W. (1999). *Letter to shareholders.* Berkshire Hathaway Inc. Annual Report.

Buffett, W. (2002). *Letter to shareholders.* Berkshire Hathaway Inc. Annual Report.

Chaffin, J. (2002, September 18). Lawyers agog as banks spill IPO beans. *Financial Times.*

Cheffins, B. R. (2003). Will executive pay globalise along American lines? *Corporate Governance, 11*(1), 8–24.

Collins, J. C., & Porras, J. (1994). *Built to last: Successful habits of visionary companies.* London: Random House.

Conger, J. J. A. (1990). The dark side of leadership. *Organizational Dynamics, 19*(2), 44–55.

Connon, H. (2003, May 18). Suffering pension worries? This lot aren't. *The Observer.*

Conyon, M. J., & Peck, S. I. (1998). Board control, remuneration committees and top management compensation. *Academy of Management Journal, 41*(2), 146–157.

Corporate governance . . . Lisbon stirs the debate. (2002/03). *European Business Forum,* Winter (12), 36–37.

Croft, J. (2003, May 30). HSBC's letter defends top pay package. *Financial Times.*

Daily, C. M., Dalton, D. R., & Cannella, A. A. (2003). Corporate governance: Decades of dialogue and data. *Academy of Management Review, 28*(3), 371–382.

Dalton, D. R., Daily, C. M., Certo, S. T., & Roengpitya, R. (2003). Meta-analyses of financial performance and equity: Fusion or confusion? *Academy of Management Journal, 46*(1), 13–27.

Davis, J. H., Schoorman, F. D., & Donaldson, L. (1997). Toward a stewardship theory of the firm. *Academy of Management Review, 22,* 20–47.

De Geus, A. (1997). *The living company.* London: Nicholas Brealey.

Finkelstein, S. & Boyd, B. K. (1998). How much does the CEO matter? The role of manageria discretion in the setting of CEO compensation. *Academy of Management Journal, 41*(2), 179–199.

Finkelstein, S., & Mooney, A. (2003). Not the usual suspects: How to use board process to make boards better. *Academy of Management Executive, 17*(2), 101–113.

Fuller, J. (2003, May 31/June 1). As the boss says: no one is indispensable. *Financial Times* (Lombard column).

Garratt, B. (2003). *Thin on top: Why corporate governance matters and how to measure and improve board performance.* London & Yarmouth, Maine: Nicholas Brealey Publishing.

Gimbel, F. (2003, July 17). Crusader sets new 'fat-cat' standard. *FTfm.*

Gimbel, F., & Targett, S. (2003, June 16). Fund managers revolt at FSA. *FTfm.*

Gladwell, M. (2002, July 22). The talent myth. *The New Yorker.*

Haskins, C. (2003, May 21). Investors need help to tackle corporate greed. *Financial Times.*

Hofstede, G. (1993). Cultural constraints in management theories. *Academy of Management Executive, 7*(1), 81–94.

Howell, J. M., & Avolio, B. J. (1992). The ethics of charismatic leadership: Submission or liberation. *Academy of Management Executive, 6*(2), 43–54.

Jost, J. T., & Major, B. (2001). *The psychology of legitimacy: Emerging perspectives on ideology, justice and intergroup relations.* Cambridge, UK: Cambridge University Press.

Kakabadse, A., & Kakabadse, N. (2001). *The geopolitics of governance.* Basingstoke, U.K., & New York: Palgrave.

Kay, J. (1997). The stakeholder corporation. In G. Kelly, D. Kelly, & A Gamble (Eds.), *Stakeholder capitalism* (chap. 12, pp. 125–141). Basingstoke, U.K.: Macmillan Press Ltd.

Kay, J. (2003, May 22). Big egos inflate executive pay, not markets. *Financial Times.*

Khurana, R. (2002, September). The curse of the superstar CEO. *Harvard Business Review,* 60–66.

The leadership challenge. (2003). *strategy+business,* Summer.

Lubit, R. (2002). The long-term organizational impact of destructively narcissistic managers. *Academy of Management Executive, 16*(1), 127–138.

Lucier, C., Schuyt, R., & Spiegel, E. (2003). CEO succession 2002: Deliver or depart. *strategy+ business,* Summer.

Main, B. G. M., O'Reilly, C. A., & Wade, J. (1993). Top executive pay: Tournament or teamwork? *Journal of Labor Economics, 11*(4), 606–628.

Main, B. G. M., O'Reilly, C. A., & Wade, J. (1995). The CEO, the board of directors and executive compensation: Economic and psychological perspectives. *Industrial and Corporate Change, 4*(2), 293–332.

Martin, R. L. (2003, January). Taking stock. *Harvard Business Review,* 19.

McGuire, J., & Matta, E. (2003). *Academy of Management Journal, 46*(3), 255–265.

Monks, R. (2002/03). Equity culture at risk. *European Business Forum,* Winter (12), 32–35.

Morse, G. (2003, January). Why we misread motives. *Harvard Business Review,* 18.

Nicol-Maveyraud, J. (2003). Mind over money. *The Psychologist, 16*(5), 240–242.

O'Reilly, C. A., Main, B. G. M., & Crystal, G. S. (1988.) CEO compensation as tournament and social comparison. *Administrative Science Quarterly, 33,* 257–274.

Pettigrew, A., & McNulty, T. (1998). Sources and uses of power in the boardroom. *European Journal of Work and Organizational Psychology, 7*(2), 197–214.

Plender, J. (2002, May 15). A flawed reward. *Financial Times.*

Plender, J. (2003, May 19). It may not be SARS but it's very contagious. *Financial Times.*

Revell, J. (2003, April 28). The latest way to hide millions. *Fortune* (European edition), *147*(8), 30–32.

Rigby, R. (2003, June 17). In search of the thin cats. *Financial Times.*

Riley, B. (2003, May 26). The last word: taking the private route. *FTfm.*

Shen, W. (2003). The dynamics of the CEO-board relationship: An evolutionary perspective. *Academy of Management Review, 28*(3), 466–476.

Stiles, P., & Taylor, B. (2001). *Boards at work.* Oxford: Oxford University Press.

Targett, S. (2003, August 11). Top funds to teach investors. *FTfm.*

Towers Perrin. (2003). Retrieved November 2003 from http://www.towers.com/towers/webcache/ towers/United_States/publications/Reports/2003 _04_Worldwide_Remuneration/WWTR_2003_ English.pdf

Useem, J. (2003, April 28). Have they no shame? *Fortune* (European edition), *147*(8), 23–29.

Wallowing in wages. (2002, April 6). *The Economist,* 57–58.

Westphal, J. D., & Zajac, E. J. (1995). Who shall govern? CEO-board power, demographic similarity and new director selection. *Administrative Science Quarterly, 40*, 60–83.

Westphal, J. D., & Zajac, E. J. (1997). Defections from the inner circle: Social exchange, reciprocity and the diffusion of board independence in US corporations. *Administrative Science Quarterly, 42*, 161–183.

Zajac, E. J., & Westphal, J. D. (1995). Accounting for the explanations of CEO compensation: Substance and symbolism. *Administrative Science Quarterly, 40*, 283–308.

18

RESPONSIBLE SHAREHOLDING AND INVESTOR ENGAGEMENT IN THE U.K.

JANE COLLIER

The last 50 years have witnessed increasing opportunities for those investing their money in equities to express their concerns about the ethical behavior of companies. The increase in the number of ethical retail funds in the U.K. and the spread of shareholder activism on the part of pension funds and charitable foundations in the United States, combined with the uncertainties of globalization, global warming, and environmental degradation, have together increased the significance of corporate social responsibility (CSR) as a factor in financial investment decisions. For instance, one of the major U.K. asset management companies has recently announced that they are selling part of their holding of BP shares because of concerns over safety issues in BP's Alaskan operations. BP's safety problems were widely publicized over a number of months, and the asset managers have been in continual dialogue with the company, but they believe that BP needs to ensure full compliance with Alaskan safety procedures and efficient resumption of oil supplies before they can fulfill the expectation of socially responsible investors.

The aforementioned developments form the backdrop to the subject matter of this chapter. In the U.K., regulatory changes over the past five years have generated an "evolutionary shift" in institutional investment, one that has sharpened the CSR focus of the financial sector. The result has been that socially responsible investment (SRI), as it is now called, is becoming not only one of the fastest growing areas of finance but also one of the major factors affecting the material well-being of people holding pension funds and other financial assets. In July 2000, a regulation under section 35 of the 1995 Pensions Act created a statutory obligation for all pension funds to have a Statement of Investment Principles.

This statement was to make explicit not only the types of investment held but also the balance between investments, risk, return, and realizations. Trustees are now required to indicate in the Statement of Principles

a. the extent to which social, environmental, or ethical principles are taken into account by trustees in the selection, retention, and realization of their investments;

b. the policy (if any) directing the rights (including voting rights) attached to investments.

As an example of how the second of these might work in practice, one major institutional investor, the Co-operative Insurance Society (CIS), has made a commitment to exercise its vote on every motion put to the general meetings of the companies in which shares are held and to publish its voting record on its Web site. It votes on average six times more frequently than other institutional investors and is mainly engaged at annual general meetings (AGMs) with evaluating proposed executive remuneration schemes in the light of CIS responsible shareholding benchmarks.[1]

The 2000 regulatory initiative was not designed to alter portfolio choice behavior. It required only disclosure on the part of pension funds, and there was no element of compulsion to justify investor choices. However, since no government would have required funds to act against the interests of beneficiaries, the legislation did contain the implication that there was no conflict between fiduciary duty and socially responsible investment decisions. This contravened the received view that SRI investment would necessarily bring lower returns and thus notionally breach fiduciary requirements, and it was this interpretative shift that brought about the "mainstreaming" of SRI in the U.K.[2]

How can the U.K. government's move towards regulation be explained, given that in principle pension funds were bound to adhere to the requirements of "fiduciary duty"? One answer was that there was a shift of legal opinion during the '90s on the interpretation of trust law which made it clear that so long as the interests of the beneficiaries were paramount, funds were perfectly entitled to have an ethical investment policy (Sparkes, 2002, p. 8).[3] Another was that the evolving geopolitics of an unregulated global market economy[4] and the potential consequences of this for corporate behavior strongly influenced government opinion. How were global companies—many of whom had worldwide sales greater than the GDPs of some first-world countries—to be encouraged to take CSR seriously? The only potential countervailing power was the influence of powerful stakeholders such as investors. No other stakeholder group could wield such potential influence. Still more pressure for change came from U.K. government fears that corporate governance failures and corporate excesses in terms of pay raises and golden handshakes had their roots in the indifference of major shareholders who acted like absentee landlords rather than like responsible stakeholders. Expectations that regulation might change all this were voiced by the Minister of State with responsibility for pensions, Stephen Timms. He "put the emphasis on 'engagement,' i.e., the belief that institutional shareholders should use their power as shareholders to press for change from the corporate sector—this could be by quiet dialogue, or more aggressively through shareholder activism or direct use of shareholder voting power" (Sparkes, 2002, p. 12).

This chapter focuses on stakeholder responsibility and the "engagement" by institutional investors in the U.K. context with companies whose shares they hold.[5] The importance of a company's relationship with its stakeholders is normally perceived by the company in terms of risk management and consequent favorable reputation effects, although of course the stakeholders may see its primary significance in terms of some kind of social benefit. "Stakeholder management" then becomes a matter of the company managing, perhaps even manipulating, the relationship and communication between itself and its stakeholders (Wheeler & Sillanpaa, 1997). In this view, the company is the dominant partner, and stakeholders are on the receiving end of the relationship. Institutional investor engagement reverses that balance. However, we find very little in the stakeholder literature dealing with the alternative perspective where the stakeholder is the one calling the shots (Frooman, 1999). When we consider that institutional investment accounts for almost 70 percent of equity investment in the U.K. market, that information flows between investor institutions are very nearly "perfect," and that institutional collaboration is frequent, swift, and effective, we get some sense of the potential power of this stakeholder sector.[6] The next section analyzes the development of socially responsible investment. I then look at the role of institutional investors as corporate stakeholders. I assess the nature and legitimacy of investor pressure on companies and attempt to clarify its rationale in governance terms. The following section sets investor engagement within the theoretical perspectives of stakeholder theory and agency theory, and the final section of the chapter looks at the dynamics of the process of "engagement" by which investors can influence CSR behavior in specific cases and considers the conditions of possibility for its success.

What Is Socially Responsible Investment?

The term *socially responsible investment* originated in the United States and, broadly speaking, has been used there to refer to "shareholder activism," that is, the filing of resolutions and shareholder voting behavior at AGMs. Whereas in 1998 more than 200 resolutions were filed at U.S. AGMs by shareholders concerned about the impact of corporate actions on the environment and on society, in the U.K. shareholder activism in this sense was virtually nonexistent. In the 10 years preceding 1998, just two shareholder motions were filed at U.K. AGMs (Taylor, 2000).

Until recently, responsible shareholding in the U.K. was covered by the term *ethical investment*. The original mode of ethical investment was for specialized retail funds to avoid or "screen out" companies producing products or undertaking

activities that did not accord with the ethical principles put forward by the fund managers. Screened funds are advantageous in that they provide a vehicle whereby people can invest their savings in line with their own beliefs and values. However, exclusion and avoidance can in theory lead to fund underperformance because whole sections of the market are excluded and thus portfolio balances cannot be optimized.[7] Screened funds are therefore not suitable in cases such as pension fund investment where client financial interest is paramount.[8] "Shareholder activism" for ethical retail funds consists in signaling approval or disapproval of corporate actions by voting behavior and by "exit" strategies (i.e., selling shares), but given that these funds represent a tiny proportion of the market share, trading is likely to have little impact on corporate decision making.

A broader approach is taken by funds that operate "positive screening," where companies are chosen from each sector for their record on social, environmental, and ethical issues ("best in class") based on the view that such best-practice companies will tend to outperform their peers because they run less operational risks and hence less reputation risk. Alternatively companies can use criteria derived from their own specific mandate or chosen policies.[9] In either case, funds operate on the premise of a link between corporate social responsibility (CSR) and shareholder value, and although evidence is conflicting, there are enough pointers to suggest that the link is positive (CIS, 2002a; Cook & Deakin, 1999b; DelGuercio & Hawkins, 1999; Sparkes, 2002). Funds request that companies provide information on their CSR status and encourage them to follow the guidelines on social reporting drawn up by the Association of British Insurers (2001a, 2001b), which specifies the disclosures that companies should be expected to make in its annual report on the assessment of risks and opportunities arising from CSR matters.

Although the term *socially responsible investment* has in one sense become an umbrella term for all modes of "ethical" investment management in the U.K., including screened retail funds, in another sense—and this is the sense in which the term is used in this chapter—it is taken to refer to situations where major investors (insurance companies and pension funds) seek to optimize returns on portfolios by investing across the market and then engaging with companies to encourage them to improve their CSR performance in the firm belief that good CSR management will improve shareholder returns. Engagement strategies allow funds to demonstrate to clients and others that they can be serious about the social and environmental impacts of the companies they invest in while at the same time maintaining their desired portfolio balances. Engagement is based in "voice" and "loyalty" rather than in "exit" responses, since selling shares is a last-ditch fund response. It should be emphasized that funds regard "engagement" as a process whereby they aim to achieve change over time in the CSR policy and performance of the company, hence improving shareholder value. "Engagement" thus targets both governance and CSR policy and practices. The methods of engagement used can range from informal contacts to shareholder resolutions at AGMs to the use of media pressure and public protest, but the preferred engagement strategy is that of quiet dialogue and rational discourse. Only when this fails are more activist strategies undertaken. It is in all cases essential to create and maintain relationships within the engagement process, since the building of trust is vital if there is to be ongoing dialogue. From the other perspective, companies need loyal shareholders if they are to feel secure. They know that SRI funds do not seek to achieve their objectives by selling shares (with consequent effects on share price and the possibility of a hostile takeover), but rather by putting pressure on companies to align their practices with CSR norms. Collaboration is thus in the best interests of both companies and the shareholders.

A number of recent studies have attempted to uncover the various realities behind the practice of stakeholder engagement in the U.K. (CIS, 2002b; Coles & Green, 2002; Dresner, 2002; Gribbin & Olsen, 2003; McLaren, 2002; Pearce &

Ganzi, 2002). Several findings are common to these studies. The first, and perhaps the most surprising, is that pension funds (the target of the 2000 regulatory initiative) are among the slowest to adopt engagement practices. Funds appear to be reluctant to monitor the activities of their managers in assessing corporate SEE profiles. Good practice is seen in only a handful of funds, and poor practice is the norm (Coles & Green, 2002). Managers appear to have wide discretion to choose the mode of engagement, and collaboration is common, particularly where knowledge on issues such as human rights, corruption, and climate change can be pooled. This was a predictable finding given that the existence and expertise of in-house SRI teams is patchy across the whole institutional sector. There also appears to be a general dislike of strategies threatening the buildup of trust that can emerge from face-to-face encounters with managers (Slinger, 1999). This may account for the reluctance to bring NGOs into collaborative engagement situations. Finally, there is evidence that norms and standards are gradually emerging, and that SRI is becoming "professionalized." There is now a Responsible Investor Network in the U.K., which serves as a focus for collaborative investor initiatives on both company-focused and issue-focused matters of common concern. It should be noted that these initiatives in no way contravene the legal constraints on investors acting in concert (Coles & Green, 2002, p. 11).

INSTITUTIONAL INVESTORS AS STAKEHOLDERS

A company's stakeholders are those who are affected favorably or adversely by the achievement of its objectives (Freeman, 1984). Stakeholders hold a "stake" in the company; they have something that is "at risk," something they can gain or lose as a result of the way in which corporate assets are used. In the latter part of the twentieth century it became fashionable (in the United States in particular) to regard shareholders as "owners" of those assets and to see managers and directors as "agents" who should put shareholders' interests and shareholder value at the top of the agenda.[10] In practice, shareholders are the owners only of their shares, that is, of financial instruments, and property rights are distributed widely among the participants in the corporate enterprise (i.e., among the stakeholders).[11] Property rights theory would maintain that efficiency is best attained by putting decision making and control rights in the hands of those whose responsibility it is to bear the risks associated with the use of those assets (Becker, 1979; Blair, 1998; Demsetz, 1967).

The risks borne by different stakeholders vary in kind. Some stakeholders have explicit contracts (employees, investors), some have implicit contracts (customers), and others stand in a noncontractual relationship with the company (Jensen & Meckling, 1976). For these latter stakeholders, the potential risk lies in the possibility that the company may externalize its own internal risks and thus create negative environmental or other impacts. For those in a contractual relationship with the company, the risk is that the company may fail to fulfill its contracts. For shareholders the situation is different. Shareholders are residual claimants to the firm's income; they take what is left over after other claims have been met, and the risks associated with being "last in line" are factored into their contract. By the same token they have appropriate incentives to encourage companies to retain a proportion of profits and allocate them to capital investment as opposed to paying high levels of dividend (Easterbrook & Fischel, 1991).

The problem with this picture is that it is incomplete. Stakeholder risk is generally much greater than is indicated in the contractual arrangements, and thus shareholders are rarely the only residual claimants. Suppliers have risks connected with "asset specificity," that is, the loss on investments they have had to make to cater to the specific needs of that company. Employees have had to acquire firm-specific skills that are nontransferable and for which they have not been able to extract proper rent from the company. Customers may lose their source of income-generating (perhaps even lifesaving) products or equipment, and so on. It is frequently the case that the rights and obligations associated with stakeholder risks are not recognized in governance structures and not adequately compensated. As Margaret Blair points out, participants in the corporate governance debates of the past few years have discredited the notion that corporations should be run in the interests of all the stakeholders, but if by *stakeholders* we mean those who have significant firm-specific investments, then the case for corporate governance reforms becomes more persuasive (Blair, 1998, p. 200).

I do not believe that reforms of this nature are likely, particularly if they imply some form of stakeholder governance. It might indeed be argued that stakeholders who have firm-specific investments, such as employees, already have contractual and other ways of protecting their interests. However, if we accept the principle of financial theory that the returns from an investment should be proportional to the risk involved, then good governance must ensure some way of establishing equitable distribution as between different risk bearers. It will be the mark of the well-managed company that all stakeholders are treated justly in this sense. Lydenberg and Paul argued back in 1997 that "when one stakeholder benefits disproportionately, receiving disproportionately more rewards, and others receive disproportionately fewer rewards over time, we say we observe a lack of corporate social responsibility, poor social performance and poor management. . . ." (quoted from an unpublished manuscript in Sparkes, 2002, p. 41).

How is equity of treatment to be achieved? Lydenberg and Paul advocate the solution that has been effectively adopted in the U.K. by the regulatory "push" towards SRI. "Socially responsible investors aim to create and support a business environment where managers are mindful of the risks their operations impose on society, to avoid incalculable risks, and in the case of calculable risks to be as equitable as possible in minimizing societal costs, along with compensating for their imposition" (Sparkes, 2002, p. 42).

In governance terms, then, engagement on the part of institutional stakeholders seeks to redress the imbalances of governance systems, which by their very nature prioritize shareholder risk and neglect the risks associated with other forms of stakeholding (Lydenberg, 2002). We may ask why the U.K. government allocated the responsibility of this to pension funds in the first instance. The answer may lie, conceptually at least, in the fact that these responsibilities no more than counterbalance the considerable rights and privileges accruing to pension fund operations— tax relief on contributions, employers' contributions not treated as taxable income, and immunity from capital gains tax (Sparkes, 2001, p. 203). But it is surely also the case that the adoption of SRI practices across the financial sector by the most powerful and cohesive stakeholder group is designed to give a clear signal to companies that long-term shareholder value is best created by responsibility in business.

Investor Engagement and Stakeholder Theory: A Dissonance

Stakeholder literature provides few guidelines by which the phenomenon of investor engagement can be theorized. In the first place, stakeholder theory is characterized either by a concern for the development of the theory itself (Donaldson & Preston, 1995; Jones, 1995) or by an almost exclusive focus on stakeholders from the perspective of the organization, either in terms of how they can contribute to strategic management or in terms of how they can be "managed" (Clarkson, 1995; Freeman, 1984; Jones & Wicks, 1999). Other perspectives take a more relational approach in that they focus on implied stakeholder contracts with the organization (Hill & Jones, 1992; Jones, 1995). Moving closer to a stakeholder focus on the engagement relationship, stakeholder attributes (Mitchell, Agle, & Wood, 1997), stakeholder interests (Wood,

1994), and typologies of stakeholder influence strategies (Frooman, 1999) may provide some basis for discussions of stakeholder engagement. Friedman and Miles (2002) focus on the question of stakeholder relationships. Drawing on social theory (Archer, 1995), they present a fourfold configuration of relationship possibilities based on two distinctions—first, whether relationships are compatible or incompatible in terms of sets of ideas and material interests, and second, whether relationships are necessary or contingent. It is clear that at the level of stakeholder relationships, investors stand in mutually binding relationships with the companies whose shares they hold that are both necessary and contingent. However, although these are significant aspects of the relationship, this typology tells us little about the process of engagement, and nothing about its likely outcome.

One reason why it is so difficult to regard investor engagement as a "typical" example of organization-stakeholder relations is that engagement is in the first instance designed to improve the welfare not of investors but of the wider group of stakeholders. This is not an example of stakeholder altruism but rather of "enlightened self-interest" on the part of investors, given that there is a clear present and future relationship between CSR performance and shareholder value. A further difficulty arises from the fact that institutional investors (in the U.K.) tend not to be sole actors in an engagement situation but rather to be part of a network of institutions holding that organization's shares. This can be characterized as a "social network" of which the organization is an integral part (Rowley, 2000). Funds exchange information and coordinate engagement activities; they share behavioral expectations and to some extent create shared norms. There is always the possibility of funds acting as "free-riders" (Blair, 1995), but their very presence in the situation adds weight, even if the work of engagement has been done by someone else. "Investor initiatives," where a number of funds (both U.K. and international) agree to target a specific issue with one or more companies, are becoming increasingly common.

The response of the organization to pressure from such a network will depend on a number of factors, not least the organization's "centrality" in terms of being able to control relationships within the network (Oliver, 1991; Pfeffer & Salancik, 1978). Strong organizations in dense networks will compromise, attempting to negotiate and pacify stakeholders. The better organized and informed investor institutions are, and the higher the importance of their loyalty to the firm, the more subordinate the role of the organization becomes in the negotiating process (Rowley, 1997).

Investor stakeholders, as we have seen, are atypical in terms of stakeholder theory, but the organizations with which they engage are equally atypical in terms of agency theory. The fact of the matter is that investor engagement will work only if accountability in companies is embedded in corporate practices and procedures in an open and transparent manner. In the "agency theory" view of organizations, processes of accountability are viewed only in terms of accounting evidence. In terms of their effects on people, they can be characterized as "individualizing" because they encourage managerial distrust and opportunism and create a climate where individuals are judged and disciplined by others in the light of evidence of performance and shareholder value (Roberts, 2000). In such an organization, stakeholder interests are unimportant. Relationships are competitive and instrumental; the self-seeking individual of agency theory is reinforced in self-understanding by the promise of executive pay structures that bear little relationship to performance and reward those who manage to get to the top of a competitive rather than collaborative hierarchy.

The alternative scenario, and one which may be more realistic in organizations subject to rapid change processes, is the situation where processes of accountability are designed and implemented not as a constraint on the powerful but as an organic feature of organizational life. The significance of power and hierarchy fades as "socializing" and dialogic relationships create interdependent managerial "selves" prepared to enter into transparent stakeholder relationships that are reciprocal and consensual rather than hierarchical and coercive. In this climate of openness, strong relationships of this sort engender mutual loyalty. Managers are prepared to listen and to collaborate because they do not feel threatened, and the effectiveness of shareholder "voice" helps to overcome managerial barriers to trust and possible lack of openness to SRI initiatives. Socialized processes of accountability are thus the basis on which SRI investors can build. They allow rejection of the pessimism inherent in the agency theory view of accountability and focus instead on creating and defining the relational processes that underpin responsible shareholding.

INVESTOR ENGAGEMENT AS "CRITICAL COOPERATION"

We now need to examine the way in which processes of accountability can work in a situation of engagement. The relationship between companies and their investors is continually changing in response to evolving expectations and changing circumstances. The interests of both parties (their needs, desires, concerns, and fears) may conflict or converge in any given set of circumstances (Covey & Brown, 2001); however, the interests of both parties are underpinned by basic realities that are relatively stable. For instance, SRI investors will actively seek to effect change in corporate CSR practice or policy, and here their interests may conflict with those of companies, but they also need to achieve share price stability or enhancement for their clients, and here their interests will converge with those of the companies. Companies, on the other hand, will be interested in their reputation and its possible effect on share price (so converging interests here), but also in cost-effective management, which may mean in practice the creation and non-internalization of externalities (so conflicting interests here) (see Table 18.1).

Table 18.1   Converging Interests

Converging Interests

		Low	High
Conflicting Interests	High	Conflict	Critical cooperation
	Low	Nonengagement	Cooperation

SOURCE: Adapted from Covey & Brown, 2001.

The most common investor engagement scenario is therefore one of "mixed interests," where both conflicting and converging interests are high. The pattern of interaction is thus one of "critical cooperation" where mixed interests are dealt with by means of a mix of cooperative and confrontational behavior (Covey, 1996; Covey & Brown, 2001; Savage, 1989). Such relationships will be ambiguous in the sense that parties to the engagement will be working simultaneously with and against the interests of the other. Clearly each party will seek to achieve its own objectives, but more important than anything is the ongoing maintenance of the relationship as trusting and respectful. Engagement is by its very nature an ongoing process; there is a considerable literature that highlights the dangers of using negotiating strategies that restrict information, are narrowly focused, or are threatening and destructive of relationships and hard-won trust (Covey & Brown, 2001).

The key question thus relates to the "framing" of the engagement process. Differences in interests in a situation of engagement are "framed" in three ways. First, negotiations are embedded in the power of parties to determine outcomes by influencing others, controlling agendas, and generally attempting to swing the situations their way. Shareholder activists may have power to focus media attention on the problem in hand, directors may have power to influence board decisions, and managers may have power to withhold crucial information. Using power to resolve disputes leads easily to a "lose-lose" outcome.

Second, negotiations can be overshadowed by recognized and enforceable rights possessed by either party. Rights in an engagement situation are grounded in the responsibilities that institutional investors have to their clients on the one hand, and in managerial autonomy to run a successful business on the other. Rights may also belong to the "subjects" of investor engagement, as in the case of child labor or the rights of Rio Tinto workers in Australia. The existence of rights can be acknowledged and respected, and conflicts can be mutually resolved accordingly. Alternatively, rights can be challenged, ignored, or swept aside. The third factor that influences the outcome of the engagement situation is the extent to which participants communicate with and manage relations with their various stakeholder constituents. At all points in the negotiation, the support of other stakeholders is crucial to meaningful outcomes.

Successful engagement has to be based in (a) a balancing of power asymmetries in terms of the recognition of both parties that each has the potential to harm the other, (b) the acknowledgment of integral rights and responsibilities, (c) intensive communication and relationship building so as to create a framework for the negotiating of core interest differentials, and (d) management of relations with other key stakeholders such as employees, savers, customers, and financial institutions (Covey & Brown, 2001).

INVESTOR ENGAGEMENT: THE APPROACH

Much of what can be called investor engagement is low profile and frequently remains that way over a long period of time. Sometimes engagement escalates, and very occasionally there is no lead-in in terms of relationship building, but rather immediate confrontation either by exposure in the media and/or by high-profile intervention at AGMs. The low-profile building blocks that precede the processes of critical cooperation are described by an analyst working for CIS (CIS, 2002c) as follows.

Defining the Issue

An issue or concern can come to our attention in a number of ways. It might be a letter from a customer, a media article, or a contact from a nongovernmental organization (NGO). We also conduct sector reviews; companies in specific sectors often face similar challenges and risks, but their responses to these vary greatly. By evaluating a sector, we can more easily spot companies that are not adequately dealing with matters of social or environmental concern.

Once a concern has been identified, our next step is to contact the company directly to find out more detailed information and to get its views of the issue. The first stage of engagement is very important because it signals to the company that the issue is of significant interest to one of its major shareholders. We usually write to a member of senior management; this way, even if we decide not to pursue the issue further, there is a good chance that it will be managed more closely following our inquiry or expression of concern.

Evaluating the Response

How do we evaluate the company's response? We consider this in the light of best practice in other companies and adherence to globally recognized standards. However, each case has a unique context, depending on events, company history, culture, leadership, and operations, and hence our judgment as to whether the company is taking appropriate responsibility must be fresh each time. Our evaluation allows us to decide whether we need to pursue the issue further with the company. This decision is discussed by the Responsible Shareholding Committee, which in addition to staff from the responsible shareholding unit also includes the chief investment manager, head of equities, and head of investment research.

We base our decision on criteria such as the following:

- *Has the company taken the best possible decision or action in the circumstances?*

- *Is the incident exceptional, or is it the result of inadequate policies and management processes?*
- *Does the issue present a risk to the value of the business?*
- *Will the company's actions have a negative impact on CIS customers, our primary stakeholders?*
- *What capacity do we have to provide suggestions as to how the issue could be better managed?*

Taking the Issue Further

This last question is the key to the success of the engagement process. The responsible shareholding unit may have knowledge of best practice by other "investee" companies that can be applied to the issue. Many NGOs have clear ideas about how companies can address certain concerns, and so we consult them when appropriate. We have another great resource in our own social accountability program: Can our own experience in areas of social and environmental responsibility be helpful to other organizations?

If we are dissatisfied with the outcome of our written correspondence with the company, the next step in the engagement process is to meet company representatives to discuss the matter. Wherever possible we will bring a proposal or recommendation for action by the company. We then ensure that ongoing communication with the investee company enables us to monitor the actions that are being taken to address our concerns (quoted from CIS, 2002c).

INVESTOR ENGAGEMENT: THE PRACTICE

The account just given essentially refers to the "quiet dialogue" low-profile aspect of investor engagement, where mixed interests are explored in a nonthreatening way. An alternative scenario is where engagement is from the outset high profile, using power positions to engage in rights debates. That kind of scenario can be the result of escalation; alternatively it can emerge in

AGMs around corporate governance issues. The following cases are examples of these two scenarios.

Case 1

This case involved the selling of medicines, particularly anti-AIDS drugs, to third-world companies (CIS, 2002b). In February 2002, Oxfam, an NGO, ran a campaign called Cut the Cost and published a briefing document on a U.K. pharmaceutical company, GlaxoSmith-Kline (GSK), in which it criticized its pricing policies, and in particular its participation in a court case brought by 39 of the world's largest pharmaceutical companies against the South African government. This case sought to block the government's right to import cheap (generic) anti-AIDS drugs. The South African government had passed a Medicines Act in 1987 that the companies maintained was in contravention of TRIPS (Trade-Related Aspects of Intellectual Property Rights). Clearly this represented a threat to GSK and to the other companies involved. It also represented a threat to investors. Not only were these groups likely to be alarmed by the threat to corporate reputation of Oxfam's campaign, but long-term shareholder value in this sector depends on worldwide patents, and the increased use of generic drugs as patents expire represents a negative scenario of unknown proportions.

Investors used the Oxfam onslaught to emphasize to GSK the seriousness of the threat represented by the widespread criticism of the companies involved in the South African case. Meanwhile in South Africa, grassroots movements, supported by NGOs, persuaded GSK and the 38 other companies to pull out of the court case. Although initially defensive, the company responded by taking on-board the need to communicate more effectively with investors. It created a new board committee of non-execs to consider CSR issues, and in June 2002 it published its "Facing the Challenge" report emphasizing the third-world bias of its R&D and its resolve to place increased emphasis

on differential pricing so as to benefit third-world countries.[12]

Case 2

A high-profile situation emerged at the 2002 AGM of EasyJet, a U.K. no-frills airline. The airline was founded by Stelios Haji-Ioannou in 1995 and became a public company in 2000. Mr. Haji-Ioannou (who controlled 58 percent of the £1.5 billion shares) continued as chairman and chief executive, being reappointed each year by the Easy Group through its agreement with the airline that licenses the EasyJet brand. In return for the brand, Easy Group would name the chairman (Adams, 2002). At the AGM, CIS (a minority shareholder) voted against accepting the board's report and recommendations, arguing that the way in which the chairman was appointed, the lack of independence of nonexecutive directors (who were paid with share options), and the company's failure to adopt an environmental impact policy demonstrated severe corporate governance failings. "This is a 'yellow card' for EasyJet," said a CIS spokesman, "and we want to work with the company to get this right." No further actions were taken, but a month later Mr. Haji-Ioannou suddenly announced that at the next AGM he would resign not just from the chairmanship but also from the board in order to pursue his career as a "serial entrepreneur." He announced that he would sell part of his holding of EasyJet shares to finance his new initiatives. CIS had recognized throughout that the creation and development of EasyJet represented a major achievement on the part of Mr. Ioannou, and it was certainly never their intention to encourage him to leave the board. It would have preferred to enter into an engagement process, but this was not to be.

A moment's reflection will show that these two cases represent very different sets of engagement dynamics. We can analyze these in terms of the four necessary conditions for successful engagement previously outlined.

Balancing Power Asymmetries

In the first case, the power advantage might have been with GSK initially, especially in view of investor sensitivity to the perceived vulnerability of long-term shareholder value, but it was diffused by Oxfam's intervention, and this helped investors to enter into negotiations with GSK on even terms. GSK was at first defensive but eventually open and collaborative, and useful new CSR measures were taken. Result: substantial mutual influence.

In the second case, there was an initial display of power by the company, matched by implicit investor threats. Given the nature of the power asymmetries, no dialogue was possible.

Acknowledging Critical Rights

In the first case, the real rights at stake are the rights of the third-world poor, and they had no voice. NGO interests served only as surrogates for these. The company was sensitive to rights-based arguments both from Oxfam and from investors and sought support for their new CSR and governance initiatives. Investors perceived the predicament facing GSK. Result: the possibility of active ongoing engagement.

In the second case, rights were all on the side of the investors, as the EasyJet chairman was openly and patently flouting the governance code of best practice. Dialogue was not appropriate here since the EasyJet chairman refused to listen to the arguments of the investors.

Negotiating Mixed Interests

In the first case, it would appear that in spite of the opening up of contact between GSK and investors/NGOs, the company might feel uncomfortable if the engagement situation were to go any further than occasional informal contacts. Furthermore, it might maintain that its current differential pricing initiatives demonstrate that it is committed to helping the third world independently of external pressure (CIS, 2002b).

In the second case, negotiation would have been inappropriate if not counterproductive.

Managing Stakeholders

In the first case, stakeholders—other investors/NGOs on the one hand and GSK corporate partners (from board members to research teams to financial planners) on the other—were well to the fore as the situation evolved.

In the second case, the primary relevant stakeholders were the savers whose interests CIS was trying to protect. CIS had done detailed research on how FTSE 100 companies and others were meeting corporate governance requirements, and they were very sure of their ground.

CONCLUSION

This chapter has sought to describe and conceptualize the growth of SRI and the process of investor engagement as it is practiced in the U.K. It began by tracing the emergence of socially responsible investment from its beginnings in the ethical retail fund market to its present manifestation as the "engagement" of pension funds, insurance funds, and others with the companies whose shares they hold with a view to improving their CSR performance and governance structures over the longer term. The chapter then considered the role and status of the institutional stakeholder as risk bearer and made the point that socially responsible investment is not about prioritizing shareholder interests, but rather about redressing the balance of governance systems that prioritize the claims of shareholders while neglecting the fact that other stakeholders are also risk bearers. This perspective implies that the phenomenon of SRI sits uneasily within the confines of both stakeholder and agency theory.

The fascination of the SRI issue lies in the example of countervailing stakeholder power it presents. However, although it is easy enough to theorize the process of engagement, it is less easy to pronounce whether or not investor engagement improves overall CSR. It is possible to point to substantial changes for the better in certain companies, but it is not possible to know whether improvements would have happened anyway, or indeed whether those same companies, or others, are finding new ways to circumvent promises and commitments to improved social performance.

Furthermore, there is no one mode of investor engagement. Engagement is about seeking change; in this it differs from dialogue, which has no stated objective. However, different investors see the problem in different ways. Some are "best practice" investors; they attack the problem schematically, identifying areas of potential improvement, holding informal discussions with companies involved, supporting corporate change initiatives, using voting rights to reinforce their position, and building strong relationships in tandem with strong governance structures. Others take a more strategic approach, seeing unfocused dialogue as a vehicle for uncovering areas of potential interest for future engagement. Yet others focus sharply on shareholder value, seeing CSR engagement as to some extent instrumental rather than merely substantive. There are also those who see the achievement of substantive CSR gains as more important than the maintenance of long-term relationships within an engagement situation. However, it is almost certainly the case that different approaches will coalesce as collaborative investor initiatives become more frequent and more sophisticated

NOTES

1. In spite of the mandatory provisions of the Combined Code of Governance, violations are the rule rather than the exception. In 2002, half the FTSE 100 companies had remuneration committees that were not independent, one-fifth had a majority of nonexecutive directors who were not independent, and three-quarters paid more to their auditors in nonaudit fees than in audit fees.

2. Between 1997 (before the regulatory changes were announced) and 2001, the total of SRI funds in the London market rose from £22.7 billion to £224.5 billion—a tenfold increase. At the beginning of that period, the major SRI investors were churches and charities; by 2001 pension funds and insurance companies were the major players. By summer 2000, 59 percent of pension funds were incorporating SRI principles into their investment process (Sparkes, 2002, p. 345). But from 1998 onwards mutual insurance companies, local authorities, trade unions, and institutional investors had also been moving towards building SRI principles into their investment management strategies.

3. In the past, there has been a great focus on the fiduciary duty of trustees, and this has often been interpreted, perhaps willfully by some, as ruling out any possibility of undertaking socially responsible investment or shareholder activism. However, the emergence of engagement as an alternative (or addition) to traditional screened portfolios and the generally increased sophistication of investment activists have weakened the traditional arguments. But there is a leap to be made from convincing trustees they are able to be socially responsible investors while meeting their fiduciary duties to convincing them that SRI is something they should do, in spite of a widespread belief that there is a clear financial case for good governance, and that other CSR activities, such as a company's relations with stakeholders or its employment practices, will over time also have an increasing impact on the bottom line (Gribbin & Olsen, 2003).

4. I am not speaking here about deregulation, but rather about the unwillingness or lack of ability of governments in emerging markets and others to provide a regulatory basis that would ensure or at least encourage corporate social responsibility in multinational companies within their jurisdiction.

5. The use of terminology here implies that the term *stakeholders*—all those affected by the operations of the company (Freeman, 1984)—includes investors, that is, those financial institutions and funds putting money into corporate equity and debt. Investors as stakeholders can in theory wield a power for good that is greater than that possessed by any other stakeholder group.

6. It can be argued that investor power is as yet potential rather than fully realized. Recent figures for share ownership in the London market are as follows: U.K. insurance companies, 20 percent; U.K. pension funds, 20 percent; rest of world, 32 percent; individuals, 15 percent; others, 17 percent. It is estimated that only about 15 percent of equity investment is "socially responsible investment" in the sense of the Pensions

Act amendment, which means that in principle companies could ignore organized investor engagement strategies. However, potential reputation effects are likely to negate that possibility.

7. There have been a number of studies on this point; these are analyzed in CIS, 2002b, chap. 2. The overall conclusion would appear to be that the costs of lower portfolio diversion are probably outweighed by the benefits of better stock selection.

8. Many funds using engagement strategies hold fully diversified portfolios and are thus in a position to optimize portfolio returns. About 25 percent of U.K. pension funds are invested "passively" against major indices such as the FTSE 100, and the managers of these funds are among the most active in terms of shareholder engagement. In contrast to these, retail "ethical" funds, such as CIS Environ, restrict diversification by investing in line with predetermined criteria. In the case of the CIS Environ Trust, for instance, the majority of funds are invested in companies that improve the environment, human health, and safety; the remainder are invested in companies considered to improve the quality of life. About 30 percent of the U.K. equity market matches Environ investment criteria, and about 75 percent of Environ funds are invested in the U.K. market.

9. For instance, the CIS Environ Fund (a retail fund) invests in companies whose activities improve the environment, human health, and safety. The principles underlying this choice pattern stem from the principles of the Co-Operative Movement.

10. This view is not substantiated in U.K. law. The company is a legal person in its own right, and the fiduciary duty of directors is to the company in the first instance.

11. Part of corporate "property," or assets, is owned by the corporation; here we refer to physical and financial assets. Much of corporate property is intangible and is owned by different groups of stakeholders; here we think of skills and knowledge, goodwill, creativity, commitment, and so on.

12. See the GSK Web site at http://www.gsk .com/index.htm. However, investor concerns about the deteriorating health situation in emerging markets and its impact on long-term share value continued to grow, and in March 2003, 12 major institutional investors presented the pharmaceutical sector with a proposed code of practice detailing the issues of concern and suggesting areas for disclosure in annual reports of listed companies. The full document can be accessed at http://www.henderson .com.

REFERENCES

Adams, R. (2002, March 16). CIS shoots at EasyJet. *The Guardian*. Retrieved from http://www .guardian.co.uk/business/story/0,3604,668390,00 .html

Archer, M. S. (1995). *Realist social theory: The morphogenic approach.* Cambridge: Cambridge University Press.

Association of British Insurers. (2001a). *Investing in social responsibility: Risks and opportunities.* London: ABI.

Association of British Insurers. (2001b). *Disclosure guidelines in socially responsible investment.* London: ABI.

Becker, L. C. (1979). Property theory and the corporation. In M. Hoffman (Ed.), *Proceedings of the Second National Conference on Business Ethics.* Washington, DC: University Press of America.

Black, B. S. (1998). Shareholder activism and corporate governance in the United States. In P. Newman (Ed.), *The new Palgrave dictionary of economics and the law.* Basingstoke: Macmillan.

Blair, M. (1995). *Ownership and control: Rethinking corporate governance for the 21st century.* Washington: Brookings Institution.

Blair, M. (1998). For whom should corporations be run? An economic rationale for stakeholder management. *Long-Range Planning, 31*(2), 195–200.

CIS. (2002a). *Responsible shareholding, past, present and future.* Manchester: Co-operative Insurance Society.

CIS. (2002b). *Sustainability pays.* Report by Forum for the Future and PIRC. Retrieved from http://www.cis.co.uk

CIS. (2002c). *Social Accountability Report 2001.* Retrieved from http://www.cis.co.uk/sar2002/ default.asp

Clarkson, M. B. E. (1995). A stakeholder framework for analysing and evaluating corporate social performance. *Academy of Management Review, 20*, 92–117.

Coles, D., & Green, D. (2002). *Do pension funds invest responsibly? A survey of current practice on socially responsible investment.* Retrieved from http://www.justpensions.org

Cook, J., & Deakin, S. (1999a). *Stakeholding and corporate governance: Theory and evidence on economic performance.* Research Paper 1 for UK Company Law Review. London: Department of Trade and Industry.

Cook, J., & Deakin, S. (1999b). *Empirical evidence on corporate control.* Research Paper 10 for UK Company Law Review. London: Department of Trade and Industry.

Covey, J. C. (1996). Critical cooperation? Influencing the World Bank through policy dialogue and operational cooperation. In J. Fox & L. D. Brown (Eds.), *The struggle for accountability: The World Bank, NGOs, and grassroots movements* (pp. 81–120). Cambridge: The MIT Press.

Covey, J. C., & Brown L. D. (2001). *Critical co-operation: An alternative form of civil society-business engagement* (Institute of Development Research Report 17:1). Hauser Center for Non-Profit Organizations, Harvard University.

Deakin, S. (2002). Squaring the circle? Shareholder value and corporate social responsibility in the UK. *George Washington Law Review, 70*(5/6), 1701–1711.

DelGuercio, D., & Hawkins, J. (1999). The motivation and impact of pension fund activism. *Journal of Financial Economics, 52*(3), 293–364.

Demsetz, H. (1967). Towards a theory of property rights. *American Economic Review, 57,* 347–359.

Donaldson, T., & Preston, L. E. (1995). The stakeholder theory of the corporation: Concepts, evidence and implications. *Academy of Management Review, 20*(1), 65–91.

Dresner, S. (2002). *Assessing engagement: A survey of UK practice on socially responsible investment.* Retrieved from http://www.justpensions.org

Easterbrook, F. H., & Fischel, D. R. (1991). *The economic structure of corporate law.* Cambridge, MA: Harvard University Press.

Freeman, R. E. (1984). *Strategic management: A stakeholder approach.* Boston: Pitman.

Friedman, A. L., & Miles, S. (2002). Developing stakeholder theory. *Journal of Management Studies, 39*(1), 1–21.

Frooman, J. (1999). Stakeholder influence strategies. *Academy of Management Review, 24*(2), 191–206.

Ghoshal, S., & Moran, P. (1996). Bad for practice: A critique of the transaction cost theory. *Academy of Management Review, 21*(1), 13–47.

Gribbin, C., & Olsen L. (2003). *Will pension funds become more responsible? A survey of member-nominated trusts.* Retrieved from http://www.justpensions.org

Hill, C. W. C., & Jones, T. M. (1992). Stakeholder agency theory. *Journal of Management Studies, 29,* 131–154.

Jensen, M., & Meckling, W. (1976). Theory of the firm: Managerial behaviour, agency theory and ownership structure. *The Journal of Financial Economics, 3,* 305–360.

Jones, T. M. (1995). Instrumental stakeholder theory: A synthesis of ethics and economics. *Academy of Management Review, 20,* 404–437.

Jones, T. M., & Wicks, A. C. (1999). Convergent stakeholder theory. *Academy of Management Review, 24*(2), 206–214.

Lydenberg, S. D. (2002). Envisioning socially responsible investment: A model for 2006. *Journal of Corporate Citizenship, 7,* 57–77.

McLaren, D. (2002). *Engagement practices in socially responsible investment: Competing paradigms of governance and the emergence of standards.* MBA dissertation, Judge Institute of Management Studies, University of Cambridge.

Mitchell, R. K., Agle, B. R., & Wood, D. J. (1997). Towards a theory of stakeholder identification and salience: Defining the principle of who and what really counts. *Academy of Management Review, 22*(4), 853–886.

Myners review of institutional investment in the UK: Final report. (2001, March). HM Treasury, U.K.

Oliver, C. (1991). Strategic responses to institutional processes. *Academy of Management Review, 16*(1), 145–179.

Pearce, B., & Ganzi, J. (2002). *Engaging the mainstream with sustainability: A survey of investor engagement on corporate SEE performance.* Report by Forum for the Future and Finance Institute for Global Sustainability. Retrieved from http://www.forumforthefuture.org

Perrow, C. (1986). *Complex organizations: A critical essay* (3rd ed.). New York: McGraw Hill.

Pfeffer, J., & Salancik, G. R. (1978). *The external control of organizations: A resource-dependence perspective.* New York: Harper and Row.

Roberts, J. (2000). *Trust and control in the UK system of corporate governance: The individualising and socialising effects of processes of accountability.* Judge Institute research papers in management studies, WP22/2000.

Rowley, T. J. (1997). Moving beyond dyadic ties: A network theory of stakeholder influence. *Academy of Management Review, 22*(4), 887–891.

Rowley, T. J. (2000). Does relational context matter? An empirical test of a network theory of stakeholder influence. In J. M. Logsdon, D. J. Wood, & L. E. Benson (Eds.), *Research in stakeholder theory, 1997–1998: The Sloan Foundation minigrant project* (pp. 21–38). University of Toronto, Clarkson Centre for Business Ethics.

Savage, G. T., Blair, J. D., & Sorenson, R. L. (1989). Consider both relationships and substance when negotiating strategically. *Academy of Management Executive, 3*(1), 37–49.

Slinger, G. (1999). Spanning the gap: The theoretical principles that connect stakeholder policies to business performance. *Corporate Governance: An International Review, 7*(2), 136–151.

Sparkes, R. (2001). Ethical investment: Whose ethics, which investment. *Business Ethics: A European Review, 10*(3), 194–205.

Sparkes, R. (2002). *Socially responsible investment: A global revolution.* London: John Wiley & Sons.

Swift, T. (2001). Trust, reputation and corporate accountability to stakeholders. *Business Ethics: A European Review, 10*(1), 16–26.

Taylor, R. (2000). How new is socially responsible investment? *Business Ethics: A European Review, 9*(3), 174–179.

Taylor, R. (2001). Putting ethics into investment. *Business Ethics: A European Review, 10*(1), 53–60.

Taylor, R. (2002). Science and ethical investment. *Business Ethics: A European Review, 11*(1), 77–85.

Useem, M. (1996). *Investor capitalism: How money managers are changing the face of corporate America.* New York: Basic Books.

Wheeler, D., & Sillanpaa, M. (1997). *The stakeholder corporation.* London: Pitman.

Wood, D. (1994). *Business and society* (2nd ed.). New York: Harper Collins.

19

INSTILLING MORAL COMPETENCE IN A MULTINATIONAL

A Technical Issue

CATHERINE SMITH

PIETER KROON

Today's discourse on business ethics is marked by a wide variety of terms such as *sustainability, corporate citizenship, responsible business practices, triple bottom line, corporate social responsibility, stakeholder dialogue*, and *socially responsible investing*. These words and phrases are all well established and often used interchangeably by companies, NGOs, investment managers, and academics alike. Nevertheless, there is still debate as to their meaning and the relationship between them. Is stakeholder dialogue the same as corporate governance? Some companies would say yes, others would say no. Is corporate citizenship the same

thing as corporate social responsibility? Again, opinions differ. The differences are also cultural. In continental Europe, the terms *sustainability* and *sustainable development* are more common than in Anglo-Saxon countries such as the United States, where the focus is more on *corporate social responsibility*.

The term *sustainable development* achieved international allure since it appeared 15 years ago in the Brundtland report *Our Common Future*. For the layperson, *sustainable* means something like *long-term*. That was also the essence of the Brundtland definition, but with a twist. It added the element of balancing different long-term

AUTHORS' NOTE: The authors would like to thank Diane Lange for her contribution to this chapter.

interests. The report defined *sustainable development* as "development which meets the needs of the present without compromising the needs of present and future generations." The idea was to achieve economic development in such a way that it did not undermine the human and natural environment.

From Brundtland's original definition, the concept of the *triple bottom line* gradually rose to the fore. The triple bottom line can be seen as a general direction for how to apply Brundtland's ideas about sustainable development to the business sector. John Elkington is generally credited with coining the term. The idea behind the triple bottom line is that a company creates more value over the long run and encounters fewer risks if it takes environmental issues (the *P* of *planet*), social issues (the *P* of *people*), and financial considerations (the *P* of *profit*) into consideration than a company that focuses purely on the *P* of *profit*. The right balance between the three *P*s is deemed to contribute to a more sustainable world along the vision of Brundtland—and much more.

Triple P thinking has gained widespread acceptance in the business world. According to the Global Reporting Initiative, more than 3,000 companies around the world are now voluntarily reporting on their Triple P performance. An international survey carried out by KPMG in 2002 found that 45 percent of the Fortune Global Top 250 companies are currently reporting on their environmental and social performance.

How did the triple bottom line push its way into the boardroom? The first factor is globalization. As companies grew worldwide during the '90s, they became aware of the social and environmental impact their activities can have in different parts of the world. Their greater visibility has attracted the scrutiny of NGOs and social activist groups with respect to certain environmental, social, and human rights issues. The second factor is the power of the media. The growth of the Internet and the swiftness with which news from remote parts of the world now travels the globe have far-reaching ramifications for international companies, including ING. We live in the CNN world. The traditional distinction

between local news and global news is gradually blurring. This presents corporations with new challenges in managing publicity and stakeholder dialogue.

Yet is a commitment to sustainable development the same thing as being ethical? And is it possible to determine whether one company is more ethical than another? Judging from the broad acceptance of Triple P thinking and the growth of *sustainable* funds in the asset management industry, one is inclined to answer yes. The widespread acceptance of the Triple P model suggests that the combination of financial, social, and environmental factors determines whether one company is more sustainable than another—and thus more ethical. In this chapter, we will discuss that view.

The starting point for our discussion is, Is *sustainable* the same thing as *ethical*? We will begin by first taking a look at the investment management industry, where socially responsible investment (SRI) funds have grown in recent years and where the term *sustainability leader* is widely used. But what is a sustainability leader? From there, we will go on to consider the following three questions:

1. Can a company that is considered *sustainable* also be considered *moral*?

2. Can moral competence be taught inside the company?

3. What role does moral competence play in the company's risk management?

Our thesis will be that sustainable behavior is not equal to moral behavior. In some cases, sustainable behavior is a subset of moral behavior, but not always. The reason for this mismatch is that it is possible to pass the sustainability test but fail the moral test. It is also possible to pass the moral test but fail the sustainability test, as our examples will show. We will also argue that moral competence is not an option but a requirement in today's business environment. Companies that teach their staff moral competence in the business setting will be better positioned in the global marketplace than those that do not. But to do that, companies cannot rely on personal conscience alone; they must create a "company conscience," so to speak, against which all business activities, including sustainability-related activities, can be tested.

ETHICAL COMPANIES

What Makes a Company Ethical?

What makes one company more ethical than another? The fact that the company donates money to good causes? The fact that it has a code of conduct? The fact that it refrains from doing business in a country known to abuse human rights? Is it a combination of these or other factors that determines a company's moral fiber? Or none of these? The widespread acceptance of the Triple P model suggests that it is the combination of financial, social, and environmental factors that determines whether one company is more sustainable than another—and thus more ethical.

Shortcomings of the Triple P Model

It is good to point out at the outset that despite the popularity of Triple P thinking, ING Group has moved away from the Triple P terminology, though not the underlying idea. Although the Group endorses the underlying idea of the need to balance financial, social, and environmental concerns, we prefer to use the term *stakeholder dialogue* to describe that balancing act. One of the reasons we eschew the Triple P vocabulary is that the Triple P model implies that it is possible to view people, planet, and profit in isolation. We believe this is too narrow a view, since each *P* can involve various stakeholder groups. Obviously companies need profits in order to survive in the long run and in order to contribute to sustainable development in the future. But financials are not the only driver anymore. Today, companies are no longer expected to be focused on making profits alone. They are also expected to fulfill a valuable

function in society and to behave responsibly—thus the growing emphasis on corporate social responsibility. ING strives to balance short-term profitability with long-term sustainability. That is no easy task, as that balancing act requires taking many intangible factors into account. Nevertheless, in considering commercial opportunities, ING gives due concern to social and environmental concerns, as well as the impact on public opinion and our reputation. For this, the dialogue with the company's stakeholders is crucial.

What Is Stakeholder Dialogue?

Who are a company's stakeholders? The answer to that question will vary from company to company and depends on a variety of factors, such as the company's size, industry, and business strategy. ING defines *stakeholders* as all people who are interested in, dependent on, connected to, and affected by ING. We chose to break our most important stakeholders into four groups: customers, shareholders, employees, and society in general.

Customers form the basis for a company's existence. ING manages the money of more than 60 million clients worldwide. That brings an enormous responsibility. ING's clients are not only individual customers but also small- to medium-sized companies and large institutional investors, such as pension funds, with significant stakes on global capital markets. ING has a moral responsibility in this respect, which stems from the fact that few societies would function properly without well-functioning banking systems. Furthermore, many business sectors would come to a standstill without the willingness of insurers and reinsurers like ING to accept and transfer risk. As a global financial institution with influence stretching across many countries and capital markets, ING's task is therefore not only to serve the individual needs of its diverse customer base, but also to maintain the highest standards of integrity while serving them in order to contribute to the stability of financial markets.

Employees form another important stakeholder group. Financial services is a people's business par excellence. The business success of a financial services provider is directly linked to the well-being, motivation, and performance of its employees. Furthermore, the high standards of integrity previously referred to must be carried out concretely by the employees themselves.

Shareholders, the third stakeholder, are primarily focused on profitability, but there is a growing general belief that profitability cannot be viewed in isolation from a commitment to long-term sustainability. ING's aim is to balance a short-term focus on profits with a long-term focus on healthy growth and sustainability.

Society in general is different from the other three stakeholders. While customers, shareholders, and employees are groups with well-defined interests, the interests of "society" are less clear-cut. ING's relationship with "global society" is a complex tapestry of numerous "sub-stakeholders." Each sub-stakeholder represents a specific interest from a wide range of interests. Sub-stakeholders include the hundreds of nonprofit and nongovernmental organizations, dozens of national governments, national and international regulatory authorities, industry and trade groups, national and multilateral institutions such as the World Bank, regional development agencies, consumer organizations, universities, and many more.

In short, ING is not purely a shareholder-focused company but also a stakeholder-focused company. ING is committed to an equitable treatment of all four of its stakeholders and aims to balance their interests in making business decisions. Some business decisions may involve weighing the interests of one stakeholder more strongly than another, while the interests of another stakeholder may weigh more heavily in other business decisions. Stakeholder dialogue is essential in order to make responsible business decisions because it enables ING to find out what our stakeholders want. Stakeholder dialogue is also a valuable source of information about how stakeholders view certain issues. It also helps a company like ING identify who the most relevant parties are in key issues of debate.

WHAT IS A SUSTAINABILITY LEADER?

The stakeholder approach is the starting point, not only for companies like ING, but also for those who track the sustainability performance of companies like ING and who provide an opinion about whether they can be considered a sustainability leader.

One of the most important groups of players to provide such an opinion are SRI fund managers. Like a traditional fund manager, the job of an SRI fund manager is to make money for investors. Unlike a traditional fund manager, an SRI fund manager picks stocks by paying attention to sustainability criteria in addition to financial criteria, the idea being that a company that is aware of its Triple P risks and opportunities and is doing good in society is more valuable than companies where this is not the case.

Sustainability leaders are chosen based on the fund manager's own analysis, in combination with research from independent companies (or specialized departments within banks) that specialize in screening companies for their sustainability performance. Companies' own social and environmental reports—also called sustainability reports—are also a key source of information. The companies that screen companies on SRI normally make use of standardized questionnaires and surveys. SiRi is an example of a company that specializes in providing SRI research. It notes on its Web site that its global profiles reflect "all major stakeholder issues . . . including community involvement, environmental impact, employment relations, customer policies, human rights issues and corporate governance. For each issue, SiRi describes and analyzes the company's policies, management systems, reporting standards and impacts together with particular strengths and weaknesses" (SiRi Group Profiles, 2003).

Companies that score high on such surveys are usually considered sustainability leaders in their sector and are more likely to be included in sustainable funds by fund managers than other companies.

Sustainability Leader/Ethical Leader

While SRI research is a valuable source of information about a company's efforts to incorporate sustainable development into its business processes, we would argue that such surveys do not provide the last word about a company's moral fiber. Receiving the distinction of sustainability leader is certainly a vote of confidence about a company's ethical demeanor. But a sustainability leader is not the same thing as an ethical leader.

This is, in our view, an important point to emphasize because this distinction does not always seem to be clear-cut for the general public. There is a general perception that a company that is considered a "sustainability" leader in its sector must be more ethical than a company that is not best in its class in sustainability.

In fact, the investment community itself makes a distinction (though some tend to equate the two) between ethical and sustainable investment funds. An ethical fund tends to be exclusionary in terms of criteria that carry a high moral content. The criteria are therefore "absolute" in nature. The criteria of a sustainable fund, on the other hand, tend to be more relative (best-in-class) and based primarily on the Brundtland criteria of sustainable development rather than one's moral view. The criteria of sustainable funds are therefore more relational than the exclusionary criteria of ethical funds. The criteria of ethical funds are determined by the moral view of the investor who chooses to invest in such funds.

Another difference between the ethical and sustainable behavior, according to Robert Smallegange, fund manager with ING Investment Management Sustainable Investment, is that "profit is integrated into sustainable behaviour, whereas this is not the case for ethical behaviour." That is not to say that ethics and profit are opposed to each other. The two may go hand in hand, but the difference is that the sustainability concept *explicitly* takes profit into consideration.

Smallegange provides another example to demonstrate the difference between *ethical* and *sustainable*: the defense industry.

Although, morally speaking, weapons are often associated with violence and war, weapons can also serve a peacekeeping role, which will benefit the three components of sustainable development. In the Netherlands, the defense industry is usually not included in sustainable funds, but in France it can be included. Cultural differences help explain the different views in some of the more morally charged industries and their sustainability merits.

As previously noted, profit is explicitly integrated into the concept of sustainable development—and thus sustainable behavior—but it is not an inherent component in ethical behavior. But another reason the term *sustainable* should not be equated with *ethical* is that it is necessary to distinguish between a company's behavior and the company's products. It is conceivable for a company to demonstrate ethical behavior while having unsustainable products. Similarly a company can pass the sustainability test while failing the ethical test. In this case, a company may be doing a great job balancing all three *P*s even though it is active in a business sector that cannot be considered sustainable.

ING Investment Management, the largest asset management division of ING Group, has dealt with this last point by making a distinction between sustainable, nonsustainable, and neutral activities. Activities that do not pass the test of sustainability, in the view of ING Investment Management, are those that have negative effects on health, human rights, ecosystems, social structures, etc. This is in line with Brundtland's definition since negative effects on health, human rights, ecosystems, and social structures can compromise the needs of current and future generations. However, there are nonsustainable activities, such as the oil sector, that have negative effects on the environment but are unavoidable in the current situation since there is no alternative. These "unsustainable" business activities alone, however, say nothing about the company's moral fiber. One could therefore argue that a company's ethical makeup can be seen separately from the kind of business it is in. A company such as Shell may be active in an "unsustainable" sector, but it may be doing a good job when it comes to making careful and responsible decisions on the key ethical—and sustainable—dilemmas it faces in its sector.

ING's Robert Smallegange therefore argues that it is necessary to differentiate between the *actions* and *products* of a company:

> Shell products are unsustainable, because the bulk of Shell's revenues are generated from the exploration and production of non-renewable, fossil fuel resources. This means that these resources are finite and as such these resources/products are not sustainable. Another aspect is the huge environmental issue of climate change due to the release of CO_2 when its products are consumed. We therefore differentiate between a company's products and a company's behaviour. Although we recognize that products derived of fossil fuels are implicitly unsustainable, it is not possible for society to stop using them right away. There are simply too few feasible alternatives to replace fossil fuels on a large scale. It would be highly uneconomical to force a fast replacement of fossil fuel. Since sustainable development according to the Brundtland definition is about balancing people, planet and profit, clearly the profit component would make such a move "unsustainable development." We therefore rate Shell within its sector on its behaviour. In the opinion of ING Investment Management, therefore, Shell's *actions* are best-in-class in terms of sustainability.

The fact that *sustainable* does not by definition equal *ethical* is confusing not only for the general public but also for fund managers themselves. ING Investment Management's Smallegange concedes that there is indeed disagreement in the investment management community about whether a company that is recognized as a sustainability leader can also be regarded as more ethical than other companies in its sector. As we have already seen, an ethical fund is not the same thing as a sustainable fund. "However," argues Smallegange, "companies that have been identified as sustainability leaders are more *likely* to be more ethical." The reason, he says, is that such companies are deemed to have management systems, policies, and internal controls in place that are likely to *lead* to ethical decisions.

Furthermore, making the policies and management systems transparent and open puts pressure on a company to follow through on promises made, because the company has subjected its policies to outside verification.

What have we established so far in our discussion? First, while SRI questionnaires and sustainability surveys are valuable sources of information about a company's sustainability performance, they do not reveal the whole story about a company's moral fiber. They can pretty accurately reveal whether a company's products and services are "sustainable," and they can reveal whether a company is doing good in society. But when it comes to answering the question of whether company A is more moral than company B, they only scratch at the surface. To answer that question, we therefore need to look further than a company's products alone. We need to look at the company's actions and the behavior of the people who work there. That is because there is a difference between *doing good* and *doing the right thing*. Doing good is relatively easy. Doing the right thing is not always easy because it can involve dilemmas. *The Random House College Dictionary* (1982) defines a *dilemma* as making a choice between two equally undesirable alternatives. Deciding to donate money to a good cause, however, is a fundamentally different type of decision than deciding whether to do business in a country that is known for its human rights abuses. SRI surveys provide a general indication of whether company A is doing a better job at doing the right thing than company B based on what is known about the company's management systems, policies, and codes and procedures. Let us now look more closely at the importance of such procedures, policies, and systems in shaping ethical decision making.

ETHICAL DECISION MAKING

Decision Making and Moral Competence

Information about such policies and procedures, codes of conduct, statements of values and principle, internal controls, and risk management systems are all clearly important since they provide an overall framework for ethical engagement within the company—a "shell," so to speak, within which ethical decision making can take place. But there is still a margin of uncertainty. A company may have all the right policies and procedures in place, but, as we argued before, it can pass the sustainability test while failing the ethical test, and vice versa. That margin of "ethical uncertainty" would appear to lie in the actual decision making within the company. The decision-making process of management and staff—the steps that are taken before solving an ethical dilemma—goes to the core of a company's ethical makeup. However, the *actual* decision-making process is not captured in SRI questionnaires, which only survey the procedures and policies that are *believed* to govern decision making.

Types of Decisions

Thousands of decisions are made each day in a large company. The majority of them involve individual deliberation. Thus, they are largely invisible to the outside world. Furthermore, the vast majority of decisions made each day do not involve ethical dilemmas.

There are two types of decisions: macro and micro decisions. *Macro* ethical choices are those for which the company has already developed clear instructions, policies, or guidelines. An example is a company's policy on E-mail. A company that clearly prohibits the use of the company E-mail system for personal use in its code of conduct has provided clear instructions about how to act if an employee considers sending a personal E-mail on company time. When a policy is created, the issue is no longer a dilemma but a clear black-and-white issue. Doing otherwise would be acting unethically because (although some employees might not see anything wrong with it) it would conflict with the company's "conscience," which has been formalized through the creation of the policy.

But suppose the company had no policy in place governing the use of E-mail. In this situation, the decision of whether to send a personal E-mail using the company system would be left to the discretion and choice of the individual concerned. It would become, therefore, a *micro* ethical decision. A micro ethical decision is one that is left to the individual discretion of the employee, the outcome of which can vary based on the individual's own moral views. Some individuals would not see anything wrong with sending a personal E-mail through the company system and do it anyway. Other individuals would not send the E-mail because they would not consider it the right thing to do, even though the policy did not exist (yet).

Types of Decision Makers

Just as we can distinguish between two types of decisions in a company, there are also two types of decision makers in the company: macro and micro decision makers. *Macro* decision makers are those with substantial leverage both within and outside the company. These include (a) the top executives in the company and (b) the company itself as a moral actor in its own right. For example, the decision by ING not to do business in Burma is an example of ING as a company taking a moral stance as a company and reorganizing its business activities accordingly. Macro ethical decisions are usually high-profile ones, with the decision usually resulting after a lengthy dialogue with outside stakeholders. *Micro* decision makers are individual staff and managers below the executive level.

Common Principles for Moral Competence

Despite the difference in leverage between these two types of decision makers, the same degree of moral competence must be present at both levels. Furthermore, the principles of moral competence must be the same at both the macro and micro level. Macro decision makers should not be expected to have a higher—or lower—degree of moral competence than micro decision makers or be subject to different principles. The reason is that ethical dilemmas can arise at all levels of the organization, regardless of one's position and status. A moral dilemma at the micro level is no less important than one at the macro level. Moral competence therefore becomes the binding element of equality through the organization. All staff and management must be subject to the same principles of moral competence.

Moral competence consists of two steps: first, the ability to spot an ethical dilemma, and second, knowing how to deal adequately with the dilemma. Staff and management can be trained in this by showing them the steps that should be taken and the choices they need to make in order to "do the right thing" in the face of a dilemma. As mentioned earlier, the intrinsic element of a dilemma is that it is not a black-and-white issue. It is a gray area. It involves having to choose between undesirable or controversial alternatives. A company cannot leave all ethical decision making to the personal conscience/values of its own employees alone. It is therefore necessary to *create a conscience* by formally and *explicitly* laying down the values and principles against which dilemmas in the company can be tested, both internally and externally, and against which the values of individual staff can be tested. The E-mail issue just described was one example of this. Ultimately, moral competence should become a "technical" decision, removed from personal conscience. Management and staff should be trained to act according to the "company conscience," but this must first be created and laid down in certain predefined principles and values.

The "Mean" in the Business Context

Moral competence in companies shows some similarities with the idea of moral competence once articulated by Aristotle. For him, "virtues are modes of choice, or involve choice" (Aristotle, trans. 1973, book 2, chap. 5, p. 1006a). Eventually, virtue should become a matter of habit. Moral virtue must have the quality of aiming at the intermediate (the mean) between two extremes. "Virtue is a kind of mean, since . . . it aims at which is intermediate . . . Virtue, then,

is . . . concerned with choice, lying in a mean, i.e. the mean relative to us, this being determined by a rational principle" (Ibid., book 2, chap. 6, p. 1107a). Choice is voluntary, and "the voluntary would seem to be that of which the moving principle is in the agent himself, he being aware of the particular circumstances of the action" (Ibid., book 3, chap. 1, p. 1111a). Practice, teaching, and habit are all crucial. The ultimate objective is "excellence in deliberation" (Ibid., book 6, chap. 9, p. 1142b), which involves reasoning (" . . . he who deliberates inquires and calculates" [Ibid., book 6, chap. 9, p. 1142b]).

Aristotle helps us understand that it is *necessary to differentiate* when making moral choices. This is clearly the case in the business context. It is not always easy to find the right mean to different kinds of business dilemmas. His theory on the particulars reveals that the proper reaction under one set of particulars might be the wrong reaction under another set of circumstances. There is much practice and experience involved, and the right solution in one set of particular circumstances might be the wrong one in another.

A good example of the difficulty in finding the right "mean" is ING's choice to do business in China but not in Burma. Both countries have been singled out for human rights abuses. So isn't it the right thing to refrain from business in both countries? Or should the company differentiate?

In this particular case, ING chose to differentiate. Why? In terms of Burma, the difference is that the country is not making any effort to improve its human rights record and there is no indication that the human rights abuses will stop any time soon. The military regime is not even interested in a dialogue with the international community. In 1997, ING closed its Burma representative office, and since then, ING has no longer been active in the country. ING does business with clients that are active in Burma, including IHC Caland, an offshore company. But in 2002, a consortium of national and international banks, including ING, stipulated that its financing could not be used for the Burma project.

In China, on the other hand, the human rights situation appears to be improving. In contrast to

Burma, China is engaged in a dialogue with the international community on human rights and has at least formally stated its commitment to improve the situation and to comply with UN regulations. Its membership in the WTO is expected to be an additional catalyst to improve its human rights record. After decades of closure, the country is gradually opening up to the West, which cannot be said of Burma.

Indeed, ING's business activities in China are important and continue to grow. ING operates two life insurance joint ventures and has commenced a fund management joint venture. ING also advises the Chinese government on pension reform. Within ING's strategy, China is a core growth market with good long-term prospects.

What are the trade-offs of ING taking such an ethical stance? One could argue that ING loses out on business—and thus the *P* of profit—by not doing business in Burma. However, ING sees it differently. Doing business in Burma would create a reputational risk, which, in turn, could cause greater damage to our profit. Looking at it another way, ING might even *win* new business as a result of its ethical stance in Burma. By forgoing a short-term profit, there may be long-term financial benefits.

As this example shows, the right ethical choice for a dilemma like the one of Burma versus China—i.e., finding Aristotle's mean—depends on the circumstances. It involves weighing the stakes, analyzing the situation, and assessing the risks on a case-by-case basis. The "mean" for the dilemma in Burma is not the right "mean" for China, given the particulars of each dilemma.

Another example of the difficulty of finding the right solution is a dilemma ING faced in Indonesia. In Indonesia, it is possible to buy a license to start an oil palm plantation. Oil palm plantations are an environmentally sensitive industry. ING was faced with the dilemma that what is legal is not necessarily ethical. Furthermore, to what extent can a financial services provider such as ING be held accountable for the actions of clients who are engaged in a business that many might consider unethical due to its

detrimental impact on the environment? Do we want to finance an industry that is politically, socially, and environmentally sensitive? And if so, should we subject our financing to certain conditions that help protect the environment and social structures?

On the one hand, nonfinancial aspects are becoming more important in credit lending activities. ING introduced guidelines to help account managers assess the environmental, ethical, and social impact of specific transactions. We are, however, just at the beginning of that process.

Unlike the ethical choice ING made with respect to its client IHC Caland in Burma— whereby ING stipulated that financing could not be used whatsoever for its Burma project—ING adopted another solution in Indonesia. While ING chose to *eliminate* all financing for projects in Burma, ING chose to *sharpen* its credit conditions for projects in Indonesia. We laid down conditions requiring that projects for the development of oil palm plantations meet the regulations of the World Bank's Forest Policy.

A crucial point here again is that the "right" solution for Burma may not be the "right" solution in Indonesia—or any other countries for that matter. The dilemmas ING has faced up to now have demonstrated that decisions concerning ethical dilemmas have to be made on a case-by-case basis and should be based on the company's own values. In making the final choice, ING's compass is not "what do we have to gain?" but "what do we and others stand to lose?"

TEACHING MORAL COMPETENCE

The Business Principles

Deciding how to handle a macro ethical dilemma in Burma or China is normally dealt with at the top corporate level. Such dilemmas usually attract wide media attention, as do the decisions about how to deal with them. But what about the micro ethical dilemmas ING management and staff may encounter in their daily work? We argued earlier that identifying and resolving ethical dilemmas—i.e., moral competence—must be subject to the same principles. The manner in which top management decides to deal with high-profile dilemmas, such as whether to do business in Burma, must be subject to the same principles as the manner in which employees deal with dilemmas in their day-to-day work. How can staff be equipped with the tools that enable them to "do the right thing" in the face of different particulars?

At ING, the answer lies in the business principles. Defining and communicating the ING Business Principles in 1999 was the first step ING took in formally developing a framework for ethical engagement in the company and thus creating the necessary "company conscience." The business principles are the starting point for all behavior and business relationships at ING. Micro and macro ethical dilemmas are therefore subject to the same principles. They are a matter of upholding the highest ethical standards of conduct and thus protecting the reputation of the company.

The general business principles are broken down into eight sections: personal conduct, employee relations, environment, international operations, communications, community relations, economic policy, and competition. The business principles articulate the company's common values (integrity, entrepreneurship, professionalism, responsiveness to clients, teamwork) and contain a number of operating principles (for a full description of the ING business principles, please see http://www.ing.com). For example, the operating principle on competition says that markets flourish within an ethical framework and that no one at ING is permitted to disparage or undermine a competitor or use unethical means to obtain an advantage for ING. The principle on international operations says that ING respects different cultures and does not intervene in politics or party political matters, but that within the legitimate role of business ING reserves the right—after careful consideration—to speak out on matters that may affect its employees, shareholders, or customers. ING continues to refine its business principles. For example, a new principle on human rights is likely to be added in order to provide more guidance on some of the human rights dilemmas ING faces in doing business around the world.

The business principles go a step beyond the regulatory and legal baseline of doing business. They confront our managers and staff with the fact that while some business practices, such as cheating a competitor, may be legal in some places, they are not permitted according to ING's principles. The business principles provide guidelines to staff all over the world for all aspects of doing business, but they leave sufficient flexibility for specific local and cultural differences. The business principles also serve as an international policy framework to all stakeholders. This framework enables decision making at the operational level throughout ING based on the same standards.

The Cascade Approach

ING adopted a cascade approach to spread the business principles in the organization. The *cascade approach* means that the business principles are formulated and adopted at the top—by the macro decision makers in the organization—and spill over into the rest of the organization through continuous training and communication. The first step in this process was for the executive board to communicate the business principles to ING's top opinion leaders (called the Top 200) and get their commitment. The Top 200, in turn, are responsible for training ING employees in the business principles in their own business units. Since 1999, training in the business principles has taken place for the majority of ING staff worldwide. The business principles have also been incorporated into the core curriculum of the ING Business School.

TRAINING

In the training materials, staff and managers are presented with exercises concerning various dilemmas that could arise in day-to-day business. For each dilemma, an example is given of a situation that might occur. For the exercises on bribery, for example, participants are taken through the following exercise:

Peter is a young manager in charge of opening a new branch office in a developing country. He is new to the country and has relied heavily on you to advise him on doing business there. You are Peter's supervising manager, live in a nearby city, and have several years more experience than Peter in the company and that country.

Peter: *"I just got off the phone with the contractor who is installing our phone system. He let me know that there is a tremendous amount of government paperwork to go through and that the process could take months. I'm supposed to have this office open in three weeks. Did you run into this problem?"*

You reply: *"Well, yeah, that kind of thing is a reality here. Tell me, did he recommend any solutions?"*

Peter: *"He said that if I was to pay a special 'processing fee,' I could stop worrying about it, he'd take care of everything."*

You: *"Did you ask him for details?"*

Peter: *"No, I'm not really sure I want to know. I think I'm just going to pay the money and move things along. I've got enough to worry about. Besides, whatever is going on, he's doing it, not me."*

Question: *What advice would you, as his supervising manager, give to Peter?*

In order to solve the dilemma, the participants are taught to engage in self-reflection. The ING business principles clearly state that bribery of any form is unacceptable, but the main point of such exercises is to fine-tune the antennas of the people who work at ING by teaching them (a) how to spot a dilemma and (b) what to do in order to make the responsible decision. For all dilemmas, employees are trained to ask themselves the following:

Are my intended actions legal?

Am I being fair and honest?

Will my actions stand the test of time?

How will I feel about it afterwards?

How will it look on the front page of my newspaper?

Could I justify it to my family?

The second crucial point is that ING Group can issue policies, procedures, and guidelines about how to act in certain dilemmas, but individual employees have to do it themselves. That is why ING deems it so necessary to spread awareness of the principles and to actively train. The principles provide the tools employees need in order to make the right decision given different particulars of a given situation. Through constant training and communication, ING wants to instill that "excellence in deliberation" Aristotle referred to. The six questions above are therefore part of ING's decision-making framework. As such, they are "technical" issues and part of the company conscience. At the same time, however, they also call upon personal conscience.

In the end, ING's objective is that with the business principles in the back of everyone's mind, corporate social responsibility and ethical self-reflection should not be an extra task for our management and staff but a second nature that ensues from the way we conduct our business. Through such training, the business principles should ultimately become a habit and lead to "excellence in deliberation." However, it is still a learning process for everyone at ING that entails trial and error.

MONITORING MORAL COMPETENCE

Moral competence cannot just be taught. To be effective, it must also be monitored on a structural basis. In the last few years, monitoring integrity in the company and guarding the company's reputation have begun to play a much more prominent role at ING. The business principles and code of conduct have been embedded into ING's overall risk management approach. Policies for both risk management and compliance policy are still being developed.

Monitoring takes place at two levels: compliance and risk management. At the Group level, ING has in place a compliance department that monitors risks in the area of reputation and integrity. Compliance officers are embedded in all levels of the organization. It is their responsibility to make sure that the code of conduct is being fulfilled and to make employees aware of transgressions of the code of conduct if they occur. The total number of compliance officers active worldwide in ING stands at approximately 500. In 2002, monitoring programs were expanded so that the compliance officers could gain a better insight into various compliance issues.

Making sure the ING business principles are observed is an important part of the monitoring programs ING has in place. The compliance officers must report whether business principles have been broken, whether there have been investigations by regulators, and whether there have been cases of fraud in the organization, among other issues.

The business principles and the code of conduct have also been embedded in ING's overall risk management approach. Breaches of business principles and the code of conduct are classified as operational risks. *Operational risk* is the risk of loss resulting from inadequate or failed internal processes, people, and systems or from external events. Operational risk includes things such as internal and external criminal activities (burglary, money laundering), business disruption (due to storm, earthquakes, political unrest, breakdown of IT systems), control failures (for example, the failure to file reports in time with regulators), client and business disruption (disputes with clients, deceptive sales practices, faulty products, improper due diligence).

Although these types of risks have always been around, in every type of company, it has only been in recent years that operational risk has been identified as a separate risk category that needs to be measured, monitored, and mitigated. Not all operational risks (such as earthquakes, failure of IT systems) are linked to the business principles. However, all breaches of business principles are operational risks. They are ethical breaches that can lead to incidents that can carry a heavy price tag. Seemingly small missteps—whether intentional or not—can have huge effects. It therefore makes sense for companies to pay attention to their ethical culture and to monitor it.

As part of the new Basel Accord for capital adequacy, all large financial institutions are required to create an operational risk management function. Starting in 2006, financial institutions like ING will have to set aside a portion of their capital to cover their operational risk. The better a company manages its operational risk, the lower the capital charge. The quality of the company's operational risk management can thus affect its capital position and earnings. We would argue that the systematic teaching of ethical decision making, as captured in the business principles, can help reduce operational risk.

We would also argue that operational risk management is not just the domain of financial institutions, but that all types of companies could benefit from installing their own operational risk manager. Operational risk is linked closely to compliance and can help a company determine how strong its own ethical fiber is.

ING established a specialized staff organization for operational risk management in 2000 in order to make operational risks more transparent and to support management in monitoring and managing them. Like the rollout of the business principles, ING's operational risk management function is also being deployed in a top-down cascade model approach.

CONCLUSION

The debate on corporate social behavior is evolving all the time, and so is the terminology being used. In this chapter, we looked more closely at the meaning of some of the terms used in the discourse. We argued that *sustainable* is not the same thing as *ethical*. Just because a company is ranked as the sustainability leader in its sector does not mean by definition that it is the ethical leader. Ethical behavior is not necessarily sustainable behavior, although the two are often equated in practice. We argued that the biggest difference between ethical and sustainable behavior is that profit is explicitly integrated into the concept of sustainable behavior, whereas profit is not a condition for ethical behavior. The right decision from an ethical point of view might be the wrong decision from a sustainable point of view, and vice versa.

Based on some examples at ING Group, we went on to show that there are no hard and fast answers for solving business dilemmas. By their very nature, dilemmas are rarely black-and-white issues. Borrowing some ideas of Aristotle, we argued that solving ethical dilemmas in business must be done on a case-by-case basis, based on the particular circumstances and on the corporate values and guidelines. This requires practice. We described the crucial role the business principles play at ING in providing a compass for ethical decision making. We argued that a company must create its own "conscience" by codifying its principles and values and continually teaching them. ING is still at the beginning of this journey. The ultimate objective is for the business principles to become second nature to staff and management and for them to call upon the principles with every business decision where a dilemma may be embedded. The fact that they are a formal part of the company's operational policies and internal procedures means that moral competence has become a "technical" issue.

The business principles are all about giving management and staff the tools to do the right thing in day-to-day business. That is much harder than the decision to donate money to a good cause. Deciding whether to donate money to a charity (doing good) is a fundamentally different type of decision than whether to serve clients who do business in countries with human rights abuses (doing the right thing). Moral competence is not necessarily required for the first, but it is definitely necessary for the second.

Doing good is good, but it's even better to do the right thing. Those companies with strong business principles in place should succeed in doing both.

REFERENCES

Aristotle. (1973). *Nicomachean ethics.* In R. McKeon (Ed.), *Introduction to Aristotle.* Chicago: University of Chicago Press.

Banerjee, S. B. (2002, August). *Contesting corporate citizenship, sustainability, and stakeholder theory: Holy trinity or praxis of evil?* University of South Australia. Presented at the Academy of Management Conference, Denver, CO.

Calpers sticks to ethical stance. (2003, February 20). *Financial Times.*

De comeback van de commissaris. (2003, March). *Management Scope.*

De Jonge, J. (2003, February 19). Doctrine of shareholder value losing more and more status. *Het Financieele Dagblad.*

Dunn, C. P. (1996). *Stakeholder interests and community groups: A new view.* International Association for Business and Society annual meetings. Retrieved from http://www.rohan.sdsu.edu

E. M. Meijers Instituut. (2002). Report of the symposium *International dimensions of responsible entrepreneurship.* University of Leiden.

Global Ethics Monitor. (2003, January 31). *Dutch ABP's stake in Innovest consultancy shows SRI entering mainstream.* Retrieved from Global Ethics Monitor Web site.

Haksever, C., Chaganti, R., & Cook, R. G. (1999). *A model of corporate value creation.* Retrieved from http://www.sbaer.uca.edu/Research/1999/SBIDA/99sbi195.htm

ING Group. (2001, November 10). *Operational risk management: Definitions and framework* (working document).

ING Investment Management, Sustainable Growth Fund. (2002, August). *Human rights and the responsibility of companies* (working paper).

ING Investment Management Sustainable Investments. (2002). *Annual report.*

Jeurissen, R. J. M. (Ed.). (2000). *Business ethics: A good thing.* The Netherlands: Van Gorcum & Comp.

Kapstein, E. (2001). The corporate ethics crusade. *Foreign Affairs*, September/October.

Litvin, D. (2003, May 12). Ethical goals will not stop criticism of business. *Financial Times.*

Moody-Stuart, M. (Sir). (n.d.). Principes moet je kunnen controleren (interview). *Elan, 3.*

Profits from the righteous path. (2003, April 3). *Financial Times.*

SiRi group profiles. (2003, December). Retrieved from SiRi Group Web site at www.sirigroup.org/services.shtml

Yu, L. (2003). The perception of deception. *Sloan Management Review, 44*(3).

Name Index

Subject Index

ABOUT THE EDITOR

George G. Brenkert is Professor of Business Ethics and Director of the Georgetown Business Ethics Institute. He is current Editor-in-Chief of *Business Ethics Quarterly,* the journal of the Society for Business Ethics, of which he is also a past president. He is a member of the Executive Committees of the Society for Business Ethics and the Association for Practical and Professional Ethics, and a Fellow of the Ethics Resource Center. He serves on the Editorial Boards of *Business Ethics: A European Review* and of *Business and Society Review.* He received his doctorate from the University of Michigan.

ABOUT THE CONTRIBUTORS

Ronald E. Berenbeim is a Principal Researcher and Director of the Conference Board's Working Group on Global Business Ethics Principles. Formerly a director of Guaranty National Corp., Mr. Berenbeim served on the National Association of Corporate Directors' Blue Ribbon Commission on the Professional Board.

Norman E. Bowie is the Elmer L. Andersen Chair in Corporate Responsibility at the University of Minnesota, where he holds a joint appointment in the Departments of Management and Philosophy. He has been a fellow at Harvard's Program for Ethics and the Professions and has served as Dixons Professor of Business Ethics and Social Responsibility at the London Business School.

Jane Collier is Senior Research Associate at the Judge Institute of Management at the University of Cambridge in Management Studies. She is Fellow and Director of Studies in Economics and Management Studies at Lucy Cavendish College.

David Collins is a former member of the executive committee of Johnson & Johnson with responsibility for a number of operations, including McNeil Consumer Products, the makers of Tylenol. He is also the former president of HealthCare Products, a consumer products division of Schering-Plough.

Richard De George is University Distinguished Professor of Philosophy and Business Administration and Director of the International Center for Ethics in Business at the University of Kansas. He is a past president of the American Philosophical Association; of the International Society of Business, Economics, and Ethics; and of the Society for Business Ethics.

John W. Dienhart is the Boeing Frank Shrontz Chair for Business Ethics at Seattle University. He is also the director of the Northwest Ethics Network, an independent group whose membership includes businesses, nonprofits, and government agencies.

Thomas Donaldson is the Mark O. Winkelman Professor of Legal Studies at the Wharton School of Business, University of Pennsylvania. He is a Trustee of the Carnegie Council on Ethics and International Affairs, a past president of the Society for Business Ethics, and an associate editor of the *Academy of Management Review.*

Thomas W. Dunfee is Kolodny Professor of Social Responsibility in Business at the Wharton School of Business, University of Pennsylvania. He was Vice Dean in charge of Wharton's Undergraduate Division, 2000–2003. He is past president of the Academy of Legal Studies in Business, a former editor-in-chief of the *American Business Law Journal,* and a past president of the Society for Business Ethics.

Georges Enderle is the Arthur and Mary O'Neil Professor of International Business Ethics at the Mendoza College of Business, University of Notre Dame. He is President of the International

Society of Business Economics and Ethics (2001–2004) and one of the cofounders of the European Business Ethics Network.

Alan S. Glazer is the Henry P. and Mary B. Stager Professor of Business at Franklin & Marshall College, Lancaster, PA. He was the Associate Director of the Independence Standards Board's Conceptual Framework Project. He serves on the editorial board of the *Journal of Accountancy* and is a CPA in Pennsylvania.

Henry R. Jaenicke is the C. D. Clarkson Emeritus Professor of Accounting at Drexel University. He was the Director of the Conceptual Framework Project of the Independence Standards Board.

Pieter Kroon was Head of Public Affairs of ING Group until 2003. In this function, Mr. Kroon was responsible for government and society relations, sustainability issues, and corporate values. He was also a member of various working groups within the industry dealing with sustainability issues, including the Netherlands Bankers' Association (NVB), the Dutch Association of Insurers (VvV), the International Chamber of Commerce (ICC), and World Business Council for Sustainable Development (WBCSD).

Josep M. Lozano is Professor and Director of the Department of Social Sciences at the ESADE Business School in Barcelona, Spain. He is also Director of the Institute for Individual, Corporations and Society (IPES) at ESADE. He is the ESADE representative in the European Academy of Business in Society, which was cofounded by ESADE.

Henk van Luijk is Professor Emeritus at the Universiteit Nyenrode, The Netherlands Business School. He is the former director of the European Institute of Business Ethics at Nyenrode University and the former chairman of the European Business Ethics Network. He is a member of the board of the International Society of Business, Economics, and Ethics and of the Knowledge and Information Centre for Corporate Social Responsibility of the Dutch Ministry of Economic Affairs.

Susan McGrath, CPA, is a Managing Director at VERIS Consulting, a firm providing due diligence, internal audit outsourcing, litigation support, and other specialized accounting and auditing services with a focus on the insurance industry. She is a former director on the staff of the Independence Standards Board and has written on auditor independence issues for professional journals.

Bruce Moats is the Corporate Vice President of Worldwide Government Affairs & Public Policy for Levi Strauss & Co. (LS&CO.). An advisor to the CEO of LS&CO., Mr. Moats is a member of the LS&CO. Executive Committee on sourcing. He was named by the UN/ILO to represent over 3,000 U.S. businesses in the May 2001 tripartite meeting of experts on HIV/AIDS.

Eleanor R. E. O'Higgins is on the faculty of the Smurfit Business School at University College Dublin. She is on the editorial board of *Business Ethics: A European Review* and is currently Director of the International Theme Committee of the Academy of Management.

Steven A. Rochlin is Director of Research and Policy Development at the Boston College Center for Corporate Community Relations. He is the principal investigator for a global business survey project called "The State of Corporate Citizenship" and co–project director of a project called "Integrating Corporate Citizenship Across the Business."

Arthur Siegel is currently a consultant and corporate director. Previously, he was executive director of the Independence Standards Board and before that a partner in Price Waterhouse, where he was vice chairman of the firm in charge of its audit practice. He has served as chairman of the American Institute of CPA's SEC Practice Section executive committee and on the Emerging Issues Task Force and the Financial Accounting Standards Advisory Council of the Financial Accounting Standards Board.

Catherine Smith is Chief Operating Officer for ING U.S. Financial Services, heading all customer service operations and IT for the U.S. business lines. During 2001, Ms. Smith was President of Health, Education, and Government Distribution for ING Aetna Financial Services. Prior to 2001, she was Chief Financial Officer for Aetna Financial Services.

Laura J. Spence is Senior Lecturer at Brunel University, London, U.K. She is Coordinator of Brunel Research in Enterprise, Sustainability, and Ethics. Since 1998 she has served on the executive committee of the European Business Ethics Network.

Manuel Velasquez is the Charles J. Dirksen Professor of Business Ethics at the University of Santa Clara, where he holds appointments in the Department of Management and the Department of Philosophy. He is a past president of the Society for Business Ethics and current Chair of the Department of Management.

Frank Vogl is President of Vogl Communications, Inc., a strategic management consulting firm in Washington, DC. He is a cofounder, former Vice Chairman, and Advisory Council member of Transparency International; a member of the Board of Directors of the Ethics Resource Center and a founding fellow of the ERC's Fellows Program; and a Trustee of the Committee for Economic Development.

Johan Wempe is Partner of KPMG, Director of KPMG Sustainability, and Professor in Corporate Social Responsibility & Sustainability at the Rotterdam School of Management of the Erasmus University in Rotterdam. He is a member of the Standing Committee on Corruption and Extortion of the ICC.